Discourse Studies – Ways and Crossroads

STUDIES IN LANGUAGE, CULTURE AND SOCIETY
Edited by Łucja Biel, Andrzej Kątny and Piotr Ruszkiewicz

VOLUME 11

PETER LANG

Karolina Broś / Grzegorz Kowalski (eds.)

Discourse Studies – Ways and Crossroads

Insights into Cultural, Diachronic and Genre Issues in the Discipline

PETER LANG

Bibliographic Information published by the Deutsche Nationalbibliothek
The Deutsche Nationalbibliothek lists this publication in the Deutsche Nationalbibliografie; detailed bibliographic data is available in the internet at http://dnb.d-nb.de.
Library of Congress Cataloging-in-Publication Data
A CIP catalog record for this book has been applied for at the Library of Congress.

This publication was financially supported by the
Institute of Applied Linguistics and Faculty of Applied Linguistics,
University of Warsaw.

ISSN 2195-7479
ISBN 978-3-631-73948-8 (Print)
E-ISBN 978-3-631-73949-5 (E-Book)
E-ISBN 978-3-631-73950-1 (EPDF)
E-ISBN 978-3-631-73951-8 (MOBI)
DOI 10.3726/b12713

Peter Lang – Frankfurt am Main · Bern · Bruxelles · New York ·
Oxford · Warszawa · Wien

This publication has been peer reviewed.

www.peterlang.com

Table of contents

Introduction

The papers in this volume are selected contributions submitted by speakers at the international linguistic conference *GlobE 2015*, organized on 14th–16th May 2015, at the Institute of Applied Linguistics, University of Warsaw. In accordance with the title of the conference, *East–West European Forum on Discourse*, the presentations then delivered and the follow-up papers published in this collection represent major lines of research in the broadly understood Discourse Studies as undertaken at different academic centres Europe-wide and beyond. Despite the geopolitical dichotomy expressed verbatim in the title (which was intended to be thought-provoking rather than provocative), the conference has proved that there can be distinguished certain approaches, methods and topics of Discourse Analysis which attract scholars' attention regardless of their specific academic, cultural etc. affiliations. On the other hand, diversity of the research topics addressed truly reflects the heterogeneity of Discourse Studies, which in turn has fully justified the sense of the 'forum' format, as the conference was meant to be.

Considering that the leitmotif of the 2015 edition of *GlobE* was "Past, present and future of discourse studies", the speakers and contributors hereto were welcome to refer back to more distant, though by no means invalidated, theories, concepts and approaches in the field, and juxtapose them with the more recent and/or mainstream analytical models. On the other hand, we were looking forward to considerations on the possible directions which Discourse Studies may follow in the years to come. We are glad that such reflections also resurface in the papers in the volume, providing many issues for further reflection.

Finally, the title of this volume itself, *Discourse Studies: ways and crossroads*, in its metaphoric binomial, intentionally alludes to the second collection of *GlobE* proceedings, *Bridges and barriers in metalinguistic discourse*[1] (Duszak and Okulska, 2006). The two publications do indeed share many similarities, the most evident being the contention that the diversity of research perspectives within Discourse Studies is in the end its asset, opening space for interdisciplinary work, rather than an obstacle to reaching a consensus among manifold schools and viewpoints. The latter would otherwise be imminent unless co-operation is established and maintained among scholars from many disciplines. Endorsing this principle, *GlobE* conference and its proceedings have since their beginnings featured contributions

1 Duszak, A., & Okulska, U. (Eds.) (2006). *Bridges and barriers in metalinguistic discourse*. Frankfurt am Main: Peter Lang.

by linguists, sociologists, social psychologists, philologists, media analysts, and many others.

The present volume is divided into four parts. The first, ***Discourse Studies: Theoretical considerations***, includes papers concerning theoretical aspects of Discourse Analysis, also approached from the perspectives of philological and literary studies, or (new) media research. The latter, in particular, identifies several challenges posed by recent technological developments to more traditional models in Discourse Analysis, not always capable of grasping e.g. multi-semiotic intricacies of multimodal discourses. Consequently, it is postulated that closer attention should be paid to models originating in Multimodal Discourse Analysis. Also, as is argued by the authors, with new platforms of communication entailing new ways of expression, research should be centred on the resulting hybrid multimodal genres, new modes of human interaction, communication strategies etc., discussed here in both theoretical and practical terms.

The author of the first paper, **Danuta Ulicka**, examines the problems of transfer of scientific terms and concepts originally coined in Russian by such scholars as M. Bakhtin or V. Shklovsky into other languages and scientific cultures. Against a detailed picture of socio-historical and political context of the Soviet Union in the 1920s and 1930s, Danuta Ulicka presents a not less complex story behind the origins of such terms as Shklovsky's *defamiliarization* or Bakhtin's *vnenakhodimost* or *heteroglossia*. On this basis she demonstrates that the translatological tendency to unify the often complex scientific terminology results in the monologization and homogenization of its polysemy as found in the discourses of Bakhtin or Shklovsky – to the evident detriment of the originality of their scholarly thought. Ulicka argues that, although possibly aimed at mediating meanings between source and target cultures, such practices eventually have a negative effect on intercultural dialogue.

In the second paper in this section, **Katarzyna Molek-Kozakowska** looks at the ontological problem of reciprocal definition of Discourse Studies and Media Studies, in particular in interdisciplinary research. In this respect, however, she argues that the assumption of an interdisciplinary nature in the relevant works is often a rhetorical stratagem rather than an actual methodological approach developed by their authors. Molek-Kozakowska notes that there exist important discrepancies between the two discussed disciplines, which inhibit genuine interdisciplinarity. Still, in the light of the complementary nature of the methodological tools offered by media analysts and discourse studies specialists, more attention should be paid in future to resolving the existing issues and seeking new ways of interaction between these disciplines.

Problems with the application of more traditional models of text linguistics to analyzing digital discourse are discussed by **Radostina Iglikova**. Following a detailed analysis of selected discourse definitional criteria originating in text linguistics, discourse analysis and Computer-Mediated Communication discourse analysis, the author focuses on the *efficiency* principle as applicable to both printed text and text 'born digital'. She argues that, although technologically advanced and multimodal, the majority of the discourse produced online is still text-based, and hence shares many features with traditional texts – despite the former's being 'born digital' rather than transposed from analogue resources. As a result, researchers should be able to remodel the traditional methods of text analysis drawing on the abundant literature and well-established methodologies, rather than invent brand new analytical models.

In the final paper in this section **Iga Maria Lehman** focuses on the concept of *identity* as a dichotomous and dynamic notion, encompassing individual and collective aspects of the social *self*, both being in constant interplay. In her study she takes the linguistic anthropology perspective on the issue of identity formation of academic writers. The process is shown to be dependent upon participation in discourse activities characteristic to the academic discourse community of which a given scholar is a member, for instance writing scientific texts. The latter in turn provide data which enable the analyst to identify specific identity-formation factors involved in their creation.

The second part of the volume, ***(New) Media Discourse***, includes case-studies whose authors take a closer look at both printed and digital mass-media. The topics discussed are approached from a variety of Discourse Analysis frameworks, including comparative text analysis, Critical Discourse Analysis and corpus-based Discourse Analysis.

The section opens with a study by **Tatiana Karpilovitch**, who presents a comparative analysis of problem feature articles published in American and Belarusian press. More specifically, she looks at the key semantic and pragmatic features of the genre. In the former case, she discusses the superstructure of the problem feature article, and compares the presence and arrangement of the specific moves in the relevant texts published in the two countries. In the latter case, the author analyzes pragmatic markers whereby specific moves in the relevant texts are expressed. Karpilovitch demonstrates that the two media cultures generally structure problem feature articles in a similar way, the main discrepancies resulting from systemic differences between the two language systems and different expressive styles rather than differences in the genre's architecture or information structure.

By contrast, **Małgorzata Sokół** analyzes a digital genre: she investigates Polish academic weblogs in terms of the use of different verbal constructions expressing epistemic modality. Given the increasing popularity of the new media in public discourse, and their widespread use in knowledge-disseminating and opinion-making, members of the academia have also adapted the genres of digital communication to debate, persuade and argue on various academic (and not only academic) issues. As the author shows, the Polish language offers a vast diversity of epistemic modality verbs, whereby academic bloggers can express their points with a different load of argumentative power. An in-depth analysis of specific cases enables the author to identify various rhetorical and pragmatic objectives which the bloggers may want to achieve in communicating their arguments and negotiating their truth-value with the audience.

The paper by **Grzegorz Kowalski** also discusses a digital genre, namely project presentations at Internet crowdfunding platforms. The author investigates how these texts use the Problem-Solution structure to justify the rationale behind developing a particular project, and how they discursively construct the project's intended target group. A comparative analysis is employed to distinguish possible differences in the application of the related discourse strategies in local- and global-impact crowdfunding platforms.

The section concludes with two articles featuring Critical Discourse Analysis methodology. In her study on newspaper discourse **Desislava Cheshmedzhieva-Stoycheva** compares and contrasts argumentation strategies used by advocates and opponents of nuclear power. The study is based on a corpus of newspaper articles published in *The New York Times*, *The Independent* and *Dnevnik*, which therefore enables the author to juxtapose specific discourse strategies used by the relevant actors in American, British and Bulgarian societies, respectively. Despite certain nuances in the discourses of the opposite fractions concerned, many of which being related to the different sociopolitical realities, it is shown that in general pro- and anti-nuclear media texts apply similar discourse strategies. Specifically, they share similar topoi, imagery, metaphors, and refer to similar emotions and events, to name but a few aspects.

Ecological issues are likewise addressed by **Oleksandr Kapranov**. The author discusses climate change discourse from a diachronic perspective, based on a corpus of annual reports by British Petroleum. With the application of corpus-research tools and statistical analysis, involving words and expressions referring to global warming and other climate issues, he demonstrates that the general message on climate change communicated by the company is not subject to significant diachronic variation. Rather, it is expressed as a stable part of the company's general policy on ecological issues.

The papers in the third part of the volume, ***Discourse in professional domains***, discuss discourses as employed in diverse professional contexts. Particular attention is given to institutional and business domains operating in international and cross-cultural contexts, in both private and public sectors.

The section opens with **Britt-Louise Gunnarsson**'s multidimensional study of the interaction between global business and corporate communication, and how the changes on the labor market influence and are influenced by corporate discourse. The author takes three directions in her research – multilingual company culture, language policy and multicultural workplace – which all confirm the hypothesis that worker mobility, global orientation and flexibility are key values for the operation of multinational companies. Not surprisingly, computer-mediated communication has become the primary platform for corporate interaction and English the primary language used in such environments.

A similar topic is addressed by **Catharina Nyström Höög**, who takes a relatively new genre, *platform of values*, under scrutiny in her analysis of Swedish public-sector communication practices. The study, involving CDA methodology and tools of multi-modal discourse analysis, shows that the texts representing this genre commonly employ the 'soft steering' approach, with both verbal and visual means used to describe positive qualities of the institution, establish its authority, and negotiate responsibility. Crucially, the author identifies three components inherent to the *platform of values*: nominal constructions referring to core values and positive qualities, mood metaphors and visual resources adjusted to the intended goal of the text.

A cross-cultural perspective is also found in the paper by **Agnieszka Kiełkiewicz-Janowiak** and **Magdalena Zabielska**, who analyze doctor-patient communication practices between Polish migrants and British healthcare providers. The empirical material, elicited through narrative interviews and ethnographic methods, points to certain differences between English and Polish healthcare practices. In particular, the authors argue that greater awareness of the cultural specificity of healthcare and the way in which it is provided is crucial for doctor-patient interactions in multi-cultural environments. Also, the authors recommend that professional medical training for healthcare staff working in migrant environments should be informed by linguistic research so that they can better address their patients' needs.

This section ends with **Grażyna Anna Bednarek**'s comparative analysis of Polish and US courtroom discourses, focusing on their respective inquisitorial and adversarial procedures of witness examination. The author points to linguistic and cultural heterogeneity of courtroom discourse, and argues that the two types of witness examination procedures should be treated as different linguistic genres shaped by specific cultural, historical and social contexts in which both legal systems operate.

The final section of the volume, ***Discourses of power and politics***, brings together studies concerning power relations and political issues in contemporary societies. The dominant approach followed by the authors is Critical Discourse Analysis, providing tools suitable to analyze the multidimensional interplay between discourse and power. Here one of the recurrent themes is the complex networking between political (and more generally public) discourse and (mass) media, which is addressed more generally in attempts to develop a relevant theoretical model, and more practically in case studies focusing on particular instances of the said phenomenon.

In the first paper in this section, **Małgorzata Rzeszutko-Iwan** takes judicial and media discourses as a point of departure for an analysis of the relationship between knowledge, power and order, which concepts she draws from Foucault's theory of discourse. Following this perspective, she argues that order is manifested through knowledge and power, which, in turn, can be expressed both verbally and non-verbally (through symbolic forms) and shape public discourse. Excerpts from courtroom interaction and media interviews show how certain discourse devices can be used as institutional tools to warrant order. Thus, the categories of knowledge, power and order are shown to be interdependent and complementary elements of public discourse.

A multi-aspect analysis has been performed by **Adam Warzecha**, who discusses the phenomenon of shockvertising in public discourse on the example of controversies related to the Polish black-metal performer Adam 'Nergal' Darski. The author confronts diverse opinions formulated by different social actors, including Church authorities, politicians of various parties, journalists, social organizations etc. He discusses the subsequent stages of the process, from shockvertising of local impact, then gathering its impetus to become a nationwide issue, and eventually becoming the subject of political and religious scandalization. The author points to the power of political discourse and its hegemonizing nature when confronted with other public domains, e.g. religion or mass culture.

Expressing institutional power in political discourse is also the topic addressed by **Julita Śmigielska**, who discusses legitimation strategies used in Vladimir Putin's speech on the annexation of Crimea. Her CDA analysis shows that the main conceptualization frame of the discourse in question is constructed on the basis of thesis–antithesis pattern, with subsequent statements referring to positive values of the in-group vs. negative ones of the out-group. Argumentation which is used to validate this division is chiefly based on historical and legal references.

The same political context is discussed by **Ludmilla A'Beckett**, who analyzes instances of the metaphor RUSSIANS AND UKRAINIANS ARE BROTHERS in Russian and Ukrainian public discourse. The author argues that despite the common use of the metaphor in both contexts, there is neither agreement as to its validity nor uniformity as to the ways in which it is expressed or otherwise referred to in discourse. This discrepancy is claimed to be a corollary of different political attitudes and ideologies advocated by the authors of the texts analyzed.

The final paper in the volume, written by **Sahadete Limani-Beqa**, proposes a new framework for critical analysis of political transformation discourse. Application of the model is illustrated with mediatized political speeches concerning Kosovo. As the author argues, several analytical tools need to be combined in order to conduct a thorough linguistic and sociopolitical research into the discursive events in question.

We dedicate this volume to the memory of Professor Anna Duszak, founder of the *GlobE* conference and co-editor of all the previous conference volumes.

Karolina Broś and Grzegorz Kowalski
Warsaw, August 2017

Prof. dr hab. Anna Duszak (1950–2015)

Professor Anna Duszak was… It is difficult to write about her in the past tense, remembering her exceptional energy, with which she undertook new research projects, and which she engaged in her daily scientific, teaching and managerial work at the Institute of Applied Linguistics, University of Warsaw. Each research topic she analyzed, each lecture she delivered, and each idea which would contribute to the development of the Institute, she executed from the beginning to the end, not accepting any stopgap, understatement or improvisation. At the same time her strong belief in any endeavour undertaken motivated her colleagues to jointly achieve the intended goal.

One can simply write "she was the director of the Institute", but this sentence sounds like a cliché. Whoever had the opportunity to meet Professor Duszak knows that in this case the word 'director' is a misnomer. A name for an organizational rank, a label of professional classification, it imposes a frame which defines the institutional hierarchy of positions. Yet I am sure that those who knew Professor Duszak would skip this official title, and say simply "she was the Institute", with no hyperbole whatsoever.

Affiliated with the University of Warsaw throughout her entire academic career, Professor Duszak was a linguist of worldwide reputation. Initially a member of the Department of Modern Languages, she later became a founder and leading scholar at the Faculty of Applied Linguistics. It is at the University of Warsaw that she was awarded the successive degrees: master's (in applied linguistics, 1973), doctoral (in humanities, 1979), *habilitacja* (in humanities, 1987), and eventually, in recognition for her scientific achievements and academic work, full professorship (2004).

Respected by her colleagues and admired by students, she was the dean of the Faculty of Applied Linguistics (1993–1999) and director of the Institute of Applied Linguistics (2002–2008 and 2012–2015). Within the Institute she was the head of the Department of Language Communication (2001–2006), which was then renamed Department of Sociolinguistics and Pragmatics (2006–2011), and recently transformed into the Department of Discourse Studies, which Professor Duszak founded and headed since 2011. She organized and co-ordinated several team-projects within the Department, and founded two of its key international linguistic conferences: *GlobE* (since 2002) and *Political Linguistics* (with the Department of Pragmatics, Institute of English, University of Łódź, since 2007). In addition, Professor Duszak co-ordinated large-scale interdisciplinary and inter-university research projects, including *Swoi – inni – obcy* [Ours – others – strangers] or a Polish anthology on comparative Systemic-Functional Discourse Analysis. An advocate of an interdisciplinary approach to discourse studies also in university education, she was a co-founder of new MA studies "Language and Society", run by the Institute of Applied Linguistics and Institute of Sociology, University of Warsaw, since 2015.

She also organized many seminars, workshops and lectures delivered by eminent scholars, who always gladly accepted her invitation to Warsaw. Herself she was likewise invited to many universities, both in Poland and abroad (e.g. University College of London, 1972–1973; University of Kansas, 1977–1978; University of California in Berkeley, 1984–1985; University of Cologne and University of Hamburg, 1990–1992; Saarland University in Saarbrücken, 1996; University of Vienna, 1997), benefiting from scholarships granted by Fulbright, Humboldt and Batory foundations. She delivered guest lectures at renowned academic institutions and participated in a number of linguistic conferences, where she was welcomed as a keynote speaker. She much esteemed international contacts among scholars, not only within her field, and befriended many, with whom she cooperated and exchanged results of academic work. Being up-to-date with global linguistic community was her priority, also in those difficult times when international co-operation and mobility – now so widespread and obvious – were much restricted in Poland.

In the course of her academic career Professor Duszak was an active member of several scientific institutions and societies, including Polish Academy of Sciences (Committee of Terminology, Committee of Linguistics, and Committee of Science Studies); International Pragmatics Association; Polish Applied Linguistics Society; Polish Cognitive Linguistics Society; Scientific Council for Colleges of Foreign Language Teachers; Societas Linguistica Europeae.

She published more than one hundred works – monographs, volumes and research articles – in renowned Polish and foreign publishing houses and journals. She edited several collections, including *Culture and Styles of Academic Discourse* (1997); *Us and Others, Social Identities Across Languages, Discourses and Cultures* (2002); *Speaking from the Margin: Global English in a European Perspective* (with U. Okulska, 2004); *Identity, Community, Discourse: English in Intercultural Settings* (with G. Cortese, 2005); *Bridges and Barriers in Metalinguistic Discourse* (with U. Okulska, 2006); *Korpusy w angielsko-polskim językoznawstwie kontrastywnym: Teoria i praktyka* (with E. Gajek and U. Okulska, 2006); *Krytyczna analiza dyskursu. Interdyscyplinarne podejście do komunikacji społecznej* (with N. Fairclough, 2008); *Globalization, Discourse, Media: In a Critical Perspective* (with J. House and

Ł. Kumięga, 2010); *Language, Culture and the Dynamics of Age* (with U. Okulska, 2011); *Systemowo-funkcjonalna analiza dyskursu* (with G. Kowalski, 2013); *Tekst naukowy i jego przekład* (with A. Jopek-Bosiacka and G. Kowalski, 2015); *Academic (Inter)genres: between Texts, Contexts and Identities* (with G. Kowalski, 2015). She was also one of the three academic editors-in-chief of the Cambridge Polish-English/English-Polish dictionary (2003). To this list one should add numerous reviews, which she wrote as an affiliated reviewer for such journals as *English for Academic Purposes, Journal of Pragmatics, Łódź Papers in Pragmatics, Papers and Studies in Contrastive Linguistic, Prague Journal of English Studies, Tekst i dyskurs*, or *Text and Talk.*

Professor Duszak is recognized worldwide for her many contributions to the field of contrastive rhetoric, in particular in relation to academic styles. The results of her analysis of similarities and differences between Polish academic style against Anglo-Saxon and Teutonic ones are presented in such articles as "Academic discourse and intellectual styles" (*Journal of Pragmatics* 21(3), 1994), "Academic writing in English and Polish: Comparing and subverting genres" (*International Journal of Applied Linguistics* 8(2), 1998) or "Publishing academic texts in English: A Polish perspective" (with J. Lewkowicz, *Journal of English for Academic Purposes* 7(2), 2008). Frequent citations in scholarly literature prove the great importance of her contributions to this area of linguistic research.

Yet without doubt her best-known work is the 1998 monograph *Tekst, dyskurs, komunikacja międzykulturowa* [Text, discourse, intercultural communication], a meticulous synthesis of her main topics of research, setting the scene for Discourse Analysis in Poland. Although in the last decade some valuable publications in this field have been published in Poland, her pioneering monograph is acclaimed for its clear structure, a wide range of topics covered, an in-depth analysis of the issues raised, and an extensive bibliography. Professor Duszak wished that the book was used as an academic textbook for Discourse Analysis – and it is so at many courses and seminars at Polish universities.

Professor Duszak can therefore be considered a precursor and champion of Discourse Analysis in Poland. Her lifelong co-operation with foreign academic centers has helped Polish scholars become acquainted with theoretical tenets and methodologies of discourse studies, and then develop the Polish school of Discourse Analysis. In the course of time the approach has gathered its impetus, attracting attention of scholars at different colleges and departments countrywide, and becoming a subject of study of many Polish linguists, sociologists, media analysts, social psychologists etc. Their works, often fragmented and uncoordinated, have recently been systematized within the framework of an inter-university consortium of Discourse Analysis, one of the founders and active participants being Professor Duszak.

It should be remembered that although Professor Duszak devoted much attention to Discourse Analysis, she also focused on many other areas of linguistics. At the beginning of her academic career she published works on contrastive grammar, followed with research into text linguistics, pragmatics and sociolinguistics. In the course of her academic career she also made contributions to the field of intercultural communication, in particular in the context of cross-cultural diversity of academic styles and discourses, but also in the broader perspective of anthropological linguistics and contrastive rhetoric. In recent years she became an important contributor to Critical Discourse Analysis, social semiotics, and Multi-modal Discourse Analysis.

Professor Duszak was also a remarkable academic teacher. At the Institute of Applied Linguistics she taught many subjects, including practical, descriptive and contrastive English grammar, semantics and pragmatics. In particular she gained her academic reputation with her insightful lectures in text linguistics, ethnolinguistics and Discourse Analysis, each of which she supported with interesting examples, using a variety of media materials. Popular among students, her lectures attracted many of her future MA and PhD candidates; she supervised numerous master's theses and doctoral dissertations, in particular in the field of Discourse Analysis.

I also had the honour to attend her PhD seminar and write the PhD dissertation under her supervision. At that time Professor Duszak was elected director of the Institute of Applied Linguistics, which to some extent worried her PhD students, as we feared that at least some seminars be postponed or even cancelled due to her official duties. We were, however, wrong – Professor Duszak was always true to her firm principle that there is time for students and there is time for managerial duties, and both must be kept apart. We had long discussions, listened to her advice and critical assessments, and shared with her our ideas. Once a part of the dissertation was completed, we would discuss it thoroughly, page by page, until all problems were solved and doubts dispelled.

Professor Duszak introduced her PhD students to the often uneasy academic reality, sometimes throwing us in at the deep end. Yet she trusted us enough to, for instance, send us alone to international conferences and present the results of our joint research projects, which she co-signed with her surname. Certainly, this signature was like a stamp of quality to the paper presented, but it also entailed a great responsibility that each of her apprentices had to embark upon.

As the director of the Institute of Applied Linguistics she enjoyed much respect among her colleagues, respect gained by virtue of her knowledge, experience and kindness, rather than – as is often the case in academic institutions – sanctioned by supervisor–subordinate relations. With a unique combination of managerial skills, academic diplomacy and tact, she often reconciled her colleagues' diverse views on the research projects carried out jointly, which was not easy, given the number of areas which we dealt with.

She was a demanding person – demanding from us, but above all from herself. A great scholar, a remarkable teacher, and a respected mentor.

Professor Anna Duszak passed away on 25th December 2015.

Grzegorz Kowalski,
Institute of Applied Linguistics, University of Warsaw

In memoriam prof. dr hab. Anna Duszak

When Professor Duszak came to Torino for our 2004 international conference on *Identity, Community, Discourse: English in Intercultural Settings*, I met her at the airport. There was a moment of panic when we could not find her briefcase with her laptop and lecture notes. She went pale. We were lucky to find everything, and as we drove into town she managed to relax and said to me: "Thanks for looking after me. You are my guardian angel!" I was really moved by her personal comment, since we had never met before.

prof. Sandra Campagna, University of Turin

During that Conference, I was driving Anna for a bit of sightseeing around Torino and we stopped somewhere. The hub cap of one of my rear wheels had come off and was lying on the sidewalk. I would never have noticed, but Anna saw it immediately. That was Anna Duszak: with all her depth and intellectual concerns, she would not lose sight of practical details. I saved years of correspondence on my computer – our respective mothers passing away, prospects for holidays that never materialized, work projects, worries over the university climate, our own writing, friends. Enjoying travel, conferencing, good food and wine and conversation, her pleasure in taking care of her rose garden when winter would finally make room for the gentle sweetness of spring. And our fears and hopes through illness, her genuine surprise in realising how we all cared, how many people cared for her.

In a few lines, she was able to convey a world of reflection and feelings. We cared for each other as good friends do. I miss her courage, strength and integrity, her capacity to go straight to the heart of a problem in total frankness. Up to her last message, she was more concerned about accomplishing things for others than about herself. Never one selfish word in all these years.

Splendid mind, crystal-clear writing, genuine concern for the destiny of the next academic generation, total dedication to professional endeavours as the highest form of contribution to academic and civil society.

Remember that line from the old spiritual, "All o' God's chillun got-a wings"? I am sure, dear Anna, you taught many how to fly.

prof. Pina Cortese, University of Turin

Before I went to Warsaw for Professor Duszak's Political Linguistics Conference in May 2014, I could not really say we knew each other. Of course, like all of us,

I had read and appreciated her work over the years and I was impressed, like many of us, by her charismatic presence, her sound methodology – and her beauty – during the 2004 international research conference in Turin. I knew how close Pina Cortese felt to Anna and I have no doubt that Anna's sentiments towards Pina were reciprocal. There were so many things they shared, not only in the scientific and professional fields, that a strong bond grew between the two of them in time. Since they were both keen on involving their research groups in their wide-ranging academic initiatives, we became part of that bond ourselves. Friendly academic collaboration grew alongside, such as Michelangelo Conoscenti and Malgorzata Sokol's mutual interest in computer-mediated communication. We were invited to her conferences and cited her work in our lectures, our own writing and our student dissertations. So it became natural to think and talk of her as "Anna".

At the Warsaw conference I was struck by Anna's poise and the menschkeit she exuded in different moments of the conference: when she chaired a plenary, encouraged a neophite in her research project, played the perfect hostess or was simply there.

prof. Elana Ochse, University of Turin

In December 2004 Professor Anna Duszak organized and hosted a major international conference on *Language and Law: Legal Communication in an Interdisciplinary Perspective* at the University of Warsaw which I attended. I had first met her earlier in the year when she came to the University of Turin Sixth Centenary Conference on *Identity, Community, Discourse: English in Intercultural Settings*, and already admired her strongly independent and critical work on the styles and cultures of academic discourse. The Warsaw Conference was an important milestone for many of us working at the language and law interface (at the time considered a somewhat peripheral area of study), but it was also the moment when I was first able to fully appreciate how all this was made possible by Anna's keen acumen and genuine interest in the participants' research, by her generosity of spirit and her empathic approach.

prof. Martin Solly, University of Turin

Thanks to Prof Anna Duszak I started working at the Institute of Applied Linguistics. She called me to invite for a job interview. I accepted the offer despite other responsibilities. It was not possible to reject it because it was HER who made it, it was clear at first sight.

It was a great pleasure and honour to co-operate with Prof Anna Duszak and Dr Urszula Okulska on the book *Korpusy w angielsko-polskim językoznawstwie kontrastywnym: teoria i praktyka* [Corpora in Polish-English contrastive linguistics:

theory and practice, 2006, Kraków: Universitas]. For me, it was a unique chance to observe her way of doing research in linguistics from the point of planning, structuring, refining, editing, and finalizing but also dealing with all human, time and budgetary constraints. As the topic was rather on the side of her main academic interest – discourse analysis, she acted as a theoretician, who investigated the role of data in linguistic reflection and the role of corpora in teaching and translation. It was in tune with the first text in the book by Prof. Jan Rusiecki in which he explains the complementary functions of corpus linguistics and linguistic analysis in research in contrast to the long lasting conflict between empirical descriptivists and rationalists, especially generative grammarians. She selected the authors very carefully to fulfil her vision of the book, suggesting the topic of their articles, but providing the authors enough autonomy in their contributions. Her leadership competences in academic work were eminent. Although she treated the technical parts of the book as transitory to some extent, being aware of the fast development of digital technology and changes in its functionalities, she let the authors and co-editors contribute freely.

It was a great honour and pleasure to work with her and under her supervision, to observe her as a great linguist and scientist, and to learn from her.

dr Elżbieta Gajek,
Institute of Applied Linguistics, University of Warsaw

Professor Anna Duszak was an outstanding scholar whose innovative ideas shaped the fields of sociolinguistics and discourse studies. I have never had the chance to meet her personally. However, we had extensive correspondence starting from 2010, when she submitted a proposal to the Mouton Series in Pragmatics on cross-cultural linguistics. Both reviewers evaluated the project very positively so we accepted it. The topic was timely and groundbreaking that time so we hoped that Professor Duszak would complete the book according to schedule.

I was in contact with her all the time encouraging her to continue working on the book that would have been a very important addition to MSP. However, her health was gradually deteriorating so she had less and less time to work on the book. But Professor Duszak managed to develop the theoretical frame of the book that rested on a cognitive-semiotic-discursive view of language. She aimed to present an integrative model of language as a system and text, and an interdiscursive approach on the level of text and discourse analysis. The book was expected to offer a comprehensive and updated overview of language-focused studies in cross-cultural communication.

I find it important to write about her never-finished-book because I think she deserves the credit for recognizing the importance of the field that is called "cultural pragmatics" now. In fact, her adding a discursive perspective to the discipline was a step in the right direction. Professor Duszak's colleagues at the University of Warsaw should be very proud of having had the chance to work with such an exceptional scholar for several decades.

Istvan Kecskes, Distinguished Professor,
State University of New York, USA

While much is said and written about interdisciplinarity in modern science, its true and original applications are few. Often these are rather multidisciplinary activities, which neither 'open' nor change the disciplines involved, but merely contribute to their outcome. This was not, however, the case of the general methodology applied and intellectual approach represented by the late Professor Anna Duszak. Linguistics was not only a field of study for her, but a source of continuous inspiration for research and support for every aspect of communication and its study, truly and comprehensively understood, in the world of science as well as between people, cultures and societies. As early as in the late 1980s, Professor Anna Duszak, in collaboration with Professor Antonina Kłoskowska (Chair of the Sociology of Culture, University of Warsaw), the most eminent Polish scholar and researcher in the sociology of culture, supported and promoted an interdisciplinary perspective on the potential and diverse phenomena of symbolic culture. Her views paved the way for Polish – and foreign – study on discursive, transgressive and evolutional aspects of symbolic culture.

Her scientific works always touched the question: What next? Who else can undertake these questions? How else can one search for the answer? These questions inspired the people who worked with her, the people whom she searched for and whom she found, and the people who were glad to work with her. For Polish humanities she was a great guide, with an outstanding motivation for linking discourse theory with anthropology of communication, axiology of intercultural relations and critical analysis of symbolic culture.

With great ease she went beyond the boundaries of specific disciplines, and with equal ease she found common scientific interests with people from all continents, with whom she shared the view of man in the world of semiosis, but also of values, cognition and emotions. Effectively she implemented her skills into the operation of scientific institutions, procedures and policies to achieve their objectives in the best possible way, a talent which is not common these days. One important example of her interdisciplinary, Renaissance approach is the long-running series of *GlobE* conferences, which she endowed with the traits close to herself: being open to different types of cultural sensitivity and outlook, and being open to different models and languages of science.

dr hab. Leszek Korporowicz,
Jagiellonian University in Kraków

It is with a deep sense of sadness that I write these words in tribute to Professor Anna Duszak. I still think of Professor Duszak as my mentor who embodied all the important qualities of an eminent scholar, including inquisitiveness, commitment, excellence and intellect, which allowed her to perform pioneering work in the fields of discourse analysis, cross-cultural communication and social semiotics.

I first met her in October 2012 during the conference *Pragmatyka 2012* in Łódź. I still vividly remember the conversation we had about my academic interests and plans for my future research. Despite being very tired after a whole day of participating in different conference activities she was very generous with her time and inspired me with ideas which helped crystallize my decision on how to frame my research into the issues of identity and academic writing. In the years to come (from 2013 to 2015) I was a regular participant at the annual *GlobE* conference, conceived and chaired by Professor Duszak. The conferences focused on issues of discourse analysis in cross-cultural perspectives, both historically and currently, and created opportunities for me to gain invaluable insights into this area of studies and to benefit from the exchange of academic ideas which allowed me to develop my research interests.

Above all, I will remember Professor Duszak as a person who inspired me to conduct my research in a way which asks us to break with received and preconceived assumptions and to try to preserve the dynamics of the process of the acquisition of knowledge, seen for what it is, not for what others want us to see it as. I found this approach captured beautifully by Wallace Stevens in his poem "Study of Two Pears":

I
Opusculum paedagogum.
The pears are not viols,
nudes or bottles.
They resemble nothing else.

II
They are yellow forms
Composed of curves
Bulging toward the base.
They are touched red.

III
They are not flat surfaces
Having curved outlines.
They are round
tapering toward the top.

[…]

VI
The shadows of the pears
Are blobs on the green cloth.
The pears are not seen
As the observer wills.

dr Iga Maria Lehman,
University of Social Sciences, Warsaw

I did not meet Dr Duszak, Professor Anna Duszak, or Ania, too often – she worked in Warsaw, and I was based in Kraków, so there were no common rooms we could share and no common corridors to walk along together. And yet, over all those years, I considered myself as Ania's friend. I was honoured to get invitations to participate in the *GlobE* conferences – one of her many brain children. I came to speak at *GlobE 2013*, and – as many times before – admired Ania's courage and stamina. I knew about her condition, but her performance at the conference gave no clue to those not in the know. There is one feature that I always associated with Ania: she was a lady. She dressed like a lady, she walked like a lady, she talked like a lady. She worked as a lady; the texts she wrote were wise and elegant. And, most important of all, she never broke her rules. At the *GlobE 2013* I saw her for the last time; the standard of her performance and her conduct did not suffer in the least from her suffering. As ever, she was friendly, gentle and open to suggestions, yet firm when it came to express her opinions – on the rules of discourse, on the role of metaphor in life, on relations between human language and human condition.

prof. Elżbieta Muskat-Tabakowska,
Jagiellonian University in Kraków

Part 1.
Discourse Studies: Theoretical considerations

Danuta Ulicka

University of Warsaw, Poland

Migratory metaphors – resident terms*

Abstract: The aim of this paper is to analyze the problem of translatability of scientific terms and the related issue of translatability of scientific cultures. These questions are addressed in relation to the translation of terminological metaphors introduced into scientific circulation by Mikhail Bakhtin. The metaphors, which have been established in the humanities since the mid-20th century, are still in use in the 21st century.

Among many terms/non-terms coined by Bakhtin the most interesting are not the best known ones like *dialogue*, *polyphony* or *discourse*, which all remain the key 'tools' of 'Bakhtinological industry', but rather the ones which have come into global use recently, like *chronotope*, or those with a turbulent history, like *heteroglossia* or *exotopy*. Additional data referred to in the current discussion, which would help us to analyze translation as a relatively smooth path linking incongruent East- and West-European scientific cultures, are the key terms introduced by Russian formalists, specifically Shklovsky's widely applied terms/non-terms *ostranenie* 'defamiliarization' and *iskusstvo kak priom* 'art as device / art as technique'. These items in particular clearly illustrate the topic discussed, which has been widely analyzed on the material of literary cultures but marginalized in the context of scientific ones. The present paper thus aims to show that the translatological practice of unifying the original styles of scientific writing as are embedded in specific ideological and biographical contexts monologizes the highly appreciated and commonly declared intercultural dialogue, and in effect reproduces the Englightment's universalism.

1. Migration of terms – unification of cultures

Half a century lapsed from the time when Bakhtin created his concepts until they were transferred from Eastern to Western Europe and further to the USA, i.e. between two totally different political, social and scientific contexts. As a result Bakhtin wrote for one audience and was read by another (Gasparov, 1979, p. 113). This historically determined context in which his works were read sometimes provoked certain misunderstandings, which the Russian scholar actually found amusing. For instance, he is said to have made a jocular comment on the

* The research reported in this paper was financially supported by Polish National Science Centre (NCN) project "The Age of Theory. A Century of Polish Literary Studies", grant no. 2014/13/B/HS2/00310.

German translation of *Tvorchestvo François Rabelais*, where the second part of the title is *Volkskultur als Gegenkultur*: seeing it, Bakhtin noted that he had no intention of becoming an ideologist of the 1968 student revolt back in 1936 (Bakhtin, 1987, 2002, p. 69).

Considering that the treatise on the *grande bouffe* and the *grande* laughter was written at the time of the great famine and the raging Great Purge, it is evident that Bakhtin's concepts were adopted as ready terms rather than ideas proper. The terms (or, to be precise, metaphors, which only in consequence of global circulation became terms in international lexicons) would become separated from the source domain and its ideological burden to become terms proper. They would be reinterpreted – and overinterpreted – and sometimes even their form would be changed in translation.

Yet Bakhtin's terms were surprisingly well applicable to new cultural fields. Transformed (sometimes beyond recognition) and disseminated not only among ethnically diverse scientific languages, but also among different scientific disciplines, they were the key force that stimulated the development of the "Bakhtin Industry", as Gary Saul Morson (1986) sarcastically dubbed the West-European fascination with the scholar.

Rhetorically apt terminological metaphors were successful enough to conceal the shortcomings of the underlying concepts. For instance, *carnival* turned out to be a befitting name which abated all the controversies over the related concept. The equally apt *Menippean satire* refuted the critics' allegation of the genre's fictitiousness, which was based on insufficiently proven materials. Finally, the persuasively strong *parody* soon replaced the more comprehensive and better developed philological proposals made by Yury Tynyanov ([1921] 1977) and Olga Freudenberg ([1926] 1973).

While the concepts themselves have often been misread and/or unread even at the elementary level of linguistic competence, they eventually proved to be more influential worldwide than any other which may have been later proposed. They have achieved this status in many and complex ways. Firstly, most work in popularizing Bakhtin's concepts seems to have been done by emigrants, who acted as both reviewers and translators of his output. Their efforts were successful enough to make it canonical. Secondly, Bakhtin's ideas were well matched with the apperceptive context of the late 1960s, when they were first adopted by French structuralists, and then also by their American opponents. The whole story is well known, from the crisis of structuralism in the mid-1960s, through the expansion of political and cultural ideas in literary studies of the 1980s until the development of the policy towards otherness and the ethics of reading of the 1990s.

Yet the related debates have hardly ever touched the problem of the possible dialogue between incongruent scientific cultures. In fact, it has only been addressed by translation theorists, who focused mostly on translatability of concepts, which they assumed to be uncontroversial at all – even if it meant compromising the form and/or updating it. By contrast, the problem of translatability of the terms proper was generally neglected. And yet in Bakhtin's work, as in the works of many other "thinking philologists" (Braginska, 2004, p. 51), "scholars-writers" such as e.g. Viktor Shklovsky (Tihanov, 2005; see also Boym, 1996), or "transreason theorists" such as Aleksey Kruchenykh (Jangfeldt, 1992, p. 48), it is untranslatability of terminological metaphors that prompts scholars to revisit the question whether a true cross-cultural scientific dialogue is indeed possible and true.[1] Their untranslatability results from the fact that few (and sometimes no) equivalents can be provided for terminological metaphors without the loss of their pragmatic semantic potential, which in turn makes heretical paraphrasing a necessity.

2. Some problems of Bakhtin's poetics

As has already been mentioned, it is in French and English translations of Bakhtin's works that his semantically vague metaphors were gradually stabilized into terms, which have been in turn introduced into dictionaries of Western scientific culture since the 1960s. Considering the continuous (and ineffective) efforts to define their meaning, it becomes evident that Western scientific culture is much different to the Russian one of the first half of the 20th century. One of the reasons is that Bakhtin's language was not theoretical, or, as Julia Kristeva (1995, p. 6) observed when trying to translate his letter into French, it was not a Cartesian language. Bakhtin avoided unambiguous – or extremely monotone, as he himself put it – terms (Gogotishvili, 2003, p. 403; see also Holquist, 1981). Instead of explaining them he would rather provide complex sequences of synonyms; in fact, amplification was one of the key features of his language. Again and anew he would create variants of words he had already introduced, sometimes difficult to be distinguished from the original ones. Or he would often add new meanings to a word or, conversely, he would give a similar, if not the same, meaning to different words, or at least locate them in the same semantic field.

---

1 Certainly, I share Emilly Apter's (2013) view stressed in her *Against World Literature: on the Politics of Untranslatability*. However, in this context it is also worth recalling Bronisław Malinowski's (1923) study "The Problem of Meaning in Primitive Languages", especially Part III, where Malinowski introduced his concepts of *context* and *situation*.

Bakhtin himself pointed to the specificity of his language. Sometimes he would apparently downplay this issue, as for instance in the late work *From notes made in 1970–1971*, where he simply emphasized his "love for variations" (Bakhtin, 1986, p. 155). In this remark Bakhtin confirmed his continuous adherence to the views which he laid out in a more serious tone some thirty years earlier in his short essay *K voprosam samosoznanija i samootsenki* 'On Questions of Self-Consciousness and Self-Evaluation' from 1943: "[a]ll the following processes occur in the term (…) the meaning becomes stable, the metaphorical force decreases, polysemy is lost, and so is the play with meanings" (Bakhtin, 1996, p. 79).[2] This viewpoint was founded on Bakhtin's opposition to systemic knowledge, which, according to him, does not include any discipline of cultural studies. As he wrote a few years later in the *Notes from 1962–1963*,

> [d]efining a term (its stability and unambiguity) is only possible in terms of function and system. Without a system (as in the case of literary studies) an accurate definition of a single isolated term transforms it into a mossy stone under which the thought does not run in a swift stream
>
> (Bakhtin, 1996, p. 377).

Contrary to the common opinion, the reasons why Bakhtin used such an apparently vague and unstable language in his writing do not stem from his critique of contemporary 'formalism', nor of 'structuralism' later, but are related to the principles essential to his scientific and literary viewpoint. Among these principles one can also find traces of the Slavophilic 'Russian idea', reanimated in the 1920s by Trubetzkoy in the Eurasian movement's manifesto *Evropa i chelovechestvo* 'Europe and Mankind'. They also explain Bakhtin's strongly polemical attitude towards Baconian and Cartesian models of science.

Among other factors which contributed to the evolution of Bakhtin's style of reasoning and writing there should be listed in particular:

(1) strong attachment to **symbolism** – *symbolism* broadly understood as both theory and practice (literary, philosophical, theological, socio-political etc.) Bakhtin's attachment to symbolism evolved under the influence of the poet and philosopher Vyacheslav Ivanov. In general, Bakhtin was attracted by the symbolist idea of *artistic theurgy*, especially the creative power of speech, capable of creating concepts inaccessible (as was widely believed) to objective rational cognition. Bakhtin adopted this idea to his esthetics, so that he could freely create names of phenomena belonging to the science which

2 Russian excerpts translated by Danuta Ulicka and Grzegorz Kowalski.

he termed *symbology*, using Sergey Averintsev's (1971) term. As in the case of symbolism, he coined neosemanticisms and neologisms, applied diverse word-formation processes, paranomasias and etymologizations – not to create totally new phenomena, existing neither in language nor in reality, but in order to retrieve long-forgotten and obliterated knowledge about reality. His goal was to 'reveal' such knowledge, or to 'fathom' it, as he said, paraphrasing Ivanov's comment on Dostoyevsky's work;

(2) influence of Tadeusz Zieliński, the author of the ideology of the Third (Slavic) Renaissance and key advocate of Nietzsche's philosophy in Russia. Sublime poetic works by Zieliński and Nietzsche, along with early studies of Kierkegaard, all contributed to Bakhtin's scientific anti-Cartesianism;

(3) **phenomenology**, being the third major source of influence in Bakhtin's language. Unlike his contemporaries – Gustav Shpet and Boris Engelgardt – Bakhtin did not adopt phenomenological epistemology, to which he was generally opposed. He put the phenomenological principle "from things to concepts" to the test of neo-Kantian verification, and claimed that a thing itself, even if it exists, is only accessible as "a thing in language". Instead, Bakhtin adopted Husserlian ontology and semantics. Of course, phenomenology and neo-Kantian influences were not necessarily mutually exclusive. Still, Bakhtin adopted more elements from the former, especially its principle of not defining concepts and their free creation based on colloquial speech. This principle expresses the pragmatic belief in evoking meanings in the recipient's mind rather than their accurate determining and designating.

Rejecting the already existing terms and creating new names on the basis of colloquial speech correspond with Bakhtin's concept of understanding as a response, which concept was also supported in phenomenology. On the other hand, this concept, which subsumed *otvetstvennost' otveta* 'responding and responsibility'[3], was not only inspired by Bakhtin's favourite philosophical and poetic texts. Of equal relevance was the influence of the restrictive context of contemporary Soviet science. Scholars were forced to produce such texts and utterances which would not provoke any wrong or unwelcome associations, but only referred to the contexts as intended by the author – even if not presented verbatim in the text.

In the context of Soviet scientific policy – which was repressive not only to people, but also to all terminology deemed 'detrimental' or 'hostile' – the semantic power of an argument was fully dependent upon its 'dense' verbal structure, which could in turn activate the reader's associations. In consequence Bakhtin had to use

3 In some translations: 'answering' and 'answerability'.

clear allusions which showed the reader the actual origins of a given metaphorical term. Also, he had to guide the reader to recognize all the citations, reminiscences, and other references to the authors and works banned in the official distribution.

These skills Bakhtin mastered from Leo Spitzer's (1920) poignant work *Die Umschreibungen des Begriffes „Hunger" In Italienischen*. During WW1 Spitzer was a censor in a camp for Italian prisoners of war; his duty was to erase the banned word 'hunger' from their letters. An expert philologist, Spitzer easily found out diverse ways of paraphrasing this word, which in turn inspired his concept of double addressee: the official one and the real one.

The three above-discussed principles of Bakhtin's scientific style and the double addressee strategy, which he had to employ in Soviet political circumstances, all explain the non-transparency of his terminological metaphors. Most of them will remain unclear unless one is aware of their origins and the context in which they were created, or unless one adds some explanatory footnotes. Otherwise they can be only useful in essay-writing, whereas in the scientific domain of cultural studies they will remain silent.

3. Term as abbreviation of discursive field

The translators' misunderstanding and/or ignorance of the tenets of Bakhtin's viewpoint presented in his works resulted in the (sometimes total) loss of the semantics of his terminological metaphors in translations. This is also the case of some fundamental terms such as *vnenakhodimost'*, a particularly significant term which Bakhtin used in his early works of the 1920s to describe first the relation I–Other in the philosophy of religion, and then, once the term was adopted in ethics and esthetics, the relation between the author and the character.

In Russian the word *vnenakhodimost'* is a neologism, probably derived by Bakhtin from Jonas Cohn's philosophy of religion: the Russian word itself follows the structure of the original German term. When interpreting Bakhtin's considerations on the crisis of authorship (Bakhtin, 1979, p. 178), Tzvetan Todorov translated *vnenakhodimost'* as *exotopy* (Todorov, 1981, 1984), using the Greek root. By doing so he totally neglected not only Bakhtin's rule of creating new terms on the basis of colloquial language, but also his strong reliance on the philosophy of German neo-Kantianism (the latter being further emphasized by the reference to Volkelt's *trans-subjectivity*).

This neglect has significant consequences. Firstly, Todorov's *exotopy* is in no way related to the philosophy of religion, the field in which Bakhtin started his scientific inquiries and the field to which he continuously contributed during his academic career. If one fails to recognize this relationship, then the topics discussed by Bakhtin in his later studies (e.g. analysis of Dostoyevsky's works) and his terminology (e.g. *superaddressee*) will remain obscure. Secondly, replacing the German root with the Greek one conceals the strong impact of German scientific culture not only on the Russian one, but also on the culture of Central and Eastern Europe in general. Thirdly, it also obscures the important debate on the political model of state, which took place in Russia in the early 20th century, the debate between the advocates of so-called 'Russian idea' and the supporters of West-European liberal democracy, the latter being associated in the academic circles with the neo-Kantian conception of cognition.

Another example illustrating how the translators of Bakhtin's works neglected his viewpoint and the contemporary context is the term known nowadays as *heteroglossia*, which, however, is a more complex case than *vnenakhodimost'*. Bakhtin is generally recognized as the author of *heteroglossia* – but the truth is that he did not know this term at all. He only introduced the **notion** of *heteroglossia* to contemporary cultural studies, but not the term itself. In fact, in German and English translations of his works and their glosses the term *heteroglossia* is used as equivalent to no fewer than three names, different in form and scope of reference, and referring to different social and linguistic phenomena, namely *raznoyazychie, raznoriechie* and (less frequent) *mnogoyazychie* (Bakhtin, 1975).

To complicate the things even more, *heteroglossia*, the term nowadays ascribed to Bakhtin, is used interchangeably with *heterology*, which was created by Tzvetan Todorov. The latter was used along with *heteroglossia* in the French edition of the work, but later removed by the American translator of his monographs (Todorov, 1984). In spite of Todorov's precise terminological distinction between *raznoyazychie* (which he called 'heteroglossia') and *raznoriechie* (which he called 'heterology'), Wlad Godzich did not respect it, and nor did the translators of a part of Bakhtin's collection *Problems of Literature and Esthetics* (1975) published three years earlier as *The Dialogic Imagination* (Bakhtin, 1981). Moreover, *heteroglossia* has phrasal equivalents, defining descriptively its capacity and content: *speech diversity, social diversity of speech types* or *mix of varied and opposing voices.*[4] In some cases *heteroglossia* is also used interchangeably with *polyglossia*. The latter is in turn used interchangeably with *polylogy, multivocality* and *polyphony*, and sometimes even as a synonym of *plurilingualism*.[5]

---

4 Cf. Hirschlop and Shepherd (1989). In the 2nd edition of Hirschlop and Shepherd (Eds.) (2001) the dictionary of terms is not available any more.

5 Cf. Zbinden (1999).

In all this terminological amalgam only one thing can be stated with full certainty: heteroglossia has two fathers. The father of the **notion** *heteroglossia* is Mikhail Mikhailovich Bakhtin, the father of the **term** – the American translator of Tzvetan Todorov's monograph *Mikhail Bakhtine: le principe dialogique*. Thanks to them Bakhtin's original tripartite concept was transformed into a single term (and thus a single sociolinguistic phenomenon) in 1984, and since then it has been recognized in 20th-century humanities worldwide – to an extent that no previous term has ever been recognized.

Yet the terminological fusion of the three names coined by Bakhtin also flattened the differences between the distinctive linguistic and social phenomena to which they referred. Multilingualism (*mnogoyazychie*) in Bakhtin's sense referred to the differentiation of national languages in the context of a multilingual cultural community. It emphasized the pluralist character of such culture, capable of destroying any language likely to become universal (as in the case of Latin in the Middle Ages) or dominant (as in the case of French in the 17th and 18th centuries). In this ethnic sense multilingualism was considered by Bakhtin to be the precondition for the emergence of the novel as a genre not only in modern Europe, but also in its embryonic form in Antiquity. A synecdochical illustration of this phenomenon in Bakhtin's work is Lucian, one of the characters presented in *Iz predystorii romannogo slova* [From the Prehistory of Novelistic Discourse], a Syrian living in the Hellenic Greece, speaking Aramaic, writing in Greek, and educated by Romans (Bakhtin, 1975, p. 429).

By contrast, language diversity (*raznoyazychie*) referred to diversification of national languages (ethnolects) in the context of a multinational state community, all of which were equal in a liberal democratic state, a political form most desired by Bakhtin and social thinkers of the 1900–1920 period. Language diversity was opposed to a single, institutionally imposed language of the official public communication.

Finally, social stratification was accounted for in *raznoriechie* 'multi-speechedness', which referred to a broad spectrum of sociolects, i.e. distinctive forms of speech influenced by status, profession and rank in both official and unofficial hierarchies of language users, and of occasionalisms, which are created if necessary in situational, informal contexts of private, familial and intimate communication, and which absorb personally marked elements of speech.

To sum up, the currently used single term *heteroglossia* covers phenomena which Bakhtin – in his works of the mid-1930s and 1940s, and later of the late 1940s and early 1950s – identified at three different dimensions: macro-dimension (in the case of multilingualism, i.e. *mnogoyazychie*), micro-dimension (in the case of language diversity, i.e. *raznoyazychie*) and mezzo-dimension (in the case of multi-speechedness, i.e. *raznoriechie*). These dimensions are not separate, but intersect. For instance, neither a continuum of ethnolects nor one along which diverse national languages are located excludes the diversity of sociolects (i.e. *raznoriechie* 'multi-speechedness'). Similarly, multiple varieties of speech and diversity of its stylistic forms and genres can be observed in both the macro-dimension of national languages and the micro-dimension of social, familial and intimate languages. Metaphorically – though not without Bakhtin's credit – one can say: thanks to them we can observe the world as in physics – Einsteinian and Newtonian at the same time – simultaneously in the micro- and macro- perspectives. A single *heteroglossia* flattens this diversity of dimensions in which the phenomena covered by the term are located.

However, what is more important than the tripartite distinction proposed by Bakhtin is the origins of Bakhtin's concept and the related names. It can be assumed that the decisive role in the evolution of Bakhtin's views in literary studies was played by 'everyday life', as was also the case of the linguistic views of Polyvanov and Jan Baudouin de Courtenay, with which Bakhtin's are related. The three scholars lived in a multi-ethnic, socially and ideologically diversified melting-pot. They also shared the particular ability to perceive in a language something more than just linguistic units. Yet their views were most influenced by the specific contemporary political context.

The **notion** of *heteroglossia* first appeared in Bakhtin's works in the mid-1930s, and it was most comprehensively discussed in the essay *Slovo v romane* [Discourse in the Novel] and in the study *Iz predystorii romannogo slova* [From the Prehistory of Novelistic Discourse], both written between the years 1934–1936. The two names referring to this notion, i.e. language diversity (*raznoyazychie*) and multi-speechedness (*raznoriechie*), supplanted the **term** *polyphony* recurrent in *Problemy tvorchestva Dostoyevskego* [Problems of Dostoyevsky's Creation] published in 1929.[6]

This development of Bakhtin's theory took place in a very difficult historical context. In 1934, after the murder of Kirov, terror was omnipresent in the Soviet Union. It had not been so savage after Lenin's death, and not so much either during the first and second purges of intellectuals (1922 and 1926–1929, respectively). In 1934 the victims of terror were artists and the *intelligentsia*. It was also the year of

6 It must be remarked at this point – although this fact is obvious to bakhtinologists – that this work should not be mistaken with the well-known *Problemy poetiki Dostoyevskogo* [Problems of Dostoyevsky's Poetics] (1963); the 1929 version cannot be considered the first edition, as Wellek (1980) put it.

the trial in the so-called 'Slavic conspiracy' case, where the accused were deemed guilty of espionage for Germany. The ensuing exile was devastating for Viktor Vinogradov, Bakhtin's faithful partner in conversations on the stylistics of the novel.[7] Bakhtin, who himself was exiled for five years since 1929, returned to the central Soviet Union in 1934, but, terrified with the ongoing events, he decided to settle in a more peripheral – thus safer – region, namely in the city of Kostanay (northern Kazakhstan). Also, Bakhtin had no one to come back to.

In 1936 died Bakhtin's friend, Valentin Voloshinov, at whose funeral another friend, Boris Zubakin, was arrested, and soon afterwards executed by the firing squad. Zubakin was a representative of Bakhtin's philosophical circle of Nevel, who, despite the ban inflicted on him as an exile, arrived in Moscow to participate in the funeral of his friend, a former Freemason – Rosicrucianist, just like Zubakin himself. In 1937 Matvei Kagan died of heart attack; he was a disciple of Cohen and the actual author of the idea of Bakhtin's neo-Kantian circle in Nevel and Vitebsk. Kagan was long plagued by the fear of imminent arrest. In 1938 one of the closest friends of Bakhtin, Pavel Medvedev, was arrested and executed, and so was Yevgeny Dmitrievich Polyvanov earlier in the same year.

Bakhtin stayed in Kostanay until 1936, when his exile came to an end. He then worked for one year in Saransk in Mordovia, but fearing the raging Great Terror he left this city in early July 1937. He lodged with his friends, moving from one to another, and took up different jobs to earn for living. Finally, Bakhtin settled in Savelevo near Moscow, and later moved to the hamlet Kimry. This state of affairs lasted until 1945. Bakhtin lost his friends with whom he co-operated in intellectual exchanges, in this peculiar form of Soviet 'collective'.

Leaving aside their impact on specific biographies, the Great Terror and the Great Purge entailed an increased monologization of public life. They also enforced the obligatory use of words-axioms not only in politics, but also in all domains of artistic and intellectual creation: painting, music, theatre and literature on the one hand, and biology, mathematics, philosophy, linguistics and poetics on the other. Many and diverse movements in arts, as well as multilingualism and language diversity of methodological comments on them, were all common in intellectual and ideological contexts before the Revolution and immediately after, as long as until 1926–1932 (for instance, in the public debate on so-called formal school in musical studies, theory of fine arts and literary studies). After the mid-1930s they were all gone.

7 Cf. Ashnin and Alpatov (1994). See also Robinson (2004) and Kemp-Welsch (1991, p. 190–239).

The murder of Kirov led to the dissolution of the Soviet Writers Association, which was independent of political authorities. Even specific ethnic languages of the multi-national empire were eradicated; the All-Union Central Committee for New Alphabet (1925–1937) concentrated its activities on the unification of ethnic languages, the development of a single official 'literary language', which would flatten national and social diversities, and the introduction of a single alphabet (Cyrillic script). The precedent reform, so-called 'Bolshevik reform of orthography', which was only applied to the Russian language, was then extended to other 'national' languages (Perrie, 1998, pp. 28–30). The dire consequences of this 'linguistic engineering' (*jazykovoe stroitiel'stvo* – the term coined and applied at the time) can be observed in the poetry of Ukrainian futurists, who used two scripts in the same poem: Latin and Cyrillic (Illnytzkyj, 1977).

The above-described political context is also reflected in Bakhtin's system of concepts. The most important are names referring to social and ethical ideas: non-uniformity of language and viewpoint; multiplicity and diversity of languages, words, utterances, genres and discourses, which are now covered by a single term – *heteroglossia*. This term, evidently overused in political and cultural studies, tells more about us than about its author. It is a symbol of monophony of the post-modern thought, which advocates legitimization of the ideals of difference, otherness and heteronomy, but which in fact is dominated by one single viewpoint (and dictionary), and, by extension, one ethnolect.

4. Back to the roots

The transfer of Bakhtin's concepts did not always involve reduction, which resulted in neglecting the original names' illocutionary felicity and their perlocutionary power. An example of a successful transfer of both the concept and the name is the term (in the proper sense of this word) *chronotope*. The term was adopted by Bakhtin in 1925 after his meeting with Alexei Ukhtomsky, a Kantist, physiologist-precognitivist, and, like Bakhtin, an expert in the works of Kant, Dostoyevsky and Einstein. Bakhtin applied the term in his studies on the forms of time and space in the novel (Bakhtin, 1975, pp. 234–407).

Having said that, one should remember that in Ukhtomsky's works *chronotope* referred to the principles of the cognitive work of the mind. According to contemporary knowledge in natural sciences and philosophy, such cognitive work involved categorization of sensory data on the basis of spatio-temporal matrixes first indicated by Kant, and later confirmed by Einstein. In his empirical research carried out in the laboratory in Peterhoff Ukhtomsky developed the ideas which Bakhtin then expressed in the language of historical poetics, in his analysis of the changes in the ways of orientation in reality as reflected in the composition of time and space in the novel (Ivanov, 2009). Today Bakhtin's/Ukhtomsky's term *chronotope* returns to its roots. When interpreting Bakhtin's views, researchers go beyond the term's exclusive poetological application, and foreground its original neurosemiotic sense (Keuen, 2000).

Still, *chronotope* is an exception in the language of international humanities (its language is English – a situation far from the ideal of polyglossia). Presumably the term retained its original sense due to the fact that it has never drawn particular attention and has not been much commented upon. It seemed transparent when used in both poetological and cognitivist contexts. By contrast, Bakhtin's other terminological metaphors were usually deprived of polysemy and non-paraphrasability otherwise typical of metaphors. In consequence they became purely instrumental and turned into generally accessible tools to be used freely.

5. Domestication as monologization

Polysemantic reduction is one of the strategies of contemporary humanities, which attracts terms coined in other cultures and adapts them to its own tradition and needs. Domestication and defamiliarization co-occur.

Interestingly, *defamiliarization* is an English term, nowadays widely used, also in Poland, which is an equivalent of the terminological metaphor *priom ostranienia* 'estrangement device / defamiliarization device' coined by Viktor Shklovsky in 1914 (or even already in 1913). The expansion of the term *defamiliarization* in 20th-century humanities has no precedent, being comparable with that of *dialogue*. *Defamiliarization* is used in different fields of science – from poetics to political studies, from ethics to neurology, in theories of different arts and in their practical output. In all these different contexts it has been used interchangeably with many synonyms, e.g. *unusalizing, hindering, alienation*. *Defamiliarization* was also paralleled with certain philosophical terms, including Hegel's *Entäusserung*, Marx's *Entfremdung*, Brecht's *Verfremdung*, or Jentsch's and Freud's *Unheimliche*, and sometimes it was even assimilated with them (Tihanov, 2005). It also inspired the creation of opposite (Nikolay Krushevsky's *stereotypical device*) and complementary terms (Yuri Lotman's *null device*; Jakobson's *essential non-recognition device*). It stimulated terminological variations, in which it took the form *otstranienije*. In the light of the above facts it should be considered the model case of Wittgenstein's concept of family resemblance, whose fuzzy meaning cannot be defined. All in all, *defamiliarization* clearly shows how much important a relevant name must be to become successful in science.

Both strategies, domestication and defamiliarization, involve the application of forces which, following Bakhtin, can be named *centrifugal forces* and *centripetal forces* (Bakhtin, 1975, p. 431). The former are related with the culture of scientific monologue, which aims at the unambiguity of language, stability and definability of names-terms, methodological coherence and clarity, and adherence to once formulated assumptions, from which non-controversial conclusions must be drawn. Historically, centrifugal forces occur with the positivist and neo-positivist concept of science. By contrast, centripetal forces support heterogeneity, diversity, non-stability and ambiguity. Historically, they occur with concepts originating in hermeneutics.

The point of my argument is not that we should evaluate the strategies applied in the transfer of concepts and names proposed by Bakhtin or Shklovsky, or the transformations which their metaphors have undergone in the subsequent transfers. Rather, the history and sociology of knowledge, and the contemporary cultural concept of histories of knowledges[8] emphasize that we must understand the circumstances in which these ideas emerged, the purposes they served, how they were used in the original context, to whom they were addressed and at whom/what they were aimed. Flattening and/or neglecting these pragmatic parameters will result in ignoring the value of intercultural dialogue, which inevitably changes into a monologue.

References

Apter, E. (2013). *Against World Literature: on the Politics of Untranslatability*. London & New York: Verso.

Ashnin, F., & Alpatov, W. (1994). *Delo slavistov': 30-je gody*. Moskva: Nasledie.

Averintsev, S. S. (1971). "Simvol". In *Kratkaya literaturnaya entsiklopediya*, Moskva: Sovetskaya entsyklopediya. Retrieved from: http://feb-web.ru/feb/kle/kle-abc/ke6/ke6-8262.htm. DOA: 24.03.2016.

Bakhtin, M. M. (1975). "Slovo w romane". In *Voprosy literatury i estetiki*. Moskva: Khudozhestvennaya literatura, 72–234.

Bakhtin, M. M. (1979). *Estetika slovesnogo tvorchestva*. Moskva: Iskusstvo.

Bakhtin, M. M. (1981). *The Dialogic Imagination: Four Essays*. Edited by M. Holquist. Translated by C. Emerson & M. Holquist. Austin: University of Texas Press.

8 Following Burke (2016), 'knowledge' should be used in plural.

Bakhtin, M. M. (1986). *Speech Genres and Other Late Essays*. Edited by C. Emerson & M. Holquist. Translated by V. W. McGee. Austin: University of Texas Press.

Bakhtin, M. M. (1987). *Rabelais und seine Welt. Volkskultur als Gegenkultur*. Edited by G. Leupold. Preface by R. Lachmann. Frankfurt M.: Shurkamp.

Bakhtin, M. M. (1996). *Sobranie sochinienii*, vol. 5: *Raboty nachala 1940-kh–nachala 1960-kh godov*. Edited by S. Bocharov & L. Gogotishvili. Moskva: Russkiye slovari.

Bakhtin, M. M. (2002). *Besedy s Duvakinym*. Moskva: Soglasie.

Boym, S. (1996). Estrangement as Lifestyle: Shklovsky and Brodsky. *Poetics Today*, 17, 511–530.

Braginska, N. (2004). Slavianskoye vozrozhdenie antichnosti. In *Russkaia teoriia 1920–1930-gody. Materialy 10-kh Lotmanovskikh chtenii* (Moskva, dekabr' 2002). Moskva: RGGU, 49–80.

Burke, P. (2016). *What is the History of Knowledge?* Cambridge: Polity Press.

Freudenberg, O. M. ([1926] 1973). Proishozhdenie parodii. *Trudy po znakovym sistemam*, 6, 490–497.

Gasparov, M. (1979). M. M. Bakhtin v russkoi kul'ture XX veka. In V. V. Ivanov & Iu. M. Lotman (Eds.), *Vtorichnye modeliruiushchie sistemy*. Tartu: publisher n.a., 110–128.

Gogotishvili, L. (2003). [Kommentatorskiy blok to: M. M. Bakhtin *K filosofii postupka*] In: S. Bocharov & N. Nikolayev (Eds.), *M. Bakhtin, Sobranie sochinienii*, vol. 1: *Filosofskaya estetika 1920-kh godov*. Moskva: Yazyki slovyanskoy kultury, 351–438.

Hirschlop, K., & Shepherd, D. (1989) Glossary: Alternative Translations of Key Terms. In K. Hirschlop & D. Shepherd (Eds.) *Bakhtin and Cultural Theory*, Manchester: Manchester University Press, 190–194.

Hirschlop, K., & Shepherd, D. (Eds.) (2001) *Bakhtin and Cultural Theory*, Manchester & New York: Manchester University Press.

Holquist, M. (1981). The Politics of Representation. In S. Greenblatt (Ed.), *Allegory and Representation: Selected Papers from the English Institute 1979–1980*. Baltimore: John Hopkins University Press, 163–183.

Illnytzkyj, O. S. (1977). *Ukrainian Futurism 1914–1930. A Historical and Critical Study*. Cambridge, Mass.: Harvard University Press.

Ivanov, V. (2009). Tema chronotopa w kulture noveyshego vremeni. *Arbor Mundi/ Mirovoye Drevo*, 15, 141–163.

Jangfeldt, B. (Ed.) (1992). *Jakobson-Budietlanin. Sbornik matierialov*, Stockholm: Stockholm Studies in Russian Literature, vol. 26.

Jakobson, R. (1967). Znaczenie Kruszewskiego w rozwoju językoznawstwa. Translated by K. Pomorska. In M. Kruszewski (Ed.), *Wybór pism*. Wrocław: Ossolineum, X-XXV.

Kemp-Welsch, A. (1991). *Stalin and the Literary Intelligentsia, 1928–39*. Basingstoke: Macmillan.

Keunen, B. (2000). Bakhtin, Genre Formation, and the Cognitive Turn: Chronotopes as Memory Schemata. *Comprarative Literature and Culture*, 2(2). Retrieved from: http://docs.lib.purdue.edu. DOA: 25.03.2016.

Kristeva, J. (1995). Beseda s Iuliei Kristevoi. *Dialog. Karnaval. Chronotop*, 2, 5–17.

Kruszewski, M. (1967). *Wybór pism*. Preface by J. Kuryłowicz & R. Jakobson, Wrocław: Ossolineum.

Lachmann, R. (1970). Die «Verfremdung» und das «Neue Sachen» bei Viktor Shklovskij. *Poetica* 3, 226–249.

Malinowski, B. (1923). The Problem of Meaning in Primitive Languages. In C. K. Ogden & I. A. Richards (Eds.) *The Meaning of Meaning; a study of the influence of language upon thought and of the science of symbolism*. New York: Harcourt, Brace & co., 451–510.

Merkulov, V. L. (1960). *Aleksey Alekseyevich Ukhtomski. Ohzerk zhyzni i nauchnoy deyate'lnosti (1875–1942)*. Moskva & Leningrad: Izdatelstvo AN SSSR.

Morson, G. S. (1986). The Bakhtin Industry. *Slavic and East European Journal*, 30(1), 81–90.

van den Oever, A. (Ed.) (2012). *Ostrannenie: On "Strangeness" and the Moving Image: The History, reception, and Relevance of a Concept*, Amsterdam: Amsterdam University Press.

Perrie, M. (1998). 'Narodnost': Notions of National Identity. In K. Kelly & D. Shepherd (Eds.) *Constructing Russian Culture in the Age of Revolution: 1881–1940*. Oxford: Oxford University Press, 28–37.

Recchia, F. (Ed.) (2012). *Uniezwyklenie*, Gdańsk: Instytut Sztuki Wyspa.

Robinson, M. (2004). *Sud'by akademicheskoy elity: Otechestvennoye slavianovedenie (1917 – nachalo 1930-kh godov)*. Moskva: Indrik.

Spitzer, L. (1920). *Die Umschreibungen des Begriffes „Hunger" im Italienischen. Stilistisch-Onomoasiologische Studie auf Grund von unveröffentlichtem Zensurmaterial*, Halle: Max Niemeyer.

Tihanov, G. (2005). The Politics of Estrangement: The Case of Early Shklovsky. *Poetics Today*, 26(4), 665–696.

Todorov, T. (1981). *Mikhail Bakhtine: le principe dialogique (suivi de: Ecrits du Cercle Bakhtine)*. Edited by G. Genette & T. Todorov. Paris: Seuil.

Todorov, T. (1984). *Mikhail Bakhtin: The Dialogical Principle*. Translated by W. Godzich. Edited by W. Godzich & J. Schulte-Sasse. Minneapolis: University of Minnesota Press.

Trubetzkoy, N. S. (1920). *Evropa i chelovechestvo*. Sofia: Rosiisko-Bolgarskoe Knigoizdatiel'stvo.

Tynyanov, Y. ([1921] 1977). Dostoyevsky i Gogol (k teorii parodii). In Y. Tynyanov (Ed.) *Poetika. Istoriya literatury. Kino*, Moskva: Nauka, 284–310.

Wellek, R. (1980). *Bakhtin's View of Dostoyevsky: «Polyphony» and «Carnivalesque»*, Dostoyevsky Studies 1. Retrieved from: http://utoronto.ca/tsq/DS/01/031.shtml. DOA: 25.03.2016.

Zbinden, K. (1999). Traducing Bakhtin and Missing Heteroglossia. *Dialogism. An International Journal of Bakhtin*, 2, 41–59.

Katarzyna Molek-Kozakowska

University of Opole, Poland

Discourse Studies and Media Studies: Crossing disciplinary boundaries?

Abstract: This paper explores some of the correspondences, as well as contested points, between the discipline of Discourse Studies, which originates with linguistics and text analysis, and the discipline of Media Studies, which belongs to the domain of social sciences within communication studies. The main divergences with regard to production and reception of mediated texts, and the locus of meaning in mediated texts are presented. The implications of the often repeated postulate for crossing disciplinary boundaries are discussed. To illustrate this point I provide excerpts from abstracts of the papers recently published in the interdisciplinary journal *Discourse & Communication* to show how their authors position themselves with respect to those two disciplines. The results indicate that to negotiate a claim to interdisciplinarity successfully, linguists tend to invoke well-established production frameworks, correlate textual meanings with social phenomena, or rely on reception studies. Meanwhile, it is shown that projecting interdisciplinarity by drawing on concepts and integrating methods from concurrent fields, or presuming specific media effects of the studied texts, constitute rhetorical manoeuvers rather than actual cross-disciplinary research perspectives.

1. Introduction

Over the last four decades Discourse Studies has evolved into a diverse and accommodating field, where interdisciplinarity is encouraged, as it gives Discourse Studies an advantage over traditional approaches, which are less adequate to the purposes of investigation of many disparate practices within human communication. Traditionally delimited as a sub-discipline of (applied) linguistics, Discourse Studies was founded on such formative disciplinary influences as text linguistics, pragmatics, conversation analysis or cognitive science. Methodologically, it has diversified into several main approaches: socio-cognitive, discourse-historical, socio-semiotic, multimodal and argumentative, to name but a few. As for the main areas of interest of Discourse Studies, they include news/media, political/public discourse, or business/professional communication, each of which has preoccupied scholars of different backgrounds, but of shared identification as discourse analysts. Admittedly, the many ways of "doing discourse analysis" enrich the exploratory potential of Discourse Studies; however, they also make it less accessible and even prone to criticism for the lack of systematicity or comparability.

Against this complex and evolving background of the (inter-)disciplinary formation of Discourse Studies, I explore one interface that has both stirred some controversy and inspired productive developments in the field. In this paper I spotlight in particular the problems with the penetration of Discourse Studies into Media Studies with respect to the analysis of representations in mediated discourses. Within a tradition that dates back to the early twentieth century (cf. McQuail, 2000, for a historical overview of mass communication theories), communication and media scholars have been preoccupied with grasping the forms, functions and, most of all, effects of mediated communication, which discourse analysts have now declared to be able to be explained with their new methodologies. In fact, as pointed out by Philo (2008, p. 130), text-based discourse analysis of journalism for example has substantial problems in its ability to show the diversity of social interests and accounts and the impact of external factors such as professional ideologies on the manner in which representations are fashioned. It also has a limited capacity to inquire into such cases when one text means different things to different audiences, as text-based discourse analysis privileges the analyst's subjective reading.

Acknowledging such criticisms, this paper explores some issues of interdisciplinarity between Discourse Studies and Media Studies, demonstrating how discourse analysis of mediated communication could become a complementary perspective to Media Studies. Having said that, it is argued that Discourse Studies should not aspire to replace other methods of media scholarship, but advance it by offering a deeper understanding of how meaning is constructed through patterned use of linguistic and visual resources, not just through content and format/medium choices, as are mainly studied by journalism specialists. In this vein, the present study aims to ascertain how interdisciplinary complementarity can be articulated by tracing the ways of "doing discourse analysis" by language-oriented scholars of mediated communication. To do so, it reports on a meta-analysis of the sample of 47 abstracts published in the international interdisciplinary journal *Discourse & Communication* in 2014 and 2015. Its aim is to establish how effectively Discourse Studies and Media Studies perspectives tend to be integrated in the latest research.

2. Some contested points between Discourse Studies and Media Studies

Within the scope of Discourse Studies' methodology, particularly its critical branch (CDA), there is a constant search for adequate theoretical concepts and well-operationalized tools for "doing discourse analysis" (cf. Chilton, 2011; Krzyżanowski & Forchtner, 2016). By now, some well-accepted formulas for analyzing discourse have been claimed to be only partly sufficient and in need of development to increase the granularity and comprehensiveness of research.

For example, Halliday's (1985) socio-semiotic approach, setting the stage for discourse analyses of ideational, interpersonal and textual meta-functions in any discursive encounter, has been found limiting by analysts outside systemic-functionalist tradition.

Similarly, Fairclough's (1995) three-stage model consisting of (1) description of linguistic/textual resources used in the discourse, (2) interpretation of discursive practices with respect to authors' intentions and ideological effects, and (3) explanation of social practices that enable and sustain the discourse, though economic and elegant, has been seen as too interpretative (for a review of CDA's criticisms, see Breeze, 2011).

By contrast, Wodak's (cf. Reisigl & Wodak, 2001) holistic, heuristic and historically oriented approach applies more diverse analytic procedures and more calibrated data. It seeks to expound on the thematic facet of discourse and its multi-layered contextualization (situational, social, historical) before looking at five main strategies of presentation: reference, predication, argumentation, perspectivation/framing and mitigation/intensification through their concrete linguistic realizations. However, even this conceptual framework did not go without criticism (e.g. Žagar, 2010).

With the advent of more multimodal discourses, Kress and van Leeuwen's (1996) "grammar" of visual meaning potentials has adopted categories of traditional linguistic grammar into visual modes. Nevertheless, these categories have also been criticized as too intuitive and unsystematic (Bateman, 2008).

Against this backdrop of internal methodological debates originating within Discourse Studies, in the following three sections I discuss in more detail some contested points between Discourse Studies and Media Studies that might become obstacles to these fields' interdisciplinary complementarity if not addressed. They pertain to production, representation and analysis, and reception, respectively.

2.1. Production: Textual practices vs. professional practices

Media scholars following the tradition of the Glasgow Media Group criticize text-based discourse analysis for failing to show the origins of competing media discourses and their roots in different social interests. For instance, Philo (2008, p. 130) demonstrates how some CDA studies of news miss out on the impact of external factors such as professional ideologies on the ways how textual representations are shaped. However, although earlier discourse analytic research has focused on linguistic criticism of the press (e.g. Fowler, 1991; Hodge & Kress, 1993), or, has treated contextual factors as subordinated to discursive factors (van Dijk, 1988; Fairclough, 1989), other approaches (e.g. Bell, 1991; Richardson, 2007; Bednarek & Caple, 2012) have correlated textual practices with larger contexts of professional practices of writing journalists and editors.

Basing on their diverse approaches, media and discourse scholars tend to disagree on the degree of individuals' agency in the production of media texts. Some media discourse analysts originating in the pragma-linguistic tradition have developed tools to foreground the intentionality of the author, or the stance of writer or speaker in journalism. They would spotlight the agency of the communicators, and the degree to which their acting complies with the co-operative principle (Grice, 1975) and its focus on mutual understanding. Alternatively, some critical discourse analysts (Fowler, 1991; van Dijk, 2006) would reveal how words have been purposefully chosen and deliberately arranged to achieve a particular ideological effect. By contrast, sociological studies of media production highlight the routines and constraints of journalism as a highly structured social domain (e.g. Tuchman, 1978; Schudson, 1981). Finally, more recent studies reveal the prefabricated, patterned and generic nature of many journalistic texts (e.g. Jones & Salter, 2012), and the lack of control of an individual author over the final shape of the article or broadcast (e.g. Hoynes & Croteau, 2002).

That is why some of the scholars familiar with the editorial and managerial aspects of journalistic practice have tried to strike a balance between *agency* and *structure* (Giddens, 1991) in their methodology and research design (cf. Bell, 1991; Bednarek & Caple, 2012, 2014), for example by focusing on the discursive construction of news values. Having said that, scholars applying this approach have yet to fully acknowledge the socio-economic (McManus, 1994; Conboy, 2002) and socio-political (Capella & Jamieson, 1997; Harcup & O'Neill, 2002; McChesney & Nichols, 2011) factors that can be made accountable for certain journalistic practices, including epistemological assumptions and discursive routines (Ekstrom, 2002; Montgomery, 2007).

2.2. Representation and analysis: Content vs. meaning

Another point of controversy between Discourse Studies and Media Studies relates to methods of analysing media messages. One of the methods is content analysis, often resorted to by media scholars to reveal "the purposes, motives and other characteristics of the communicators as they are (presumably) 'reflected' in the content; or to identify the (presumable) effects of the content upon the attention, attitudes or acts of readers and listeners" (Richardson, 2007, p. 12). Richardson (2007, p. 11) distances himself from the claim that content analysis is "the objective, systematic and quantitative description of the manifest content of communication" because he doubts that interferences about the relationship between intent and content or between content and effect can validly be made, or that the actual relationship between them could be established. Another assumption which Richardson criticizes is that a study of the content can reveal the meaning of the text. This may be questionable as

> such an assumption is only really valid in the case of denotative, as opposed to connotative, meaning. For this reason content analysis usually attempts to keep the coded categories focused as much as possible on evident or unmistakable features of the text.
> (Richardson, 2007, p. 12)

This also means that some of the less definite categories of meaning tend to be left out by content analysts.

Another challengeable assumption in content analysis is that the quantitative description of a message's content is meaningful. This boils down to the frequency of occurrence of certain characteristics of content being the most important aspect of description of the communication process. But to understand why differences in frequency and distribution are significant, analysts need to investigate messages by applying contextual and constructivist approaches. In contrast to content analysis, (Critical) Discourse Analysis provides theoretical constructs and methodological tools for a more nuanced analysis with emphasis on "interpretations of the meanings of texts, rather than just quantifying textual features and deriving meaning from this" (Richardson, 2007, p. 15). Discourse analysts, through their corpus-driven studies, reveal salient patterns of collocation, grammatical structures, argumentative moves, discursive strategies, conceptual frames informing word choices and rhetorical devices, and can correlate them with contextual features to discover their functions.

In Media Studies the focus on content, not meaning or function, of the message has been reflected in the relative marginalization of such theories as technological determinism (McLuhan, 1964), and has coincided with the current treatment of rhetoric as a style-oriented sub-discipline of composition studies or oratory rather than a valid approach to mediated texts. It is only recently that style has been treated as meriting greater scholarly attention when it comes to media production and knowledge construction (Lanham, 2006). By contrast, discourse analysts have never shied away from studying the functional aspects of mediation, as their assumption is that meaning is co-constituted by form and content in context, and that register, style, rhetoric and other linguistic resources are instrumental to creating meaning.

2.3. Reception: Analysts vs. audiences

In her review of criticisms levelled against Critical Discourse Analysis, Breeze (2011) notes the tendency in CDA to eschew complex frameworks of text reception that lie at the core of communication studies (Potter, 2013). Instead of exploring audience reception studies, some CDA practitioners seem to choose an intuitive, if not naïve, understanding of how texts influence their receivers that supports their hermeneutic, language-oriented approach:

> The problem of obtaining evidence about the effects of the text on the reader or listener is one that is rarely even raised in CDA research. The bodies of research that exist in media studies or ethnography of communication are rarely even alluded to by CDA practitioners, and in general it can be stated that CDA lacks a cogent theory of audience effects and audience response that would provide support for its assertions about the influence of discourses on human subjects.
>
> (Breeze, 2011, p. 512)

By abdicating the willingness to inquire about actual 'perlocutionary' effects of mediation (considered to be beyond the scope of their research), discourse analysts may fall into the trap of circularity: they subordinate their analysis to the pre-formulated conclusion about the scope/degree of purported perloutionary effect. Moreover, without trying to check their interpretations of emergent representations, ideological meanings and hegemonic practices against the actual readings made by particular audiences, analysts project their interpretations as the most probable, even dominant ones. They privilege the analyst's perspective, even if they claim that they work with resources that belong to wider communities of practice and that their aim is to empower the public.

By contrast, since Hall's (1980) seminal work on encoding and decoding practices in broadcast texts, media scholars have taken into consideration the fact that particular audiences tend to engage in a variety of readings and responses, many of which have not been envisioned by analysts. The readers' social positioning, background knowledge or experience and interpretative literacies vary so much that a uniform 'preferred' or dominant reading is more of a coincidence than a rule. Audience-oriented studies have also revealed the degrees of active involvement of readers and readers-communicators (Lievrouw, 2011), which have rarely been taken into consideration by discourse scholars, who, in accordance with what their paradigm can prescribe, have kept postulating that readers are relatively uniform, passive and manipulable (e.g. van Dijk, 2006), without being positioned to verify that claim.

Considering that scholars in Media Studies have long been preoccupied with identifying and measuring media effects and influence (McQuail, 2000; Potter,

2013), whereas those in Discourse Studies have not considered this area to fall within the scope of their research, reception is, arguably, the aspect of research which would mostly profit from interdisciplinarity.

3. Discourse Studies of mediation: A meta-analysis

This work aims not only to review the main controversies involved in the disciplinary overlap between Discourse Studies and Media Studies, but also to illustrate how the problematic areas tend to be currently confronted by discourse analysts. Are discourse analysts willing to acknowledge criticisms coming from neighbouring disciplines and incorporate other perspectives to calibrate their methods? If Discourse Studies is to become a complementary rather than divergent or rivalling approach to mediated communication, will it admit Media Studies' insights and any attempt at reconciling the controversies?

The material for this meta-analysis is taken from 47 abstracts of all the research reports published in *Discourse & Communication* (*DCM*) in 2014 and 2015. *DCM* is an interdisciplinary impact-factor journal which aims to integrate language-oriented studies and social research on mediated communication. The choice of abstract as an object of study is motivated not only by the recent rise in the significance of abstracting and indexing of research articles for the purposes of academic access and assessment, but also by the fact that in abstracts authors need to precisely locate their studies within the increasingly multidisciplinary landscape of academic publishing. Given the need to "create a research space" (Swales, 1990) and to find a "gap to fill" with their study, writers have to not only position themselves within Discourse Studies, but also to make relevant references to neighboring fields.

Apart from its aim of reporting on the content and approach of the article, another function of the abstract is to persuade editors and readers to take interest in it; hence its likely rhetorical overlay. Indeed, one could claim that the limited space of the abstract imposes even higher demands on the authors to demonstrate the fit between the objectives of their study and the intellectual heritage of the discipline(s), as well as the scope of the journal, including the expectations of its diverse audiences.

This exploratory analysis aims to trace the main ways in which authors present their research on mediated communication and to see if they address any of the problematic aspects discussed above, and if so, what they consider to be the main strategies to achieve interdisciplinary complementarity.

Out of the 47 abstracts collected, 25 introduced a research report on mediated communication (including print/broadcast news reports, columns, lifestyle-oriented online texts and magazines, online comments and posts, advertising etc.), with the remaining abstracts being devoted to professional texts/interactions, restricted/non-mass mediated content, interpersonal computer-mediated communication etc. The gathered abstracts vary in length between 70 and 250 words. All abstracts which are excerpted here are anonymized (and treated as sampled textual material rather than authored work), and for this reason not provided with author identification. Their full versions are freely available at http://dcm.sagepub.com/. As with the theoretical sections above (cf. sections 2.1–2.3), I follow the same sequence of problematic areas in cross-disciplinary research on mediated discourse, namely the issue of production of mediated texts (section 3.1), the issue of mediated representation (section 3.2) followed with an analysis thereof (section 3.3). Similarly, as in section 2.3, I conclude with the issue of reception, explaining the nature of influence which the abstracts analyzed have on their audiences and, with regard to possible negative effects, suggesting how to rectify them (section 3.4).

3.1. Production: Contexts influencing texts

As regards the production issues, one way to signal a study's interdisciplinarity is to demonstrate how certain social transformations or economic developments cause change in the characteristics of media texts, and how this correlation between the context of production and the form of mediation is established as the main motive for the research, as in the following examples (all emphases mine):

(1) An examination of **these three phases** (…) will show how television interviewers [in Saudi Arabia, after the Arab Spring – KMK] **have shifted** from initially taking a very cautious and overtly deferential approach with interviewees, officials and public figures to adopting a more aggressive approach in the third phase.
(2) When reporting and commenting **on environmental issues of global concern**, the national media voice [in China – KMK] **may seek to achieve** attitudinal consensus with the international community while adhering to the official discourse.
(3) The corpus-driven discourse analysis [of Pakistani letters to editors – KMK] demonstrated diversity in organization patterns, […] exhibiting […] the 'seemingly chaotic realities' of **a society in transition**.
(4) These differences reflect different interview styles [in Spanish public and private media – KMK] which, in turn, **reveal different conceptions of journalism, politics and society**.

In the abstracts which position themselves as interdisciplinary in this way, an assumption is made that there is a causal link between context (e.g. Arab Spring in example 1, climate change in example 2, social transformation in example 3, or media privatization in example 4) and text (e.g. political interviews in example 1, media reports in example 2, letters to editor in example 3), one which does not have to be problematized, but illustrated. It is also assumed that larger mechanisms (structural transformations) are reflected in or exhibited through shifting discursive patterns (cf. the use of words that express new phenomena: *shifted* in example 1, *seek* in example 2, *demonstrated* and *exhibiting* in example 3, *differences* / *different* in example 4). Usually little agency or responsibility for the changing pattern is evidenced (cf. *national media voice* in example 2), which brings this kind of discourse analysis closer to the "mass communication" approach in its research design.

A similar technique for bridging Media Studies and Discourse Studies is deployed by aiming to demonstrate how (new) media technologies bring change in the structuring of media texts:

(5) The analysis shows that **social media and the press are intertwined**, with the press exerting a notable influence through social media, but social media not always being led by the press.
(6) Digital enthymemes, conversely, are texts without clear borders or any notion of moral norms. Such arguments characterized especially **user-generated, English-language discussions** concerning female celebrities.

Assuming the position which mirrors technological determinists' thinking that "medium is the message", some discourse analysts attempt to compare how digital, interactive and social media communication differs from 'traditional' one-way mass mediation in various details (cf. adverbs such as *conversely* in example 6, or *not always* in example 5). In this way they signal that meanings conveyed in and influences exerted by different media vary. This is an aspect of research in which Discourse Studies can significantly contribute to communication scholarship.

3.2. Representation: Meaning beyond the text

A few texts in the sample present mediated texts as representative of larger non-textual constructs or formations (identity, cultural values, social hierarchies and social movements). This is the type of Discourse Studies as envisioned by its champions (cf. Fowler, 1991; Hodge & Kress, 1993; Fairclough, 1995). In this approach the assumption is that texts construct, not just reflect, social meanings that need to be revealed:

(7) This paper dissects how state media in China frame narratives and represent meanings **to construct national cultural identity** in earthquake coverage.
(8) The strong presence of transformative ideologies in the verbal and visual modes underscores the potential for Spanish-language media to **represent Latin@s as powerful social actors** who stand up to negative treatment **through activism**.
(9) The data reveal that in the show LGB emancipation is framed as a personal problem and not as a socio-political issue with moral and ideological dimensions. In the end, we argue, the effect could very well be that **the show does not promote but rather – ironically – hinders LGB emancipation**.

The link between the discursive (e.g. narrative, verbal and visual mode, framing) and the social (cf. *cultural identity* in example 7, social *activism* in example 8, *LGB emancipation* in example 9) appears to be well-theorized here, in the spirit of the social constructivist alignments of CDA. However, this type of interpretation of "meaning beyond the text" needs meticulous linguistic scrutiny; in most cases content analysis alone is claimed to be incapable of yielding sufficient evidence of socio-political work that a given discourse does.

A specific case of this type of interdisciplinary endeavour is to demonstrate how media texts represent (e.g. mitigate, construct) contradictory interests and diverse ideologies:

(10) Differences are identified in the reporting strategies of *The Guardian*, *Daily Mail* and *The Sun* that provide insight into **the ideology of the British press**.
(11) How a specific happening – Hurricane Katrina – was linguistically **constructed as newsworthy in major American news media outlets**.
(12) 11 major techniques are identified by which *The Yomiuri* discursively mitigates the risks from Fukushima and **calls Japanese national identity into the service of the nuclear industry**. The article concludes with implications for understanding the impact of political discourse in mass media on other policy debates in Japan and elsewhere.

Here attention is paid to the strategic ways in which media outlets obscure the hegemonic ideologies within the social domain by naturalizing certain representations in the service of political or economic interests (of *the British press* in example 10, *major American news media outlets* in example 11, *The Yomiuri* in example 12). The 'rhetorical' nature of news media is being exposed. Also, the link with well-researched production frameworks (e.g. *newsworthiness* in example 11, political economy of the media in example 12) is established. In this way discourse analysts are to address what Philo (2008, p. 130) calls the origins of competing media discourses stemming from various social interests.

3.3. Analysis: Integrating various approaches

Such words as *interdisciplinary* or *integrating* appear in some abstracts of the papers which aim to explain how media texts should be studied to ensure the sufficient calibration of methods and the granularity of analysis:

(13) The perspective of the research is **interdisciplinary**, its methodology is qualitative, and the process guiding the textual analysis is inductive and hermeneutic. The corpus is made up of the news related to the studied legislative process.
(14) By **integrating theories** about inquiry, discourse analysis, gender, and sociolinguistics, the article makes an important contribution to the growing literature on

contemporary discourse in the media. The research was conducted on popular television cooking channels, the *Food Network* and the *Cooking Channel.*

(15) A **supplementary data set of ethnographic** semi-structured interviews with professional team sports players is also used to develop **insider perspectives** on the discursive behaviour of professional team sports players.

(16) We use **critical discourse analysis, notions of remediation and immediacy** to scrutinize discourse structures and other discursive strategies designed to conceal mediation and authorial prejudices, and to make the reader 'experience' the actual content.

Eclecticism or multidisciplinarity in the methodology of "doing discourse analysis" is declared here to 'maximize' the accuracy of the findings and to highlight the appropriateness of the explanation (cf. some of the relatively extensive listings of perspectives). Combining (*integrating* in example 14, *supplementing* in example 15) several frameworks drawn from Discourse Studies and other disciplines studying mediation is assumed to be an appropriate move towards ensuring the complementarity of perspectives. However, this can also mask an idiosyncratic or atheoretical approach, which does not help to remedy the fragmentation within the field.

3.4. Reception: The assumed effect

As mentioned in the theoretical part (see section 2.3), one of the most contested issues between Discourse Studies and Media Studies is how media texts influence the recipients. Since discourse analysts do not usually study audiences but texts, what they often do in their abstracts is declaring that a given type of media effect is to be assumed:

(17) Representations of the situation in the media **shape how** citizens understand and respond to it.

(18) These conceptual frameworks **are capable of influencing** how readers perceive and interpret news events, ultimately influencing their behavior as consumers and the financial decisions they make.

(19) The frequent presence of such negative responses to the commercial suggests that anti-immigrant sentiments continue and **possibly are intensifying** among segments of the population in the United States.

(20) The study reveals that the advertisers creatively blend verbal and visual cues in the discourse largely to **elicit certain sensibilities in the readers so as to make them think and act in the direction of** the investment offer.

(21) Moreover, the contrast of ideologies across the verbal and visual modes **may incite** the audience to participate in activism that supports Latin@ immigrants in the United States.

(22) The news content heightens anxiety and miseducates more than it enlightens readers on migration issues.

Although usually phrased rather tentatively (e.g. with such expressions as *capable of* in example 18, *possibly* in example 19, *certain* in example 20 etc.), such declarations of tangible media effects are nevertheless made, presumably to enhance the significance of a text-based study by locating it within the most extensive and highly ranking field of media communication research – the research on media influence (Potter, 2013). Despite the fact that only texts were analysed, the authors claim knowledge of these texts' perceptual, cognitive, affective, and even behavioural effects on people (e.g. *shaping understanding* in example 17, *influencing perceptions* in example 18, *intensifying sentiments* in example 19, *eliciting sensibilities* in example 20, *thinking and acting in the direction of* in example 20). This is where Discourse Studies could open to more rigorous studies of audiences, as practiced by Media Studies scholars, or include statistical, survey or ethnographic data on actual patterns of reception.

Finally, some authors make their text-based findings more relevant by including a normative or pedagogic element, namely by recommending how media texts should be changed to improve the quality of communication:

(23) This analysis suggests that despite the **call for a more cautious use** of (or even a prohibition of) the analogies discussed, participants in the debate on the Israeli–Palestinian conflicts are bound to resort to them – even if only to condemn them.

(24) The authors distinguish strategies and specific linguistic means as well as argumentation **fallacies that journalists employ** in the articles to construct the representation which is consistent with a newspaper's ideology.

(25) **A number of recommendations are made for journalists** to become cognizant of their own context models when reporting on Muslim women.

Placing the focus on normative implications (as exemplified by such words and expressions as *call for* in example 23, *fallacies* in example 24, *recommendations* in example 25), rather than just descriptive and explanatory observations, is an attempt to present Discourse Studies as pedagogically useful and applicable to solving communication-related problems.

4. Conclusion

Through a meta-analysis organized along the identified contested points related to the interdisciplinary fit between Discourse Studies and Media Studies, this study has aimed to survey how discourse analysts project their research as interdisciplinary in the abstracts of research articles submitted to *Discourse & Communication* in 2014 and 2015. I have discussed the following areas within which the authors aimed at expanding their studies beyond their language-focused disciplinary orientation:

1. how social transformations bring change in media texts;
2. how (new) media technologies bring change in media texts;
3. how media texts represent aspects beyond the text;
4. how media texts represent contradictory interests or diverse ideologies;
5. how media texts should be analysed to ensure better calibration;
6. how media texts influence the recipients;
7. how media texts should be changed to improve the quality of communication.

Although I have noted that some claims to interdisciplinarity might be exaggerated or based on presumptions or declarations, the observation which can be offered here is that despite discrepancy of perspectives between Discourse Studies and Media Studies, some *DCM* contributors representing the former field claim to genuinely enrich their analytic toolkits and procedures to accommodate insights from Media Studies. Especially notable is the reference to well-researched production frameworks (e.g. newsworthiness, political economy of the media), as well as statistical or ethnographic data on the patterns of text reception.

This study has explored some issues of interdisciplinarity between Discourse Studies and Media Studies, demonstrating how discourse analysis of mediated communication could become a complementary perspective to Media Studies. For its merits, Discourse Studies can help to advance media scholarship by offering a more thorough understanding of how meaning is co-constructed through minute but consistent linguistic and visual resources. Recent developments within Discourse Studies (e.g. corpus-driven studies, cognitive approaches, multimodal frameworks) make it a reservoir of sophisticated methods, apt theoretical constructs and reliable analytic categories.

However, in their approach to mediation, discourse analysts ought to seek to keep up with Media Studies practitioners' results to help find the main ways (though obviously not all the ways) how texts represent ideas/ideologies to media consumers. Through its qualitative approaches (thick descriptions), Discourse Studies should offer assistance in differentiating between various media genres, styles and rhetorics, but should also aim at contextualizing text analysis within specific discourse formations and professional practices. In addition, with the growth in application of various metrics (e.g., in corpus and computational linguistics, annotation techniques), Discourse Studies can help grasp patterns in text structure that had not been noticed before. Discourse analysts can also resort to ethnographies and online tools to delimit more precisely the patterns of text reception even before moving on to text analysis. Complementarity between Discourse Studies and Media Studies is to some extent fostered by such journals as *Discourse & Communication*, but more attention should be paid to addressing the contested issues, making complementary positions clearer and resolving differences where possible.

References

Bateman, J. (2008). *Multimodality and Genre: A Foundation for the Systematic Analysis of Multimodal Documents*. Basingstoke: Palgrave Macmillan.

Bednarek, M., & Caple, H. (2012). *News Discourse*. London: Continuum.

Bednarek, M., & H. Caple (2014). Why do News Values Matter? Towards a New Methodological Framework for Analyzing News Discourse in Critical Discourse Analysis and Beyond. *Discourse and Society*, 25(2), 135–158.

Bell, A. (1991). *The Language of News Media*. Oxford: Blackwell.

Breeze, R. (2011). Critical Discourse Analysis and its Critics. *Pragmatics*, 21(4), 493–525.

Capella, J. N., & Jamieson, K. H. (1997). *Spiral of Cynicism: The Press and the Public Good*. Oxford: Oxford University Press.

Chilton, P. (2011). Still Something Missing in CDA. *Discourse Studies*, 13(6), 769–781.

Conboy, M. (2002). *The Press and Popular Culture*. London: Sage.

van Dijk, T. (1988). *News as Discourse*. Hillsdale, NJ: Erlbaum.

van Dijk, T. (2006). Discourse and Manipulation. *Discourse and Society*, 17(3), 359–383.

Ekstrom, M. (2002). Epistemologies of TV journalism. *Journalism*, 3(3), 259–282.

Fairclough, N. (1989) *Language and Power*. London: Pearson Education.

Fairclough, N. (1995). *Media Discourse*. New York & London: Longman.

Fowler, R. (1991). *Language in the News: Discourse and Ideology in the Press*. London: Routledge.

Giddens, A. (1991). *Modernity and Self-Identity*. Cambridge: Polity Press.

Grice, H. P. (1975). Logic and Conversation. In P. Cole & J. L. Morgan (Eds.), *Syntax and Semantics, vol. 3*. New York: Academic Press, 41–58.

Hall, S. (1980). Encoding/Decoding. In S. Hall, D. Hobson, A. Lowe & P. Willis (Eds.), *Culture, Media, Language: Working Papers in Cultural Studies*. London: Hutchinson, 128–139.

Halliday, M. A. K. (1985). *Introduction to Functional Grammar*. London: Edward Arnold.

Harcup, T., & O'Neill, D. (2002). What is News? Galtung and Ruge Revisited. *Journalism Studies*, 2(2), 261–280.

Hodge, R., & Kress, G. (1993). *Language as Ideology*. London: Routledge.

Hoynes, W., & Croteau, D. (2002) *Media/Society: Industries, Images, and Audiences*. London: Sage.

Jones, J., & Salter, L. (2012). *Digital Journalism*. London: Sage.

Kress, G., & van Leeuwen, T. (1996). *Reading Images: The Grammar of Visual Design*. London: Routledge.

Krzyżanowski, M., & Forchtner, B. (2016). Theories and Concepts in Critical Discourse Studies: Facing Challenges, Moving beyond Foundations. *Discourse & Society*, 27(3), 253–261.

Lanham, R. (2006) *The Economics of Attention: Style and Substance in the Age of Information*. Chicago: University of Chicago Press.

Lievrouw, L. (2011). *Alternative and Activist New Media*. Cambridge: Polity Press.

McChesney, R., & Nichols, J. (2011). *The Death and Life of American Journalism: The Media Revolution that Will Begin the World Again*. New York: Nation Books.

McLuhan, M. (1964). *Understanding Media: The Extensions of Man*. Cambridge, MA: The MIT Press.

McManus, J. (1994). *Market-driven Journalism*. Thousand Oaks: Sage.

McQuail, D. (2000). *McQuail's Mass Communication Theory*. London: Sage.

Montgomery, M. (2007). *The Discourse of Broadcast News. A Linguistic Approach*. London: Routledge.

Philo, G. (2008). News Content Studies, Media Group Methods and Discourse Analysis: A Comparison of Approaches. In E. Devreux (Ed.), *Media Studies: Key Issues and Debates*. London: Sage, 78–92.

Potter, W. J. (2013). *Media Effects*. London: Sage.

Reisigl, M., & Wodak, R. (2001). *Discourse and Discrimination*. London: Routledge.

Richardson, J. (2007). *Analysisng Newspapers: An Approach from Critical Discourse Analysis*. Basingstoke: Palgrave Macmillan.

Schudson, M. (1981). *Discovering the News: A Social History of American Newspapers*. New York: Basic Books.

Swales, J. (1990) *Genre Analysis: English in Academic and Research Settings*, Cambridge: Cambridge University Press.

Tuchman, G. (1978). *Making News: A Study in the Construction of Reality*. New York: Free Press.

Žagar, I. (2010). Topoi in Critical Discourse Analysis. *Lodz Papers in Pragmatics*, 6(1), 3–27.

Radostina Iglikova
University of Shumen, Bulgaria

The pursuit of efficiency in the era of the text 'born digital'

Abstract: The following article is based on the proposition that certain elements of the theory of textuality as proposed by de Beaugrande and Dressler in their seminal *Introduction to Text Linguistics* (de Beaugrande & Dressler, 1981) can be successfully employed in the analysis of the phenomenon of the "born-digital" text (see Metz, 1993; Erway, 2010; Neal, 2015) and the discourse it pertains to – i.e. the textual content populating the innumerable pages of the World Wide Web. More specifically, the paper recognizes the opportunities as well as the challenges stemming from the inherent digital convergence, non-linearity, hypertextuality and interactiveness of the Internet as a medium, and, in turn, aims to pinpoint some of the potential benefits of approaching online discourse from the perspective of *efficiency* as a regulative principle. In this respect, the article can be regarded as an attempt at bridging the gap between tradition (in the face of text-oriented discourse analysis) and current trends (the abundant and varied literature exploring what is widely referred to as "writing for the web").

1. Introduction

The beginning of the 21st century is marked by the prevalent influence of globalization in every sphere of human life (see e.g. Giulianotti & Robertson, 2006; Robertson & White, 2007). The most obvious example of the hegemony of the 'global village' social developments and the major factor in producing and reproducing this reality is the new electronic medium comprising innumerable separate pages with information of various kinds (the World Wide Web and its websites/webpages) and the communication network created through the use of computers (the Internet, including e-mail, Facebook, Twitter, Instagram etc.) Enabling virtual communication and information exchange, these digital innovations create access to unlimited sources and amounts of information within seconds, and also provide communicative opportunities for the formation and development of communities independently of the members' location in space. In this sense, they have become the 'birthplace' of new and transformed discourses, each of which has its own affordances, requirements and specificities.

Another crucial aspect of the digital medium in its World Wide Web form stems from the immediate and unlimited access to information which it provides. This abundance is as much a curse as it is a blessing due to the constant decision-making process required for navigating such volumes of information. This has resulted in phenomena such as “information anxiety” (Wurman, 2001) and a dramatic change in the way we handle both information and our attention resources (Thorngate, 1990; Carr, 2008, 2010; Wurman, 2012). It has made it necessary for those who provide information online to make a conscious effort in order to make their discourses attractive, usable and accessible. On the one hand, this concerns Search Engine Optimization (SEO) management and has to do with the way search engines manage available blocks or chunks of information in response to user queries (Enge, Spencer & Stricchiola, 2015). On the other hand, once selected and accessed, these computer-mediated discourses are intended for the user and their specific information need(s), which makes it vital for the actual content to be usable (Nielsen, 2007) and of optimal quality in terms of processing ease.

Therefore, the notion of efficiency as a design criterion for the evaluation of the quality of texts in terms of processing the greatest amount of content with a minimum of effort is accepted as a valid principle not only for the written/printed medium, but is indeed of great value and importance in the context of the so-called “new media” or, more specifically, computer-mediated discourse.

Therefore, this new discourse is expected to exhibit specific strategies aimed at achieving efficiency. These strategies are naturally expected to rely for their fulfillment on the specific resources the medium and the communicative situation in question can provide, as they will as well inevitably face the limitations and specific requirements these factors entail.

One specific aspect of text online is the constant pressing need for reducing the length of texts, i.e. limiting and minimizing the volume of content. At the same time, this very content needs to be informative (it cannot be so short as to have low informative value) and understandable (removing too many explicit elements may cause a breach of communication).

As a result of this need, the resources which a language provides need to be employed so that the content may be configured in an appropriate way that is compatible with the economy of surface structure. In a sense, the content needs to be transformed so as to become less reliant on the surface structure and explicit statement (the words themselves). The World Wide Web as a technological phenomenon and web content in particular provide a multimodal framework which comprises various channels of informational exchange, and what is explicitly worded in textual content is only one of them.

2. The relationship between the notions of *text* and *discourse*

The notions of *text* and *discourse* are traditionally interrelated and used by different researchers in various fields of study, with each of the approaches investing the terms with a different meaning. So far no single uniform definition has been agreed upon for either of these concepts, which provides fertile ground for misunderstanding and ambiguity.

The *Routledge Dictionary of Language and Linguistics* (Bussmann, 2006) defines *discourse* as the "generic term for various types of text", while *text* is the

> linguistic form of expression of a communicative act which is individually determined (a) according to pragmatic, text-internal criteria of a communicative intention which is situation-specific and meets a corresponding listener expectation (text function), and (b) according to internal textual features, such as boundary signals, grammatical cohesion, dominant text theme, and content coherence (macrostructure, thematic development).
> (Bussmann, 2006)

The same source also briefly lists some of the various definitions and uses of the term *discourse* such as:

- connected speech (Harris, 1952);
- the product of an interactive process in a sociocultural context (Pike, 1954);
- performance (vs "text" as a representation of the formal grammatical structure of discourse) (van Dijk, 1974);
- talk (vs written prose, or 'text') (Cicourel, 1975);
- conversational interaction (Coulthard, 1977);
- "language in context across all forms and modes" (Tannen, 1981);
- process (vs product, or "text") (Brown & Yule, 1983).

Dobreva and Savova (2000, pp. 30–31) outline some of the basic trends in the understanding of the term *discourse* and its relation to *text*:

- In a narrow sense – as part of language communication, denoting a unit above sentence level with a clearly distinguishable function, or connected speech in general, any unit above sentence level;
- In a broad sense – beyond the limits of language communication; seen as equivalent to any communicative practice;
- The discourse–text relationship – the popular view regarding this question nowadays defines discourse as the "purposeful exchange of semiotic information under actual communicative conditions", and text as "the semiotic complex providing material realization for discourse in a particular situation";

- Sociological approaches – within this framework, the specific "ways of talking about things, formed in a particular sphere of social life or in connection to a particular political, ideological, intellectual… practice" are considered to be "discourses". All these spheres are controlled by institutions and are governed by a system of rules (an order of discourse) which control "what can be discussed, who and in what way can serve as a source of information, what text forms and expressions are appropriate, etc."

Fairclough (1995, pp. 54–62) uses the term *discourse* to refer to "spoken or written language use… a form of social practice", which implies that it is "a socially and historically situated mode of action, in a dialectical relationship with other facets of the social". Particular discourses are viewed as "ways of representing aspects of the world – the processes, relations and structures of the material world, the 'mental' world of thoughts, feelings, beliefs and so forth, and the social world" (Fairclough, 2003, p. 124). Fairclough also introduces the following distinctions in the framework and terminology of discourse analysis:

- The construction of a framework for critical discourse analysis of a communicative event which consists of three dimensions – text, discourse practice and sociocultural practice.
- Discourse practice (or "discursive practices") is seen as "mediating between the textual and the social and cultural" and denotes a community's "normal ways of using language" (Fairclough, 1995, p. 55), "the processes of text production and text consumption" (Fairclough, 1995, p. 57). Discourse practices are viewed in terms of networks, called *orders of discourse*.
- Sociocultural practice has various aspects, broadly divided into three groups: "economic, political (concerned with issues of power and ideology), and cultural (concerned with questions of value and identity)" (Fairclough, 1995, p. 62).
- Social institutions and domains and various areas of experience are associated with their own "order of discourse" which consists of "all the discursive types which are used there" (Fairclough, 1995, p. 55).
- Discourses (as constituents of "orders of discourse") are divided into two main types – genres ("use[s] of language associated with and constituting part of some particular social practice" which can be described "in terms of their organizational properties") and discourses ("the language used in representing a given social practice from a particular point of view", appertaining to knowledge and its structuring) (Fairclough, 1995, p. 56).
- "Text" is seen from a "multifunctional" point of view, as "simultaneously having three main categories of function, each of which has its own systems of choices: *ideational, interpersonal, and textual*" (Fairclough, 1995, p. 58, italics

used in the original). Thus any text is language use and provides "a way of investigating the simultaneous constitution of systems of knowledge and belief… and social relations and social identities" (Fairclough, 1995, p. 58). The author further emphasizes the need for a multisemiotic analysis of discourse in order to investigate "how these other semiotic modalities interact with language in producing meanings, and how such interactions define different aesthetics for different media" (Fairclough 1995, p. 58).

On the basis of the brief overview above, the present article treats the notions of *discourse* and *text* and their relationship in the following way:

- discourse in general is understood as language communication with a specific function within a specific socio-cultural situation;
- specific discourses involve particular sets of affordances, requirements, expectations and criteria for appropriateness regarding the communicative situation and its elements;
- discourses are actualized by means of the use of language (i. e. texts are the material aspect of particular discourses); the specificities of discourses, thus, can be studied through analyzing linguistic practices or, in other words, through analyzing texts;
- texts are not abstract units to be considered in isolation but rather are units of language in use, i.e. communicative units; as a result, they are inseparable from their context;
- the notion of *text* is independent of the medium of its actualization – thus, texts can be oral, written, printed or electronic (digitalized or digital).

3. Research in New Media Studies and Computer-Mediated Discourse Analysis (CMDA)

Recent developments in computer and communication technology and the emergence of the Internet and the World Wide Web as a medium have affected existing fields of research. They have also given rise to a number of disciplines and approaches which study these new phenomena from various perspectives. The vast potential for research is addressed by disciplines ranging from Computer Science and Engineering, Information Technology and Information Design, Software Engineering, Web Design, Communication Design, Human-Computer Interaction, through Marketing, User Experience, Search Engine Optimization (SEO), to Online Journalism, Discourse Studies and Linguistics.

Locher and Mondada (2014) discuss new media as an object of study for Linguistics and outline the variety of approaches and topics of interest which have emerged during the 20 years of linguistic research into computer-mediated communication. Some areas of research include New Media Studies (Murray, 2003, pp. 3–11), Internet Linguistics (Crystal, 2011), Digital Humanities (Schreibman, Siemens & Unsworth, 2004), Computer-Mediated Discourse Analysis (Herring, 2001).

The term *New Media* is taken to refer to

> those methods and social practices of communication, representation, and expression that have developed using the digital, multimedia, networked computer and the ways that this machine is held to have transformed work in other media: from books to movies, from telephones to television.
>
> (Lister, Dovey, Giddins, Grant & Kelly, 2009, p. 2)

Authors working within the broad framework of New Media Studies focus on some specific characteristics of these new methods and practices of human communication such as their non-linearity, interactivity, hypertextuality, multimodality, hypermediacy and remediation (Nielsen, 1995; Bolter & Grusin, 1999; McAleese, 1999; Landow, 2006; Vanderdorpe, 2009; Kress, 2010).

Internet Linguistics, on the other hand, envisages four aspects of studying the new language styles and forms that have developed under the influence of the Internet. These aspects include (1) the sociolinguistic perspective, with its focus on the influence of the Internet on language in terms of communication; (2) the stylistic perspective, with a focus on the effects of Internet on language change, the development of new forms and modes of expression; (3) the educational perspective, with a focus on Internet learning and education; and, last but not least, (4) the applied perspective, which researches issues like multilingualism and language diversity on the Internet (Crystal, 2011).

As a discipline, Digital Humanities has developed as an area of study at the intersection of computing and the humanities. Its contributions focus on applying digital technology to the study of digitalized or texts born digital by means of the accumulation and organization of large textual corpora, performing automated content analysis, parsing and text mining procedures (Schreibman et al., 2004).

Linguistic research focusing on New Media and the Internet (including the World Wide Web) has given rise to a number of terms referring to language as the subject of research. These include *Netspeak* (Crystal, 2011), *CMC* or *computer-mediated communication* (Herring, 2001), *CMD* or *computer-mediated discourse* (Herring & Aleksandroutsopoulos, 2015), *digital discourse*, *electronic discourse*, *e-communication*, *digitally-mediated communication* (Locher & Mondala, 2014). Specifically, studies of the system of language focus on aspects of New Media in terms of phonology, morphology, syntax, semantics and pragmatics. By contrast, studies of language as interaction investigate the specific organizational principles and norms of interaction within CMC. Cognitive Linguistics in turn discusses the effects of various digital environments in terms of cognitive overload and frustration, as well as studies the role of metaphors and semantic fields in the creation of meaning within the novel interface of CMC.

In order to discover particular underlying patterns and regularities, Linguistics applies a variety of methodological approaches – qualitative as well as quantitative, experimental as well as empirical, based on web corpora or digital ethnographies, with descriptive or theory-building aims (Bolander & Locher, 2014, pp. 14–26). The World Wide Web and new technology offer immense possibilities for the accumulation, storage, organization and analysis of vast amounts of data, where the entire Internet can serve as source (the 'web as corpus' approach, see Hundt, Nesselhauf & Biewer, 2007, pp. 1–6) or individual researchers can compile custom-made corpus data for their specific purposes (the 'web for corpus' approach, see Hundt et al., 2007, pp. 1–6).

Initially introduced in 1995 by Herring (see Herring, 2001), the term "computer-mediated discourse analysis" (CMDA) is construed as

> an approach to researching online interactive behavior [...] CMDA applies methods adapted from language-focused disciplines such as linguistics, communication, and rhetoric to the analysis of computer-mediated communication (Herring 2001). It may be supplemented by surveys, interviews, ethnographic observation, or other methods; it may involve qualitative or quantitative analysis; but what defines CMDA at its core is the analysis of logs of verbal interaction (characters, words, utterances, messages, exchanges, threads, archives, etc.). In the broadest sense, any analysis of online behavior that is grounded in empirical, textual observations is computer-mediated discourse analysis.
>
> (Herring, 2004, p. 339)

Herring and Aleksandroutsopoulos (2015, p. 127) define *Computer-Mediated Discourse* (CMD) as "the communication produced when human beings interact with one another by transmitting messages via networked or mobile computers, where 'computers' are defined broadly to include any digital communication device". This phenomenon is also referred to as "computer-mediated conversation, digital conversation, digital discourse, digital language, electronic discourse, electronic language, Internet language, and new media language" (Herring & Aleksandroutsopoulos, 2015, p. 144).

4. Writing for the Web

The popularity and ubiquity of computer-mediated communication has given rise to a vast body of literature concerning writing for the Web (Krug, 2006; Nielsen, 2008; Stolley, 2011; Redish, 2012), which proposes guidelines for creating successful texts for the digital medium. Experts in the field emphasize the importance of following these guidelines in order to compensate for the "impatience" of web users, the extremely limited resources of time and attention which people are generally willing to spend on any particular item of web content. In fact, all these guidelines are designed to promote processing ease, i. e. *efficiency*, understood as the processing of the largest possible amount of content in minimum time and with minimum (physical and mental) effort. Since the notion of *efficiency* pertains to the textual aspect of communication (it is, after all, a regulative principle of textuality), it is a narrower concept than that of *usability*, proposed by Nielsen (2012) as "a quality attribute that assesses how easy user interfaces are to use", which also "refers to methods for improving ease-of-use during the design process". The latter is defined by these five quality components (Nielsen, 2012):

- "Learnability: How easy is it for users to accomplish basic tasks the first time they encounter the design?"
- "Efficiency: Once users have learned the design, how quickly can they perform tasks?"
- "Memorability: When users return to the design after a period of not using it, how easily can they reestablish proficiency?"
- "Errors: How many errors do users make, how severe are these errors, and how easily can they recover from the errors?"
- "Satisfaction: How pleasant is it to use the design?"

The decidedly hands-on and 'holistic' nature of this type of literature makes it stand out against the background of traditional linguistic research. As a result, however, there emerge several important weaknesses of this practical approach to discussing and analyzing the quality of a digital text:

- Although most authors are determined to point out the importance of the quality of the content itself and its priority over other aspects of Web-based communication – as Redish (2012, p. 1) puts it, "visitors come for the content" – there are usually no specific criteria for evaluating the quality of such texts from a linguistic perspective;
- Guidelines are usually limited to formulaic statements about the design and organization of texts, without providing a general framework of reference pertaining to textual specificities and crucial linguistic notions such as cohesion and coherence, for example;
- The terms *efficiency* and *effectiveness* are either used interchangeably or simultaneously, perhaps in an attempt to emphasize the general idea of economy, brevity, clarity and practicality, which they denote in everyday discourse.

One particular assumption of this efficiency-focused approach to providing training, instruction and assistance to potential website creators seems to be that people presumably need specific instruction in order to figure out and tune up the marketing and PR strategy of their website and make it correspond with their company's or their personal goals. What follows is that they need knowledge and practice in order to master web design and information architecture or at least hire a specialist. Also, they need to get to know their target audiences and include content (information) which is valuable for visitors and present it in the visitors' words. The task of actually generating that very content itself, however, is given little attention and coverage in literature in the field. What is available are merely (not very long) lists of so-called "tricks" for keeping things simple and brief (see Krug, 2006; Nielsen, 2008; Stolley, 2011; Redish, 2012).

It would follow, then, that in order to be able to write successful digital texts (or, in other words, generate quality content) one only needs to practice applying the tricks in a consistent way. If this is indeed the case, we may not be very far away from the day when software will be able to generate valuable content and produce high-quality texts on its own, provided it has been fed the right amount of data concerning the target audience's interests and vocabulary, the company's marketing and advertising plans, and an algorithm of rules similar to the ones below:

- Content = conversation (Redish, 2012, p. 2);
- Home pages-content-rich with few words (Redish, 2012, p. 74);
- Continue the conversation quickly (Redish, 2012, p. 79);
- Write in fragments (Redish, 2012, p. 98);
- Focusing on conversations and key messages (Redish, 2012, p. 125);
- Give people only what they need (Redish, 2012, p. 126);
- Cut! Cut! Cut! And cut again! (Redish, 2012, p. 132);
- Start with your key message (Redish, 2012, p. 136);
- Key message first = inverted pyramid style (Redish, 2012, p. 136);
- Announcing your topic with a clear headline – use a statement, question, call to action (Redish, 2012, p. 170);
- Exploit the power of parallelism (Redish, 2012, p. 181);
- Write short, simple sentences (Redish, 2012, p. 198);
- Use the imperative in instructions (Redish, 2012, p. 199);
- Write in the active voice (most of the time) (Redish, 2012, p. 208);
- Keep paragraphs short (Redish, 2012, p. 218);
- Lists and tables may be even better (Redish, 2012, p. 218);

Although keeping things short and simple make for good mottos (as exemplified in the list of pieces of advice on web writing above), both *short* and *simple* are relative and not absolute notions. This very relativity, or the principle of employing constant trade-offs between saying too little (and thus being unclear) and saying too much (and consequenstly being redundant and losing the readers' attention) is precisely what textual efficiency as a principle for the evaluation of the design of texts stands for.

5. The textlinguistic perspective – constitutive standards of textuality, cohesive devices and the regulative principle of efficiency

In this sense it would seem that specific aspects of the well-developed theoretical construct of Textlinguistics and Text-oriented Discourse Analysis could prove to be useful tools for assessing the quality of textual web content. More specifically, the cohesive devices each language possesses and their potential for compacting surface structure could offer a more integrated approach to the evaluation of textual content. Therefore, what follows is a brief overview of some of the key notions in the field of Textlinguistics which are considered to be highly relevant to assessing the quality of textual content in general, and texts on the Web in particular.

According to de Beaugrande, text is "the naturally occurring manifestation of language" (de Beaugrande, 1980), whose decisive trait is that it is "a communicative occurrence" (de Beaugrande & Dressler, [1981] 2002). It must meet "seven standards of textuality", which function as "constitutive principles [...] of textual communication: they define and create the form of behaviour identifiable as textual communicating, and if they are defied, that form of behaviour will break down" (de Beaugrande & Dressler, 2002). These standards include the following:

- the standard of *cohesion*, which "subsumes the procedures whereby surface elements appear as progressive occurrences such that their sequential connectivity is maintained and made recoverable. The means of cohesion include the grammatical formatting of phrases, clauses, and sentences [...], and such devices as recurrence, pro-forms and articles, co-reference, ellipsis, and junction";
- the standard of *coherence*, which "subsumes the procedures whereby elements of knowledge are activated such that their conceptual connectivity is maintained and made recoverable. The means of coherence include: (1) logical relations such as causality and class inclusion; (2) knowledge of how events, actions, objects, and situations are organized; and (3) the striving for continuity in human experience.

Cohesion is upheld by continual interaction of text-presented knowledge with prior knowledge of the world";

- the standard of *intentionality*, which "subsumes the text producer's attitude that a given language configuration is intended to be a cohesive and coherent text; and that such a text is an instrument in following a plan toward a goal";
- the standard of *acceptability*, which "subsumes the text receiver's attitude that a language configuration should be accepted as a cohesive and coherent text";
- the standard of *situationality*, which "subsumes the factors that make a text relevant to a current or recoverable situation";
- the standard of *informativity*, which "is the factor of the relative uncertainty about textual occurrences or occurrences within a textual world as opposed to possible alternatives";
- the standard of *intertextuality*, which "subsumes the relationships between a given text and other relevant texts encountered in prior experience, with or without mediation. [...] Intertextuality is the major factor in the establishment of text types".

On the basis of the aforementioned seven standards of textuality, de Beaugrande and Dressler (2002) envision the existence of at least three "regulative principles [...] that control textual communication rather than define it". These are also referred to as "design criteria" (de Beaugrande, 1980), and serve to control "the constitution and use of texts" and "distinguish the quality of a sample already admitted as a text" (de Beaugrande, 1980). Thus, having already established that a particular sample is a text, the analysis proceeds with establishing the quality of the text in terms of the three principles:

- the principle of *efficiency* – it depends on the use of a text "in communicating with a minimum expenditure of effort by the participants" (de Beaugrande & Dressler, 2002), and "results from [the] utilization [of text] in communication with the greatest returns for the least effort, so that PROCESSING EASE is promoted" (de Beaugrande, 1980);
- the principle of *effectiveness* – it depends on a text "leaving a strong impression and creating favourable conditions for attaining a goal" (de Beaugrande & Dressler, 2002); i. e. it has to do with the "intensity of impact on text receivers, promoting processing depth, and upon its contribution toward the producer's goal, constituting the relevance of text materials to steps in a plan" (de Beaugrande, 1980);
- the principle of *appropriateness* – it has to do with "the agreement between [the textual] setting and the ways in which the standards of textuality are upheld" (de Beaugrande & Dressler, 2002); thus it depends "on the proportionality

between the demands of a communicative situation and the degree to which standards of textuality are upheld" (de Beaugrande, 1980).

Drawing upon Halliday and Hasan's (1976) notion of *cohesion* and the *cohesive devices* which every language provides for ensuring surface connectivity, or connectivity of surface expression, de Beaugrande (1980) distinguishes certain classes of cohesive devices on the basis of their contributions to efficiency. He considers those to be among the main resources of language for achieving optimal processing ease:

- *recurrence* – the repetition of expressions with the same or different reference;
- *definiteness* – the extent to which an entity is considered to be identifiable and recoverable from context;
- *co-reference* – the application of different surface expressions to refer to the same entity;
- *anaphora* – co-reference via a pro-form following a lexical expression;
- *cataphora* – co-reference via a pro-form preceding a lexical expression;
- *exophora* – the application of a pro-form to an entity not expressed in the text;
- *ellipsis* – the carrying forward of conceptual content by means of using noticeably incomplete surface expressions;
- *junction* – the devices which serve to connect surface expressions while signalling relationships pertaining among elements of the conceptual text-world knowledge; subtypes are conjunction, disjunction, contrajunction and subordination.

In his view, these devices of cohesion contribute to textual efficiency in several ways:

- by compacting the surface expression;
- by enabling the omission of surface elements;
- by carrying forward relevant elements for further modification, expanding, development etc.;
- by signaling knownness, uniqueness or identity;
- by providing a balance between repetition and variation.

6. Concluding remarks

The present article has briefly touched upon some linguistic and discursive issues which are directly related to recent technological and communicational developments such as the popularity of the World Wide Web and the so-called "digital shift" or "digital turn" (see Westera, 2013) in media and communication. The unique specificities of the World Wide Web as a technology, a medium and a discourse have effected qualitative changes in the ways text (textual or text-based content) is utilized. Consequently, it becomes more and more obvious that text needs to be transformed instead of transferred, and to be "re-born" as digital instead of being mechanically "digitalized" (the equivalent of reproducing it on a screen instead of on paper). The nature of this "digital turn" with its immediate effects upon text-based computer-mediated communication has further emphasized the importance of optimizing the quality of text in terms of processing ease.

One fundamental notion in the field of Textlinguistics is the regulative principle of efficiency, which governs the design and utilization of texts with regard to ensuring the aforementioned processing ease. Recent developments in technology and communication, however, have resulted in the overwhelming popularity of the World Wide Web and, respectively, have effected the evolution of a new phenomenon – the text "born digital". In the light of these developments and their undeniable significance, it would seem justified to revisit the issue of text-evaluation in terms of the efficiency principle with a newly added emphasis on the specificities and requirements of this qualitatively new type of content and its context of appearance (the webpages of the World Wide Web).

In spite of its potential and claims to multimodality, however, the World Wide Web still remains a highly textual medium, whose content draws upon existing and well-established forms of communication. Mapping the notions, views, methodology and theoretical background of well-developed disciplines such as Textlinguitics, Text-oriented Discourse analysis, Comparative Linguistics etc. onto popular modern approaches (some of which have been mentioned in this article) would help analysts with different theoretical backgrounds to relate what we already know about text and to establish systematic connections and points of reference between the paradigm of text-oriented linguistic research and analysis and the new paradigm of digitality, the World Wide Web and its digitally born text(s).

The purpose of this article is to emphasize the relevance and importance of establishing an algorithm of transference and emulation of information and understanding between and among the existing vast amounts of research and theoretical work and the newly emerging reality of the digital text. In this way this approach precludes the necessity for all disciplines dealing with electronic discourse to start anew, from scratch, as if text never existed before the Internet era, or as if digital text were a phenomenon which miraculously came into being instead of emerging, developing and evolving on the basis of and in a dialectic relationship with printed text.

References

Bolander, B., & Locher, M. A. (2014). Doing Sociolinguistic Research on Computer-Mediated Data: A Review of Four Methodological Issues. *Discourse, Context & Media*, 3, 14–26.

Bolter, J., & Grusin, R. (1999). *Remediation: Understanding New Media*. Cambridge, Mass. & London, England: The MIT Press.

Brown, G., & Yule, G. (1983). *Discourse Analysis*. Cambridge: Cambridge University Press.

Bussmann, H. (2006). *Routledge Dictionary of Language and Linguistics*. Translated and edited by G. Trauth & K. Kazzazi. London: Routledge.

Carr, N. (2008). *The Big Switch: Rewiring the World, From Edison to Google*. New York & London: W.W. Norton & Company.

Carr, N. (2010). *The Shallows: What the Internet Is Doing to Our Brains*. New York & London: W.W. Norton & Company.

Cicourel, A. V. (1975). Discourse, and text: Cognitive and linguistic processes in studies of social structure. *Versus*, 33–84.

Coulthard, M. (1977). *An Introduction to Discourse Analysis*. London: Longman Pearson Education.

De Beaugrande, R. (1980). *Text, Discourse and Process. Toward a Multidisciplinary Science of Texts*. Retrieved from http://www.beaugrande.com/TDPOpening.htm. DOA: 01.11.2012.

De Beaugrande R. A., & Dressler W. ([1981] 2002). *Introduction to Text Linguistics*. Retrieved from http://www.beaugrande.com/introduction_to_text_linguistics.htm. DOA: 01.11.2012.

van Dijk, T. (1974). *Philosophy of Action and Theory of Narrative*. Mimeo: University of Amsterdam.

Dobreva, E., & Savova, I. (2000). *Tekstolingvistika: Uvoden Kurs*. Shumen: Konstantin Preslavsky University Press. [Добрева, Е., Савова, И. „Текстолингвистика: Уводен курс“. Шумен: УИ „Епископ Константин Преславски“.]

Enge, E., Spencer, S., & Stricchiola, J. C. (2015). *The Art of SEO. Mastering Search Engine Optimization. Third Edition*. Sebastopol, CA: O'Reilly Media, Inc.

Erway, R. (2010). "Defining 'Born Digital'". Retrieved from http://www.oclc.org/content/dam/research/activities/hiddencollections/borndigital.pdf. DOA: 01.01.2017.

Fairclough, N. (1995). *Media Discourse*. London: Hodder Arnold Publication.

Fairclough, N. (2003). *Analysing Discourse. Textual Analysis for Social Research*. London: Routledge.

Giulianotti, R., & Robertson, R. (2006). Glocalization, Globalization and Migration: the Case of Scottish Football Supporters in North America. *International Sociology*, 21(2), 171–198.

Halliday, M. A. K., & Hasan, R. (1976). *Cohesion in English*. London: Longman Group, Ltd.

Harris, Z. (1952). Discourse analysis. *Language*, 28(1), 1–30.

Herring, S. C. (2001). Computer-mediated discourse. In D. Tannen, D. Schiffrin, & H. Hamilton (Eds.), *Handbook of Discourse Analysis*. Oxford: Blackwell, 612–634.

Herring, S., & Aleksandroutsopoulos, J. (2015). Computer-Mediated Discourse 2.0. In D. Tannen, H. E. Hamilton & D. Schiffrin (Eds.), *The Handbook of Discourse Analysis. Second Edition*. Oxford: Wiley Blackwell, 127–151.

Hundt, M., Nesselhauf, N., & Biewer, C. (2007). Corpus Linguistics and the Web. In M. Hundt, N. Nesselhauf & C. Biewer (Eds.), *Corpus Linguistics and the Web*. Amsterdam: Rodopi, 1–6.

Kress, G. (2010). *Multimodality. A Social Semiotic Approach to Contemporary Communication*. London & New York: Routledge.

Krug, S. (2005). *Don't Make Me Think: A Common Sense Approach to Web Usability. 2nd Edition*. Berkeley, CA: New Riders.

Landow, G.P. (2006). *Hypertext 3.0. Critical Theory and New Media in an Era of Globalization*. Baltimore: The Johns Hopkins University Press.

Lister, M., Dovey, J., Giddins, S., Grant, I., & Kelly, K. (2009). *New Media: A Critical Introduction. 2nd Edition*. London & New York: Routledge.

Locher, M. A., & Mondada, L. (2014). Linguistics and the New Media. *Dichtung Digital: A Journal of Art and Culture in Digital Media* 44. Retrieved from http://www.dichtung-digital.de/en/journal/aktuelle-nummer/?postID=2538. DOA: 01.12.2015.

McAleese, R. (1999). *Hypertext. Theory and Practice*. Exeter, England: Intellect.

Metz, R. 1993. "Borndigital". Retrieved from http://www.rafimetz.com/borndigital/. DOA: 01.01.2017.

Murray, J. (2003). Inventing the Medium. In N. Wardrip-Fruin, & N. Montfort, (Eds.), *The New Media Reader*. Cambridge, Mass. & London, England: The MIT Press, 3–11.

Neal, J. (2015). "Preserving the Born-Digital Record". Retrieved from https://americanlibrariesmagazine.org/2015/05/28/preserving-the-born-digital-record/. DOA: 01.01.2017.

Nielsen, J. (1995). *Multimedia and Hypertext. The Internet and Beyond*. Mountain View, CA: Academic Press.

Nielsen, J. (2007). “Show Numbers as Numerals When Writing for Online Readers”. Retrieved from http://www.nngroup.com/articles/web-writing-show-numbers-as-numerals/. DOA: 01.10.2015.

Nielsen, J. (2008). “Writing Style for Print vs. Web”. Retrieved from http://www.nngroup.com/articles/writing-style-for-print-vs-web/. DOA: 01.10.2015.

Nielsen, J. (2012). “Usability 101: Introduction to Usability”. Retrieved from http://www.nngroup.com/articles/usability-101-introduction-to-usability/. DOA: 01.10.2015.

Pike, K. L. (1967). *Language in Relation to a Unified Theory of the Structure of Human Behavior*. 2nd Edition. The Hague: Mouton & Co.

Redish, J. (2012). *Letting Go of the Words*. San Francisco: Elsevier.

Robertson, R., & White, K. E. (2007). What Is Globalization?. In G. Ritzer (Ed.) *The Blackwell Companion to Globalization*. Oxford: Blackwell Publishing, 62–63.

Schreibman, S., Siemens, R., & Unsworth, J. (Eds.) (2004). *Companion to Digital Humanities*. Oxford: Blackwell.

Stolley, K. (2011). *How to Design and Write Web Pages Today*. Greenwood: ABC-CLIO, LLC.

Tannen, D. (Ed.). (1981). *Analyzing discourses*. Georgetown University: Gurt.

Thorngate, W. (1990). The Economy of Attention and the Development of Psychology. *Canadian Psychology*, 31(3), 262–271.

Vanderdorpe, C. (2009). *From Papyrus to Hypertext. Toward the Universal Digital Library* (English translation). Urbana & Chicago: University of Illinois Press.

Westera, W. (2013). *The Digital Turn: How the Internet Transforms Our Existence*. Bloomington, IN: Authorhouse.

Wurman, R. S. (2001). *Information Anxiety 2*. Indianapolis: QUA.

Wurman, R. S. (2012). “Information Anxiety: Towards Understanding”. Scenario 05: Extraction. Retrieved from http://www.scenariojournal.com/article/richard-wurman/. DOA: 01.12.2015.

Iga Maria Lehman

University of Social Sciences, Warsaw, Poland

Language use in cultural contexts: Towards an integrative view of academic writer identity

Abstract: My approach to writer *identity* is based on the premise that the concept of the self consists of two fundamental self-representations: the *individual* (personal) *self* and the *collective* (social) *self*, which are in a constant state of flux, interacting with each other in many complex ways. Although there is a general consensus that these two parts of *identity* are social, there is, however, significantly less agreement on the nature of the interactions between them. My purpose in this paper is to outline a framework to investigate *identity* as constituted in academic texts with reference to the theory and practice of linguistic anthropology.

1. Introduction

Since the last decade of the 20th century the relationship between language and culture has been to a large extent the subject of research of such subfields of linguistics as linguistic anthropology (Duranti, 1997, 2009), sociolinguistics (Hymes, 1974; Gee 1990, 2012; Kramsch, 2002), intercultural and translation studies (Baker, 2006; House, 2009) as well as second language acquisition (SLA) and foreign language teaching (Freeman, 2004; Lantolf & Thorne, 2006; Atkinson, 2011). Intensive studies of the language/culture relationship have focused on the following areas of research: (1) how cultural differences are constituted and manifested through various forms of language use, with a particular emphasis on discourse practices (Hinds, 1987; Duszak, 1994, 1997; Kowalski, 2015); (2) how culturally different conceptual systems and value categories are included in the semantic and pragmatic systems of various languages (Wierzbicka, 1992, 1997); and (3) how socialization processes contribute to the formation of different types of sociocultural identities (Pavlenko & Lantolf, 2014). Although extensive research into the language/culture interface has provided a lot of meaningful results, there is an aspect of it that seems unclear and problematic, namely, research activities inspired by the Whorfian hypothesis, according to which language and culture are an inseparable whole. This contention manifests itself in such assertions as "language and culture are inseparable", "language is culture and culture is language", and "language and culture are interwoven", which are frequently found in the research area that forms my point of departure, i.e. the study of the influence of culture on the writer's self-representation (Connor, 1996, 2011; Duszak, 1997; Atkinson, 1999; Vassileva, 2000).

2. Research on language use in specific cultural contexts

For the past forty years the impact of cognitive and cultural aspects on written discourse has been a research area in the field of intercultural rhetoric, known in its earlier incarnation as contrastive rhetoric. First proposed by American applied linguist Robert Kaplan (1966), it attracted the attention of SLA researchers and teachers interested in how people navigate rhetorically within and across cultures. Kaplan's work was considerably extended by Connor (e.g. 1996, 2011) to consider not only the comparative studies of cultural thought patterns in intercultural education, but also to include studies of interactions in which writers from a variety of linguistic, cultural and social backgrounds negotiate their identities through oral and written discourse.

However, the conceptual basis of intercultural rhetoric has been strongly questioned ever since it first emerged as an area of research and pedagogical interest. The strongest controversy is to be found around the assertion that there is an inseparable link between language and culture, which leads to essentializing writers by neglecting to consider individual variations in written discourse. Because of this evident drawback in research assumptions, the field has been criticized for insensitivity to cultural differences (cf. Scollon, 1997; Spack, 1997; Zamel, 1997), for supporting the cultural dichotomy between the East and the West, and for the alleged resultant promotion of the superiority of Western writing (e.g. Kubota, 1999, 2001). In addition, Kubota (1999, 2002) accused contrastive rhetoric research of stereotyping writers by suggesting that someone thinks, speaks or writes in a certain way because of their cultural and linguistic background.

This simplified view of language and culture has been opposed in other research, specifically Freadman (2001) and Kramsch (2002, 2004), according to which the complexity of the relationship between language and culture should be emphasized and a more comprehensive analysis of the structure of this complexity is necessary. Although I share this approach to the language-culture nexus, it is not my intention to oppose the idea that there are clear links between language and culture in various aspects of communication, but to contribute to the clarification of insights into the nature of this correlation.

My approach is based on an integrative concept of language in which a study of language involves viewing language as an integral part of culture, society and an individual's unique cognitive processes. Undoubtedly, language use is always cultural because it is imbedded in a larger socio-cultural context on which it leaves its trace, and also because it is, in itself, a form of cultural practice. However, when exploring the relationship between language and culture, it is critical to distinguish between language and culture at the global level on the one hand, and language and culture at the local level on the other.

At the global level, the language-culture relationship is approached as a phenomenon realized in two forms: as a psychological/cognitive experience and as a social experience. Language and culture can be viewed as psychological/cognitive phenomena in the sense that human beings are equipped with species-typical mental predispositions, and as social experience which develops in the course of their social life.

In the global perspective, it is not possible to separate language from culture because linguistic practice is always rooted in a broadly defined cultural context. By contrast, at the local level, a wide range of cultures and languages can be encountered because we are confronted with different forms of language practice on a daily basis. This includes other (non-native) languages, and language varieties and registers. What is more, we can also identify specific products of language practice, such as differences in meaning, norms, values, beliefs and worldviews. Written language is to be found at both local and global levels, yet it is only when we examine English as a second language, or a particular instance of written discourse, that we move to the local level in order to describe those linguistic instantations which are not only influenced by a particular culture, but can also be universal. In every language there are some universal aspects which it shares with other languages and some elements which are unique to it. Consequently, all languages are, to varying extents, bearers of both linguistically specific and linguistically universal features. This observation applies to cultural products, artefacts and relations: some are culture-specific and have a limited scope of influence, while others are assumed to be shared by a wide variety of societies. Therefore, it needs to be clarified that the differences between languages and cultures are relative.

What follows is that it is only natural to draw a logical line between talking about language in the global sense (i.e. general theoretical issues of language as a vehicle of communication) and at the local level (i.e. with reference to a particular instance of language use). It is, in my view, the lack of a clear distinction between the global and the local levels that leads to confusion in terms of the relationship between language and culture. Along these lines Lévi-Strauss, in a paper given at a conference for linguists and anthropologists in Indiana in 1952, writes the following:

> [i]t has seemed to me on many occasions that we have unconsciously, in the course of the same discussion, slipped from one level to another… Initially, the interest has been with the relationship between *one* language and *one* well-defined culture…We have also discussed at another level where **the question asked is no longer that of the relationship between *one* language and *one* culture but rather between language and culture in general.**
>
> (Lévi-Strauss, 1958, p. 77; italics used in the original, bold-type emphasis mine)

The complex problem of the interplay between language and culture has been successfully addressed by both research and practice in linguistic anthropology, which relies on "[a]ny solid piece of work that could give a sense of (i) the importance of language(s) for an understanding of culture and society and (ii) the relevance of cultural and social phenomena of an understanding of language(s)" (Duranti, 2009, pp. 1–2). Given the wide scope of investigative interests, research findings within the field provide a comprehensive account of the meaning of linguistic messages within the contexts in which they are produced and interpreted. The commitment of linguistic anthropology to contextualized language makes it possible to study the language/culture relationship from a 'language in culture' perspective that includes both the global and local levels of this relationship.

The name 'linguistic anthropology' coexists with such subfields of anthropology as anthropological linguistics and sociolinguistics (along with ethnolinguistics in the United States). Although these disciplines are frequently perceived as synonymous, there are some important differences in the methods, goals and academic affiliations of the scholars involved. First of all, the research interests of the three subfields appear to follow separate paths: anthropological linguists center their research on 'language and culture' (Nuckolls, 1996; Schieffelin, Woolard & Kroskrity, 1998), sociolinguists shift their research focus to 'language as culture' studies (Labov, 1972, 1997; Gee, 1990, 1999), and the analysis of linguistic anthropologists relies on a 'language in culture' perspective (Gumperz & Hymes, 1964; Duranti, 1997). Furthermore, the term 'anthropological linguistics' demonstrates stronger links with the discipline of linguistics than with the discipline of anthropology by viewing "[l]inguistics as a tool for training social or cultural anthropologists to do fieldwork" (Duranti, 2009, p. 31). Despite the initial convergence of research interests (such as language variation and the importance of context), the current approach in linguistic anthropology adopts a constructivist view of social categories (e.g. Salzmann, 1993; Hanks, 1996; Duranti, 1997; Foley, 1997), and therefore rejects the radical division between dependent and independent variables as is otherwise supported in sociolinguistics (Roberts & Rousseau, 2003; Chambers, 2009).

Rooted in the knowledge of historical and current scholarship which cuts across the fields of linguistics and anthropology, linguistic anthropology explains the role which language plays in those human activities that constitute the social life of individuals and communities. The discipline thus focuses on the understanding of the cultural organization of a given activity (e.g. speaking or writing) through linguistic and ethnographic scrutiny. According to Duranti (2009, p. 1), "[i]f we want to understand the role of languages in people's lives, we must go beyond the study of their grammar and venture into the world of social action, where words are embedded in and constitutive of specific cultural activities". Duranti then goes on to explain that an in-depth language study "[s]tarts from utterances but always looks for fabric within which such utterances are shaped and meanings are produced".

All in all, the theories and methods of linguistic anthropology draw strongly on linguistic diversity, grammar in use, the role of speaking in social interaction, the organization and meaning of conversational structures, and the notion of participation as a unit of analysis. It seems clear then that these theories and methods can be successfully applied to investigate writing as a semiotic system which creates meaning and writer identity, the interplay of individual (the agency of participants) and environmental (social structures and social practices) factors.

In view of the above considerations, the premise of this paper is that, with the ever-deepening linguistic and cultural texture of contemporary societies, languages permeate cultures and cultures permeate languages. I therefore propose that as a consequence of this development, linguistic and cultural practices evolve and change likewise, and are exchanged through a variety of social networks via transnational patterns of communication, creating the origins of a global multicultural identity. In this process, certain cultural elements mix with one another, others become similar to each other, and still more retain their distinctiveness. In my approach I follow the path of linguistic anthropologists who "have ventured into the study of everyday encounters, language socialization, ritual and political events, scientific discourse, verbal art, language contact and language shift, literacy events, and media" (Duranti, 2009, p. 5).

3. Textual realization of individual/personal and collective/ social selves

My approach to writer identity is based on the premise that the concept of the self consists of two fundamental self-representations: the *individual* (personal) *self* and the *collective* (social) *self*. In other words, individuals define their identities in two basic ways: (a) in terms of their unique traits and (b) in terms of group membership (Sedikides & Brewer, 2001; Lehman, 2015).

Specifically, the individual self is formed by differentiating oneself from others. It is that aspect of the self which is a product of one's cognition, personality and life history, and which distinguishes the individual within their social context. This form of self-representation relies on interpersonal comparison processes and is associated with the motive of protecting or enhancing the person psychologically (Markus, 1977; Sedikides, 1993; Brewer & Gardner, 1996).

By contrast, the collective self is constructed within the social groups with which the individual identifies and by contrasting their in-group membership with relevant out-groups. This form of self-concept is constructed socially and constituted on the basis of origin and characteristics shared with other individuals or groups. Turner, Hogg, Oakes, Reicher and Wetherell (1987, p. 50) argue that the collective self is a "shift towards the perception of self as an interchangeable exemplar of some social category and away from the perception of self as a unique person". In sum, the collective self rests on intergroup comparison processes and is connected with the motive of protecting or enhancing the in-group (Brewer & Gardner, 1996).

It is assumed that these two aspects of identity coexist within the same individual and that they are both social, in that they are located in specific social and cultural contexts (Simon, 1997). Therefore I argue for the value of viewing identity as a socio-cultural phenomenon that emerges from and is situated in contexts of discoursal interaction, rather than a stable structure constituted primarily by the individual's cognitive processes and personality features. This dynamic nature of authorial identity was evidenced by the findings of my own semi-ethnographic study[1] (Lehman, 2014) designed to qualitatively test the validity of the hypothesis that each academic text is an act of identity influenced by individual (the agency of participants) and social factors (social structures and social practices). This inquiry sought to understand how student writer identity is affected by writing in 'the space between' two languages and two cultures and, specifically, how students' acquisition of cultural and linguistic knowledge of the second language is reflected in their writing in Polish and in English. I found that dual authorial self is constructed by a new perspective acquired due to the knowledge of two languages and two cultures, and that it is a dynamic concept which cannot be determined entirely by any socio-cultural or institutional factors, but is unique for each writer and can be negotiated and changed.

---

1 This study was a part of my PhD research project on "The co-construction of authorial identity in student writing in Polish and English," published in the on-line series *Studi@ Naukowe* (http://www.sn.ikla.uw.edu.pl/).

My approach focuses on the interplay between the two self-representations. I argue that these two aspects of the self are equally important in constituting authorial identity.[2] This view involves specifying the determinants of the formation of both aspects of the self, along with the circumstances that cause one self to take precedence over the other. From this perspective, the individual self and the collective self can be perceived as complementary, mutually exclusive, or entirely independent.

Although there is a general consensus that both parts of identity are social, there is, however, significantly less agreement on the nature of the interactions between individual and collective selves. Are they cooperating partners, staunch opponents or distant acquaintances? The key questions that should be formulated here to begin the inquiry into the nature of the relationship between these two aspects of writer identity are as follows.

1. Can particular features of individual and collective selves be traced in specific linguistic instantiations?
2. And if so, what do they reveal about the nature of this relationship?

To obtain reliable research results concerning writer identity, the line of inquiry should focus on both specific features of language and the influence of culture and society on the individual language user, allowing for the investigation of communicative language use by specific groups of people.

The central argument I put forward here is the one formulated by Grucza (2002, pp. 45–46): *Językowa tożsamość ludzi stanowi niewątpliwie najistotniejszy, centralny współczynnik "całej" tożsamości ludzi* [People's linguistic identity remains undoubtedly the most important, central constituent of the 'whole' human identity]. Inspired by this observation, I argue that writers' textual self-representations can be analyzed on the basis of their idiolects[3] and polylects[4]. According to Grucza

2 As I argue elswhere (Lehman, 2014), my approach to authorial identity can be supported by Fairclough's view of the relationships between language and identity. Fairclough takes up the 'translinguistic' ideas of Bakhtin and asserts that "[t]he matching of language to context is characterized by indeterminacy, heterogeneity and struggle" (1992, p. 42). Authorial identity in the context of academic writing has also been investigated in other studies including Ivanič (1998), Hyland (2002), Pittam, Elander, Lusher, Fox and Payne (2009).

3 *Idiolect* is a language which comprises a set of rules unique for an individual speaker-listener (Grucza, 1983, p. 300, translation mine).

4 *Polylect* is a language shared by a group of two or more speakers-listeners which is governed by a set of rules common to all the actual speaker-listeners who belong to that group. Examples of polylects are languages of ethnic groups that define themselves as

(2002), every language internalized by its owner/bearer (an individual's idiolect) contributes to the formation of both their personal and collective identities. This is made possible due to the four basic functions every language serves – constitutive, cognitive, distinctive-identificational and communicative (Grucza, 2002), contributing to the creation of a multidimensional identity in which an individual's idiolect intersects with diverse internalized polylects.

> *W istocie języki ludzkie są [...] najpierw i przede wszystkim pewnymi „faktami" całkiem osobistymi poszczególnych ludzi, ich właściwością całkiem „prywatną". Każdy idiolekt każdego konkretnego człowieka jest najpierw i przede wszystkim współczynnikiem jego osobowości. Natomiast pewnym faktem społecznym jest on o tyle, o ile „zbiega się" z idiolektami innych ludzi (ewentualnie innych członków danej wspólnoty), czyli o tyle, o ile „mieści się" on w obrębie ich polilektu. Wynika z tego w sposób zgoła oczywisty, że rzeczywiste języki ludzkie w rozumieniu idiolektów są pewnymi współczynnikami konstytuującymi zarówno osobową (prywatną), jak i zbiorową (społeczną) tożsamość swoich właścicieli, w tym także ich poczucie przynależności do określonej wspólnoty językowej i/lub komunikacyjnej.*
>
> (Grucza, 2002, p. 46)

> [In fact, human languages are (...) predominantly certain, rather personal 'facts' of particular individuals, their 'private' property. Every 'idiolect' of each specific person is first of all a constituent of their personality. Yet it remains a particular 'social fact' to the extent that it overlaps with the idiolects of other people (or other members of a particular community), in other words to the extent that it 'fits' within the scope of their polylect. It goes without saying that real human languages understood as idiolects are particular factors which constitute both individual (personal) and collective (social) identity of their owners/bearers, including their sense of belonging to the particular linguistic and/or communicative community.]
>
> (translation mine; Lehman, 2015, p. 175)

Also, thanks to Grucza's (2009) distinction between anthropocentric linguistics and culturology on the one hand, and paradigmatic linguistics and culturology (e.g. disciplines whose objects construct linguistic paradigms, models or patterns) on the other, texts can be viewed as products of specific people who identify themselves with two cultures: *idioculture*[5] and *polyculture*[6].

---

nations, and include the following: dialects, socio-dialects, ethno-dialects and nation-dialects (Grucza, 1983, p. 300, translation mine).

5 *Idioculture* defines culture at the individual's level by focusing on an individual as the locus of cultural creation, especially with reference to their own language use (i.e. *idiolect* in Grucza's 1983 sense; see footnote 3).

6 *Polyculture* re-specifies culture at the group level, as properties shared by two or more people along with the language they use (termed *polylect* by Grucza, 1983), it also identifies properties through which objects become the bearers of their own idioculture.

4. Identity construction in academic texts

Since every act of social interaction is embedded in a context which is constituted by an individual's communicative purpose and their social relationships, the two aspects of identity of a specific language user (in the case of this paper: an academic writer) can change quite radically from one act of writing to another. This understanding of 'context', which Halliday (1978, with Hasan 1989) calls 'context of culture', and what Fairclough (1989, 2003) calls 'institutional' and 'societal' context, is undoubtedly the most powerful aspect of academic writing because of the competing discourse traditions, norms and practices pertaining to culture, institution and society. Each decision an academic writer makes is affected both conventionally and creatively by these influences. Therefore, academic writer identity analysis usually involves research into the context of culture/language interactions, because the way student writers build coherence and cohesion in their texts, how they establish logical connections between ideas and order them into a meaningful argument differs from one writing culture to another. According to Duszak (1997, p. 2), cross-cultural differences in writing styles have been mainly observed in such aspects of discourse organization as global and local structures in texts, levels of explicitness and metatextual cueing, degrees of redundancy and distribution of salience, and linearity and complexity in form and content development.

Moreover, academic writers' linguistic choices ultimately reveal tensions between the rhetorical conventions of a given discourse community, along with the relations of power institutionally inscribed in it, and the author's preferences, which are shaped by the author's personal and socio-cultural experiences. Therefore, my approach to the formation of academic authorial identity has a certain affinity with Hyland's (2009) concept of performance, which he explains in the following way: "[w]e perform identity work by constructing ourselves as credible members of a particular social group, so that identity is something we do, not something we have" (Hyland, 2009, p. 70).

In writing fiction the writer has full freedom to choose the 'voice' they want their audience to hear and freedom to disguise their identity, whilst in academic writing they find themselves in a rather restricted position. On the one hand, they have to obey conventionalized values, beliefs and propositional content of academic communication, and institutionally sanctioned rules for organizational structure of the written work, while on the other hand academic writing is also about self-representation, choosing the voice authors want their audience to hear. Recent research has pointed to this individualistic/personal aspect of academic writing, arguing that writers establish credibility by projecting an identity invested with individual authority, displaying confidence in their evaluations and commitment to their ideas (Tang & John, 1999; Matsuda, 2001; Hyland, 2004; Clark & Ivanič, 2007).

Many characteristics of academic writing produced by students reflect their institutional and social positions, as evidenced in Gruber, Rheindor, Wetschanow, Reisigl, Muntigl and Czinglar's (2006) study, which showed how institutional and social positions occupied by student-writers pervade their writing and shape their discipline-specific identities. Firstly, students write because they have to fulfil a specific task and in order to become competent members of a specific discourse community. Gruber et al. (2006) found that students of different disciplines are aware of this kind of double identity in differing ways; for example, history students often view themselves as 'junior scientists' whereas business students view themselves as 'students' in a transitory situation as they are hoping to enter the business world as soon as possible. Therefore, the self of an academic author is a relative concept: writers perceive themselves and, consequently, present themselves to a greater or lesser degree as authors. Some of them draw strongly on other authorities, which leads to the dilution of the writer's voice; others assume a strong authorial stance.

Since academic writers differ significantly in how they establish authority for the propositional content of their writing and how they build logical connections between ideas and order them into a meaningful argument, it is essential to analyze their authorial identity through issues of legitimization (credibility of assertions), coherence and interdiscursivity, which involves "intertextual relations to conventions" (Fairclough, 1992, p. 104). Specifically, legitimization in discourse involves conceptual as well as linguistic aspects which can be approached from a number of perspectives, including cognitive, sociopsychological, textual and analytical, as well as using corpus linguistics, and/or critical discourse analysis (Cap, 2013, p. 64). Each of these perspectives requires an enactment of credibility of the speaker/writer, which, in academic text, concerns the author's voice, i.e. the author's position, opinions and beliefs, as well as the way they develop and sustain their arguments.

My purpose in this paper is to propose an approach to research on academic writer identity within the field of linguistic anthropology which would involve viewing language as an integral part of culture, society and one's unique cognition. To achieve this goal, I suggest the use of a methodology based on a two-dimensional framework for studying discourse, at the macro level and the micro level, as applied in critical discourse analysis (CDA) (Wodak & Meyer, 2001; Fairclough, 2003; Duszak, House & Kumięga, 2010), thereby providing a more integrative view on academic writer identity.

At the macro level, the analysis of academic texts should involve aspects of legitimization and interdiscursivity in order to investigate the relationship between the text and broader social processes. Here, the analysis of legitimization in academic texts can be carried out by examining the representations of social actors, considering such parameters as genericization and specification, assimilation and individualization, as well as nomination and categorization (see van Leeuwen, 2008). Although originally designed to investigate how social actors are represented in text (e.g. third persons, the people about whom the text speaks), van Leeuwen's (2008) framework can be applied to investigate textual manifestations of the writer's voice to identify who is part of the in-group and how and to what extent individuality is accounted for. According to Ivanič (1998), interdiscursivity is a central concept for any theory of language and identity because it explains how writers make particular discoursal choices by drawing on the text types which are made available to them. This macro-level aspect of interdiscursivity can be measured by Lehman's (forthcoming) Evaluative Parameter of Interdiscursivity, an evaluative tool designed to measure students' alignment with the rhetorical conventions of their discourse communities, as demonstrated through such aspects of discourse organization as linearity in form and content, explicitness and metatextual cueing and distribution of salience.

At the micro level, the analysis can focus on the linguistic features and devices employed to make the text coherent and cohesive. Therefore, text samples are examined for the cohesion of the explicit text and the coherence of the mental representation of the text using Coh-Metrix (a computational tool that produces indices of linguistic and discourse representations and contains a description of 108 indices incorporated into the website Coh-Metrix version 3.0; see McNamara, Louwerse, Cai & Graesser, 2005).

Assuming that an author's self-representation depends on aspects of individual self, such as writer agency and intentionality, and aspects of collective self, including socio-cultural experiences and the institutional context, an examination of writer identity with the use of the concepts of legitimization, interdiscursivity and coherence will contribute to the conceptualization of the discursive construction of identities of academic writers.

5. Conclusion

As argued in this paper, two aspects of academic writer identity, individual and collective self, are in a constant state of flux. They are continuously re-shaped by social processes of adjustment to writing conventions established by specific discourse communities and the writers' own interpretations of their personal and socio-cultural experiences.

To sum up, the framework proposed in this paper accentuates the interplay between individual and collective aspects involved in processes of identity formation of an academic writer. Positioned within the theory and practice of linguistic anthropology, it adopts the view that language is an activity born out of social life and individual experiences, which has consequences for writers as members of particular discourse communities.

References

Atkinson, D. (1999). Culture in TESOL. *TESOL Quarterly*, 33, 625–654.

Atkinson, D. (2011). A Sociocultural Approach to Second Language Acquisition: How mind, body, and world work together in learning additional languages. In D. Atkinson (Ed.), *Alternative Approaches to Second Language Acquisition.* New York: Routledge, 143–166.

Baker, M. (2006). *Translation and Conflict: A Narrative Account.* New York & London: Routledge.

Brewer, M. B., & Gardner, W. (1996). Who is this "we"? Levels of collective identity and self representations. *Journal of Personality and Social Psychology*, 71, 83–93.

Cap, P. (2013). *Proximization. The pragmatics of symbolic distance crossing.* Amsterdam & Philadelphia: John Benjamins.

Chambers, J. K. (2009). *Sociolinguistic Theory: Linguistic Variation and Its Social Significance.* Malden: Wiley Blackwell.

Clark, R., & Ivanič, R. (2007). *The Politics of Writing.* London: Routledge.

Connor, U. (1996). *Contrastive Rhetoric: Cross-cultural Aspects of Second Language Writing.* Cambridge: Cambridge University Press.

Connor, U. (2011). *Intercultural Rhetoric in the Writing Classroom.* Michigan: The University of Michigan Press.

Duranti, A. (1997). *Linguistic Anthropology.* Cambridge: Cambridge University Press.

Duranti, A. (2009). Lingistic anthropolology: history, ideas, and issues. In A. Duranti (Ed.), *Linguistic Anthropology. A Reader.* Chichester, UK: Wiley-Blackwell, 1–59.

Duszak, A. (1994). Academic discourse and intellectual styles. *Journal of Pragmatics*, 21, 291–313.

Duszak, A. (1997). Cross-cultural academic communication: a discourse-community view. In A. Duszak (Ed.), *Culture and Styles of Academic Discourse.* Berlin: Mouton de Gruyter, 11–39.

Duszak, A., House, J., & Kumięga, Ł. (2010). *Globalization, Discourse, Media: In a Critical Perspective / Globalisierung, Diskurse, Medien: eine kritische Perspektive.* Warszawa: Wydawnictwa Uniwersytetu Warszawskiego.

Fairclough, N. (1989). *Language and Power.* London: Longman.

Fairclough, N. (1992). *Discourse and Social Change.* Cambridge: Polity Press.

Fairclough, N. (2003). *Analyzing Discourse: Textual analysis for social research.* London & New York: Routledge.

Foley, W. A. (1997). *Anthropological Linguistics: an introduction.* Oxford: Basil Blackwell.

Freadman, A. (2001). The culture peddlers. *Postcolonial Studies,* 4(3), 275–296.

Freeman, D. (2004). Language, sociocultural theory, and L2 teacher education: Examining the technology of subject matter and the architecture. In M. R. Hawkins (Ed.), *Language Learning and Teacher Education: A Sociocultural Approach.* Clevedon: Multilingual Matters, 169–197.

Gee, J. P. (1990). *Social Linguistics and Literacies: Ideology in Discourses.* Basingstoke: Falmer Press.

Gee, J. P. (1999). *An introduction to discourse analysis: theory and method.* London & New York: Routledge.

Gee, J. P. (2012). *Social Linguistics and Literacies.* London: Routledge.

Gruber, H., Rheindor, M., Wetschanow, K., Reisigl, M., Muntigl, P., & Czinglar, C. (2006). *Genre, Habitus Und Wissenschaftliches Schreiben - eine empirische Untersuchung studentischer Texte.* Wien: LIT-Verlag.

Grucza, F. (1983). *Zagadnienia metalingwistyki. Lingwistyka – jej przedmiot, lingwistyka stosowana.* Warszawa: Państwowe Wydawnictwo Naukowe.

Grucza, F. (2002). Język (narodowy) – tożsamość (narodowa) – integracja europejska. In E. Jeleń, M. Rauen, M. Świątek & J. Winiarska (Eds.), *Zmiany i rozwój języka oraz tożsamości narodowej – trendy w procesie integracji europejskiej. Referaty z konferencji Kraków, 11–13.X. 2001.* Kraków: Księgarnia akademicka, 25–49.

Grucza, F. (2009). *Diskurse als Mittel und Gegenstände der Germanistik. Materialien der Jahrestagung und der internationalen wissenschaftlichen Konferenz des Verbandes Polnischer Germanisten abgehalten an der Warmia und Mazury Universität, 8–10. 05.2009 Olsztyn.* Warszawa: Stowarzyszenie Germanistów Polskich.

Gumperz, J. J., & Hymes, D. (1964). The Ethnography of Communication. *American Anthropologist,* 66 (6), part II, 137–154.

Halliday, M. A. K. (1978). *Language as Social Semiotic: The social interpretation of language and meaning.* London: Edward Arnold.

Halliday, M. A. K., & Hasan, R. (1989). *Language, Context and Text: Aspects of language in a social-semiotic perspective* (2nd edition). Oxford: Oxford University Press.

Hanks, W. F. (1996). *Language and communicative practices*. Oxford (UK) & Boulder (CO): Westview.

Hinds, J. (1987). Reader vs. writer responsibility: A new typology. In T. Silva & P. K. Matsuda (Eds.), *Landmarks Essays on ESL Writing*. New Jersey: Hermagoras Press, 63–73.

House, J. (2009). *Translation*. London: Oxford University Press.

Hyland, K. (2002). *Teaching and Researching Writing*. Harlow: Longman.

Hyland, K. (2004). Disciplinary interactions: Metadiscourse in L2 postgraduate writing. *Journal of Second Language Writing*, 13, 133–151.

Hyland, K. (2009). *Academic Discourse: English in A Global Context*. London: Continuum.

Hymes, D. (1974). *Foundations in sociolinguistics: An ethnographic approach*. Philadelphia: University of Pennsylvania Press.

Ivanič, R. (1998). *Writing and Identity: The Discoursal Construction of Identity in Academic Writing*. Amsterdam: John Benjamins.

Kaplan, R. B. (1966). Cultural thought patterns in inter-cultural education. *Language Learning*, 16, 1–20.

Kowalski, G. (2015). *Claim-making and Claim-challenging in English and Polish Linguistic Discourses*. Bern: Peter Lang.

Kramsch, C. (2002). Introduction. How can we tell the dancer from the dance?. In C. Kramsch (Ed.), *Language Acquisition and Language Socialization: Ecological Perspectives*. London: Continuum, 1–30.

Kramsch, C. (2004). Language, thought, and culture. In A. Davies & C. Elder (Eds.), *Handbook of Applied Linguistics*. Oxford & Malden, MA: Wiley-Blackwell, 235–261.

Kubota, R. (1999). Japanese culture constructed by discourses: implications for applied linguistic research and English language teaching. *TESOL Quarterly*, 33, 9–35.

Kubota, R. (2001). Discursive construction of the images of U.S. classrooms. *TESOL Quarterly*, 35, 9–38.

Kubota, R. (2002). The author responds: (Un)Raveling racism in a nice field like TESOL. *TESOL Quarterly*, 36(1), 84–92.

Labov, W. (1972). *Sociolinguistic Patterns*. Philadelphia PA: University of Pennsylvania Press.

Labov, W. (1997). Linguistics and sociolinguistics. In N. Coupland & A. Jaworski (Eds.), *Sociolinguistics: A Reader and Coursebook*. London: MacMillan, 23–24.

Lantolf, J. P., & Thorne, S.L. (2006). *Sociocultural theory and the genesis of second language acquisition*. Oxford: Oxford University Press.

van Leeuwen, T. (2008). *Discourse and Practice: Tools for Critical Discourse Analysis*. New York: Oxford University Press.

Lehman, I. M. (2014). The role of identity in student writing in English and in Polish. *Kwartalnik Neofilologiczny*, 3(14), 601–611.

Lehman, I. M. (2015). Academic identities: individual and collective 'selves'. In A. Duszak & G. Kowalski (Eds.), *Academic Inter-Genres: between Texts, Contexts and Identities*. Warszawa: Peter Lang, 167–187.

Lévi-Strauss, C. (1952). Linguistics and Anthropology. A paper presented at a Conference of Anthropologists and Linguists at Bloomington, Indiana.

Lévi-Strauss, C. (1958). *Anthropologie structurale*. Paris: Plon.

Markus, H. (1977). Self-schemata and processing information about the self. *Journal of Personality and Social Psychology*, 35, 63–78.

Matsuda, P. K. (2001). Voice in Japanese written discourse: Implication for second language writing. *Journal of Second Language Writing*, 10, 35–53.

McNamara, D. S., Louwerse, M. M., Cai, Z., & Graesser, A. (2005). Coh-Metrix version 3.0. Retrieved from http://cohmetrix.com. DOA: 01.03.2017.

Nuckolls, J. B. (1996). *Sounds like Life: Sound-symbolic Grammar, Performance, and Cognition in Pastaza Quechua*. Oxford: Oxford University Press.

Pavlenko, A., & Lantolf, J. P. (2014). Second language learning as participation and the (re)construction of the selves. In J. P. Lantolf (Ed.), *Sociocultural Theory and Second Language Learning*. Oxford: Oxford University Press.

Pittam, G., Elander, J., Lusher, J., Fox, P., & Payne, N. (2009). Student beliefs and attitudes about authorial identity in academic writing. *Studies in Higher Education*, 34(2), 153–170.

Roberts, I., & Roussou, A. (2003). *Syntactic Change: A Minimalist Approach to Grammaticalization*. Cambridge University Press.

Salzmann, Z. (1993). *Language, culture, and society: An introduction to linguistic anthropology*. Boulder: Westview Press.

Schieffelin, B. B., Woolard, K., & Kroskrity, P. (1998). *Language Ideologies: Practice and Theory*. New York: Oxford University Press.

Scollon, R. (1997). Contrastive rhetoric, contrastive poetics, or perhaps something else? *TESOL Quarterly*, 31, 352–363.

Sedikides, C. (1993). Assessment, enhancement, and verification determinants of the self-evaluation process. *Journal of Psychology and Social Psychology,* 65, 317–338.

Sedikides, C., & Brewer M. B. (2001). *Individual self, relational self, collective self.* Philadelphia: Psychology Press.

Simon, B. (1997). Self and group in modern society: Ten theses on the individual self and the collective self. In R. Spears, P. J. Oakes, N. Ellemers & S. A. Haslam (Eds.), *The social psychology of stereotyping and group life.* Oxford: Blackwell, 318–335.

Spack, R. (1997). The rhetorical construction of multilingual students. *TESOL Quarterly,* 31,765–774.

Tang, R., & John, S. (1999). The 'I' in identity: Exploring writer identity in student academic writing through the first person pronoun. *English for Specific Purposes,* 18, 23–39.

Turner, J. C., Hogg, M. A., Oakes, P. J., Reicher, S. D., & Wetherell, M. S. (1987). *Rediscovering the social group. A self-categorization theory.* Oxford: Blackwell.

Vassileva, I. (2000). *Who is the author? A contrastive analysis of authorial presence in English, German, French, Russian and Bulgarian academic discourse.* Sankt Augustin: Asgard Verlag.

Wierzbicka, A. (1992). *Semantics, Culture and Cognition: Universal human concepts in culture-specific configurations.* New York: Oxford University Press.

Wierzbicka, A. (1997). *Understanding Cultures Through Their Key Words: English, Russian, Polish, German, Japanese.* New York: Oxford University Press.

Wodak, W., & Meyer, M. (2001). *Methods of Critical Discourse Analysis.* Sage Publications.

Zamel, V. (1997). Toward a model of transculturation. *TESOL Quarterly,* 31, 341–343.

Part 2.
(New) Media Discourse

Tatiana Karpilovitch

Minsk State Linguistic University, Belarus

Semantic and pragmatic structure of problem feature articles in American and Belarusian media discourse

Abstract: The paper proposes an integrated approach to analyzing semantic and pragmatic structures of discourse on the example of problem feature articles from American and Belarusian press. A prototypical semantic structure of this genre has been singled out, which consists of two categories: *the essence of the problem* and *ways of solving the problem*. The pragmatics of semantic categories is revealed through the use of evaluative lexis, modal units, stylistic devices, and opinion making utterances. The cross-linguistic study of problem feature articles from American and Belarusian media discourse has shown the prevalence of similar properties in the semantic and pragmatic structures of this genre. The differences lie in the use of some language units and stylistic devices which are predetermined by the systemic differences between English and Belarusian, and also by the traditions of using expressive language means in the two media cultures.

1. Introduction

Various approaches have been proposed to formalize the semantics of text and discourse (e.g. Minsky, 1975; Schank & Abelson, 1977; Thorndyke, 1977; van Dijk & Kintsch, 1983; Mann & Thompson, 1988; Swales, 1990). Some of these theories have provided the basis for computer summarization systems aimed at automatic generation of secondary documents, i.e. summaries and abstracts of texts and discourses (Hahn & Reimer, 1999; Marcu, 1999; Karpilovitch, 2003). Summaries, as concise representations of the source discourse, include factual (semantic) information. In contrast to the tools of automatic summarizing and abstracting, a new trend in natural language processing, *opinion mining* is aimed at developing computer algorithms for extracting pragmatic information from discourse). This new field in applied linguistics has stimulated research in formalizing the pragmatic plane of discourse for its further implementation in the systems of opinion mining and sentiment analysis (Devitt & Ahmad, 2007; Pang & Lee, 2008; see also Karpilovitch, 2014), which are of great importance for various types of business and government intelligence applications.

This paper is devoted to a cross-cultural analysis of problem feature articles from American and Belarusian newspapers, with the aim of identifying shared and context-specific language means which signal the semantic and pragmatic structures of this media genre in the two lingua-cultures. Apart from providing conclusions drawn from a cross-cultural and cross-linguistic study, the analysis offers results which can be used in the linguistic information base of opinion mining algorithms.

The paper consists of four sections: in section 1 the necessity of analyzing the formal markers of the pragmatic plane of discourse is grounded; section 2 outlines the theoretical premises of the integrated approach to the study of discourse semantics and pragmatics. Section 3 presents the analysis of problem feature articles excerpted from American and Belarusian media discourses; the conclusions are given in section 4.

2. Theoretical frame

In order to formalize the pragmatics of discourse, in particular to identify and classify language markers that convey pragmatic information and determine the rules of their search in discourse, I have developed an integrated semantic-pragmatic approach to discourse analysis. The underlying theoretical principle of this approach is the thesis that discourse semantics and pragmatics are interrelated and genre-dependent. On the one hand, discourse semantics without considering its pragmatics is indefinite and incomplete because pragmatics sets personal, temporal and local boundaries for semantics, which characterize, in the first place, the interaction between the addresser and the addressee. As van Dijk (1985, p. 189) observes,

> [m]eaning and aspect are just one aspect of discourse, closely intertwined with surface, structural, pragmatic, cognitive, and interactional features, so that also in this respect any semantic analysis exhibits the disadvantages of a partial description.

On the other hand, it is evident that pragmatics cannot exist without semantics inasmuch as pragmatic information is inferred from the logical and semantic organization of discourse. In other words, pragmatic meaning is closely connected to semantic meaning, which determines both the choice of language items and the presentation of the necessary facts in a certain order. The difference between the two planes then results from the fact that discourse semantics characterizes the content of the discourse generated by the addresser, while pragmatics allows him/her to convey ideas to the addressee in the most effective way.

In my approach, the pragmatic plane of discourse includes the characteristics of the participants, their goals, communicative strategies, tactics, and also language means necessary to be realized in discourse. In fact in each discourse there can be found certain words, expressions and other linguistic phenomena which have a special pragmatic load. They include e.g. evaluative lexical units, emotive words, stylistic devices or different means of foregrounding important information in discourse. For instance, the contribution of evaluation language units to discourse pragmatics is clearly shown within the framework of the Appraisal theory, which is concerned with

> the systematic analysis of evaluation and stance as they operate in whole texts and in grouping of texts; it considers the social functions of these resources, not simply as the means by which individual speakers/writers express their feelings and take stands, but as the means by which they engage with socially-determined value positions.
>
> (White, 2011, p. 14)

In applied linguistics, there is a tendency to consider and represent semantic and pragmatic information as a unity because understanding is achieved by the integrated implementation of semantic and pragmatic knowledge. Thus, we can draw the conclusion that the effect of discourse on the addressee is produced by the interaction of discourse semantics and pragmatics. This is why whenever we analyze the pragmatics of discourse we must as well take into account its contents, i.e. the semantics.

In my research, discourse semantics is associated with *superstructure*, that is semantic structures of discourse genres. This term was first introduced in the theory of Teun van Dijk and Walter Kintsch (1983), alongside the notion of a *macrostructure*. Superstructure is defined as a conventional global scheme of discourse which "may be made explicit in terms of the specific categories defining a discourse type". By contrast, macrostructures "are the semantic content for the terminal categories of these superstructural schemata" (van Dijk & Kintsch, 1983, p. 189). In a concise form, macrostructures can be expressed by headlines, thematic sentences or summaries.

Though the authors argue that superstructure is the overall *form* of a discourse (van Dijk & Kintsch, 1983, p. 189, emphasis mine), in their analysis of news stories they identify not only formal categories such as *headline*, *lead*, *summary* or *introduction*, which are, in fact, parts of a prototypical newspaper article, but also categories which are semantic in nature, such as *previous information*, *actual information*, *background*, *opinion*, *events*, *consequences*, etc. The authors show that the order of these semantic elements is determined by discourse generation strategies (van Dijk & Kintsch, 1983, pp. 243–245). That is why in this analysis of newspaper feature articles I use the term *superstructure* in the sense of a semantic structure typical of a given discourse genre.

The psychological reality of superstructures as conventional mental schemata was proved in a number of experiments made by cognitive psychologists and psycholinguists. They showed that authors who regularly create discourse of a certain genre are guided by superstructures which are present in their minds (Liddy, 1991, pp. 55–56). While the content of any two texts – no matter if it represents the same or different genres – is always different, there is always a conventional structural scheme that is reflected in the discourse.

While considering the notion of superstructure I should point out that it is different from the term *composition*, which is often used in discourse linguistics, text linguistics and genre analysis (Matveeva, 1990). Composition is defined as a form of discourse (or text) structuring into semantic blocks which are comparatively complete in the discourse space. Some common semantic blocks include *summary*, *introduction*, *main body* and *conclusion*. These elements are formal in the sense that, firstly, they are discrete units, and, secondly, they are located in specific parts of discourse (e.g. introduction – at the beginning, conclusion – at the end). Consequently, they can be easily identified by the reader. As my analysis of media discourse genres shows, as opposed to compositional blocks, superstructural categories can be found in different parts of the discourse space; moreover, they can be interspersed and recursive.

The notion of superstructure is a lingua-cognitive parameter used for the description of a discourse genre given that superstructural semantic categories are identified on the basis of their 'surface' realization in discourse and are inferred mainly from the meanings of specific lexical and grammatical units of discourse, not from an "external knowledge base" (Sinclair, 1992, p. 82). Consequently, for most of the superstructural categories it is possible to define a set of language markers which will signal each of these categories in a particular discourse genre. Such markers include lexical items (lexemes and phrases, in either case representing different parts of speech), lexical clichés, lexico-semantic and lexico-syntactic structures. Also, a superstructure of a discourse genre can comprise a number of semantic categories but not all of them are always represented in a concrete discourse representing this genre. That is why I suggest that we differentiate between a *prototypical* and a *detailed* superstructure. The former includes categories which are regularly represented in a discourse belonging to a given genre; in other words, prototypical superstructures are the most frequent. By contrast, the latter includes all possible semantic categories which can form a given genre; the detailed superstructure is therefore much less frequent than the prototypical superstructure.

For the purposes of a linguistic analysis the semantics and the pragmatics of a discourse genre can be studied separately, but in real discourse they are inseparable and interconnected. I will demonstrate this by means of an analysis of problem feature articles from American and Belarusian media discourse.

3. Analysis and Discussion

Using the above-mentioned theoretical premises, I analyzed the media discourse genre of a feature article in American and Belarusian press. In particular, for close consideration, I chose only those articles which were devoted to the description and discussion of topical problems in different spheres of public life: politics, economy, culture, sports, lifestyle, etc. For the relevant discourse, I use the term *problem media discourse*; for the genre in question – *a problem feature article.*

Problem feature articles chosen for the analysis were taken from American newspapers: *The New York Times*, *The Wall Street Journal*, *The Seattle Times* and *USA Today*, and Belarusian newspapers: *Звязда* 'The Star' and *Рэспубліка* 'The Republic'. All of them were published in the time period 2009–2015. Forty articles were selected for each language.

The superstructures of problem feature articles under study were defined on the basis of logical text analysis and the method of language markers described in Section 2. As a result, the following semantic categories were singled out: *the essence of the problem, the causes of the problem, the description of the problem situation, the effect of the problem on society,* and *ways of solving the problem*. The analysis has shown that only two of these categories are present in the majority of the articles under consideration: *the essence of the problem* and *ways of solving the problem,* and, consequently, they form the prototypical superstructure of the problem feature article.

The semantic categories were defined on the basis of their language representation in the discourse. For instance, among the nouns associated with the category *the essence of the problem* some typical examples in English and Belarusian media discourse are, respectively: *challenge, clash, concern, hurdle, problem, restriction, question, trouble*; *канфлікт* 'conflict', *незадаволенасць* 'dissatisfaction', *праблема* 'problem', *пытанне* 'question'. The semantic analysis of these words shows that most of them have an evaluative meaning, which is disclosed in their dictionary definitions. As an example let us consider the definition of the noun *problem* in the meaning which is realized in the semantic category *the essence of the problem*: "an unsettled matter demanding solution or decision and requiring usually considerable thought or skill for its proper solution; an issue marked by usually considerable difficulty, uncertainty or doubt with regard to its proper settlement;

a perplexing or puzzling question" (*Webster's third new international dictionary*, 1986, p. 1807). This definition contains such evaluative lexical units as *unsettled, proper, difficulty, uncertainty, doubt, perplexing, puzzling*, alongside relatively neutral items: *matter, solution, discussion, thought, skill, issue*, etc. As can be seen in this example, the meanings of linguistic exponents of the superstructural categories present in problem feature articles demonstrate the unity of semantics and pragmatics.

In discourse, this connection between semantics and pragmatics can be further emphasized by the use of evaluative attributes: ***daunting*** *challenge*, ***tough*** *challenge, a* ***growing*** *problem*; ***набалелая*** *праблема* 'a **painful** problem', ***хвалюючае*** *пытанне* 'an **exciting** question'; phraseological units: *галаўны боль* '*fig.* headache', *закрываць вочы* 'close one's eyes', metaphors: *a black box, заглушка раздору* 'a gag to discord', and other expressive linguistic means.

The language markers of the category *the essence of the problem* are often found in the formal initial parts of the newspaper articles under study: headlines (see examples 1 and 2), subtitles (see examples 3 and 4), and leads (see examples 5 and 6).

(1) Montana coal railroad's delay reflects **hurdles** for exports.
(*The Seattle Times*, 20.07.2014)

(2) *Абарона беларускіх брэндаў становіцца* ***пытаннем*** *нацыянальнай бяспекі краіны.*

[Defending Belarusian brands is becoming **a question** of national security]
(*Звязда*, 13.07.2013)

(3) Employers, workers **clash** on pay and benefits; IRS to take closer look at classifications.
("Contractor' Label Provokes Legal Disputes", *The Wall Street Journal*, 19.10.2009)

(4) *Калі трухлявыя дамы перастануць быць* ***"галаўным болем"*** *для мясцовых жыхароў?*

[When will shabby houses stop being a **headache** for the local people?]
("А знос і сёння там" [No pulling down yet]", *Звязда*, 17.09.2014)

(5) Applying for a mortgage for many home purchasers not only is **a tough challenge**, but one that ends unhappily – they get rejected.
("Red flags bankers see when you seek a loan", *The Seattle Times*, 20.07.2014)

(6) ***Праблема*** *яшчэ і ў тым, што спіртныя напоі нікому з бацькоў і ў галаву не прыйдзе прапаноўваць дзецям, а гаджэты падсунуць нават маленькаму дзіцяці, каб проста яго заняць ці супакоіць.*

[**Another side of the problem** is that parents will never offer alcohol to their children but as for gadgets, they will give them even to a little kid just to entertain or calm him/her].
("Выхапіць з павуціння" [To snatch out from the web], *Звязда*, 03.06.2016)

The integrated character of semantic and pragmatic meanings is also evident in the use of evaluative lexis in the discourse realization of the semantic categories discussed, examples of which are given in the above excerpts, e.g. *closer*, *get rejected*, *unhappily*; *бяспека* 'security', *трухлявы* 'shabby', *супакоіць* 'calm'. With such lexical items the author directly expresses positive or negative evaluations of the problem raised in the article.

The category *the essence of the problem* can also be verbalized with negative predicates or words with negative meanings indicating different kinds of bans, obstacles and misdoings which create problems and conflicts (see examples 7 and 8).

(7) Microsoft is imposing new **restrictions** on those who work for the company through vendors and temp agencies.
("Microsoft to restrict contractor access", *The Seattle Times*, 20.07.2014)

(8) *Два гады* ***не працуе*** *цэнтр рэабілітацыі інвалідаў пад Брэстам.*
[The recovery center for disabled people near Brest has been out of work for two years already]
("Зацяжны рамонт" [Slow repairs], *Звязда*, 25.04.2013)

However, the analysis has also shown that media discourse does not always contain explicit indicators of all the semantic categories in question. Thus, the category *the essence of the problem* can also be disclosed by listing the actions performed by the conflicting sides (see examples 9 and 10).

(9) *Пенсіянер з вёскі Ліпск, якая знаходзіцца ў палескай зоне раёна* ***прад'явіў прэтэнзіі*** *суседцы Ніне Гапановіч, якая на сваім участку* ***рассыпала***, *на думку Івана Пятровіча, празмерную колькасць мінеральных угнаенняў, ад чаго вада ў яго калодзежы сапсавалася.*
[The retired man from the village Lipsk, which is situated in Polesie zone of the region, **laid claims** to his neighbour Nina Gapanovich, who **had used** too many fertilizers on her piece of land, and as a result, the water in the well of the plaintiff was spoiled.]
(*Звязда*, 12.12.2011)

(10) Sandra Person Burns **used to love browsing and shopping** online. Until she **realized** she **was being tracked** by software on her computer that she **thought** she **had erased**.
("Code that tracks users' browsing prompts lawsuits", *The New York Times*, 21.09.2010)

Opposite to the category *the essence of the problem*, one can find the second prototypical category of problem feature articles – *ways of solving the problem* – which is usually signaled in the discourse by explicit language markers. The indicators of this category are, in the first place, sentence structures with direct or indirect speech and the social status of the person whose opinion is given, for instance in the corpus analyzed: *chief executive*, *founder of the investment firm*, *Microsoft spokesman*, *college president*, *managing consultant*; *дырэктар Дэпартамента дзяржаўнай інспекцыі працы* 'director of the state department of labor inspection', *намеснік галоўнага ўрача* 'deputy chief doctor', *міністр адукацыі* 'minister of education', *старшыня сельсавета* 'chairman of the village council', *настаяцель храма* 'church dean', etc. These indicators are usually combined with verbs and verbal phrases denoting a speech activity (e.g. *add*, *comment*, *confirm*, *say*, *tell*, *write*; *адзначыць* 'note', *гаварыць* 'say', *звярнуць увагу* 'draw attention to', *каментаваць* 'comment', *лічыць* 'consider', *падкрэсліць* 'stress', *сцвярджаць* 'state', etc., see examples 11 and 12), or with an introductory prepositional phrase (e.g. *according to*; *па меркаванні* 'in the opinion of', *па словах* 'according to the words of').

(11) **Surface Transportation Board spokesman** Dennis Watson **said** the decision to bump back the schedule on the railroad study was made to accommodate the "intense interest" in the project.

("Montana coal railroad's delay reflects hurdles for exports", *The Seattle Times*, 20.07.2014)

(12) *Балонскі працэс для нас – не самамэта,* – ***падкрэслівае міністр адукацыі***. – *Ва ўмовах глабалізацыі эканомікі ёсць неабходнасць састыкоўкі сістэмы адукацыі Беларусі з сістэмамі іншых краін*

["The Bologna process for us is not an end in itself," **stresses the Minister of Education**. "In the era of economic globalization, it is necessary to connect the Belarusian system of education with the systems of education of other countries."]

("Ці ёсць у Балонскага працэсу 'пабочныя эфекты'?" [Does the Bologna process have "side effects"?], *Звязда*, 13.02.2014)

The integrated approach to the analysis of discourse semantics and pragmatics in problem feature articles made it possible to define that the second prototypical category of the newspaper articles under study is more pragmatically loaded than the first. This result can be explained by the main communicative goal of the problem feature article – to suggest possible ways of solving the topical problem, relying on the opinion of experts, analysts, representatives of the government, businesses and other institutions.

The analysis showed that the pragmatic load of the category *ways of solving the problem* is created not only by the frequent use of evaluative lexis but also by modal units, utterances expressing opinions, and stylistic devices, both lexical and syntactic. Though all these linguistic means are present in American and Belarusian media discourse, there are certain tendencies in speech behavior which are specific to either of the two media cultures.

The first difference lies in the character of modal lexical units used by the discourse participants when expressing their viewpoints on the ways of solving the problem under discussion. Specifically, American participants use modal verbs with the meaning of necessity *have to, must, need, should* more often, while Belarusian participants prefer modal adverbs *варта* 'should', *неабходна* 'it is necessary', *патрэбна* 'to need', *трэба* 'must'. These preferences can be explained by the differences in the systems of modal units of the two languages. In the English language, the modal meaning of necessity is expressed not only by modal adjectives (*indispensable, necessary*, etc.) but also by verbs, varying in the degree of necessity/obligation. By contrast, in the Belarusian language necessity is usually expressed by the predicative *павінен* 'must' and modal adverbs listed above (see examples 13 and 14).

(13) That has changed now, and there is a recognition within the company that we **have had to** change our attitude about how we approach this market.
("Nokia struggles to regain market share in the U.S.", *The New York Times*, 19.10.2009)

(14) *Тут* ***трэба*** *знайсці неабходную залатую сярэдзіну, у адпаведнасці з якой мы будзем і зарабляць самі, і ў той жа час дзяржава будзе падтрымліваць установы культуры.*

[We **should** find the golden mean here: on the one hand, we will earn money ourselves, and on the other hand, the government will support the cultural institutions.]
("Дарожная карта' для гістарычнага помніка" ["Roadmap" for a historical monument], *Звязда*, 11.07.2015)

The second difference between the two media cultures in the use of pragmatically loaded devices is the tendency to use certain stylistic expressions. Among lexical stylistic devices American participants, including the author of the newspaper article, tend to use epithets (*elaborate clothes, flamboyant presentation, fragile ecosystem, a hard-and-fast answer, intense interest, scrupulous use, thoughtful decision*, etc.), while their Belarusian counterparts quite often prefer phraseological units of different types (*выносіць на сваіх плячах* 'carry on one's broad shoulders', *залатаць дзірку* 'to patch a gap', *лёд крануўся* 'the ice has been broken', *на поўную катушку* 'in full swing', *паставіць кропку* 'to put a full stop', *у поце твару* 'by the sweat of one's brow', etc.), and colloquial words and expressions (*абкатаць* 'to roll in', *прабуксоўка* 'stagnation', *раскрутка* 'promotion', *усё ўключана* 'all included', etc.) See examples (15) and (16) for an illustration: the former features epithets, whereas the latter a phraseological unit.

(15) Some proven methods exist, including **strict** control of antibiotics in hospitals, **rapid** identification of infected patients and **scrupulous** use of isolation, hand hygiene and room cleaning protocols.

("There is no easy answer.", *USA Today*, 24.08.2012)

(16) *Пакуль найбольш даходлівая форма прывучыць да правілаў бяспекі –* ***пакараць рублём.***

[So far, the best way to make people keep to safety rules is **to punish them with a fine**.]

("Кантралёра да кожнага не прыставіш" [It's impossible to appoint an inspector to look after every person at work], *Звязда*, 05.02.2016)

While epithets, in most contexts, help to convey the addresser's emotional attitude towards the statement, phraseological units contribute to the imagery of the discourse. Though different in their pragma-stylistic functions, the above mentioned stylistic devices enhance the overall impact of the discourse content on the addressee, in the long run.

There are also some differences in the use of syntactic stylistic devices by the representatives of the two media cultures. In particular, American participants tend to use anaphoric and parallel syntactic structures to emphasize the importance of a given approach in tackling the discussed social problem, while Belarusian participants use inverted sentence structures and parcellation. See examples (17) and (18) for an illustration: the former employs anaphoric and parallel syntactic structures, while the latter parcellation.

(17) **It's not** your credit scores. **It's not** how much you've got for a down payment. **It's** your "DTIs" – your debt-to-income ratios.

("Red flags bankers see when you seek a loan", *The Seattle Times*, 20.07.2014)

(18) *Пры гэтым, выстаўляючы патрабаванні для новага ўласніка, трэба ведаць меру, каб яго не адпудзіць.* ***Бо галоўнае – захаваць гістарычны аб'ект.***

[For all this, when setting out the requirements to the new owners, it is necessary to know measure not to frighten them off. **Because the main thing is to keep the historical object**.]

("'Дарожная карта' для гістарычнага помніка" ["Roadmap" for a historical monument], *Звязда*, 11.07.2015)

The pragmatic load of the semantic component *ways of solving the problem* is also constituted by utterances expressing the speech acts of advice and recommendation (see examples 19 and 20). Imperative sentences with this meaning are supposed to have a strong impact on the reader, as the addresser appeals to him/her directly.

(19) Most important: **Postpone** your purchase until your DTI ratio tell you – yes, you can afford the house you want and lenders won't reject you out of hand.
("Red flags bankers see when you seek a loan", *The Seattle Times*, 20.07.2014)

20. ***Падключыце*** *ў свайго мабільнага аператара паслугу бацькоўскага кантролю, якая дазваляе вызначыць раён апошняга знаходжання дзіцяці.*

[**Activate** mobile service "Parents' control", which allows you to define the child's last place of location.]
("Куды знікаюць дзеці?" [Where do children disappear?], *Звязда*, 29.05.2015)

The majority of the examples given in this paper show that most of the opinion-making statements contain explicit language means of evaluation and stance (Martin & White, 2003), which can be listed in the linguistic information base of opinion mining algorithms. The identified set of language markers signaling the semantic category *ways of solving the problem* can be therefore considered another formal instrument of retrieving opinion statements from problem feature articles written in English and in Belarusian (Karpilovitch, 2014).

4. Conclusion

The discourse analysis of the problem feature article as one of media genres in American and Belarusian press has made it possible to identify the semantic categories constituting its prototypical superstructure: the essence of the problem and ways of solving the problem, which are common for both media cultures. In the discourse, the first category is marked by explicit linguistic indicators (certain words, phrases, negative predicates, etc.) and also implicitly – through context. By contrast, the second prototypical category is usually signaled in the discourse by explicit language markers: direct or indirect speech, verbs and phrases denoting speech activity.

The integrated approach to the study of semantic and pragmatic structures of the problem feature articles allows to conclude that prototypical semantic categories are closely connected with pragmatic information, although different from the point of view of their pragmatic value. The results obtained in the course of the analysis show that the pragmatic load of the prototypical semantic category, *ways of solving the problem*, is greater than that of the category *the essence of the problem*. This is conditioned by the main communicative goal of the author of a given problem feature article, i.e. to suggest ways of solving the problem relying on the opinion of authoritative personalities. The pragmatic load of the category *ways of solving the problem* is constituted by the abundance of opinion-making statements, modal units, evaluative lexis, directive speech acts, as well as various lexical and syntactic stylistic devices.

The cross-cultural analysis of problem feature articles excerpted from American and Belarusian media discourse has revealed the prevalence of similar properties in the semantic and pragmatic structures of this genre, the existence of language markers signaling prototypical semantic categories, and the use of a set of pragmatically loaded language units. The identified differences lie in the different patterns of use of particular language units and stylistic devices, which can be explained, on the one hand, by the systemic and structural differences between English and Belarusian, and on the other hand – by the different traditions of using expressive language means and rhetorical devices in the two media cultures.

References

Devitt, A., & Ahmad, K. (2007). Sentiment analysis in financial news: a cohesion-based approach. *Proceedings of the Association for Computational Linguistics*, 984–991.

van Dijk, T. A. (1985). A semantic discourse analysis. In T. A. van Dijk (Ed.), *Handbook of discourse analysis*. Vol. 2. London: Academic Press, 103–136.

van Dijk, T. A., & Kintsch, W. (1983). *Strategies of discourse comprehension*. New York: Academic Press.

Hahn, U., & Reimer, U. (1999). Knowledge-based text summarization: salience and generalization operators for knowledge base abstraction. In I. Mani & M. T. Maybury (Eds.), *Advances in automatic text summarization*. Cambridge, Mass.: MIT Press, 215–232.

Karpilovitch, T. (2003). *Modelirovanie smyslovoi compressii teksta: kognitivno-diskursivny podhod* [Modeling of text semantic compression: a cognitive-discursive approach], Minsk: MGLU.

Karpilovitch, T. (2014). Semantic and Pragmatic Interface in the Algorithms of Analyzing Media Discourse. *Vestnik MGLU. Philology*, 4, 28–35.

Liddy, E. D. (1991). The discourse-level structure of empirical abstracts: An exploratory study. *Information Processing and Management*, 1, 55–81.

Mann, B., & Thompson, S. (1988). Rhetorical structure theory: Toward a functional theory of organization. *Text*, 8(3), 243–281.

Marcu, D. (1999). Discourse trees are good indicators of importance in text. In I. Mani & M. T. Maybury (Eds.), *Advances in automatic text summarization*. Cambridge, Mass.: MIT Press, 123–136.

Martin, J. R., & White, P. R. R. (2003). *Appraisal: the language of attitude and intersubjective stance*. London & New York: Palgrave.

Matveeva, T. V. (1990). *Functsionalnye stili v aspecte textovyh kategoryi* [Functional styles in the aspect of text categories], Sverdlovsk: Izd-vo Ural. un-ta.

Minsky, M. (1975). A framework for representing knowledge. In P. H. Winston (Ed.), *The psychology of computer vision*. New York: McGraw-Hill, 211–277.

Pang, B., & Lee, L. (2008). Opinion mining and sentiment analysis. *Foundations and Trends in Information Retrieval*, 2, 1–135.

Schank, R. C., & Abelson R. P. (1977). *Scripts, plans, goals and understanding*. Hillsdale, NJ: Lawrence Erlbaum.

Sinclair, J. M. (1992). Priorities in discourse analysis. In M. Coulthard (Ed.), *Advances in spoken discourse analysis*. London: Routledge, 79–88.

Swales, J. (1990). *Genre Analysis: English in academic and research settings*. Cambridge: Cambridge University Press.

Thorndyke, P. W. (1977). Cognitive structures in comprehension and memory of narrative discourse. *Cognitive Psychology*, 9, 77–110.

Webster's third new international dictionary (1986). Springfield (Mass): Meriam-Webster Inc. Publishers.

White, P. R. R. (2011). Appraisal. In J. Zienkowski, J-O. Östman & J. Verschueren (Eds.), *Discursive pragmatics*. University of Antwerp & University of Helsinki: John Benjamins Publishing Company, 14–36.

Małgorzata Sokół

University of Szczecin, Poland

Constructing knowledge and professional identity in social media academic discourse: The study of epistemic predicates in weblogs

Abstract: Taking the discourse-based, interactional approach to epistemic modality and recognising that knowledge is social, relative and contextual, this paper aims to explore the use of epistemic predicates in a corpus of Polish academic weblogs and their role in the negotiation of bloggers' professional identity. The variety of epistemic predicates reflects bloggers' discursive choices in how they disseminate knowledge both within a given epistemic community, across disciplines and to the non-specialist audience. This, in turn, brings us closer to understanding scholars' attitudes to networked scholarship, changes in the professional roles that scholars adopt when engaged in networked scholarship, and more generally, the role of the emergent academic weblog genre in scholarly exchange.

1. Introduction

The ecologies of social media environments have created new spaces for the construction of scholarly knowledge, and for the negotiation of scholars' professional identity. This paper focuses on the genre of academic weblog, which has become a popular example of *networked scholarship*, i.e. "the emergent practice of scholars' use of social technologies and online social networks to pursue, share, reflect upon, critique, improve, validate, and further their scholarship" (Veletsianos, 2016, p. 15). An important part of networked scholarship that is realised through blogging is academics' engagement in exchange and dissemination of knowledge.

Referring to the useful distinction between *digital residents* and *digital visitors*[1], Veletsianos (2016) admits that scholars have different degrees of understanding

---

1 Following White and LeCornu's (2011) distinction, Veletsianos argues that when

> [a]pplied to networked participatory scholarship, digital residents are those scholars who understand the affordances of the participatory web for scholarship, cultivate digital identities and relationships online, and view the web as a crucial component of their work and identity. Digital visitors on the other hand are those scholars who use the web as a tool when they see a need for it.
>
> (Veletsianos, 2016, p. 36)

of the technological affordances of social media, different degrees of literacies and skills necessary to operate them, and different degrees of confidence in making themselves and their scholarship public via social media, and thus their varying engagement in the use of social media for knowledge creation. An additional complication is challenges that higher education institutions are facing today. Still,

> [g]iven that social media and online networks permeate contemporary cultures, they may present promising opportunities for addressing a number of these challenges. An evidence-based understanding of scholars' efforts, obstacles, experiences, and tensions with network scholarship might help contribute to a greater understanding of the role of digital technology on the enterprise of higher education, especially as open/digital/networked scholarship, frequently performed via social media, is seen as a radical breakthrough in how new knowledge is created and shared
>
> (Veletsianos, 2016, p. 4).

The role of blogging in the exchange and dissemination of knowledge is confirmed by the investigations into the antecedence of the academic weblog as an emergent genre of scholarly communication, as well as into scholars' motivations behind blogging: hence, the metaphors of the *visible college* (Halvais, 2006) or *virtual university* (Mewburn & Thomson, 2013) used in reference to academic weblogs.

To apply Herring, Scheidt, Bonus and Wright's (2004) earlier categorisation of blogs, academic weblogs may be viewed as *k(nowledge)-logs*, i.e. environments for knowledge sharing. According to more recent studies, academic weblogs are treated as examples of *thematic blogs*[2] (cf. Grieve, Biber, Friginal & Nekrasova's 2010 classification; see e.g. Garzone, 2014), whose generic antecedent may be the conference talk (Mauranen, 2013). As regards the reasons for blogging, the studies report such purposes of academic blogs as communication of knowledge to peers, and more broadly, to non-specialist audiences, and enhancement of interdisciplinary interaction (e.g. Halvais, 2006; Luzón, 2009; Mauranen, 2013; Garzone, 2014; Mahrt & Puschmann, 2014; Sokół, 2014; Veletsianos, 2016). In this way, blogs as part of networked scholarship can encourage and develop the pursuit of knowledge as a communal and public activity (e.g. Luzón, 2009; Puschmann & Mahrt, 2012; Mauranen, 2013; Sokół, 2015; Veletsianos, 2016).

Following the discourse-based, interactional approach to epistemic modality and recognising that knowledge is social, relative and contextual (van Dijk, 2014), this paper aims to explore the use of epistemic predicates in a corpus of Polish

2 Grieve et al. (2010, p. 303) distinguish between "personal blogs in which an author discusses their own life and thematic blogs in which an author discusses a topic other than themselves".

academic weblogs and their role in the negotiation of the bloggers' professional identity. The variety of epistemic predicates reflects bloggers' discursive choices in how they disseminate knowledge both within a given epistemic community, across disciplines and to the non-specialist audience. This, in turn, brings us closer to understanding scholars' attitudes to networked scholarship, changes in the professional roles that scholars adopt when engaged in networked scholarship, and more generally, the role of the emergent academic weblog genre in scholarly exchange.

2. Background: Discourse approaches to modality, identity and knowledge

The present study follows discourse-based approaches to modality, in which modality is viewed more broadly than a grammatical and semantic category. According to these approaches, modality as an important manifestation of subjectivity and evaluation relates to the expression of stance in discourse and plays a role in the construction of identity (e.g. Kärkkäinen, 2003; Marín-Arrese, Downing & Marín-Arrese, 2004; Englebretson, 2007; Marín-Arrese, 2011; Facchinetti, 2013; Hidalgo Downing & Núñez Perucha, 2013; Marín-Arrese, 2013; Thompson & Alba-Juez, 2014).

In traditional grammar, modality is concerned with the status of the proposition that describes the event and refers to the expression of speaker's attitudes to the content of a proposition (Palmer, 1981). As a subcategory of modality, epistemic modality "expresses the degree of commitment of the speaker to the truth of what is being said" (Palmer, 1981, p. 153), and epistemic verbs, which are the focus of the present study, belong to the main exponents of epistemic modality (cf. Nuyts, 2000; Danielewiczowa, 2002).

The application of a broader, discourse-based approach to modality offers a way to study interpersonal meanings in text. For one thing, epistemic modality is socially and interactionally motivated, and, as modal meanings are to some degree contextually determined, they may even acquire new interactive meanings and functions (Kärkkäinen, 2003; van Dijk, 2014). For another, exploring modality more broadly allows us to study speakers' attitudes and beliefs, as well as their engagement with other voices and positions constructed in text (Hidalgo Downing & Núñez Perucha, 2013).

As already stated, modality has relevance for the construction of identity, whereby identity is defined as a process of positioning (e.g. Benwell & Stokoe, 2006; de Fina, Schiffrin & Bamberg, 2006). As de Fina et al. (2006, p. 7) argue,

> [i]nvestigating levels of identity construction as a process of positioning, and discovering the means adopted to enact various positions, leads to reflecting on the many ways of doing identity, ranging from the proclamation and open assignment of membership into social categories to the enactment of different kinds of selves, to indirect conveying of alignments and disalignments, to the implicit placement of social agents into pre-assigned roles.

Modality choices may be strategically used to negotiate speakers' identity positions in text. Thus, the focus on epistemic verbs may give us a possibility to investigate bloggers' positions in relation to the knowledge claims they advance, to other voices constructed in text, and to their intended audience.

More generally, the approach adopted in the present paper aims to contribute to the study of knowledge and its relation to discourse, or to the advancement of *discourse epistemics*, i.e. a multidisciplinary research domain that can give us insights into how knowledge is acquired and shaped by discourse, how it is presupposed, implied, expressed and shared (van Dijk, 2014). In his recent work, van Dijk argues for the development of the cognitive theory of discourse and knowledge processing that will

> (i) be better grounded neurologically, (ii) be more ecologically valid through studying natural and multimodal discourse in natural communicative situations, (iii) account for context and (iv) be inspired by evolutionary insights into adaptive developments and the genetic programming of language, discourse and knowledge
>
> (van Dijk, 2014, pp. 48–49).

What is of particular relevance for the aims of this paper is that both discourse and knowledge are "produced and understood under the control of context, defined as the subjective 'definition of the communicative situation,' as it is represented by participants in dynamic **context models**" (van Dijk, 2014, p. 47; emphasis in the original). This implies that knowledge, and so the use of epistemically relevant expressions, should be studied as part of communicative situations; hence, the importance of the following social dimensions of context models: the setting, the identity, roles and relations of participants, and the goals of the communicative event (van Dijk, 2014, p. 228).

In view of the above, the study of knowledge construction in the context of the academic weblog should also take into consideration additional aspects of this communicative situation that relate to academic bloggers' roles such as expectations that knowledge will be communicated; entitlement to convey specific knowledge; constraints on the responsibility and reliability of participants in institutional contexts; the status of the weblog's intended or imagined audience; the amount of knowledge that is presupposed and shared. Ethnographic research into the academics' motives for blogging (Sokół, 2014) confirms their engagement in the exchange and pursuit of knowledge (cf. e.g. "because a blog is a tool for an open lecture", Stanisław Czachorowski, author of http://czachorowski.blox.pl/html; "[a] fairly important element is perhaps a possibility to publish in a blog some reflections, research hunches, notes, which are insufficient for a scientific paper, but a blogger may consider them worthy of sharing with others", Rafał Wójcik, author of http://abrewiacje.wordpress.com/)[3], which makes the emergent genre of the academic weblog a challenging communicative situation in which to study knowledge construction.

3. Epistemic verbs in academic weblogs: Analysis and discussion

3.1. Data and method

The present study of knowledge construction within the communicative situations of networked scholarship is focused on academic weblogs. The research material consists of 480 posts that were retrieved from the websites of 24 academic blogs run in Polish by individual scholars in the fields of humanities and social sciences (Subcorpus A, with the total number of words of 115 303, with the average of 480.4 words per post), and by scholars in natural, technical and exact sciences (Subcorpus B, with the total number of words of 184 683, with the average of 769.5 words per post).[4] With the exception of two blogs, the blogs are run under the blogger's real name. The subcorpora represent academics of various status (PhD students, PhDs and professors), and such disciplines as communication, pedagogy, sociology, history, digital philology & medieval studies, literary studies, media studies, philosophy and education (in Subcorpus A); biology and biotechnology, physics and astronomy, climatology, neurobiology, statistics and information technology (in Subcorpus B). While there can be expected possible discipline-bound and individual variation in the use of epistemically relevant expressions, the aim of the present study is to explore the general tendencies in their use in the emergent genre of the academic weblog without focusing on the said variables.

3 The quotes come from the answers to email questionnaires distributed among the authors of the weblogs under investigation (cf. Sokół, 2014; my translation of the original quotes). I express my thanks to all the bloggers who agreed to participate in the study and whose blogs were included in the corpus.

4 For the lists of weblogs in Subcorpus A and Subcorpus B, see Appendix.

The theoretical-methodological background of the investigation draws on discourse approaches to modality, identity and knowledge. The undertaken analysis is essentially qualitative and the focus is put on the use of epistemic predicates and the exploration of their role in the construction of the bloggers' identity. Therefore, the research involved the search for the occurrences of epistemic verbs according to the list established on the basis of Danielewiczowa's (2002) classification of Polish epistemic verbs of "insufficient knowledge", i.e. verbs which are semantically founded on knowledge, but which are "a group of predicates with propositional arguments in the meanings of which the lack of the epistemic subject's knowledge is implied" (Danielewiczowa, 2002, p. 374; all translations from Polish are mine). The search was conducted by means of the concordancing software Poliqarp (http://poliqarp.sourceforge.net/), a tool suitable for analysis of languages rich in inflection, originally developed for the use with the National Corpus of Polish (http://nkjp.pl).

The research aims to identify the epistemic verbs in use, explore the patterns of their use and analyse their function in relation to the bloggers' professional identity. It is assumed that the use of epistemic verbs will reflect: (1) the specificity of the communicative context of the academic weblog that merges the informal communication with more 'traditional' scholarly exchange; (2) the pursuit of the bloggers' disciplinary and individual goals, such as their engagement in the dissemination of scientific knowledge, education of the audience, as well as self-expression and self-disclosure.

In her study, Danielewiczowa groups the epistemic verbs under investigation into the following categories: (1) *myśleć że* 'think that' – grasping the ungraspable[5], (2) *sądzić że* 'reckon that' – making epistemic judgments, (3) *uważać że* 'be of the opinion that' – adopting a stance, (4) conjectures and doubts – two extremes of the epistemic scale, (5) helpful senses, i.e. what it seems to somebody, (6) *be sure that* and *be convinced that* – how much you lack in order to know and how important is justification, (7) belief and hope – mindset for the positive, (8) suspicions and fears – mindset for the negative, (9) delusions – contrary to what others may know, and (10) creating an epistemic reality. The verbs in focus are verbs denoting epistemic states, and as regards their surface structure, "they represent two-place predicates. The first argument refers to a personal epistemic subject. The other one takes the form of a subordinate clause; it is introduced by

5 When enumerating the groups of epistemic verbs, I use my translation of the descriptions of particular groups that Danielewiczowa uses in her Polish-language work (2002).

że[6] 'that' in Polish" (Danielewiczowa, 2002, p. 370). What follows is a discussion of the epistemic predicates identified in the data and the variety of their usage patterns according to the frequency of occurrence. Rather than focusing on the semantic analysis of the verbs in question, I will explore the pragmatic effects of their use in the context of the academic weblog.

3.2. *uważać, że* 'be of the opinion that'

The most frequent category in both subcorpora under investigation is the interpretative epistemic verb *uważać, że* 'be of the opinion that'. When using this verb, the epistemic subject takes a stance, often in a radical but responsible way, with the awareness that although the stance taken represents a subjective view of the world, it is well-grounded (cf. Danielewiczowa, 2002, pp. 164–165). Numerous occurrences of *uważać, że* 'be of the opinion that' used in the first-person singular indicate the blogger's responsibility and confidence: see the use of the adverb *zdecydowanie* 'decisively' when making a recommendation based on personal experience in example (1), or the introductory clause *warto więc sprostować i wyjaśnić, że* 'it is worth correcting and clarifying that' when taking a firm stance in a debate on the role of political blogging in example (2). In both cases, the blogger presents his opinion, while respectfully acknowledging the space for other, alternative voices.

(1) *Miałem przyjemność czytać końcową wersję książki i* ***uważam, że*** *zdecydowanie warto po nią sięgnąć.*

[I had the pleasure of reading the final version of the book and **I am of the opinion that** the book is definitely worth reaching for it.][7]

(BH1)

(2) *Warto więc sprostować i wyjaśnić, że: widzę potencjał transparentności tkwiący w internecie;* ***uważam, iż*** *może być on wykorzystywany do prześwietlania skorumpowanych polityków (na przykład przez blogerów politycznych tropiących przekręty);*

[It is worth correcting and clarifying that: I can see the potential of transparency in the internet; **I am of the opinion that** it can be used for scanning corrupt politicians (for instance, by political bloggers who track scam);]

(BH3)

Uważać, że 'be of the opinion that' is also used like in more 'traditional' forms of academic communication, to discuss and evaluate the literature of the subject,

---

6 Examples from the subcorpora also include the variant form of *że*, which is *iż*.

7 All the examples are quoted in the original form, with the spelling and punctuation as used in the posts under investigation. All the translations of the examples are mine.

with the indication of epistemic subjects other than the blogger, as in example (3), or in impersonal constructions, as in example (4):

(3) *Ogólnie rzecz biorąc, autorka udowadnia swoją tezę dotyczącą charakterystycznej struktury najsłynniejszych historycznych wystąpień.* ***Uważa, że*** *„najlepsze z najlepszych" przemówień i prezentacji, charakteryzują się pewną ściśle określoną strukturą – swego rodzaju linią melodyczną.*

[In general, the author proves her thesis concerning the characteristic structure of the most famous historical speeches. **She is of the opinion that** "the best out of the best" speeches and presentations are characterised by some strictly specified structure – a kind of melodic line.]

(BNH3)

(4) **Uważa się bowiem, że** liczba neuronów i ich względne rozmieszczenie w poszczególnych częściach mózgu wyznacza sprawność procesów umysłowych i – w konsekwencji – determinuje zachowanie.

[Since **there is an opinion that** the number of neurons and their relative distribution in particular parts of the brain indicates the efficiency of mental processes and – in consequence – determines behaviour.]

(BNH10)

3.3. *wydaje się [komuś], że* 'it seems [to sb] that' and *mieć/odnosić wrażenie, że* 'have/get the impression that'

Another frequent group of epistemic verbs in the data includes the verbs that express short-term, changeable epistemic states constructed on the basis of data received from the senses, i.e., at least to some extent, the epistemic subject's direct perception is involved (Danielewiczowa, 2002, pp. 186–210). The most numerous representatives of this group are *wydaje się [komuś], że* 'it seems [to sb] that' and *mieć/odnosić wrażenie, że* 'have/get the impression that', with a higher frequency of their use in Subcorpus B, i.e. the blogs by scholars in natural, technical and exact sciences. In the corpus there are no occurrences of *czuć, że* 'feel that'.

The verb *wydaje się [komuś], że* 'it seems [to sb] that' as an epistemic expression poses interpretative problems. Its meaning denotes the epistemic subject's awareness of their insufficient knowledge; it is thus close to *przypuszczać, że* 'suppose that' and *wątpić, że* 'doubt that', and refers to states which are weaker than belief and certainty. Its impersonal version, *wydaje się, że* 'it seems that' (see example 7), has the value of such modal particles as *probably*, *supposedly*, etc. (cf. Danielewiczowa, 2002, pp. 186, 188). In the corpus the verb occurs both in its personal form, e.g. examples (5) and (6), and as a metatextual expression, e.g. in example (7). As a tentative expression, it is used to express low modality. It may indicate an informal analysis of some phenomenon, as in example (5), as well as self-reflection (with reference to the blogger's professional life) and consideration of the audience, both in the offline and online worlds, as in example (6). Thus, *wydaje się [komuś], że* 'it seems [to sb] that' holds an interactive potential but is also self-revealing and potentially face-threatening for the blogger.

(5) *Tak jak panikujemy z nawłocią kanadyjską (roślina uznana za gatunek obcy i inwazyjny), a* ***wydaje mi się, że*** *jej ekspansja bardziej wiąże się z brakiem wypasu i wykaszania a nie przez wypieranie rodzimych gatunków.*

[Just as we are panicking about the Canadian goldenrod (a plant considered an alien and invasive species), and **it seems to me that** its expansion is more connected to the lack of grazing and mowing, and not to forcing out the native species.]

(BNH1)

(6) *Przygotowując tekst wystąpienia* ***wydaje mi się, że*** *mogę o pewnych sprawach nie mówić, gdyż są oczywiste, ale wynika z tego, że jednak należy szerzej analizować kwestie, gdyż nie każdy ma dostęp do kluczowych dla problemu źródeł.*

[When I prepare the text of a presentation, **it seems to me that** I may choose not to speak about certain matters as they are obvious, but it follows [from the above] that it is necessary to analyse issues more broadly, since not everybody has access to the key sources on the issue.]

(BH2)

(7) ***Wydaje się, że*** *z tej czwórki najwyraźniejsze pragnienie sukcesu przejawiał Watson – był najmłodszy, zaraz po doktoracie, zmienił właśnie specjalność z ornitologii (!!!), ponieważ wiedział, że DNA jest ważne.*

[**It seems that**, out of these four, the most visible desire for success was manifested by Watson – he was the youngest, soon after his PhD, he just changed his specialisation from ornithology (!!!), because he knew that DNA is important.]

(BNH8)

Similarly, *mieć/odnosić wrażenie, że* 'have/get the impression that' indicates uncertainty and subjectivism of the epistemic subject, but compared to *czuć, że* 'feel that', it is more objective and social, denoting the temporary state that is, at least to some extent, constructed on the basis of shared knowledge (cf. Danielewiczowa, 2002, p. 208). The occurrences of *mieć/odnosić wrażenie, że* 'have/get the impression that' in the corpus indicate the blogger's self-expression and self-disclosure, coupled with a dose of humour, as in example (8), and the verb's role in informal debate, in which the blogger's view is expressed with engagement, e.g. in example (9), or distance, as in example (10):

(8) *Uznano mnie za super profesjonalistę, ale po prostu miałem szczęście. Teraz oglądam nagranie. Zawsze* ***mam wrażenie, że*** *jestem młodszy, niż wyglądam, ale poza tym nie było źle, chociaż oczywiście sporo należałoby poprawić.*

[I was judged as a super-professional, but I was simply lucky. Now I'm watching the recording. **I** always **have the impression that** I'm younger than I look, but apart from that, it wasn't bad, although much could have been improved.]

(BNH10)

(9) ***Mam wrażenie, że*** *ostatnie słowo w tej debacie jeszcze nie padło i niedługo pojawią się nowe prace wspierające lub podważające ich wnioski. Ale o to właśnie chodzi* ☺

[**I have the impression that** the last word in this debate has not been said yet and new works will appear soon that will support or challenge their conclusions ☺]

(BNH5)

(10) *Jednak w trakcie lektury* ***odnosi się wrażenie, że*** *autorowi zabrakło czasu, objętości czy umiejętności aby bardziej rozbudować psychologicznie postaci oraz pociągnąć niektóre wątki.*

[Still, while reading, **one gets the impression that** the author lacked the time, space or skills to psychologically develop the characters or extend some plots.]

(BH7)

3.4. *wierzyć, że* 'believe that', *mieć nadzieję, że* 'hope that', *liczyć [na to], że* 'count that' and *oczekiwać, że* 'expect that'

The epistemic verbs of belief and hope presuppose positive valuation, and thus their use indicates an axiological or volitive attitude of the epistemic subject (cf. Danielewiczowa, 2002, p. 239). The most frequent representatives of this category in both subcorpora are *mieć nadzieję, że* 'hope that' and *oczekiwać, że* 'expect that'.

As Danielewiczowa (2002, pp. 261–265) emphasises, *mieć nadzieję, że* 'hope that' is a common verb that denotes an epistemic rather than emotional state and the epistemic subject's strong engagement, but also their humbleness, recognition of insufficient knowledge and uncertainty about the state of affairs referred to in the complement clause. It may also have a conventional, clichéd use. In the corpus, the verb occurs in the first person singular form, pointing to the bloggers' involvement and belief in the usefulness and success of their academically-related activities, whether it is being helpful in communicating knowledge, as in example (11), blogging as a new form of interaction between the academia and society, as in example (12), or joint educational activity, as in example (13). In addition, the use of *mieć nadzieję, że* 'hope that' serves to minimise the distance between the blogger and the audience.

(11) ***Mam nadzieję że*** *poniższy obrazek pomoże rozwiać wszelkie wątpliwości.*
[**I hope that** the image below will help dispel any doubts]

(BNH7)

(12) *Człowiek i Technologie jest – **mam nadzieję, że** udanym :) – przykładem takiej działalności.*

[Man and technology is – **I hope that** a successful :) – example of such activity]

(BH10)

(13) ***Mamy nadzieję, że** w przyszłym roku uda nam się bardziej rozbudować i wypromować ten pomysł.*

[**We hope that** next year we will be able to expand and publicise this idea.]

(BH12)

By contrast, *liczyć [na to], że* 'count that' and *oczekiwać, że* 'expect that' do not have an axiological character, and imply that the state of affairs referred to in the complement clause is barely advantageous for the epistemic subject, and so the epistemic subject does not attach to this state any positive values (Danielewiczowa, 2002, p. 269). The use of *oczekiwać, że* 'expect that' in the corpus, which is more directed to the future event than *liczyć [na to], że* 'count that', is more frequent, especially in the blogs by scholars in natural, technical and exact sciences. Both verbs are used in the impersonal form, more conventionally, which allows the bloggers to conduct more general discussions of the topics that are interesting for them and the broader public – see e.g. examples (14) and (15):

(14) *Google jest już tak ogromne, że (choć Larry stara się z tym walczyć) trudno **oczekiwać, że** będzie "spójne" – wszystkie zespoły=produkty będą idealnie współdziałać od razu*

[Google is so huge already that (although Larry is trying to fight with it) it is difficult to **expect that** it will be "cohesive" – all units=products will ideally cooperate at once]

(BNH9)

(15) *Wychodząc więc z założenia, że podręczniki są zaakceptowane przez wszystkich świętych we wszystkich ministerstwach można **liczyć na to, że** kilka sztuk się sprzeda, oraz na to, że inne wydawnictwa pójdą tym śladem.*

[Assuming that the textbooks have been approved of by all the saints in all the ministries, one can **count that** a few copies will sell, and that other publishing houses will follow in these steps.]

(BH11)

Instances of *wierzyć, że* 'believe that' are the least frequent of the verbs in this group; they include both impersonal and first-person singular forms. This epistemic verb denotes the epistemic subject's belief that is clearly realised and that is in agreement with their system of knowledge and convictions (Danielewiczowa, 2002, pp. 248–249). This is illustrated by example (16), in which the author makes a self-revealing comment about his professional activity, where the use of *wierzyć że* 'believe that' is strengthened by the adverb *mocno* 'strongly'. Example (17) includes the impersonal *wierzyć, że* 'believe that' which – negated – expresses a more 'socially' shared disbelief.

(16) Maks na co było mnie stać to publikacja w youtube, slideshare i częściowe zadowolenie z efektów, bo bardzo mocno **wierzę w to, że** materiały są wartościowe i ciężko znaleźć podobne w polskim internecie.

[The maximum that I could afford was the publication on youtube, slideshare and partial satisfaction with the effects, because **I** strongly **believe that** the materials are valuable and it is difficult to find similar ones in the Polish internet.]

(BH11)

(17) *Aż nie chce się* ***wierzyć, że*** *w serii „Nauczyciele – Nauczycielom" wyszedł już dwudziesty drugi tom.*

[It is difficult to **believe that** in the series "Teachers – For Teachers", the twenty second issue was already published]

(BH2)

3.5. *sądzić, że* 'reckon that'

Generally, *sądzić, że* 'reckon that' is a frequent epistemic verb, whose meaning, on the one hand, is close to *think*, but on the other, has a more philosophical sense of the expression *make judgements*. It is characteristic for conducting a reasoned argument and is used in contexts where a difference in stance is marked, or when there is a need for a stance to be taken. The epistemic subject is aware that their knowledge is sufficient to take a stance (Danielewiczowa, 2002, p. 140).

In the corpus, *sądzić, że* 'reckon that' appears in a variety of forms in both subcorpora, however, with substantial prevalence in Subcorpus B, i.e. the posts by scholars in natural, technical and exact sciences. In examples (18) and (19), the bloggers signal their firm voice in the discussion undertaken in the post. Example (20) illustrates a situation in which a stance is assigned to the epistemic subject other than the blogger: following academic conventions, the blogger discusses the reactions to the work of Bernard Mandeville (1670–1733). The use of the verb in the past adds to the narrative component of the post. Example (21) includes an impersonal form of the verb, used more conventionally in a general discussion of the topic.

(18) ***Sądzę, że*** *ten sam problem dotyczy wychowania muzycznego.*

[**I reckon that** the same problem concerns musical education.]

(BH6)

(19) *Nie mówiąc o tym, że po narażeniu na zakażenie nie istnieją żadne przeciwwskazania do podania szczepionki (**nie sądzę** zresztą, **że** nawet najbardziej zakamieniały antywacek protestowałby przeciwko jej zastosowaniu).*

[Not to mention the fact that after the exposure to infection there are no contraindications against the vaccine to be administered (**I don't reckon that** even the most hardened anti-vaxxer would protest against its application).]

(BNH12)

(20) *Friedrich Hayek* ***sądził, że*** *głównym motywem tej gniewnej reakcji, był fakt, iż Mandeville zakwestionował boskie pochodzenie porządku.*

[Friedrich Hayek **reckoned that** the main motive of that angry reaction was the fact that Mandeville questioned the godly origin of the order.]

(BNH8)

(21) *Określenie „duża cześć" nie jest precyzyjne, ale pozwala* ***sądzić, że*** *to właśnie ta „część" sprawia, że odbiorca jednoznacznie klasyfikuje czasopismo jako literackie.*

[The term a "large part" is not precise, but it allows us to **reckon that** it is just that "part" that makes the recipient to unequivocally classify a magazine as a literary one.]

(BH8)

3.6. *zakładać, że* 'assume that' and *uznawać, że* 'recognise that'

Zakładać, że 'assume that' and *uznawać, że* 'recognise that' are used to create an epistemic reality. They function as metatextual commentaries, whose aim is to clarify and justify what has been said, hence they are characteristic for academic discourse (Danielewiczowa, 2002, p. 317). In the corpus, *zakładać, że* 'assume that' outnumbers *uznawać, że* 'recognise that', and overall, these verbs are more frequent in subcorpus B. Their use gives evidence for the bloggers' awareness of the audience, and for the recontextualisation of scientific knowledge with the aim of making it more accessible, also to non-specialists, see examples (22) and (24). Examples (23) and (25) illustrate the use of *zakładać, że* 'assume that' and *uznawać, że* 'recognise that' in the context of literature review.

(22) *Sama strona została zablokowana po kilku dniach, aby po pewnym czasie pojawić się w nowej odsłonie.* ***Zakładam, że*** *zawiodła komunikacja na linii ministerstwo – wykonawca.*

[The website itself was blocked after a few days only to appear after some time in its new version. **I assume that** the communication between the ministry and the contractor failed.]

(BH1)

(23) Shanon, który napotkał znaczne jej ilości w okolicach Qumran, **zakłada, iż** musiała być znana i używana w czasach biblijnych.

[Shanon, who found its substantial amount in the area of Qumran, **assumes that** it must have been known and used in the biblical times.]

(BNH10)

(24) ***Zakładając, że*** *objętość poszczególnych prac pozostaje plus minus stała, można* ***uznać, że*** *wzrost liczby publikowanych stron będzie wykazywał bardzo silną korelację z liczbą artykułów.*

[**Assuming that** the size of particular works remains more or less constant, it can be assumed that an increase in the number of published pages will correlate strongly with the number of articles.]

(BNH5)

(25) **Uznano, że** opis działania i lista schorzeń, na które miałyby pomagać nie odpowiada rzeczywistości.

[**It was recognised that** the description of activity and the list of illnesses in which they would help do not correspond to the reality.]

(BNH6)

3.7. *myśleć, że* 'think that'

Myśleć, że 'think that' is a frequent epistemic verb, especially in spoken registers. It is semantically the most general, and denotes the epistemic subject's knowledge (vaguely expressed) and readiness to express it (Danielewiczowa, 2002, pp. 121–139). The use of *myśleć, że* 'think that' in both subcorpora gives evidence for informal, conversational style, where the bloggers are dynamically engaged in the explicit expression of their opinions – see examples (26) and (27). This also shows that the process of thinking is an activity that directs attention both to the author and the topic under discussion.

(26) *To jest świetny pomysł i* ***myślę, że*** *powinien zostać podchwycony również w innych szkołach.*

[It's a great idea and **I think** it should be picked up in other schools]

(BH6)

(27) ***Myślę, że*** *dzięki m.in. takim działaniom gospodarka chętnie zwraca się do środowiska naukowego z konkretnymi propozycjami.*

[**I think that** it is thanks to, among others, such actions that economy turns to the scientific community with specific proposals.]

(BNH1)

3.8. The least frequent epistemic verbs in the subcorpora

This section discusses the epistemic verbs with occasional occurrence in the subcorpora under investigation. The verbs include the representatives of three groups in Danielewiczowa's (2002) study: (1) *podejrzewać, że* 'suspect that' and *obawiać się, że* 'fear that'; (2) *przypuszczać, że* 'suppose that'; (3) *być przekonanym, że* 'be convinced that'.

Podejrzewać, że 'suspect that' and *obawiać się, że* 'fear that' represent the epistemic verbs that presuppose negative valuation of the state of affairs referred to in the complement clause, as states which are negative or unwelcomed by the epistemic subject. Specifically, *podejrzewać, że* 'suspect that' is in opposition to belief, while *obawiać się, że* 'fear that' – in opposition to hope (Danielewiczowa, 2002, pp. 276–297). Examples of these verbs in the corpus may indicate the epistemic subject's (emotional) engagement in the topic under discussion. Their use may be tentative and self-revealing, and thus, potentially face-threatening for the blogger – see examples (28) and (29):

(28) ***Podejrzewam, że*** *są to czynniki, które najsilniej przeszkadzają w legalizacji marihuany i eliminowaniu narkofobii.*

[**I suspect that** these are the factors that interfere the strongest in the legalisation of marijuana and elimination of narcophobia.]

(BNH10)

(29) ***Obawiam się, że*** *będziemy w najbliższym czasie świadkami wyszarpywania sobie kasy przez tzw. rektorów, tzw. kanclerzy czy założycieli, a ofiarami tego procesu będą STUDENCI i zatrudnieni w tych szkołach pracownicy.*

[**I fear that** we will soon witness how the so called rectors, the so called chancellors or founders [of private colleges] will be grabbing money from others, and the victims of this process will be STUDENTS and employees of these colleges.]

(BH2)

Przypuszczać, że 'suppose that' is a frequent epistemic verb that is helpful in formulating and refuting hypotheses. Although it implicates the lack of knowledge of the epistemic subject, it is important for scholarly argumentation (Danielewiczowa, 2002, pp. 168–177). In the corpus, *przypuszczać, że* 'suppose that' is used impersonally, as in example (30), or with the epistemic subject other than the blogger, as in example (31), to indicate hypothesizing.

(30) *Można więc* ***przypuszczać, że*** *permski klimat był o wiele bardziej surowy, i to niezależnie od miejsca na Ziemi, które weźmiemy pod uwagę.*

[It can be **supposed** then **that** the Permian climate was much harsher, and it is irrespective of the place on Earth which we take into consideration.]

(BNH2)

(31) *Autorzy badania* ***przypuszczają, że*** *halucynacje są syntetyzowane w mózgu w wyniku procesów poznawczych.*

[The authors of the research **suppose that** hallucinations are synthesised in the brain as a result of cognitive processes.]

(BNH10)

Finally, *być przekonanym, że* 'be convinced that' as a strong epistemic verb is used for persuasive purposes. It implies that the epistemic subject managed to overcome doubts through finding good justification. Although its use is subjective, conviction is built not only on the basis of particular knowledge about a given state of affairs, but also on more general knowledge (Danielewiczowa, 2002, pp. 230–238). Examples (32) and (33) illustrate the blogger's authoritative position in making a claim.

(32) *Tego nie dociekam, ale **jestem przekonany, że** nie ma nic lepszego w naukach społecznych, jak właśnie interdyscyplinarność kompetencyjna i badawcza młodych naukowców.*

[I do not investigate this, but **I am convinced that** there is nothing better in social sciences than competence and research interdisciplinarity of young scholars.]

(BH2)

(33) *Żeby była jasność – gdy myślę o moich latach szkolnych, było podobnie i **jestem głeboko przekonany, że** nie jest to "znak czasów" i teraz młodzież jest inna pod tym względem.*

[To make things clear – when I think about my school years, it was similar, and **I am deeply convinced that** it is not "the sign of our times" and that the young people today are different in this respect.]

(BH6)

4. Concluding remarks

The variety of uses of epistemic verbs of "insufficient knowledge" identified in the research data reflects the numerous rhetorical purposes for which weblogs are used by the members of academia, as well the professional roles they adopt in this communicative context. Academic bloggers express their engagement in the current public life, including secondary and higher education in Poland; they report on the new discoveries in the fields of their interest; they persuade, debate and argue; they present a structured reasoning; and finally, they evaluate and refer to other academic sources. In this way, they pursue many of their professional roles, and also show understanding of this new medium of scholarly exchange and successfully explore its interactive capabilities.

The bloggers whose posts have been analyzed construct their competent and authoritative professional identity, an important part of which is awareness of the audience. They know that the audience is needed and address it, even if not explicitly. The diversity of the epistemic verbs in use confirms the interactive, networking potential of weblog discourse, where the audience is invited into a dialogue.

In general, the use of epistemic verbs in the data proves the self-expressive, persuasive and collaborative nature of academic blogging discourse that merges the private and the public (institutional) aspects of the bloggers' identity. The bloggers comply with the 'traditional' norms of scholarly interaction, as well as engage in informal and indirect communication of personal content. This results from the inherent features of the weblog as a self-oriented genre as such, and the bloggers' involvement in network scholarship: constructing and sharing knowledge, and making it accessible to wider audiences of both peers and non-specialists.

The present study also shows that further investigations are needed that will take into consideration discipline-, status- and genre-dependent use of epistemic verbs in the communicative contexts of networked scholarship, studies on knowledge construction that will involve comparison of epistemic verbs with the uses of other epistemically relevant expressions.

References

Benwell, B., & Stokoe, E. (2006). *Discourse and identity*. Edinburgh: Edinburgh University Press.

Danielewiczowa, M. (2002). *Wiedza i niewiedza: Studium polskich czasowników epistemicznych*. Warszawa: Katedra Lingwistyki Formalnej UW.

De Fina, A., Schiffrin, D., & Bamberg, M. (2006). *Discourse and identity*. Cambridge: Cambridge University Press.

van Dijk, T. A. (2014). *Discourse and knowledge: A sociocognitive approach*. Cambridge: Cambridge University Press.

Englebretson, R. (Ed.) (2007). *Stancetaking in discourse*. Amsterdam: John Benjamins.

Facchinetti, R. (2013). Modal verbs in news-related blogs: When the blogger counts. In J. I. Marín-Arrese, M. Carretero, J. Arús Hita & J. van der Auwera (Eds.), *English modality: Core, periphery and evidentiality*. Berlin: Mouton de Gruyter, 359–377.

Grieve, J., Biber, D., Friginal, E., & Nekrasova, T. (2010). Variation among blogs: A multi-dimensional analysis. In A. Mehler, S. Sharoff & M. Santini (Eds.) *Genres on the Web. Computational models and empirical studies*. Berlin: Springer, 303–322.

Halavais, A. (2006). Scholarly blogging: Moving toward the visible college. In A. Bruns & J. Jacobs (Eds.) *Uses of blogs*. New York: Peter Lang, 117–125.

Herring, S. C., Scheidt, L. A., Bonus, S., & Wright, E. (2004). Bridging the gap: A genre analysis of weblogs. *Proceedings of the 37th Hawaii International Conference on System Sciences (HICSS'04)*. Los Alamitos: IEEE Computer

Society Press. Retrieved from URL http://www.csus.edu/indiv/s/stonerm/genreanalysisofweblogs.pdf. DOA: 13.03.2017.

Hidalgo Downing, L., & Núñez Perucha, B. (2013). Modality and personal pronouns as indexical markers of stance: Intersubjective positioning and construction of public identity in media interviews. In J. I. Marín-Arrese, M. Carretero, J. Arús Hita & J. van der Auwera (Eds.) *English modality: Core, periphery and evidentiality*. Berlin: Mouton de Gruyter, 379–410.

Kärkkäinen, E. (2003). *Epistemic stance in English conversation. A description of its interactional functions, with a focus on* I think. Amsterdam & Philadelphia: John Benjamins.

Luzón, M. J. (2009). Academic weblogs as tools for e-collaboration among researchers. In N. Kock (Ed.) *E-collaboration: Concepts, methodologies, tools, and applications. Volume I*. Hershey & New York: Information Science Reference, 455–462.

Mahrt, M., & Puschmann, C. (2014). Science blogging: An exploratory study of motives, styles, and audience reactions. *Journal of Science Communication* 13(3). Retrieved from journal URL http://jcom.sissa.it/archive/13/03/JCOM_1303_2014_A05. DOA: 13.03.2017.

Marín-Arrese, J. I. (2011). Effective vs. epistemic stance and subjectivity in political discourse: Legitimising strategies and mystification of responsibility. In Ch. Hart (Ed.) *Critical discourse studies in context and cognition*. Amsterdam: John Benjamins, 193–223.

Marín-Arrese, J. I. (2013). Stancetaking and inter/subjectivity in the Iraq Inquiry: Blair vs. Brown. In J. I. Marín-Arrese, M. Carretero, J. Arús Hita & J. van der Auwera (Eds.) *English modality: Core, periphery and evidentiality*. Berlin: Mouton de Gruyter, 411–445.

Marín-Arrese, J. I., Hidalgo Downing, L., & Molina, S. (2004). Evidential, epistemic and deontic modality in English and Spanish: The expression of writer stance in newspaper discourse. In R. Facchinetti & F. Palmer (Eds.) *English modality in perspective. Genre analysis and contrastive studies*. Frankfurt: Peter Lang., 121–139.

Mauranen, A. (2013). "Hybridism, edutainment, and doubt: Science blogging finding its feet". *Nordic Journal of English Studies*, 13(1), 7–36.

Mewburn, I., & Thomson, P. (2013). Why do academics blog? An analysis of audiences, purposes and challenges. *Studies in Higher Education*, 38(8), 1105–1119.

Nuyts, J. (2000). *Epistemic modality, language and conceptualization. A cognitive-pragmatic perspective*. Amsterdam & Philadelphia: John Benjamins.

Palmer F. R. (1981). *Semantics. Second edition*. Cambridge: Cambridge University Press.

Puschmann, C., & M. Mahrt (2012). Scholarly blogging: A new form of publishing or science journalism 2.0? In A. Tokar, M. Beurskens, S. Keuneke, M. Mahrt, I. Peters, C. Puschmann, T. van Treeck Timo & K. Weller (Eds.) *Science and the Internet*. Düsseldorf University Press: Düsseldorf, 171–181.

Sokół, M. (2014). The academic weblog as a semi-peripheral genre. In K. Bennett (Ed.) *The semiperiphery of academic writing. Discourses, communities and practices*. Houndsmills, Basingstoke: Palgrave Macmillan, 221–239.

Sokół, M. (2015). The academic weblog as a social networking genre. In A. Duszak & G. Kowalski (Eds.) *Academic (inter)genres: between texts, contexts and identities*. Frankfurt am Main: Peter Lang, 189–213.

Thompson, G., & L. Alba-Juez (Eds.) (2014). *Evaluation in context*. Amsterdam: John Benjamins.

Veletsianos, G. (2016). *Social media in academia. Networked scholars*. New York & London: Routledge.

White, D., & LeCornu, A. (2011). Visitors and residents: A new typology for online engagement. *First Monday* 16(9). Retrieved from journal URL http://firstmonday.org/article/view/3171/3049. DOA: 13.03.2017.

Appendix

The subcorpora used in the study consist of the posts retrieved from the following single-authored academic weblogs:

Subcorpus A (blogs run by humanities and social sciences academics)

BH1: warsztat badacza Emanuel Kulczycki <http://ekulczycki.pl/>.

BH2: pedagog <http://sliwerski-pedagog.blogspot.com/>.

BH3: popblog <http://www.piotrsiuda.pl/>.

BH4: marcin wilkowski <http://wilkowski.org/>.

BH5: Filologia cyfrowa :: Mediewistyka 2.0 <http://filologiacyfrowa.wordpress.com/>.

BH6: Komiks w bibliotece <http://abrewiacje.wordpress.com/>.

BH7: HerstoriA <http://herstoria.blox.pl/html>.

BH8: humanistyczny notatnik naukowy <http://humanistycznynotatniknaukowy.com/>

BH9: KOCHAM HISTORIĘ <http://kochamhistorie.blox.pl/html>

BH10: Człowiek i Technologie <http://czlowiekitechnologie.com/tag/blog-naukowy/>

BH11: blog.2edu.pl Obudź w sobie eduNinje <http://blog.2edu.pl/>

BH12: presscafe.eu blog o edukacji medialnej <http://presscafe.eu/>

Subcorpus B (blogs run by natural, technical and exact sciences academics)

BNH1: profesorskie gadanie http://czachorowski.blox.pl/html

BNH2: Żywa Planeta http://zywaplaneta.pl/

BNH3: http://zajaczkowski.org/

BNH4: wduch http://wduch.wordpress.com/

BNH5: borczyk~ Il nome della Rosa http://bborczyk.wordpress.com/

BNH6: Mroczna Sztuka Ogłupiania http://czajniczek-pana-russella.blogspot.com/

BNH7: Doskonale szare http://doskonaleszare.blox.pl/html

BNH8: Nie od razu naukę zbudowano http://kierul.wordpress.com/

BNH9: „Pan inżynier" dziś bada http://marekopel.wordpress.com/

BNH10: piękno neurobiologii Blog Jerzego Vetulaniego http://vetulani.wordpress.com/

BNH11: http://smarterpoland.pl/

BNH12: Sporothrix http://sporothrix.wordpress.com/

Grzegorz Kowalski

University of Warsaw, Poland

Problem-Solution text pattern and references to target groups in crowdfunding projects' presentations

Abstract: This paper analyzes the use of the Problem-Solution text pattern in crowdfunding projects' presentations, for which purpose it takes Hoey's (1983, 2001) model of Problem-Solution text as a point of reference. Hoey's model is, however, supplemented with methodologies originating in multimodal discourse analysis to grasp the multisemiotic intricacies of the genre in question, including written text, spoken text, graphics and motion pictures. Also, a critical discursive approach is employed to analyze how the projects' authors discursively construct the Problem and the Solution, and how they define the target groups for projects marketed at local and global crowdfunding platforms. In particular, the research focuses on discourse strategies applied to (1) construct local vs. global significance of the Problem and (2) to identify and positively evaluate the relevant Solution, and (3) those whereby the target group concerned is defined. Empirical material is excerpted from presentations of three crowdfunding projects marketed at the local Polish crowdfunding platform PolakPotrafi and three from the global crowdfunding platform Kickstarter.

1. Introduction: crowdfunding

Dynamically developing since approximately a decade (for statistical data, see e.g. Dushnitsky, Guerini, Piva & Rossi-Lamastra, 2016), crowdfunding has now become one of the key phenomena of Web 2.0, or a World Wide Web co-constructed through interactions by the virtual community of its users. Taxonomically, crowdfunding is sometimes related to *crowdsourcing* (e.g. Schwienbacher & Larralde, 2012), since both involve massive co-operation of Internet users to accomplish a goal pre-specified in a project by an individual or corporate author.

In crowdsourcing Internet users will voluntarily rally around the task, engaging their time, knowledge, computer's calculating power and/or other resources. While an individual contribution remains imperceptible, a large army of co-workers can indeed help to solve the problem, although the commissioning person or company can never assume that the joint input of the contributors will be sufficient to do so.

By contrast, in crowdfunding the help sought after is financial. The author presents a project to gather funds necessary for its accomplishment, and Internet users are invited to act as investors. In general the payments made to support a particular crowdfunding project are small, and consequently, and as in the case of crowdsourcing, the contribution of a single investor is often modest. Yet again, given the sheer number of the supporters involved, the eventual sum collected is often sufficient for the author to put the project into effect.

Crowdfunding did not appear concurrently with Web 2.0. Historical initiatives such as French and American fundraising for the Statue of Liberty and its pedestal, respectively, or nationwide campaigns to purchase war bonds issued during WW1 and WW2 in several countries, are frequently cited as antecedents of modern Web 2.0 crowdfunding (Lawton & Marom, 2010; Gierczak, Bretschneider, Haas, Blohm & Leimeister, 2016). However, what makes the former different from Web 2.0 crowdfunding is the scope of operation. Specifically, pre-Web 2.0 fundraisers would address local audiences, restricted by the range of traditional channels of communication (meetings, newspapers, radio and TV broadcasts). By contrast, with the development of online communication, in particular social media, fundraisers can address, attract and be supported by Web users globally, unconstrained by spatial and temporal limits of the traditional channels.

Another important element of Web 2.0 crowdfunding is *crowdfunding platforms*, which showcase projects and facilitate interaction between their authors and potential backers. Popularity of crowdfunding translates into the ever-increasing number of crowdfunding platforms established in different countries. Despite some apparent differences in their layout, general or specific areas of interest, management policies etc., crowdfunding platforms can be broadly divided into two types according to the benefit obtained by the backer, and likewise into two types according to the mode of transfer of the capital to the project's developer. Along the former line, crowdfunding platforms employ the *reward-based* system, where in return for the donation the backer obtains some good (e.g. the project's merchandise badge, adloop, piece of garment, etc., or the product itself if the project is accomplished), its value depending on the amount donated, or *equity* system, in which the backer becomes a shareholder of the enterprise and participates in future profits it makes on the sales of the product, again proportionally to the amount of the backer's investment. Along the latter line, crowdfunding platforms operate in either the *All-or-Nothing* mode, whereby the sum raised is transferred to the project's developer only if it equals or exceeds the sum applied for (otherwise the donations are returned to the backers), or the *Keep-It-All* mode, where the project's developer receives the amount raised, regardless of whether it meets the cost estimate submitted or not, as soon as the fundraising period terminates.

Of relevance for the present study is another criterion of crowdfunding platforms' diversification, namely their local vs. global operation and impact, which is discussed in the next section.

2. Local and global crowdfunding platforms

In the present study I analyse sample project presentations showcased at two crowdfunding platforms: PolakPotrafi and Kickstarter. Given the reasons discussed below the former is classified as a local platform, while the latter as a global one.

Launched in 2011, PolakPotrafi (www.polakpotrafi.pl) is the longest-running and biggest Polish reward-based crowdfunding platform, operating in the All-or-Nothing mode. In the first year it promoted 15 projects, backed with 75,000 PLN (approx. 19,000 USD) in total, and gathered 4000 users. In 2013 the total funds surpassed 1 million PLN (approx. 250,000 USD). The data for May 2017 are as follows: 17+ million PLN (approx. 4.4 million USD) raised in total, 2968 projects supported[1], 183,462 registered backers, 385,615 PLN (99,500 USD) being the biggest sum raised for a single project, 3688 backers being the biggest number of supporters of a single project, and 129% of the intended sum raised being the average result for a successful project (www.polakpotrafi.pl; DOA: 25.05.2017). The range of projects is broadly defined as "all kinds of ideas, proposals and intentions, or a plan of organized activities aimed at achieving a particular goal" (http://www.pi.gov.pl/PARP/chapter_86197.asp?soid=793EC92A184A4685B42D671C25EE2AA4; DOA: 25.05.2017, translation mine); there are no limitations on the maximum target sum to be raised or the duration of the fundraising campaign. The platform charges the 7.4% fee on the project + 2.5% on the payments made.

By contrast, Kickstarter, launched in 2009, is a leading global crowdfunding platform, often used as reference by platforms operating locally (PolakPotrafi is sometimes described as *polski Kickstarter* 'Polish kickstarter', see e.g. http://di.com.pl/crowdfunding-w-polsce-polski-kickstarter-skonczyl-rok-45492; DOA: 25.05.2017). Like PolakPotrafi, Kickstarter follows the All-or-Nothing

1 No information provided on the proportion of successful and declined projects; according to the data available from the Polish Agency for Enterprise Development, the platform has successfully promoted a few hundred projects (http://www.pi.gov.pl/PARP/chapter_86197.asp?soid=793EC92A184A4685B42D671C25EE2AA4; DOA: 25.05.2017).

principle for promoting reward-based projects. The projects it promotes also fall into diverse thematic fields, their goals being limited only by five general rules:[2]

- Projects must create something to share with others;
- Projects must be honest and clearly presented;
- Projects can't fundraise for charity;
- Projects can't offer equity;
- Projects can't involve prohibited items.

(https://www.kickstarter.com/rules?ref=faq-basics_whatfor; DOA: 29.05.2017)

Kickstarter's statistics confirm its dominant position in the global crowdfunding market. By 11th May 2017 the platform has raised 3.035 billion USD, of which 2.65 billion USD was provided for successful projects. So far 352,440 projects have been launched, of which 124,524 were successful and supported with the required or higher sum. The backers' base is 12.9 million people, including 4.1 million regular supporters, who made 38+ million donations in total. Most Kickstarter projects submitted call for 1000–9999 USD (56% of successful projects); 230 successful projects claimed a budget of 1+ million USD.

While it should be essential for a project's author to reach as broad audience as possible, and hence attract as sizeable group of potential backers as possible, it is evident that particular platforms impose certain limitations on the projects' authors and/or backers. In consequence, none of the currently operating crowdfunding platforms can be claimed to be a truly global one. These limitations can be broadly distinguished into legal, linguistic and symbolic.

Legal limitations on the use of crowdfunding platforms are specified in their respective conditions of application, agreements with the users and corporate policies. In addition, there apply external documents including relevant rules of law in force in a given country, in particular concerning cash flow or taxation. This is also the case of the two platforms discussed in the present study. Kickstarter was originally open only to projects submitted by US residents, and only since 2012 has gradually extended the fundraisers' base to residents of the "UK, Canada, Australia, New Zealand, the Netherlands, Denmark, Ireland, Norway, Sweden, Germany, France, Spain, Italy, Austria, Belgium, Switzerland, Luxembourg, Hong Kong, Singapore and Mexico" (https://www.kickstarter.com/

2 PolakPotrafi.pl follows a similar policy. It should be noted that in 2016 the platform's founders established a sister entity, *Polak Pomaga* 'a Pole helps', which runs a charity foundation and related charity crowdfunding platform.

help/faq/creator+questions#faq_41823; DOA: 29.05. 2017), which still excludes the vast majority of people. A Kickstarter applicant must hold a permanent address in one of the countries specified, a valid ID document issued therein, and a bank account with a credit or debit card run by a bank in the country of residence. No limitations are introduced for potential backers. As for PolakPotrafi, projects are only accepted from persons holding an account in a bank operating in Poland (https://polakpotrafi.freshdesk.com/support/solutions/articles/14000015522-czy-musz%C4%99-by%C4%87-polakiem-aby-stworzy%C4%87-projekt-; DOA: 29.05.2017).

The language barrier is the second obstacle for reaching global audience. While English seems to be a natural choice for platforms wishing to attract its most sizeable portion, other platforms seem to target local communities by showcasing project presentations in national languages with relatively limited number of speakers. The former is the case of Kickstarter: although the platform's managers invite projects' portfolios prepared in any language, a caveat is made that the platform supports French, German and Spanish. Also, the English version is recommended at least as supplementary. Also, all video materials are required to contain English subtitles (https://www.kickstarter.com/help/faq/creator+questions?ref=faq_nav#GettStar; DOA: 29.05.2017). As for PolakPotrafi, the platform's regulations do not provide information on the preferred or required languages; however, all the projects currently (as for 29.05.2017) showcased are in Polish, a few of them containing videos subtitled in other languages (e.g. French in *Baza Księżycowa pod Krakowem* 'Moon base near Kraków', https://polakpotrafi.pl/projekt/baza-ksiezycowa-pod-krakowem?utm_source=projects, DOA: 29.05.2017; see section 5.1.3).

Finally, platforms can feature certain symbolic means of including or excluding particular groups of potential users, be it projects' developers or backers. For instance, the name of the Polish platform reproduces the well-known Polish idiom *Polak potrafi* 'a Pole can / will do', which in this context emphasizes the platform's focus on projects created by Polish authors. This symbolic bias as conveyed in the cunning intertextual use of the idiom is further reinforced verbatim in the platform's policy:

> *PolakPotrafi.pl ma na celu uświadomienie społeczeństwu,* ***jak wiele mamy fascynujących talentów, z których możemy być dumni****. Nie wszyscy robią show aby zostać dostrzeżonym przez stacje telewizyjne, ale wielu zasługuje na co najmniej takie wyróżnienie. My* ***chcemy wyróżnić wszystkich, którzy chcą stworzyć wspólnie lub samodzielnie lepszą Polskę****.*
>
> [PolakPotrafi.pl aims to make society aware of **how many fascinating talents we have, talents that we can be proud of**. Not every one of them is making a show to be noticed by

TV stations, but many of them deserve at least such a distinction. **We want to distinguish all those who wish to create – in teams or individually – a better Poland.**]

(https://polakpotrafi.freshdesk.com/support/solutions/articles/14000015494-kto-mo%C5%BCe-za%C5%82o%C5%BCy%C4%87-projekt-na-polakpotrafi-pl-; DOA: 22.05.2017)

As can be noted, the use of the inclusive *we* in the first sentence clearly establishes a sense of national community not only between the platform's managers and project creators addressed, but also extends to backers and Polish society in general. Also, the final sentence emphasizes that priority is given to projects of local (countrywide) impact, encouraging the potential developers to position the country's welfare as the overriding principle in their ideas.

3. Problem-Solution text pattern in discourse

3.1. Problem-Solution text pattern: Hoey's (1983) model

The Problem-Solution pattern has been widely discussed in literature in the field of Discourse Analysis as one of the major frames of text organization in different written and spoken genres (e.g. McCarthy, 1991; Dudley-Evans, 1994; Paltridge, 1996; Flowerdew, 2003, 2008). A seminal work by Michael Hoey *On the surface of discourse* (1983) has provided a general structure of the pattern, which was developed in more recent studies of his (e.g. Hoey, 1986, 2001; Hoey & Winter, 1986) and adopted – with possible modifications – by other scholars (see the preceding list of references). Starting with an assumption that texts are a "visible evidence of a reasonably self-contained purposeful interaction between one or more writers and one or more readers, in which the writer(s) control the interaction and produce most of (characteristically all) the language" (Hoey, 2001, p. 11), Hoey notes that texts of particular genres are structured in a culturally predictable manner, providing lines along which writer–reader interaction unfolds. From among the many possible patterns he discusses e.g. Goal-Achievement, Opportunity-Taking, Knowledge-Filling, Question-Answer, and Problem-Solution, the latter considered to be "arguably the most common pattern of all" (Hoey, 2001, p. 123).

According to Hoey (2001), the Problem-Solution pattern consists of four basic steps: Situation, Problem, Solution, and Result/Evaluation. Specifically, Situation presents a broader context in which a specific Problem is identified. The latter triggers off a Solution, which is supposed to rid of the Problem and restore orderliness to the Situation. The Result of the Solution is simply acknowledged or, alternatively, its eventual effectiveness is subject to some Evaluation. The general Problem-Solution pattern is shown in Figure 1 (further optional stages are not discussed here).

Figure 1. Problem-Solution pattern (Hoey, 2001, p. 127)

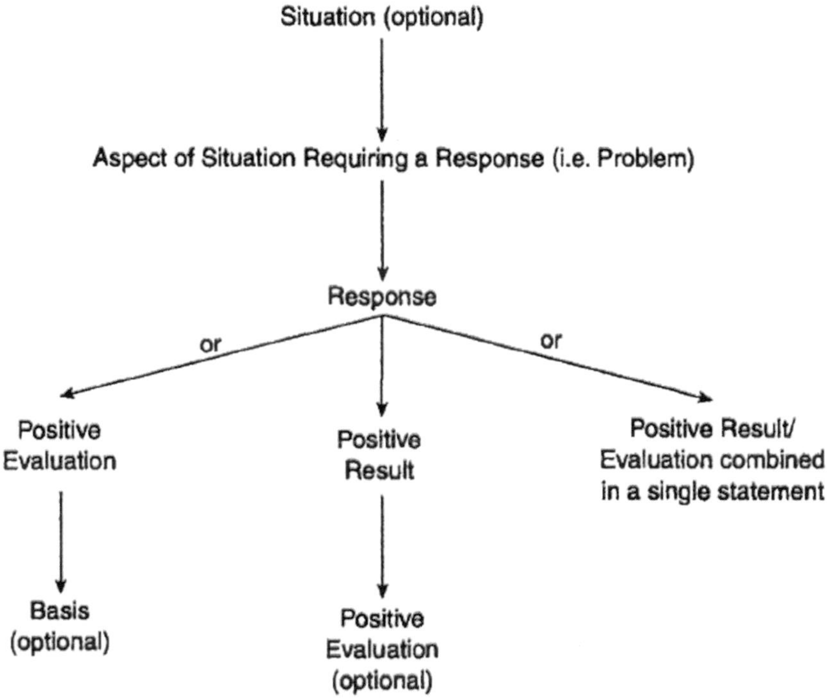

According to Hoey (2001, p. 128), elements of the Problem-Solution pattern are identifiable on the surface of discourse by specific triggers, including lexical and grammatical ones. The former are keywords such as *problem/issue/challenge* or *solution/answer* (see also Winter, 1977; Jordan, 1984). Pragmatically, lexical triggers are classified into *inscribed signals* (explicitly referring to problem or solution, e.g. *solution*, *problem*, *challenge*), *inscribed evaluations* (alluding to problem or solution in their semantics, e.g. *unfortunately*), and *evoking signals* (presuppositions requiring more general commonsense knowledge to be properly understood as signaling a problem or solution, as in *had no money*). By contrast, grammatical triggers include relevant markers of sentence subordination and discourse markers (see Jordan, 1984)[3], and also certain syntactic constructions e.g. direct questions to the reader. The latter act as verbatim markers of the text's interactive

3 Hoey (1983) discusses in detail how clause relations can co-align with components of the Problem-Solution pattern. Specifically, he finds the Cause and Consequence

character, whereby the author can refer to (1) the Situation as a shared experience familiar to him-/herself and the reader, and (2) the Problem which this shared Situation entails and which affects as much the author as it does the reader.

Identifying the triggers and associating them with a particular discourse pattern are basic steps in the analytical framework described by Hoey (2001). Some authors, in particular Flowerdew (2008), have recently postulated that corpus analysis may help elicit triggers of the respective components of the Problem-Solution pattern in large-scale corpora. Having said that, it should be remembered that triggers are context-bound elements of discourse and they are not distributed evenly across discourses and genres. In general,

> [t]he greater the knowledge that the reader shares with the writer, the less need there is for the writer to make explicit linguistic reference to the pattern being followed, since the significance of the information being provided will be quite obvious to the reader.
> (Hoey, 2001, p. 128)

Also, the boundaries of the components of the Problem-Solution pattern do not always correlate with the boundaries of grammatical units, be it clauses, sentences or paragraphs, which can make their delimitation relatively challenging. Finally, to complicate the task even more, the components can appear in a non-linear order, and may be recurrent in a given text (see e.g. McCarthy, 1991, p. 28; Flowerdew, 2008, p. 2).

One of the genres of which the Problem-Solution pattern is characteristic is advertisement, which is also analyzed by Hoey (2001, p. 128–129). The Problem-Solution pattern in advertisements clearly fits into the business process, in particular in terms of demand creation and management. Once the addressee of the advertisement acknowledges that the Problem affects him or her in a Situation he or she experiences, and that the Solution offered by the advertiser is (or at least might be) an effective remedy, such a person becomes a potential customer, and the advertiser's role is now to maintain the customer's demand to the point that he or she acquires the product.

3.2. Problem-Solution text pattern in crowdfunding projects' presentations

Crowdfunding projects cover a wide array of fields of human activity, which do not always involve a clearly recognizable Problem nor propose an apparent

---

relation to frequently represent the Problem-Solution relation, and Instrument and Achievement relation to frequently represent the Solution-Result relation.

Solution. This is particularly the case of artistic projects, which refer to aesthetic preferences of certain people. In other words, while a successful artistic project will answer a market demand, it does not constitute a Solution as understood in Hoey's (2001) terms.

By contrast, crowdfunding projects in the categories *Technologia* / Technology, which I have chosen for this analysis, usually concern a tangible device supposed to solve a particular Problem identified by their developers. In addition, such a Solution is shown to be innovative: it is supposed to fit into a market niche so far unoccupied, and in turn attract the attention of consumers aware of this niche and thus likely to recognize the relevance of the device marketed. It can thus be expected that presentations of innovative technological devices promoted at crowdfunding platforms would employ the Problem-Solution pattern on the one hand, and refer to marketing mechanisms of demand and consumer needs and wants on the other. While the present paper focuses only on the former, it would be wrong (and often impossible) to separate the two aspects: an aggregate analysis is therefore welcome.

My general hypothesis is that a crowdfunding project's presentation is an advertising text based on the Problem-Solution text pattern, at least in relation to projects in the categories *Technologia* / Technology analyzed. As an advertising text, it promotes a project with the perspective of its accomplishment thanks to the backers' financial support. In the case of technological devices the presentation will depict the Problem which the project is to solve. To show the Problem's relevance to potential backers the Problem should be presented in the light of a Situation known to them. The more common the Situation and the more familiar the related Problem, the greater the number of people affected thereby, and thus the greater the chances to attract a group of backers sizeable and generous enough to ensure the project's accomplishment. Strategic management of the Problem-Solution text pattern and skilful use of the relevant discursive means are then prerequisite for the developer to gather support from beyond the tried-and-true FFF (Family, Friends, Fools) circle of backers.

Unlike Hoey (2001), I do not limit my analysis to text. Other channels, largely employed in the digital medium, may be equally employed to promote a crowdfunding project. Different media, including videos, sounds and images, can complement, amplify or otherwise highlight, replace etc. the textual content, be it depiction of the Situation, identification of the Problem, presentation of the Solution, or demonstrating the Result/Evaluation.

4. Methods, materials and research hypotheses

4.1. Methods and materials

Using a discursive approach, the present study compares and contrasts presentations of six crowdfunding projects, three excerpted from Kickstarter and three from PolakPotrafi. I intend this preliminary research to provide the grounds for a more extensive study. A multi-modal approach is applied to duly consider the possible role of the spoken and written content as well as visual and sound elements in the presentations in question.

The projects analyzed were selected on the basis of the following criteria. They all represent the *Technologia* / Technology category, which statistically constitutes a major group of projects in the crowdfunding platforms (#2 category, 12.2% of the total of the ongoing projects at Kickstarter; #2 category, 12.5% of the total of the ongoing projects at PolakPotrafi; data for 25th May 2017). Projects in this category usually feature innovative devices, and these, as has been noted above, are more prototypical examples of Solutions than, say, artistic undertakings.

From among the numerous projects in the *Technologia* / Technology category I selected the three (for each platform) which were completed successfully before 25th May 2017 and which were supported by the greatest number of backers.[4] The project's success, in most of the cases analysed supported with the sum exceeding the sum applied for, and a substantial number of backers provide a general indication that the device proposed is perceived as a relevant and promising Solution to the Problem addressed.

4.2. Research hypotheses

1. *The project provides a Solution to a Problem of a certain group*

Assuming that the project presents a Solution to a certain Problem, there must be a certain group directly concerned with the Problem and hence potentially interested in being provided with a Solution thereto. The group may be small in size, yet sizeable enough for the author to anticipate the possible market interest in the Solution proposed. In other words the Solution may address a niche Problem, but the latter cannot be purely hypothetical.

---

4 Two projects from the *Technologia* category at PolakPotrafi (production of accordions and soap manufacturing) were rejected as they involved rather handcraft than technology in its proper sense. Similarly, to eliminate artisanal or otherwise non-technological projects, the combined tag *Innovative + Technology* was applied for Kickstarter projects.

2. *The group concerned with the Problem is referred to in the project's presentation*

It is assumed that the project's presentation will refer to the group concerned with the Problem, with any or all modes of communication available (text, speech, images, video, sound etc.), in order to indicate that the Problem is real and not hypothetical, and in turn to prove the relevance of the Solution proposed.

3. *Projects launched at local crowdfunding platforms will address local groups and provide Solutions to local Problems; projects launched at global crowdfunding platforms will address global groups and provide Solutions to global Problems*

This is the key research question which I would like to examine in the present study. As has been stated above (section 2), certain barriers and exclusion mechanisms applied by various crowdfunding platforms, including Kickstarter and PolakPotrafi, determine their respective audiences and, what follows, the size of the potential backers' base. From the point of view of the author of a project it is a strategic decision at which platform his or her project should be marketed, keeping in mind the said variables.

5. Analysis

5.1. PolakPotrafi projects

5.1.1. *efood – baza produktów*

E food – baza produktów 'efood – products database' (https://polakpotrafi.pl/projekt/efood?utm_source=projects; DOA: 29.05.2017) is the most successful PolakPotrafi project in the category *Technologia*, which attracted 430 backers and raised 17,251 PLN against 9,000 PLN applied for.

The Problem-Solution pattern is recurrent in the project's presentation, appearing already in the introduction of its promotional video (https://youtu.be/haHTWzuxpuU; DOA: 12.06.2017). One of the authors poses the question:

> *Dlaczego na producentów alkoholu i papierosów nakłada się obowiązek informowania o szkodliwości spożycia, a nie oczekuje się tego od producentów żywności?*
>
> [Why are alcohol and cigarette manufacturers obliged to inform about these products' harmful effects, while food manufacturers are not expected to do so?]
>
> (00:00:10–00:00:17)

The first clause refers to the Situation: that there are legal regulations[5] for tobacco and alcohol manufacturers to label their products with information about their detrimental effects is part of consumers' commonsense knowledge. The second clause draws on this knowledge: there are no similarly strict regulations for food manufacturers to inform about potentially harmful ingredients. Awareness of the latter fact helps the audience perceive this state of affairs as the Problem.

In the next part of the video (00:00:30–00:00:50), however, the Situation-Problem structure is redefined. Instead of referring to commonsense knowledge one of the project's developers presents a personal narrative:

> *Siedzieliśmy przy stole na wyjeździe, zaczęliśmy oglądać opakowania, no i okazało się, że nikt nic nie wie, co jest w tych produktach, które spożywamy. A na dodatek nie mamy internetu, nie mamy jak sprawdzić co jest co.*
>
> [We were sitting at the table on a trip, we started to examine the packages, and it turned out that nobody knows what is in the products we eat. And we do not have Internet at that, and we have no way of checking what is what.]

As the narrative unfolds, it becomes clear that its role is to emphasize the relevance of the Problem to average consumers. Even if the story refers to a specific event – a short trip with friends – similar experiences are likely to be familiar for the peers of the project's developers. Correspondingly, while the climax of the story recapitulates a discussion of the diners on this particular occasion, it can be assumed that similar debates can occur in similar contexts. Thus on the surface the narrative refers to a personal Situation and a personal Problem, but considering their ordinary character they can be interpreted by the readers as general Situation and general Problem, respectively, and thus provide the rationale for the Solution proposed in the following part of the video.

The general – rather than personal – relevance of the Problem is further accentuated in the coda of the story, which evokes the well-known metaphorical representation of sheep led to the slaughterhouse, in this context representing ignorant consumers: *no i dobra bierzemy to i idziemy być może jak owieczki na*

5 See, for example, Article 11 of *WHO Framework Convention on Tobacco Control* (http://apps.who.int/iris/bitstream/10665/42811/1/9241591013.pdf?ua=1; DOA: 12.06.2017); Hammond (2011); "Health Warning Labeling Requirements" of the International Alliance for Responsible Drinking (http://www.iard.org/policy-tables/health-warning-labeling-requirements/; DOA: 12.06.2017); EU legislation (e.g. Directive 2001/37/EC of the European Parliament and of the Council of 5 June 2001 on the approximation of the laws, regulations and administrative provisions of the Member States concerning the manufacture, presentation and sale of tobacco products).

rzeź [all right, we accept it and we go perhaps as sheep to the slaughter]. The verbal content is accompanied with the matching visual representation of a sheep herd, cramming into a narrow interior (00:00:51).

Apart from the metaphor of sheep led to the slaughterhouse the promotional video also uses other cliché elements in the construction of the Problem-Solution sequence. One of them is the catchphrase *Lubimy jeść* [We like to eat], representing a common truth (Situation) of the general public (cf. the inclusive 1st person plural pronoun). The Situation is thus again redefined, and so is the ensuing Problem: *ale czy wiemy co jemy?* [but do we know what we eat?]. The question form signals that the issue at hand is indeed a Problem, to which an answer (Solution) should be sought.

The Situation-Problem-Solution sequence is also a recurrent discourse organizational pattern in the textual part of the project's presentation, in particular in the section *Idea*. Its opening paragraph integrates the Situation with the discursive construction of the target group:

> *efood opracowaliśmy z myślą o ludziach takich jak my. Nie jesteśmy sportowcami, modelkami na diecie ani matkami karmiącymi (co pokazuje płeć niektórych członków zespołu). Ale lubimy wiedzieć co jemy i jak to na nas wpływa.*
>
> [We have developed efood for people like us. We are not sports people, models on diet or feeding mothers (as the gender of some of the team's members shows). But we like to know what we eat and how it affects us.]

The Situation as presented in this excerpt refers to average consumers and their daily eating routines. It is assumed that they will be interested in learning about the effects of food ingredients on their health. Since eating routines are inherent to human life, the authors assume that the interest in "what we eat" is equally universal, and thus the application should meet the expectations of the authors themselves as much as of average consumers ("people like us"). As in the video commentary, the target group is defined negatively, i.e. by excluding narrow groups of food-conscious persons (sports people, models and feeding mothers), in consequence leaving a major part of society within the scope of the application's potential customers/users.

While the Problem is not stated explicitly in this excerpt ("we like to know what we eat" presupposes that "we do not always know what we eat"), the second paragraph in the *Idea* section names the Solution ("our application") and its operation: *Dlatego nasza aplikacja weryfikuje produkty spożywcze pod kątem dodatków chemicznych* [This is why our application verifies food products for chemical additives].

The next section in the project's description, *Jak działa aplikacja* [How the application works], complements the Problem-Solution pattern by providing elements of Evaluation. First, negative Evaluation is applied for alternative Solutions available to consumers. Here Evaluation directly points out to the negative Result of applying these alternative methods: *trzeba przeczytać tony książek i zakuć setki dziwnych terminów* [you have to read tons of books and cram hundreds of strange terms]. Application of these alternative methods is then evaluated as tedious, monotonous and boring (*żmudne, monotonne i nudne*). By contrast, the efood application is positively Evaluated, and in turn becomes the most suitable Solution: *efood to zmienia i jest zawsze pod ręką – bez potrzeby dostępu do internetu* [efood changes that and is always at hand – no need for Internet access].

Turning now to the definition of the target group, as has been stated above, in the project's description there are recurrent references to the application's relevance for a broad group of users, potentially global. Firstly, the application addresses a Problem recognized worldwide (lack of labeling alimentary products for potentially harmful ingredients, see footnote 5). Secondly, the description contains clichés e.g. *Lubimy jeść* [We like to eat] (00:00:58) or *W końcu jesteśmy tym, co jemy* [All in all we are what we eat] (00:02:05–00:02:06), which may be interpreted as cultural universals (if the inclusive 1st person plural pronoun is understood as generic). Thirdly, even if a reverse strategy of indirect referring to the target group is applied – e.g. when the authors claim that "This is for people who are not food freaks" (*To jest dla ludzi, którzy nie są food freakami*) (00:02:07–00:02:12) – they exclude a relatively narrow group, whereas the actual target group encompasses "all others".

Having said that, it should be noted that in the final sections of the project's description, *Pomysł na wspólny rozwój aplikacji* [Idea for joint development of the application] and in particular *Trochę o nas* [Something about us], the authors suggest that the application's primary market is Poland:

> *Aplikacja efood opiera się na dwóch fundamentach: – wspieraniu świadomej konsumpcji; – interakcji z użytkownikami. Co to dokładnie oznacza? [...] pomożecie nam wesprzeć świadomość żywieniową* ***innych Polaków****.*
>
> [The efood application is based on two foundations: – supporting conscious consumption; – interaction with users. What exactly does this mean? [...] you will help us support the nutritional awareness of **other Poles**.]
>
> (emphasis mine)

In another fragment one of the authors makes a pun of the platform's name (in the first sentence) and the idiom which it reproduces (in the second sentence). In doing so he refers to Polish people as potential users of the application: *Wierzymy w siłę Polak Potrafi. Wiemy, że* ***Polak potrafi zadbać o swoje zdrowie*** [We believe in the power of Polak Potrafi. We know that **a Pole can take care of his/her health**] (emphasis mine).

5.1.2. *Nowatorski longboard elektryczny z panelami słonecznymi*

Nowatorski longboard elektryczny z panelami słonecznymi [Innovative electric longboard with solar panels] (https://polakpotrafi.pl/projekt/nowatorski-longboard-elektryczny-z-panelami-slonecznymi?utm_source=projects; DOA:29.05.2017) is the second most successful PolakPotrafi project in the category *Technologia*, which attracted 230 backers and raised 21,281 PLN against 6,000 PLN applied for.

In comparison with the e-food application, the longboard project's presentation employs the Problem-Solution pattern to a lesser extent and contains fewer references to the target audience. Instead, most information concerns technical issues and product specification. Also, elements of the Problem-Solution structure are sometimes presupposed rather than stated explicitly, as is the case of the opening paragraph of the project's presentation:

> *Masz przeczucie, że najbliższe lata to czas energii odnawialnej i pojazdów elektrycznych? Ja też, dlatego połączyłem te dwie rzeczy! Przedstawiam Wam pierwszego takiego elektrycznego longboarda z panelami słonecznymi!*
>
> [Do you have a feeling that the coming years are the time of renewable energy and electric vehicles? Me too, so I joined these two things! I present you the first such electric longboard with solar panels!]

The first sentence presents the Situation, yet hypothetical (future-oriented) rather than real, which in turn justifies the use of the question form and the speculative construction *Masz przeczucie, że* ... [Do you have a feeling that ....] The following answer *Ja też* [Me too] presupposes the author's and audience's shared belief in renewable energy and electric vehicles being widespread in the near future[6]. The Problem is not stated at this point, and in turn one cannot identify the longboard as the Solution yet.

The bulk of the description provides technical specifications of the longboard, and it is only towards the end of the text that the Problem-Solution structure resurfaces, though the former element is presupposed rather than phrased verbatim:

> *Jest to pierwszy elektryczny longboard, z takimi osiągami, w takiej cenie! Dodatkowo: czas ładowania do pełna to tylko 2h, a maksymalna waga użytkownika przekracza 110kg! Nie trzeba martwić się o panele, ponieważ są one bezpiecznie zamknięte wewnątrz deski.*

---

6 This belief recurs in the later part of the project's description: *Szał na pojazdy elektryczne dopiero się zaczyna* [The hype for electric vehicles has just begun]

> [This is the first electric longboard, with such performance, at such a price! In addition: the full load time is only 2h, and the maximum weight of the user exceeds 110kg! You do not need to worry about the panels because they are securely locked inside the board.]

In fact, the Problem is rather puzzling due to the ambiguous meaning of *pierwszy* 'first': the Problem can be either (1) lack of similar longboards (the Problem then being a market niche), or (2) drawbacks of similar products already available, which the longboard is claimed to overcome. Another excerpt suggests that the former option is actually the case: *Jest to innowacyjny pomysł,* ***na całym świecie nie ma produkowanych desek tego typu*** [This is an innovative idea, **there are no boards of this type in the world**] (emphasis mine). On the other hand, comparative constructions *z takimi osiągami, w takiej cenie* [with such performance, at such a price] presuppose that there is some product of reference against which the comparison in favour of this longboard is made – no further details are, however, provided.

The comparative constructions used in the above excerpt also express positive Evaluation of the longboard (Solution), and presuppose negative Evaluation of unidentified competing products. Specifically, they emphasize that the longboard has the competitive edge in terms of performance and price, and is also characterized by short battery load time (shorter than usual for solar panels?) and relatively high user's weight limit.

Also, the solar panel longboard is claimed to be a Solution over the Problems posed by traditional longboards or electric-powered longboards, especially those related to time-effectiveness, energy-saving and economy:

> *Przez ostatnie dwa miesiące powoli budowałem prototypową deskę z wbudowanymi wewnątrz panelami słonecznymi, które umożliwiają ciągłe ładowanie deski –* ***oszczędzają tym samym czas, energię i pieniądze!***
>
> [For the last two months I have slowly built a prototype board with built-in solar panels which enable continuous charging of the board – **saving time, energy and money!**]
> (emphasis mine)

While the text discursively constructs the longboard as the Solution, its specific qualities are also presented as Solutions in their own right (hereinafter "Specific Solutions"). When discussing the prototype construction the author makes negative Evaluation of the elements used therein, indicating that scarce funds are responsible for the low quality of certain components. The next longboards are to be fitted with components which would solve the Problems inherent to those temporary ones, including *wydajne panele słoneczne, porządne trucki i duże koła, mocny silnik, wysokiej klasy ESC, nowe baterie litowo polimerowe, balancer do bezpiecznego ładowania* [efficient solar panels, good tracks and large wheels, powerful engine, high-quality ESC, new lithium polymer batteries, balancer for safe charging]. As can be noted, each element is modified by an attribute which provides the positive Evaluation element to each Specific Solution in the list.

As for references to the longboard's target group, they are few and far. One example appears in the project's promotional video (https://youtu.be/BZnddChNrpQ; DOA: 12.06.2017), namely a slogan which suggests a possibly global relevance of the product, or at least the author's (true?) ambition to market it worldwide: *Stwórzmy razem ostateczny produkt, którym będę chciał podbić świat* [Let's create together the final product that I want to conquer the world with] (00:00:50–00:00:53).

Aspirations for reaching the global customer are reiterated in two additional videos: one posted on the final day of the crowdfunding campaign (https://youtu.be/3T9SWnLz-ng; DOA: 12.06.2017), and one presenting the project's update (https://youtu.be/H2eQCsI4FMY; DOA: 12.06.2017). In the former the author announces that the project was successfully accomplished and that it will be continued with the aim of global marketing the product: *Pamiętajcie, że to jest dopiero początek całej przygody. Podbijamy razem świat. Polak Potrafi to był tylko pierwszy krok* [Remember that this is just the beginning of the whole adventure. We conquer the world together. Polak Potrafi was just the first step] (00:00:39–00:00:47). In the latter video a new threshold for the crowdfunding campaign is stated along with the goal of brand development and worldwide promotion. Again the target group of potential customers is identified in the global perspective: *Mam nowy cel: chcę uzbierać 20000 złotych* […] *chodzi o zbudowanie całej marki. Chodzi o zrobienie czegoś, aby o tej desce usłyszał cały świat.* [I have a new goal: I want to raise 20000 PLN […] it's about building the whole brand. It's about doing something so that the whole world hears about this board] (00:00:43–00:00:55)

5.1.3. Baza księżycowa pod Krakowem

Baza księżycowa pod Krakowem [Lunar base near Kraków] (https://polakpotrafi.pl/projekt/baza-ksiezycowa-pod-krakowem?utm_source=projects; DOA: 29.05.2017) is the third most successful PolakPotrafi project, which attracted 188 backers and raised 69,230 PLN against 60,000 PLN applied for.

Unlike the other two projects discussed before, this project has a primarily scientific character, for it involves the construction of an analog Moon/Mars habitat in Poland. This fact affects the line of argumentation followed in the project's presentation, also in terms of Problem-Solution text pattern and definition of the target group. Specifically, as is discussed below, the authors of the project frequently focus on the national aspect of their undertaking, indicating the pioneering character of the habitat in Poland and Europe.

The Situation and the Problem are first mentioned at the beginning of the project's promotional video (https://www.youtube.com/watch?time_continue=1&v=wqnKxhamQhY; DOA: 12.06.2017), when one of the projects' coordinators, dr Agata Kołodziejczyk of European Space Foundation, asks the audience two questions:

> *Kto z was nie wyobrażał sobie jak to jest żyć na obcej, niegościnnej planecie? Kto z was chciałby być świadkiem jak ląduje pierwszy człowiek na Marsie?*
>
> [Which one of you did not imagine how it looks like to live on an alien, inhospitable planet? Which one of you would like to witness how the first man on Mars lands?]
>
> (00:00:11–00:00:20)

Both these questions, rhetorical in character, touch upon the general human curiosity concerning space exploration, and for this reason presuppose the affirmative answer. This excerpt discursively constructs the foundations for both the Situation and the Problem: the Situation refers to the shared experience of curiosity-driven speculation how living on a different planet or first landing on Mars will look like, while the related Problem refers to the similarly shared awareness that at the moment neither of these undertakings can be accomplished.

In the following part of the commentary the project is presented by another participant, Wojciech Gołębiowski of SKA Polska:

> *Wspólnie z grupą uczelni i firm zajmujących się badaniami kosmosu chcemy zbudować w Polsce analogową bazę planetarną do przeprowadzania symulacji załogowych misji księżycowych lub marsjańskich. Będzie to pierwsza na świecie tak duża i zaawansowana baza.*
>
> [Together with a group of universities and companies dealing with space research, we want to build an analog planetary base in Poland to simulate manned Moon or Mars missions. This will be the first so large and advanced base in the world.]
>
> (00:00:31–00:00:45)

This passage does not name the Solution to the Problem mentioned by dr Agata Kołodziejczyk: accomplishment of the analog Moon/Mars habitat does not warrant changing one's vision of living on another planet into a more palpable experience, be it in the role of a witness or a participant. Nor can it be assumed that the habitat can somehow accelerate the Mars exploration programme. Instead, Wojciech Gołębiowski redefines the Problem: it is habitats already operating, which are presupposed to be smaller and less advanced (implicit negative Evaluation). The analog Moon/Mars habitat is believed to be the Solution also to this Problem. As such, it is also positively Evaluated verbatim (*pierwsza na świecie tak duża i zaawansowana baza* [the first so large and advanced base in the world]).

In another part of the promotional video the Problem is once again redefined, with its national relevance brought into focus. In the following excerpt dr Agata Kołodziejczyk refers to the project's innovative character as a lever to shift Poland to the vanguard of research on lunar missions:

> *Potrzebujemy waszego wsparcia, aby Polska mogła znaleźć się w czołówce badań nad misjami kosmicznymi na Księżyc, a także w przyszłości na inne planety i inne księżyce.*
>
> [We need your support so that Poland can be at the forefront of research on space missions to the Moon, and in the future also to other planets and moons.]
>
> (00:00:49–00:01:01)

The project of the analog Moon/Mars habitat is presented here as the Solution to the Problem of Poland being a minor participant in research on space missions to the Moon, other planets and moons. The element of Evaluation (*znaleźć się w czołówce* 'be at the forefront') indicates that the habitat is an effective remedy to this Problem.

Another example of this line of argumentation used for constructing the Problem-Solution is found in the text of the project's presentation. In the section *O projekcie* [About the project] the authors highlight its pioneering role: *Chcemy zbudować pierwszy w Polsce i jeden z pierwszych w Europie analogowy habitat kosmiczny.* [We want to build an analog space habitat, the first in Poland and one of the first in Europe]. In terms of the Problem-Solution construction this statement is complementary to the claim made in the video commentary by Wojciech Gołębiowski that the habitat will be bigger and more advanced than any other already operating. The Problem is also associated with the market niche, though in the local scale: no similar habitat operates in Poland and only few operate in Europe. The commonsense expectation that this gap (Problem) should be somehow filled will justify the construction of the habitat (Solution).

The next passage in the text of the project's presentation discusses scientific aspects of the project, and in consequence the Situation, Problem and Solution are redefined, the focus being changed from the habitat's national relevance to its scientific value. At the beginning the term 'habitat' is defined: *Habitat to baza, w której przebywać będą przyszli kolonizatorzy najpierw Księżyca a potem Marsa* [Habitat is the base for future colonists, first of the Moon and then of Mars]. The definition presents the colonization of the Moon and Mars as self-evident, and as such it should be accepted by the audience (Situation).

Should there arise any skepticism, in the later part of the same paragraph the authors refer to the opinions of space agencies, whose authority is boosted by the attributes 'powerful' and 'international', and self-evidence of the future manned flight to the Moon by the adjective 'logical':

> *Potężne międzynarodowe agencje kosmiczne patrzą na Księżyc jako logiczny krok poprzedzający misję na Marsa. To tam odbędą się pierwsze załogowe lądowania na innym globie od czasu misji Apollo.*
>
> [Powerful international space agencies perceive the Moon as a logical step before the mission to Mars. This is where the first manned landing on another globe will take place since the Apollo mission.]

The above-described Situation entails a Problem: *Dlatego ważne jest, aby dogłębnie zrozumieć jak zachowuje się załoga podczas długiego pobytu w zamknięciu oraz izolacji od świata zewnętrznego.* [It is therefore important to understand in depth how the crew reacts to a long stay in isolation and isolation from the outside world.] The Problem is marked here as essential (*ważne jest* 'it is important') so that the audience become aware of its relevance and urgency of finding an effective Solution.

The Solution is immediately presented:

> *Wychodzimy na przeciw przyszłym potrzebom badawczo-naukowym i budujemy w Polsce analogowy habitat, który posłuży jako platforma do nauki. Wiedzę tak zdobytą będzie można potem wykorzystać, kiedy przyjdzie czas na budowę prawdziwej bazy.*
>
> [We address in advance the future research and scientific needs, and we are building an analog habitat in Poland which will serve as a research platform. The knowledge gained can be used when the time comes to build the real base.]

A link with the Problem is signaled by the noun *potrzeby* 'needs', whereas the Solution is signaled by the constructions *Wychodzimy na przeciw* 'We address in advance', *posłuży jako* 'will serve as' and the participle *zdobytą* 'gained', which all semantically convey a positive Evaluation element of the Solution proposed.

The project's presentation ends with a bold-typed slogan which again refers to the national relevance of the project: *Polska ma szansę stać się liderem tego typu badań!* [Poland has a chance to become the leader of this type of research!] The slogan repeats the national aspect of the Problem: that Poland lags behind in space research programmes, whereas the analog habitat provides an opportunity (Solution) to move the country the forefront in this domain.

As far as the definition of the project's target group is concerned, the analog Moon/Mars habitat may seem of little direct relevance for the general public, inasmuch as it serves primarily research purposes. As a result, the target group would be much narrower than that of the *efood* application or the longboard (see sections 5.1.1 and 5.1.2), and in turn the project's presentation may not refer so much to the more mundane needs of average customers as the descriptions of the other two projects. The analysis shows that at least two target groups are identified in the Moon/Mars habitat's presentation: scientists (e.g. *budujemy w Polsce analogowy habitat, który posłuży jako platforma do nauki* [we build in Poland an analog habitat, which will serve as a platform for research]) and habitat residents, selected from a group of volunteers, who will live in the habitat for a specified time[7]. It is also anticipated that the habitat may be a venue open to visitors, and hence may attract the general public.

Interestingly, at one point of the commentary it is emphasized that the volunteers' selection criteria may prioritize participants of specific age and nationality: *Analogowa baza planetarna to szansa dla wielu młodych Polaków* [An analog planetary base is a chance for many young Poles] (00:01:03–00:01:05).

5.2. Kickstarter projects

5.2.1. LightSail: A Revolutionary Solar Sailing Spacecraft

LightSail: A Revolutionary Solar Sailing Spacecraft (https://www.kickstarter.com/projects/theplanetarysociety/lightsail-a-revolutionary-solar-sailing-spacecraft?ref=tag; DOA: 25.05.2017) is the most backed and successful Kickstarter project in the category *Technology + Innovative* (as for 25th May 2017), gaining 1,241,615 USD, against 200,000 USD applied for, from 23,331 backers.

The project, a solar-powered space sail, is presented in the promotional video (https://ksr-video.imgix.net/projects/1744252/video-535670-h264_high.mp4; DOA: 12.06.2017), which discusses the details of the craft and points out its advantages over other, already operational types of space propulsion. Consequently, LightSail is discursively constructed as the Solution, whereas alternative types of propulsion are claimed or at least presupposed to have some deficiencies, and hence constitute the Problem. This contrast is further emphasized with markers of positive Evaluation of the Solution and/or negative Evaluation of the Problem, e.g. "With solar sailing in principle you can **go vast distances** and do it **in relatively small amounts of time**" (00:01:18–00:01:23; emphasis mine), or "We can go to the moon **and beyond for a very low cost**" (00:01:36–00:01:39; emphasis mine), or "Solar sailing can take us to the moon, to other planets, and **even** to interstellar space. Your help with our Kickstarter campaign can help drive the future of cube SATs for **low-cost exploration**." (00:01:43–00:01:54; emphasis mine)

In the later part of the film the Problem and the Solution are, however, redefined: LightSail is presented as the Solution to the Problem which is no longer

7 The first casting is reported to have attracted 50+ candidates for six places in the first two-week mission in the habitat (https://polakpotrafi.pl/projekt/baza-ksiezycowa-pod-krakowem?utm_source=projects; DOA: 13.06.2017).

scientific or technical, but administrative and political, as pointed out by Neil deGrasse Tyson, Board member of the Planetary Society, which manages the project:

> You know NASA. You pay tax, tax money and that goes to fund NASA and then somebody else decides what NASA does. In the Planetary Society the membership decides so there's a sense of participation, I think, is without equal. And when you see the thing launched, you say "Hey, I had something to do with that directly". That's a good feeling. (00:02:15–00:02:37)

The Problem as discursively constructed in the above excerpt concerns the monopoly of a governmental agency to carry out space research in the USA. While NASA is funded with US residents' taxes, taxpayers have limited influence on the agency's decision-making process, and cannot contribute to its research programmes. The LightSail project is claimed to provide the Solution to this Problem: (1) organizationally, as the project's decision-making process operates democratically within the Planetary Society, which invites new members without strict criteria for entry, and (2) financially, as crowdfunding entails voluntary and goal-specific support, and also provides more transparency for the investor than taxpaying does for the taxpayer. In the course of the project's presentation references to these two aspects overlap, a consequence of which is the related synthesis of the roles of the audience addressed: financial investors and decisionmakers in/contributors to the LightSail research project.

The two above-discussed facets of the Problem-Solution structure (technological and administrative/political) are often shown to be mutually related. For instance, there is the financial consideration mentioned: the technological Problem (costly rocket-propulsion space programmes) is related to the administrative/political Problem (costly rocket-propulsion space programmes are run by NASA – and funded from taxes), which are contrasted with the technological Solution (cost-effective solar-powered LightSail) and the administrative/political Solution (LightSail is developed by an NGO and funded from voluntary donations).

This synthesis of the two aspects of the Problem and the Solution is perhaps best expressed in the address of Bill Nye, CEO of Planetary Society. The passage begins as follows:

> Imagine it: unlimited free energy from the Sun will provide CubeSats with propulsion and revolutionize access to space for low-cost citizen projects – projects like ours or by teams of students and faculty at universities.

Here Nye recapitulates the Problem and the Solution, alluding to their twofold nature (technological and political/administrative). He integrates elements of Evaluation with each of them, either verbatim (in the case of the Solution: "unlimited free energy" as propulsion; "low-cost citizen projects") or implicitly (in the case of the

Problem: limited and costly energy of rocket-propulsion spacecraft; costly government projects related to NASA rocket-propulsion spacecraft).

The next part of Nye's address refers to the technological aspect of the LightSail (Solution), attributing positive qualities to it (positive Evaluation), and presupposing that their opposites are inherent to the current space programmes (Problem): "This means that spacecraft, especially small ones like CubeSats, **won't have to carry heavy fuels into orbit**, and that the **acceleration will be continuous**." (emphasis mine)

Then Nye addresses the political/administrative aspect: "Even better, this is a journey that is directly funded by the world's citizens, like you, rather than by governments. LightSail™ is truly 'the people's spacecraft'." The discourse marker "even better" suggests that the political/administrative aspect is more significant to Nye than the technological one. Again, the LightSail (Solution) is positively Evaluated, in this case with reference to democratic axiology: the concepts of "world's citizens" and "the people's" are contrasted with "governments".

In the remaining part of his address Bill Nye refers to both aspects of the Problem and the Solution, the latter being complemented with markers of positive Evaluation, e.g. "LightSail is a **huge contribution** to space science and exploration" (emphasis mine), or "To learn more about this **amazing** project, check out our dedicated website ..." (emphasis mine). The same role is played by the metaphor of pathfinder, presupposing the limited exploration capacity of rocket-propulsion spacecraft, and, in the light of the attributes given to LightSail, also its costliness: "we will use CubeSats **to open new paths** beyond Earth and, one day, potentially to other planets with an **inexpensive, inexhaustible** means of propulsion" (emphasis mine).

Positive Evaluation of the Solution seems to intensify as Nye's address progresses, leading to the climax in the last two sentences. First, the author refers to LightSail as "this **epic** point in space exploration history" (emphasis mine), and then ends on an even more audacious note: "LightSail propulsion truly holds the promise – dare I say it? – to change the world!" Both these statements increase the disparity between the Problem and the Solution, the former already reaching its operational limits, and the latter being promising enough to be worth implementing.

Representing the Problem and the Solution in relation to NASA and its space programmes vs. Planetary Society's LightSail is also found in another passage from the project's presentation (text):

> Over 19,000 backers and another 42,000 Planetary Society members joining together to power a mission to demonstrate a CubeSat propulsion system at a fraction of the cost of a government program. With each of us doing just a little bit more, we can make big thing happen. That's the power of democratized space exploration!

In the above excerpt the authors of the project contrast their venture with a government space programme, stressing the former's social character (cf. the use of numbers referring to the people involved financially and organizationally) and cost-effectiveness (as compared with expenditures and costs inherent to "a government program"). In the second part of the excerpt the Problem-Solution is formulated in political terms, also alluding to the fundamental values of a democratic system, as expressed with the inclusive 1st person plural pronouns ("each of **us**" and "**we** can make…"). In the same line of argumentation, one of the sections' headlines reads "LightSail: **The People's** Spacecraft" (emphasis mine), placing the project in line with democratic axiology, and presupposing that current spacecraft technologies are anything but.

Of relevance for this topic is *The Impact* section, which recapitulates the essence of the Problem and the Solution, along with their negative and positive Evaluation, respectively. However, unlike in the previous sections, NASA is no longer represented as the antagonist, but a possible beneficiary of the Solution – provided that it considers abandoning rocket-propulsion programmes (thus eventually solving its Problem, at least from LightSail developers' point of view):

> Through this program, **we're making it possible for other groups, including NASA, to utilize this innovative propulsion technique** on CubeSats and other small spacecraft – opening the door to a huge variety of low-cost missions throughout the solar system. With LightSail as the pathfinder, CubeSats propelled solely by sunlight will be able to regularly leave Earth for interplanetary destinations.
>
> (emphasis mine)

Let me now turn to the way(s) the target group of the project is defined in discourse. As has been noted in section 5.1.3, the authors of a primarily scientific space-related project need to cope with the problem of its limited direct relevance for the general public. In the case of the analog Moon/Mars habitat this issue was addressed by (1) inviting any person interested to take part in the casting for voluntary residents of the habitat, and (2) emphasizing the national identity of the project (e.g. the first analog habitat in Poland, an opportunity for many young Poles etc.) By contrast, the authors of the LightSail focus on democratic values and social dimension of the project to show its general significance and to address a relatively broad audience as its target group, not only in terms of co-financing the project, but also in enabling them to have a say in the decision-making process as members of Planetary Society. In other words, however niche a space research project is and however narrow a target group it usually concerns, the LightSail project – and analog Moon/Mars habitat alike – overturns this stereotype.

Finally, speaking about the project's presentation, it should be noted that apart from promotional videos and the body text, the project's Kickstarter website also contains distinct frames which either present key content (e.g. the project's step-by-step schedule) or reiterate the project's authors' key opinions, often in an abbreviated form, similar to marketing slogans. As for the latter, a relevant example is found below the project's step-by-step schedule:

> Once these milestones have been achieved, we will demonstrate solar sailing is the future of citizen-funded, low cost, accessible space exploration. You can help make this revolutionary dream a reality and become part of something truly historic.

This concise form recapitulates the main advantages of the Solution, hence the accumulation of markers of positive Evaluation: "the future […], citizen-funded, low cost, accessible […] revolutionary […] truly historic". Another frame, one concluding the project's description, ends with a powerful statement by Bill Nye ("Together we can change the world"), which emphasizes the project's relevance in the global scale, and defines humankind as its target group. The statement rephrases the claim Bill Nye made in his address ("LightSail propulsion truly holds the promise – dare I say it? – to change the world!"; see above).

5.2.2. Ossic X

"OSSIC X: The first 3D audio headphones calibrated to you" (https://www.kickstarter.com/projects/248983394/ossic-x-the-first-3d-audio-headphones-calibrated-t?ref=tag; DOA: 25.05.2017) is Kickstarter's 2nd most backed and successful project in the category *Technology + Innovative* (as for 25th May 2017), gaining 2,708,472 USD, against 100,000 USD applied for, from 10,263 backers.

The project is presented on the basis of the Situation-Problem-Solution structure, which already appears at the beginning of the promotional video (https://ksr-video.imgix.net/projects/2317622/video-639733-h264_high.mp4; DOA: 18.05.2017). The Situation is presented as follows:

> Sound is arguably the most important of the senses: it conveys emotions, tells stories and helps us navigate our world. While we can only see what is directly in front of us, we can hear everything from all around all of the time.
>
> (00:00:00–00:00:14)

As can be noted, the Situation states a general truth ("Sound is arguably the most important of the senses"), which is justified with commonsense arguments derived from everyday experience ("it conveys emotions, tells stories and helps us navigate our way"). Inclusive 1st person plural pronouns represent these experiences as shared by the speaker and the audience.

The second sentence of the above excerpt signals the approaching transition to the Problem, which indeed follows in the narrative: "When was the last time your headphones made you feel like you were actually there? Not just identifying the sound but feeling transported?" (00:00:14–00:00:22) Here the Problem is stated in the question about a personal experience, which presupposes (especially when combined with the second question) a particular answer as intended by the author ("Long time ago" appears to be the case here).

The Solution is announced forthwith – "I would like to introduce you to the Ossic X" – which is followed with a summary of technical qualities of the product, integrated with their positive Evaluation (*advanced, incredibly realistic*): "OSSIC X headphones combine advanced 3D audio algorithms with head tracking and anatomy calibration to create incredibly realistic 3D sound." (00:00:29–00:00:38)

It should be noted that the Situation-Problem-Solution sequence presented at the beginning of Ossic X's promotional video is constructed not only at the textual level (in the off commentary), but also with background sound effects and images. Specifically, when the Situation is presented, the video shows a woman, zooming in on the profile of her head, on which motion images of nature phenomena are displayed (e.g. the blooming flower). The images are paired with sounds of nature in the background. When the narrator turns to the Problem, both the images displayed on the woman's face and the accompanying sounds change dramatically. Now there can be seen images of man-made artifacts, specifically noise-generating ones (presented in the crescendoing order: street traffic, rock concert, space shuttle start). They are accompanied with the equally crescendoing background noise in the video, which eventually drowns the off comment. The ear-piercing drone then ends abruptly as the woman puts on Ossic X headphones and the narrator introduces them as the Solution. The woman turns to en face, and the previously dim interior is brightened: the woman and her headphones are now clearly visible.

In the further part of the video the Situation-Problem-Solution structure is reproduced, though with more focus on technical aspects of headphones: inaccurate technology of traditional headphones (Problem) and advanced sound-reproducing technology used in Ossic X (Solution). First, the narrator draws the Situation, referring to the audience's commonsense knowledge embedded in everyday experience: "In real life sound comes from everywhere and the way you hear the world is unique only to you." (00:01:19–00:01:24) This fragment is illustrated with a video excerpt depicting an anonymous man walking down the street, with different common sources of sound being marked with animated circles representing the spreading sound waves.

Then comes the transition point between Situation and Problem, marked with the contrastive conjunction *but*:

> It is based on your position in space, the size of your head, even the shape of your ears but with traditional and even surround sound headphones these elements are not taken into account. In effect you are removed from the sound equation. This makes for an incredibly small audio experience where sounds can only come from a few places instead of anywhere.
>
> (00:01:24–00:01:43)

Before the transition point the Situation mentions three variables crucial to understanding the Problem (other headphones) and the Solution (Ossic X): while the former largely ignore these variables, the latter takes them all into account. The verbal explanation is supplemented with a simplified graphic illustration of the three variables, which are later crossed out so as to represent the fact that they are largely neglected in traditional headphones.

The Solution is then discussed in detail by Ossic's CEO Jason Riggs, who points out its qualities (positive Evaluation): "OSSIC X is the **world's first** headphone that **instantly** calibrates to the listener, creating the **ultimate** 3D listening experience" (emphasis mine). Two visual examples are used to represent the sound quality rendered by Ossic X headphones: feeling like being at a concert while actually riding a train, and feeling like being at the cinema while actually watching TV at home. Further positive Evaluation of Ossic X is provided by experts, e.g. Ty Ahmad-Taylor, CEO of THX, Ossic's contractor ("it was really **revolutionary**", 00:02:17–00:02:18, emphasis mine) or German Heller, co-founder of 3-Dar, a VR, film and animation studio ("Ossic is really bringing a **whole new** element here [...] it's a **more powerful** feeling of being there", 00:02:46–00:02:56, emphasis mine). These other voices contribute to the favorable representation of the Solution (see also below).

Next the video focuses on certain technological aspects of Ossic X, in particular its capability of customizing the parameters to the user's individual anatomy. The Problem-Solution structure is also applied in this context. The speaker (Ossic's CTO Joy Lyons) first signals the Problem (How to create an accurate and realistic sound experience?), and then claims that Ossic X employs technological solutions which effectively address this Problem: "The key to creating an accurate and realistic sound experience is knowing the listeners individual auditory anatomy and how it influences the way we hear sound." (00:03:51–00:03:59)

When the commentary progresses, presenting different aspects of the headphones' self-adjustment to individual needs, the video shows a sequence of anonymous individuals of different age, gender and ethnicity, illustrating Ossic X's automatic adaptability to different cranial and ear anatomies. Diversity of the individuals presented confirms the broad target group as intended by the product's developers.

The functionally corresponding sections in the main text of the project's presentation are *The background* and *The Ossic solution*. The former covers the Situation and the Problem, and presents the general context of sound reception by humans (Situation) and the limitations of traditional headphones (Problem):

> WE ALL HEAR THE WORLD DIFFERENTLY BASED ON OUR ANATOMY
> How we hear the world is not a one-size-fits all situation. It's our physical anatomy that plays a critical role in defining how sound enters our ears. This is called our head related transfer function, or HRTF. Our individual HRTF is based on:
>
> - Our position in space
> - The size of our head
> - The shape of our ears

The section's opening claim (capitalized) states a general truth (cf. inclusive 1st person plural pronouns) and presupposes the shared character of the experience described. The main paragraph begins with a transition-point sentence: it refers to the Situation ("we hear the world"), but also presupposes a possible Problem ("is not a one-size-fits all"). Then the author explains the role of individual anatomy in sound reception, and specifically of HRTF (head related transfer function).

While the first paragraph does not identify the essence of the Problem, the next part states it directly ("traditional headphones"):

> TRADITIONAL HEADPHONES DON'T ACCOUNT FOR OUR ANATOMY
> With traditional headphones the listeners anatomy is not taken into account. This makes for an incredibly small listening experience, where sound remains close to your head rather than around you. This leads to:
>
> - A "close to your head" listening experience
> - Inaccurate ability to place sounds in space
> - Degradation in overall sound quality

The paragraph also enumerates the drawbacks of traditional headphones, repeating the main point of criticism (traditional headphones neglect the user's individual anatomy) in the headline and the first sentence. Once identified, the Problem is negatively evaluated ("doesn't take into account", "not taken into account", "incredibly small […] experience"). Further critical remarks appear in the bullet-point list.

The Solution is presented only in the following section, *The Ossic solution*:

> CALIBRATION PUTS YOU BACK INTO THE LISTENING EQUATION
> OSSIC X calibrates to the individual listener's head and ear feature, **increasing** overall sound quality and **ensuring** the **most accurate** sound placement, making for a listening experience that's ten times **more immersive** than current technologies.
>
> HOW IT WORKS
> The OSSIC calibration process starts as soon as you put the headphones on. The data is **instantly** paired with our **smart** algorithms to determine **accurate** sound playback based on your anatomy and position. No laboratories required.
>
> (emphasis mine)

The section also opens with a general claim, in the headline ("Calibration puts you back into the listening equation"), which is accompanied with a graphic representation of Ossic X's calibration to individual anatomical and environmental parameters. The following two paragraphs discuss the details of the calibration technology, providing technical details of the Solution and their positive Evaluation.

The promotional video ends on an audacious note: "Together we can shape the future of audio."[8] This final claim confirms the product's innovative potential and puts future customers into the active role of contributors to its eventual success.

Coming back to the main text of the project's presentation, the Problem-Solution text pattern is a recurrent structure here. As early as in the introductory section (*Introducing OSSIC X*) the Solution (Ossic X) is presented, and its advantages are listed (positive Evaluation). By contrast, the Problem (traditional headphones) is rather presupposed than stated, and so are its specific drawbacks:

> THE WORLD'S MOST ADVANCED 3D AUDIO HEADPHONE
> OSSIC X is the world's first 3D audio headphone that instantly calibrates to the listener, increasing the sense of auditory space, and acoustically recreating the way you hear the world everyday. By pairing advanced 3D audio algorithms with head-tracking and individual anatomy calibration, we deliver incredibly accurate 3D sound to your ears. Experience music like never before. Get more immersed in virtual reality. Bring gaming to the next level.

As can be seen, the Solution is shown to have global relevance (***world's** most advanced…*; ***world's** first 3D….*) Markers of positive Evaluation include superlative adjectives (*most advanced*), ordinal number *first*, and verbs denoting the headphones' superior position in comparison with others (*increasing*). References to shared experience (*the world everyday*) indicate that the product is targeted at the general public rather than a specific group of customers (the question of

8 Cf. a similar claim made in the final sentence of LightSail's description: "Together we can change the world!" (section 5.2.1).

defining the target group in Ossic X's description is discussed below). In the last three sentences of the above passage there appear imperative clauses, which place the reader in the role of the potential customer of Ossic X. Also, each of these sentences contains a comparative element (*like never before*; *more immersed*; *to the next level*), which further emphasizes Ossic X's (Solution) superior position over traditional headphones (Problem). The comparison between the Problem and the Solution is also reproduced graphically: the former shows a human figure located on a 2D plane, whereas the latter reproduces the same image but with additional circles encapsulating the figure in a 3D sphere. Commonsense knowledge is sufficient to indicate the advantage of the latter in terms of rendering surround sound.

The Situation-Problem-Solution pattern also structures the section *Benefits of Ossic X 3D audio*, which opens with a brief argument referring to commonsense knowledge (Situation); its taken-for-granted truth-value is stressed with 1st person plural inclusive pronoun:

> Audio is a crucial part of the way we experience content. By implementing accurate 3D audio, any content can take the listener to new places by improving the following [...]

The second sentence presupposes the possible Problem – Is "accurate 3D audio" rendered by all sound technologies? – which is then confirmed as actual Problem since Ossic X is claimed to "improv[e] the following". That the Solution is indeed Ossic X is already signaled in the title of the section, specifically in the marker of positive Evaluation *benefits*.

Also the following subsections are structured along the Situation-Problem-Solution pattern, each of them discussing a different context of application for Ossic X: *Ossic X for virtual reality*, *Ossic X for gaming*, *Ossic X for movies*, and *Ossic X for music*. For instance, *Ossic X for virtual reality*, like the section's introductory passage, opens with a general claim referring to the author's and the audience's shared knowledge:

> In virtual reality, sound is key. With accurate 3D sound we can give a sense of space and direct your attention to elements outside your field of view for a more immersive experience.
>
> - Drastically **improved** sound localization
> - **Increased** sense of presence
> - Accurately render sound in any x,y,z coordinate in space
>
> (emphasis mine)

The second sentence presupposes the possible Problem – Is "accurate 3D sound" rendered by all VR sound devices? Again the Problem is presupposed to be real (not all VR sound devices render 3D sound accurately), as the comparative *more immersive* indicates. As is announced in the headline, Ossic X is the Solution to this Problem, also in the light of its qualities (positive Evaluation) listed underneath – note that they also employ comparative lexis (*improved*, *increased*) to presuppose Ossic X's advantage over other headphones.

Finally, one should mention the section *Creating the next generation of 3D audio*, which specifies the areas of the project which the crowdfunding campaign is to support. It also features elements of the Problem-Solution pattern, but redefines the Problem for which Ossic X is supposed to provide the Solution:

> Our goal is to not only develop a product, but help educate the world on the potential of what a 10X improvement in audio immersion can sound like. To do this, we need your support from this initial campaign to not only fund our production, but also get the word out about what we're developing.

In the above passage the Problem is stated in a more abstract way than before, namely in terms of global consumers' ignorance of the accurate sound rendering, unattainable with traditional audio systems but already achievable with Ossic X. Consequently, the Solution does not lie as much in delivering the ready-made product as in educating the potential customers about Ossic X's advantages over alternative products. As can be assumed, social media marketing might play a crucial role in this task ("get the word out about what we're developing").

As far as defining the target group for Ossic X is concerned, relevant signals are interwoven in the Problem-Solution structure. In general, the project's presentation foregrounds Ossic X headphones' multi-purpose applicability, listing such contexts of use as virtual reality, gaming, movies, and music listening. Considering that each of these contexts has its relatively broad group of participants, their sum constitutes a large and diversified target group of potential customers. This is further emphasized in the commentary by means of mass nouns e.g. *people* ("our mission is to change the way people hear sound") and the frequently used general 2nd person pronoun (e.g. "we deliver incredibly accurate 3D sound to your ears", or "OSSIC changes the way you listen to music").

Representing a broad and diversified global target group is not only achieved verbally, but also visually: at least fifteen anonymous persons are shown in Ossic X's promotional video with Ossic X headphones on. Apart from the product's testers, there are also users presented in everyday situations: playing computer games, listening to music at home or when commuting, playing musical instruments, etc. They differ in age, gender and ethnicity, which all contribute to the discursive (multi-modal) construction of the target group as broad, global and diversified.

Of particular relevance to this issue is the concluding section of the project's presentation, "Help us shape the future of the audio". The title itself underlines the product's global relevance, and expresses the authors' intention to reach customers worldwide. The focus on the global impact to be achieved jointly by Ossic X's developers and the backers resembles similar marketing slogans used in the presentations of the solar-power longboard (*Stwórzmy razem ostateczny produkt, którym będę chciał podbić świat* [Let's create together the final product that I want to conquer the world with], see section 5.1.2) and LightSail ("Together we can change the world", see section 5.2.1). This claim is then rephrased in the passage's thematic sentence: "We're redefining the way we hear audio in headphones".

5.2.3. Knocki

Knocki: Make Any Surface Smart (https://www.kickstarter.com/projects/knocki/knocki-make-any-surface-smart?ref=ta; DOA: 25.05.2017) is the third most backed and successful Kickstarter project in the category *Technology + Innovative* (as for 25th May 2017), gaining 1,144,399 USD, against 35,000 USD applied for, from 8,897 backers.

As far as the Problem-Solution pattern is concerned, a cursory glance at Knocki's presentation reveals that its authors base their argument on the product's multiple applications in daily routines, presenting (in text, images and videos alike) everyday activities performed without (Problem) and with (Solution) Knocki. The problem, however, is that while Knocki is shown to facilitate many daily routines, and hence should be targeted at a relatively broad, global target group, most of its functions are operational only in so-called smart houses, which in turn largely limits the group of potential customers.

The Problem-Solution pattern is recurrent in the project's promotional video and its text description. In the former (https://ksr-video.imgix.net/projects/2424950/video-668848-h264_high.mp4; DOA: 22.06.2017) it appears at the beginning of the commentary:

> We are surrounded by technology. It is entering our homes and helping us automate daily tasks. But I find myself thinking there has to be a more natural and accessible way to control the devices around us. If the goal of automation is to simplify our lives, why does it feel so complicated? Our goal as a company is to solve this. Say hello to Knocki.
> (00:00:02–00:00:25)

The Situation is delineated in the first two sentences of the above passage. Inclusive 1st person plural pronouns account for the taken-for-granted character of the propositions, which refer to shared experience of the speaker and the general public. The transition point between the Situation and the Problem is marked with the contrastive *but*, which introduces a personal opinion of the author ("But I find myself thinking…") The Problem itself, however, is presupposed rather than stated verbatim, by means of the comparative ("more natural and accessible way") and the adverb of degree *so* used in the following rhetorical question. These discursive devices indicate that (1) there exist certain Solutions to the Problem of automating daily tasks, yet (2) these Solutions are neither natural nor easily accessible, and, importantly, are complicated, and so (3) they constitute another Problem in themselves. The Solution to the latter Problem – Knocki – is identified in the concluding part of the passage.

Next the speaker presents the Solution in detail, along with its positive Evaluation. The focus of positive Evaluation is on the product's compact size, multi-functionality (paired with ease of use) and customizability:

> Knocki is a **small elegant** device that **instantly** transforms ordinary surfaces in your environment into remote controls. Using Knocki couldn't be **easier**: Take it out of the box, pick a place to put it, select a surface to attach it to, and then define all the things you'd like Knocki to do. Knocki **can control** a **wide** variety of devices around us but the **true beauty** of our technology is that what it **can do** is **only limited by your imagination**.
> (00:00:27–00:00:57, emphasis mine)

In other parts of the commentary Knocki (Solution) is positively Evaluated in relation to its other qualities, e.g. its compatibility with popular smart applications ("You can enjoy using Knocki from **anywhere**. The number of devices and software that Knocki interact with is **rapidly growing** every day", emphasis mine), or esthetics and design ("[w]e **carefully** chose every material and finish for Knocki [...] Knocki **blends in** in your environment and also looks **beautiful** on your surfaces", emphasis mine).

The same Problem-Solution structure is recapitulated in the text of the project's description:

> **Turn Any Surface into a Remote Control**
>
> Technology should make our lives easier, so why does controlling it feel so complicated? An endless maze of mobile apps, smart switches, and other interfaces create a confusing and fragmented experience.
>
> We believe there's a better way – Knocki offers the simplest, most natural, and accessible way to control the world around you. You've never seen anything like it!

Unlike the commentary in the promotional video, the above passage does not present the Situation explicitly, and immediately proceeds to the Problem. The Problem is stated in the rhetorical question ("why does controlling it feel so complicated?"), following a general claim ("Technology should make our lives easier"). The Problem is therefore identified with current home-use technology, which is negatively Evaluated for its complication and lack of compatibility, which in turn translates into the users' necessity to manage "an endless maze of mobile apps, smart switches, and other interfaces". The resulting confusion and "fragmented experience" add further elements of negative Evaluation of the Problem. The Solution is brought with Knocki, positively Evaluated as "a better way" and, more specifically, praised for its simplicity, ergonomics and ease-of-use ("simplest, most natural, and accessible").

Interestingly, Knocki's presentation contains elements of "comparative advertising", much more evident than in any other projects discussed so far. Specifically, Knocki is contrasted with sound- and voice-control technologies and smart switches, some of which are identified with actual brands. This comparison, in favour of Knocki, also involves the Problem-Solution pattern to show advantages of the Solution (Knocki) as set against the drawbacks of alternative technologies.

Problem-Solution-based comparative advertising appears in Knocki's promotional video, with critical remarks expressed about "technologies that rely on sound or voice control", negatively Evaluated as "unreliable and confusing to use" and likely to "be triggered accidentally". The commentary is supplemented with related images of problems caused by sound- and voice-control applications: a man who claps his hands and incidentally switches on the floor lamp rather than the TV set as intended, or the smartphone displaying the message "Didn't get that" in consequence of misrecognizing the voice command. Comparative advertising is most evident in the use of the image of the Clapper, a popular American sound-activated electrical switch for household appliances.

Yet it is in the main text of the project's description that Problem-Solution-based comparative advertising is presented in great detail, in two sections, *What About Voice Control?* and *What about Smart Switches and Buttons?* The titles of the sections reflect the possible questions a potential customer can ask, based on his/her knowledge of alternative technologies (voice controlled devices and smart switches/buttons, respectively). This hypothetical dialogue between the reader/customer and Knocki's developers enables the latter to compare Knocki with alternative technologies, and point out the advantages of the former (Solution) against the drawbacks inherent to the latter (Problem). The two sections also contain many markers of Evaluation, both positive towards the Solution and negative towards the Problem.

The first section, *What About Voice Control?*, begins with delineating the Situation: "Voice control is everywhere", which claim refers to commonsense knowledge grounded in the consumers' everyday experience. The next sentence refers to specific solutions (using the company's and product's registered names), which are shown to be potentially useful, but in the end prove not to be free of certain drawbacks (Problem): "Services like Apple's Siri and Amazon's Alexa can simplify tasks, but often don't work as expected."

Then follows a list of four specific Problems inherent to voice control technologies, each being juxtaposed with the Solution offered by Knocki: *Background sounds, Can distrurb others, It often misunderstands*, and *Can't use multiple voice controllers in the same space.* Due to space limitations I will illustrate the Problem-Solution pattern as is used in the last passage:

> **Can't use multiple voice controllers in the same space:** Good luck putting a voice controller on your nightstand, and then another one on your partner's nightstand. You'll have both controllers responding simultaneously creating smart home chaos. Knocki recognizes gestures on a specific surface so you can have multiple Knockis in the same room or other space without conflict. Knocki allows you to personalize controls to the surfaces near you.

The passage identifies as the Problem inherent to voice-control technology the fact that the user "[c]an't use multiple voice controllers in the same space". In an ironic comment ("Good luck…") the author signals a possible Problem. First, the Situation is constructed, referring to a shared-experience context (a couple in the bedroom): "putting a voice controller on your nightstand, and then another one on your partner's nightstand". Should the effect of this Situation be difficult to be derived, it is presented in the next sentence ("You'll have both controllers responding simultaneously"), with the ultimate consequence being vividly depicted as "smart home chaos". The second part of the passage presents Knocki as the Solution to the Problem, along with its positive Evaluation ("recognizes […] without conflict […] allows").

Voice-control technology is identified as the Problem also visually, in the adjacent image which depicts three voice-control devices, including two applications in mobile phones. Voice-control technology is negatively Evaluated, here with a brief ironic slogan: "voice works… kinda".

A similar comparison between Knocki and alternative technologies is presented in the next section, *What about smart switches and buttons?* As in the preceding section on voice-control devices, the section's introductory sentence acknowledges potential advantages of smart switches and buttons ("Smart buttons and switches can also automate tasks"), which is, however, outbalanced by their several drawbacks ("but they have a few "pressing" problems"). Again Knocki is shown to be superior to alternative technologies due to a number of reasons, each of which is discussed in a separate section: *Don't blend in, Must be pressed or flipped, Not as reliable or responsive*, and *Limited functionality.* To illustrate how they are structured along the moves of the Problem-Solution pattern I analyse the first passage:

> **Don't blend in:** Wall switches and buttons aren't so pretty to look at. Knocki can be placed under or behind surfaces, so you don't even have to see it to use it. But if you do mount it within view, it blends beautifully with your surfaces.

The passage refers to the context of household and its appliances familiar to readers/customers ("wall switches and buttons"), i.e. the Situation. This context entails the Problem: wall switches and buttons "aren't so pretty to look at". Knocki is then presented as the Solution to this Problem, along with its positive Evaluation referring to the two possible ways of installation: hidden ("you don't even have to see it") and displayed ("it blends beautifully with your surfaces").

Finally, the Problem-Solution pattern is found in the concluding section of the text of the project's presentation, *Our story*, where it is employed to present the origins of the idea behind Knocki:

> **Our Story**
>
> Co-founders Jake & Ohad have been friends for years, but their "aha moment" happened more recently over a family get-together. They were watching one of their small children stacking up boxes to reach a light switch. That observation led them to ask a simple question, "Why not turn walls and other common surfaces into control interfaces?"
>
> That was the spark that set them on their path to develop Knocki, and this Kickstarter campaign marks an exciting milestone. Building a successful company, growing a talented team, and developing an amazing product is full of hard work and perseverance, and we thank you for supporting us as we bring Knocki to the world!

As can be noted, the passage opens with a personal narrative, which refers to the context of a family meeting (Situation), a shared experience for the general public, and a specific event which occurred on this occasion – a child trying to reach a light switch – similarly familiar to most readers/customers.[9] The event itself is discursively constructed as the Problem, alluded to in the image of the child needing to stack up boxes to reach the switch, and then signaled in the *Why not...* question. Searching for the answer to this question, from realizing the essence of the Problem (the "aha moment") to the ready-made product, denotes a gradual process of developing the Solution. The Solution itself is positively Evaluated in the later part of the passage ("**amazing** product", emphasis mine), and so are the project's fundraising campaign ("**exciting milestone**", emphasis mine), the company ("a **successful** company", emphasis mine) and its staff ("**talented** team", emphasis mine). The passage ends with repeating the company's intention to

---

9 A similar example is found in the presentation of the *efood* project (see section 5.1.1), where the narrative presents a short trip of friends as a point of departure for identifying the Problem and developing the Solution.

market the product worldwide due to its assumed relevance to the global customer ("we bring Knocki to the world").

As for defining the target audience, at one point of the promotional video Knocki's CEO, Jake Boshernitzan, claims "We couldn't be more excited about how this product is going to change lives and bring joy to **people everywhere**" (00:03:13–00:03:18, emphasis mine), which shows that the intended target group is global general public.

Knocki's developers envisage that their product will be widely used in households, and hence the customer base would be broad and diversified. A relevant example is the following passage from the promotional video's off commentary:

> Knocki [...] transforms ordinary surfaces in your environment into remote controls. Using Knocki couldn't be easier: Take it out of the box, pick a place to put it, select a surface to attach it to, and then define all the things you'd like Knocki to do. Knocki can control a wide variety of devices around us but the true beauty of our technology is that what it can do is only limited by your imagination.
>
> (00:00:27–00:00:57)

Due to its key qualities (in particular ease of use and customizability) the device is supposed to meet diverse expectations of individual customers, and its installation and operation should pose no problem even to an unskilled user. All these aspects considered, Knocki should theoretically attract attention of anyone. Theoretically, since – as is later noted in the commentary – Knocki is primarily designed for smart home use, and otherwise it offers a relatively limited number of functions ("But even if you're new to the smart technology world you can still use Knocki for simple functions around your home").

As can also be noted in the passage above, the authors address the reader as if he or she already were the user of Knocki: a sequence of the imperative clauses resembles a step-by-step installation procedure as is often featured in electronic devices' instruction booklets ("Take it out of the box, pick a place to put it, select a surface to attach it to, and then define all the things you'd like Knocki to do.")

A corresponding section in the main text of the description is *Who is Knocki for?*, which reiterates the claim that the product is perfectly useful when paired only with a smart phone and Wi-Fi internet connection:

> Knocki isn't just for people with smart homes or high-tech offices. Knocki works well anywhere with a WiFi internet connection. It allows you to "tap" into many powerful functions, even if your only smart device is an iPhone or Android phone.

As a result, the intention to reach a broad global group of customers is maintained. Having said that, it should be noted that the remaining part of the subsection *Who is Knocki for?* focuses on the householders of smart homes, using smart technologies on an everyday basis:

> But if you already have a few smart devices, you can immediately expand what Knocki can do, and transform "dumb" surfaces all around your home or office into intelligent interfaces.

A unique discursive strategy applied in Knocki's both promotional video and text description is what I term "micro-narratives", which are short flashes of daily routines, easily identifiable with particular contexts (in terms of participants, time, location, artifacts, scripts, causal, temporal and other relations of events, etc.) by the audience as their shared experience. For this reason some if not most of the micro-narratives are incomplete, beginning *in media res*, lacking some form of introduction, climax or conclusion, which elements the viewer can supplement referring to his or her knowledge. Micro-narratives strengthen the message that Knocki should be useful for "people everywhere", and in turn define the product's target group as the global general public. Also, at least some micro-narratives are built on the Problem-Solution pattern.

There are no fewer than eleven micro-narratives presented in Knocki's promotional video, and consequently they constitute more than a half of its running time. The micro-narratives show anonymous persons performing everyday activities, and also indicate how Knocki performs its function in them. The micro-narratives include the following (in order of appearance):

1. A man is in the backyard of his house, unaware of the delivery man approaching the front-door. The delivery man knocks, which instantly activates the Knocki smart phone application, displaying the message "Someone at front door". The man opens the door and is given a package. (00:00:46–00:00:58);
2. Two couples are watching a film in the living room. One person taps the table to pause the film in order to bring snacks, and then taps again to resume the film. The Knocki message reads "Play / pause" (00:00:59–00:01:04);
3. A woman is sleeping in her bed. When the alarm starts ringing, she taps the nightstand to snooze the alarm. She turns back and sleeps again. The Knocki message reads "Snooze + coffee" (00:01:05–00:01:12);
4. A boy is playing in his bedroom and then goes to bed. With a tap he turns off the light. (00:01:14–00:01:24);
5. A couple is sitting on the sofa, watching the TV in the living room. The woman wraps herself in a blanket. The man taps the armrest to activate the Nest thermostat, which is shown to be interfaced with Knocki. The Knocki message reads "Activate Nest" (00:01:27–00:01:38);

6. A woman puts her handbag on the kitchen countertop and starts rummaging through its contents. Unsuccessful, she taps on the countertop, which instantly activates the ring of the mobile phone in the handbag. The Knocki smart phone application displays the message "Find phone" (00:01:44–00:01:54);
7. A man in the bathroom activates the Knocki smart phone application to turn on a music player ("Play music") (00:02:22–00:02:24);
8. A teenager walks into his bedroom, places his schoolbag on the floor, and turns on the notebook. He taps the desk, upon which his mother – being away from home – receives the message "Hayden is home" with the Knocki smart phone application (00:02:25–00:02:32);
9. A lady on the wheelchair enters the living room and taps the wall, which switches on the light. The Knocki message reads "Lights on/off" (00:02:33–00:02:35);
10. The father holds his sleeping daughter in his arms, walks into her bedroom, and puts her to bed. Tapping the wall, he switches the night lights into the dimmed mode; another tap starts a lullaby in the music player. The father kisses his daughter goodnight. The Knocki message reads "Night light + lullabies" (00:03:15–00:03:28);
11. The previous story continues. The father now goes to bed himself and taps the nightstand to activate the night alarm. The Knocki message reads "Night mode", with the activated house alarm device seen in the background (00:03:30–00:03:38).

As has been noted above, the plot of some micro-narratives is clearly structured along the moves of the Problem-Solution pattern. The micro-narratives depict various Situations, that is everyday events as can be experienced by the general public, most of which entail some Problem, e.g. in (6) the woman may spend considerable amount of time searching for her phone; in (10) the man may not be able to dim the lights and start the music player as long as he keeps the child in his arms. However, all these Problems seem to be solvable without the use of Knocki: if the latter does offer a Solution, it consists in simplifying time-consuming, uncomfortable and otherwise bothersome procedures.

As for positive Evaluation of the Solution, it proves to be effective in each micro-narrative, as is signaled with the relevant Knocki message displayed. Also, the characters' reactions (facial expression, gestures, etc.) suggest their positive reactions to the desired course of events, e.g. the householder in (1) is smiling when receiving the package; the couple in (5) exchanges smiles; the woman in (6) looks with relief when her mobile phone starts ringing; the mother in (8) smiles upon receiving the message that her son is already at home.

Apart from (re)constructing the Situation-Problem-Solution pattern, the micro-narratives also contribute to defining the product's target group. Following the company's intended global marketing policy (cf. "this product is going to change lives and bring joy to people everywhere"), the micro-narratives represent a heterogeneous group of characters, diversified in terms of age, gender and family status. The target group can then be identified as non-specific global customers.

6. Discussion

The analysis has confirmed that project presentations at Internet crowdfunding platforms use the Problem-Solution text pattern to identify a particular Problem to which the given project is to provide a Solution. The Problem-Solution pattern has also been shown to co-occur with passages identifying the product's target group, i.e. the group directly concerned with the Problem and hence potentially interested in being provided with a Solution thereto.

In line with the first research hypothesis, i.e. *The project provides a Solution to a Problem of a certain group*, it has been found that projects vary in terms of the target group, from the general public (e.g. householders in the case of Knocki) through broad social groups (music listeners, computer gamers, VR users and film viewers in the case of Ossic X) to more specific groups, e.g. nationally restricted (e.g. Polish consumers in efood).

As for the second research hypothesis, i.e. *The group concerned with the Problem is referred to in the project's presentation*, it has been found that projects' presentations employ different channels to express the Problem-Solution structure and define the target group. These include verbal channels (written and spoken), motion pictures (e.g. micro-narratives in Knocki) and images (graphic icons, photographs etc.) Importantly, these different semiotic modes have been shown to interact to co-construct both the Problem-Solution sequence and the project's target group. A multimodal discourse analysis approach has thus proven relevant to analyze the research topic.

Finally, the third research hypothesis – that projects launched at local crowdfunding platforms will address local groups and provide Solutions to local Problems, while projects launched at global crowdfunding platforms will address global groups and provide Solutions to global Problems – has been generally confirmed. In particular it has been confirmed in so far as systemic barriers and exclusion mechanisms are concerned, especially the language barrier which excludes non-speakers of minor languages from becoming familiar with and supporting projects marketed at local platforms, e.g. PolakPotrafi. As a result, presentations of projects marketed at local platforms frequently refer to the national significance of the project, as is the case of the analog Moon/Mars habitat or the efood application.

Yet it is not always true that local platforms promote projects of local relevance. For instance, the solar longboard is intended to attract global interest, even if the promotional materials are currently available only in Polish. Similarly, despite the recurrent emphasis on its pioneering character in Poland and opportunities offered to Polish research, the analog Moon/Mars habitat is expected to produce research results of potential interest to US and European space agencies.

On the other hand, the authors of projects which seem to be relatively niche ones, and hence directly concern a small target group, often employ discourse strategies to construct their more general relevance – and hence extend the scope of the target group. This can be found, e.g. in the space-related projects – LightSail and the analog Moon/Mars habitat. The former emphasizes the democratic mechanism in the decision-making process, inviting any and all persons interested to join Planetary Society and in turn negotiate the future directions of research on LightSail and its space destinations. In the case of the analog Moon/Mars habitat the authors invite volunteers to participate in the simulated space mission, which dispels the possible belief that the habitat is generally a scientific project.

Finally, the results of the study show that multimodality plays an important role in projects' presentations at Internet crowdfunding platforms. In all six examples analysed the project's presentation employs written text, spoken text (promotional videos' off commentary and appearances of company representatives, experts, testers), motion pictures (promotional videos), also with visual effects, and graphic elements (e.g. highlight frames, citation boxes etc.) All these modalities have been shown to be functionally related, although in different ways. For instance, in the case of spoken text and motion picture in the project's promotional video the former can present certain functions of the product promoted in the crowdfunding campaign, while the latter will simultaneously display examples of how these functions are used in real life. This pattern, which I will call *Concretization*, appears e.g. in Knocki's promotional video, in the form of micro-narratives illustrating the real-life applications of the device.

By contrast, static graphic elements, in particular frames and boxes, integrate text with graphic icons to present certain highlights of the project (*Highlighting*), e.g. list of its components and basic specifications (solar longboard project), or suggestions of possible applications (Knocki project). On the other hand, frames and boxes seem particularly useful to simplify the explanations of otherwise sophisticated mechanisms of advanced technology projects, as can be seen especially in Knocki or Ossic X projects' presentations. Finally, frames and boxes can also re-quote – in full or in part – utterances of the project's developers and experts originally cited in the main body of the project's description and/or its promotional video (*Re-quoting*), with relevant examples found e.g. in the LightSail project's website.

Even the channels of otherwise secondary importance for the meaning-making (compared with verbal content or motion pictures) prove to be instrumental in the marketization of the project when integrated with other channels. This is the case of Ossic X's promotional video and its play with (1) sound (the crescendoing noise followed with sudden silence), concomitant with (2) images (of noise-generating artifacts and Ossic X headphones, respectively), and (3) spoken text (off commentary fading and then coming to a normal pitch once Ossic X headphones are shown).

7. Conclusion

Taking Hoey's (1983, 2001) Problem-Solution text pattern as the initial point of reference, the present study has shown that the original model can hardly be applicable to grasp the complex multisemiotic interplay of channels applied in descriptions of projects marketed at Internet crowdfunding platforms. The study shows the importance of applying multimodal discourse analysis, supplemented with a critical discursive approach, to identify and interpret the ways these multiple semiotic systems contribute to the construction of the respective stages of the Problem-Solution pattern on the one hand, and to the definition of the project's target group on the other.

Crowdfunding is currently in its heyday worldwide, and new Internet crowdfunding platforms are created to promote innovative projects, be it locally or globally. Likewise, the number of projects increases, in geometrical rather than arithmetical progression. Consequently, their authors need to be innovative not only in terms of the project itself, but also in the use of promotional strategies to indicate the project's relevance to a target group sizeable enough to warrant sufficient financial backing. It can thus be expected that in the course of time projects' presentations may exploit multimodality in ways other than currently observed, and/or rework discourse strategies of advertising so as to make the given project conspicuous against the mass of others. It is thus recommended that future research addresses the topics analysed in this paper on a regular basis.

References

Dudley-Evans, T. (1994). Variations in the discourse patterns favoured by different disciplines and their pedagogical implications. In J. Flowerdew & M. H. Long

(Eds.) *Academic listening: Research perspectives*. Cambridge: Cambridge University Press, 146–158.

Dushnitsky, G., Guerini, M., Piva, E., & Rossi-Lamastra, C. (2016). Crowdfunding in Europe: Determinants of platform creation across countries. *California Management Review*, 58(2), 44–71.

Flowerdew, L. (2003). A combined corpus and systemic-functional analysis of the Problem-Solution pattern in a student and professional corpus of technical writing. *TESOL Quarterly*, 37(3), 489–511.

Flowerdew, L. (2008). *Corpus-based Analyses of the Problem-solution Pattern: A Phraseological Approach*. Amsterdam: John Benjamins.

Gierczak, M. M., Bretschneider, U., Haas, P., Blohm, I., & Leimeister, J. M. (2016). Crowdfunding: Outlining the New Era of Fundraising. In D. Brüntje & O. Gajda (Eds.) *Crowdfunding in Europe. State of the Art in Theory and Practice*. Springer: Cham et al., 7–23.

Hoey, M. (1983). *On the surface of* discourse. London: George Allen & Unwin.

Hoey, M. (1986). Overlapping patterns of discourse organisation and their implications for clause relational analysis of problem-solution texts. In C. R. Cooper & S. Greenbaum (Eds.) *Studying Writing*, London: Sage, 187–214.

Hoey, M. (2001). *Textual Interaction: An Introduction to Written Discourse Analysis*. London: Routledge.

Hoey, M. & Winter, E. (1986). Clause relations and the writer's communicative task. In B. Couture (Ed.) *Functional approaches to writing: Research perspectives*, London: Frances Pinter, 120–141.

Jordan, M. P. (1984). *Rhetoric of everyday English texts*. London: Allen & Unwin.

Lawton, K., & Marom, D. (2010). *The Crowdfunding Revolution: Social Networking Meets Venture Financing*, thecrowdfundingrevolution.com.

McCarthy, M. (1991). *Discourse Analysis for language teachers*. Cambridge: Cambridge University Press.

Paltridge, B. (1996). Genre, text type, and the language learning classroom. *ELT Journal*, 50(3), 237–243.

Schwienbacher, A., & Larralde, B. (2012). Crowdfunding of entreprenurial ventures, In D. Cumming (Ed.) *The Oxford Handbook of Entrepreneurial Finance*. New York: Oxford University Press, 369–391.

Desislava Cheshmedzhieva-Stoycheva

University of Shumen, Bulgaria

Nuclear power discourse in *The New York Times*, *The Independent*, and *Dnevnik*

Abstract: Nuclear power is a debatable issue. While statistics show it to be a low-cost source of energy, it also entails large investments in the development of new plants and, importantly, involves risk factors around their operation. Chernobyl and Fukushima Daiichi are only two of the numerous examples of nuclear plant accidents that come to mind.

Provoked, on the one hand, by the public debates and the referendum which followed on the development of a new atomic power station in Belene, Bulgaria, in 2013, and on the other hand, by concurrent international debates over similar projects in the UK and the US, this paper analyses the ways in which an American, a British and a Bulgarian newspapers present the conflicting issue of the development of nuclear power plants in the three respective countries in 2013. Using CDA as the main approach of analysis the paper compares and contrasts the ways in which these three different cultures view the said issue as reflected in their national media.

1. Introduction

Currently there are heated debates over the pros and cons of nuclear energy, many of which appear in media discourse. Certain events, such as the disaster in Chernobyl in 1986 and more recently the accident at Fukushima Daiichi in 2011, have fostered reassessment of some countries' policies towards nuclear power and its production. The issue is complex as nuclear power is considered both cheap and environmentally clean in the sense that it does not involve carbon emissions; at the same time, however, development of new nuclear plants requires considerable investments and the completion of the projects themselves takes time.

Being a substantial part of a country's economy, nuclear power is also a political issue, which in the cases where plants are state owned is also associated with public budget financing. Therefore, discourse on nuclear power is part of political discourse as well.

Last but not least, nuclear energy entails the problems of danger, safety and risk management related to accidents, radiation, and other hazardous consequences.

All these nuances of the topic as they emerge in discourse on nuclear power make it complex, but also one which is interesting to analyse.

2. Theoretical background

The topic of nuclear power can be considered a highly debatable issue. On the one hand, nuclear power raises negative associations with weapons of mass destruction, while on the other, nuclear power plants can provoke similarly negative attitudes, related to the risk factors associated with their maintenance and operation in general.

The discourse on nuclear power as employed by the three newspapers analysed meets the definitional criteria of *discourse* as understood by Fairclough in CDA approach as "a social activity and mutual influence, [and also] people who interact in real social situations [as well as] a social creation of reality, [and] a kind of knowledge" (1995, p. 18). Also, it shows how the media – through their discourses – do not only influence but also create reality (cf. Fowler, 1991; Cottle, 2000). In particular this study shows how discourse on nuclear power in the three newspapers analysed reflects all positive as well as negative sides of nuclear power, and at the same time constructs its image by means of various linguistic devices.

As an important social issue nuclear power enjoys high interest in the press. The topic meets several of the criteria of newsworthiness as set forward by Galtung and Ruge (1965), being politically, economically, environmentally, and socially significant. The role of the media reporting on nuclear power is also important inasmuch as the way they present the information on the issue can shape the attitudes of the general public. Referring to the study at hand, the fact that the topic of nuclear power has managed to generate no fewer than 700 articles published within one year is indicative of the highly mediatized nature of the issue, and can be considered instrumental for raising and shaping social awareness of it. This correlation clearly corresponds with the observation made by Allan, Adam, Carter and Beck (2000, p. 5) that "public awareness and concern for environmental issues correlates with the relative amount of coverage being generated by the news organisations", i.e. broader coverage triggers higher social awareness.

The role of the media in communicating nuclear issues and risks, and hence in constructing social attitudes towards nuclear power, is also discussed by Perko, Turcanu, Geenen, Mamane and Van Rooy (2011, p. 22), who, quoting Gamson and Modigliani (1989), state that it is actually the media that predetermine political interest in this issue by dedicating much attention to the topic, and thus presenting it as substantial. Similarly, talking about mediatized risks of contemporary society as varied as nuclear fallout and industrial toxins, Cottle (2006, p. 123) quotes Beck

(2001, p. 33), stating that the media bring to the fore the "'unseen side-effects of industrial production' and help turn these into 'global ecological flashpoints'".

3. Corpus and methods of analysis

The corpus of articles for this study is comprised of publications which appeared in the electronic versions of the American *The New York Times* (NYT), the British *The Independent* (IN), and the Bulgarian newspaper *Dnevnik* (DN). The articles were selected by the keyword "nuclear" in NYT and IN, and its Bulgarian equivalent *атомен* (along with its feminine and plural derivatives: *атомна* and *атомни*[1]), which initially provided a large number of articles covering a broad range of topics verging from nuclear arms to types of family organization. All articles were then reviewed one by one applying "nuclear plant" and its Bulgarian equivalent, i.e. "атомна електроцентрала", as a filter. Thus, the final corpus of articles dealing with matters related to nuclear power plants numbered 700 articles (56 published in *The New York Times*, 135 in *The Independent*, and 509[2] in *Dnevnik*) published in 2013.

The reason to choose these three newspapers in particular was the fact that they are all considered quality press. My intention was to focus on objective reporting without the sensational twist of tabloids.[3]

In contrast to previous studies on the topic (cf. Gamson & Modigliani, 1989; Perko et al., 2011), which used mainly Content Analysis, in this analysis I have applied both Content Analysis and Critical Discourse Analysis. The CDA was preferred for its integrative character as "any discursive 'event' (i.e. any instance of discourse) is seen as being simultaneously a piece of text, an instance of discursive practice, and an instance of social practice" (Fairclough, 1993, p. 4; Huckin, 1997; Todorova, 2015).

4. Analysis

Looking at the corpus of articles on nuclear power, it can be observed that the opinions presented there vary: some define nuclear power as environmentally

---

1 In Bulgarian adjectives are gender and number motivated.

2 The reason for the considerable number of articles published in the Bulgarian *Dnevnik* was that the period of research coincided with various public debates and the referendum which followed them on the development of a new atomic power station in Belene – a project which was generally considered ridiculous and unnecessary as Bulgaria had an operative nuclear power plant and no shortage of electricity.

3 Tabloids could be explored as an interesting source for further studies on the topic as their language might differ from that of quality press.

friendly, others as costly, and still others advocate closing down of nuclear power plants due to the high risks they pose in case of an accident. Inevitably, however, and irrespective of the stance taken, each nuclear power discourse at one point or another refers to scare, panic, danger and/or risk, i.e. emotions that are negative in nature. Therefore, it can be argued that in general the negative connotations of the term *nuclear* as presented in newspaper discourse exceed the positive ones by far.

Although this study is based only on publications related to nuclear power generation for civil purposes, thereby the focus being mostly on nuclear discourse related with nuclear power plants, some of the texts analyzed (five in total) contain references to the threat which even nuclear power generation for civil purposes could pose to world peace:

(1) Nonproliferation experts have expressed concern that the light-water reactor under construction in Yongbyon **could be a cover for making bombs**. North Korea itself has threatened to use **all its nuclear facilities to expand its arsenal**.
(NYT, 24.12.2013)

(2) I welcomed that prospect because I thought that **Iran would renounce its support of terror** around the world, a role that won it the State Department's ranking as the **No. 1 state sponsor of terrorism**. Not for a second did I think that the issue on the negotiating table would be **Iran's development of nuclear weapons**.
(NYT, 25.11.2013)

As examples (1) and (2) show, the intertwining between the two domains: the civil and the military one, is an indelible part of the debate on nuclear power. As can be seen in example (1), while such lexemes as *light-water reactor* or *nuclear facilities* refer to devices which generally serve the civil sector, they are mentioned along with *concern*, *cover*, *bombs* and *arsenal*, which in turn are mostly associated with military activities and strategies.

In both above examples one can also clearly notice the influence of stereotypes about the two nations concerned: on the one hand there is an image of North Korea as an "international outlaw", especially strong in American psyche (cf. Savada, 1993) (see example 1); on the other hand, example (2) describes Iran explicitly as a "sponsor of terrorism". Thus, the two examples present two belligerent nations involved in the development of nuclear power facilities which could only provoke concerns in Western societies, especially bearing in mind the possibility of nuclear weapons falling into the hands of terrorists.

The topic of danger in nuclear power discourse is also existent in the context of non-military, civil applications due to the possibility of leakages. Therefore, it is not surprising that many of the articles on the topic of nuclear risks contain references to Fukushima and Chernobyl as two of the biggest accidents in the history of nuclear power.

In the period of analysis (year 2013) references to Fukushima Daiichi's[4] aftermath were especially numerous (NYT – 47, IN – 6, DN – 41) as the process of removal of the radioactive fuel rods was ongoing through a bigger part of the analysed period. The significance of the risk factor in nuclear production was further intensified through the use of intertextual references to other sources discussing the accident at Fukushima Daiichi nuclear power plant. For instance, the people living in the neighbourhood of Fukushima are described as *evacuees* and *nuclear refugees*[5] (as in example 3). The second collocation is particularly interesting as it links two different discourses: that of nuclear power and that of war, political upheaval and/or persecution as reasons for fleeing one's own country. The end-result is forlorn cities, towns or even countries. This idea of abandonment and lifelessness is presented through the reference of *a ghost town*, which denotes the town of Fukushima (see example 3). The associations which this reference brings are with the accident in Chernobyl, in which context the same phrase has been used to refer to Pripyat in Ukraine:

(3) The Disaster Is Over, but **the Effects on a Nation Are Not** /h/[6].

> […] **Most of the evacuees**, also known as **nuclear refugees**, are middle-aged or older people who have been relocated from Futaba […]. Crowded in dormitory-like conditions, subsisting on bento box meals, they await word that never comes of when they might return to their homes in **what is now a ghost town**.
>
> (NYT, 10.12.2013)

This association is further reinforced through the use of the verb *spook* from the same semantic domain as *ghost town*, as shown in example (4):

(4) Removing Fuel Rods Poses New Risks at Crippled Nuclear Plant in Japan /h/

> It was the part of the Fukushima Daiichi nuclear power plant that **spooked** American officials the most, as the complex **spiraled out of control** two and a half years ago.
>
> (NYT, 10.11.2013)

The idea of fear conveyed through the use of the verb *spook* as well as the uncontrollable nature of any nuclear disaster stated explicitly in example (4) are further

---

4 For an analysis of emotions and types of reports on the aftermath of Fukushima see Perko et al. (2011, pp. 50–52)

5 Both terms have been used in the documentary *Nuclear Nation* (directed by Atsushi Funahashi), which focused on Fukushima Daiichi nuclear disaster and was released on 10th February 2012.

6 Abbreviations used: /h/ - headline, /sh/ - subheadline

intensified through the use of the generalizing phrase *global terror* used in the reference to the removal of rods in example (5):

(5) On '**Global Terror**' and the Fukushima Fuel Move /h/ [...]

Since October, an **apocalyptic message** has been making the rounds of anti-nuclear blogs, crystallized in this headline on a post by longtime anti-nuclear campaigner Harvey Wasserman: 'Dear Climate Scientists, Please Note **the Global Terror** at Fukushima Four.'

(NYT, 18.11.2013)

To sum up the discussion so far, the key message conveyed through all the references highlighted in examples (3–5) and further emphasized by the association with apocalypse in example (5), is fear related with nuclear power: fear of environmental disaster and fear of possible death caused either through mass destruction or radiation.

As stated by various sources, such as the UN Scientific Committee on the Effects of Atomic Radiation and Nuclear Regulatory Commission (see *Sources, Effects and Risks of Ionizing Radiation: United Nations Scientific Committee on the Effects of Atomic Radiation 2013 Report*; *Radiation: effects and sources, United Nations Environment Programme*, 2016), the effects of radiation exposure on people and the number of actual victims cannot be precisely defined as the effects of radiation (cancer, for example) might be exhibited in the course of many years. Probably that is why, whenever the articles analyzed cite accounts of the people exposed to radiation and suffering from it, they refer to Chernobyl rather than Fukushima as the former had occurred earlier and its effects are already visible:

(6) In a 2008 report, it [the UN Scientific Committee on the Effects of Atomic Radiation] found that as of 2006, the radiation health effects of Chernobyl were essentially **limited to** the **more than 6,000 cases of thyroid cancer** reported in children and adolescents who were exposed at the time of the accident. The report said that more cases can be expected **in coming decades.** This represents **a public health catastrophe** of the first magnitude.

(NYT, 06.11.2013)

(7) Settled in New York, but Still *Within Chernobyl's Reach* /h/

[...] While no one can say for certain what caused her cancer, doctors told her that **it most likely had been caused by living and working so close to Chernobyl, Ukraine**, [...] Doctors said that her son Yan, who was born in Belarus in **1989**, and later suffered a rash of health problems, including cysts, sores and tooth loss, **might also have been affected by the radiation** that blanketed the region

(NYT, 02.12.2013)

Both the scientific analysis conducted by the UN Scientific Committee on the Effects of Atomic Radiation (cited in example 6) as well as the personal account in example (7) present an apocalyptic picture, already evoked in the previous examples (especially examples 4 and 5). At the same time, these excerpts can boost panic as they speak of more cases of people already affected but still to be revealed as well as of the post-radiation effects being transferred through generations. The use of the contradicting notions of *limited to* and *more than* in example (6) is also interesting, especially bearing in mind that the time reference starts from 1986, then goes through 1989 and 2006, and continues within the next *decades* (in plural!) to reach the status of *a public health catastrophe*. All these linguistic devices intensify the problem of radiation-related health problems and show the scale which the new accident in Fukushima could possibly reach.

A publication in *Dnevnik* voices the same threat out loud:

(8)[7] ***Регулаторната база оставя стотици хиляди души в Япония в нужда.*** *В тази ситуация могат да се окажат реално и хората, които живеят в държави с ядрени реактори,* ***алармират от Грийнпийс.***

[**The regulatory base leaves hundreds of thousands of Japanese in need**. This could turn out to be the situation of all people who live in countries with nuclear reactors, **warn people from Greenpeace**.]

(DN, 11.03.2013)

(9) With a Plant's **Tainted Water** Still Flowing, **No End to Environmental Fears** /h/

(NYT, 24.10.2013)

As the above examples show, nuclear power discourse which is critical towards operating nuclear power plants stresses the invisible global threat of radiation-related health problems (see examples 4–7) or environmental hazards (see example 8) and their aftermath (see example 9). By contrast, discourse critical towards closing down nuclear power plants refers to the threat of energy shortages, and thus creates a fear that is old-forgotten in the developed world:

(10) Fear of the **Dark** /h/

(NYT, 09.11.2013)

In *The Independent*, too, there are several articles that touch on that issue and present it as an important one:

(11) the industry has warned of **the impact of shortages**. Last week Ian Marchant, boss of Centrica's rival SSE, warned 'there is **a very real risk** of the lights going out' in Britain, saying the government was significantly underestimating the scale of **the capacity crunch** and **warning** the country could face **electricity blackouts** within three years.

(IN, 25.03.2013)

7 Translations of the original examples in Bulgarian into English are done by the author.

As can be seen in the above example, references to power shortages employ metaphorical imagery suggesting potential restrictions and shortages, e.g. the noun phrase *capacity crunch* in example (11). This type of threat is all the more significant as it usually occurs at the time of highest demand for electricity, i.e. during the cold part of the year, which can cause serious problems in both household and public contexts. Such a scenario, depicted with emotionally charged lexis expressing concerns, e.g. *risk*, *impact*, *warning* and *capacity crunch* in example (11), can be viewed as a culturally specific phenomenon, more distressing to Western nations than, for instance, Eastern and Central European ones. In fact, energy outages would not possibly create as much panic in Bulgaria, where such phenomena used to be quite frequent in the past and still happen from time to time even nowadays.

The topic of danger and the ensuing fear are inevitably connected with the topics of safety and risk management. All the three newspapers analysed feature articles on the possible improvement of safety regulations or the safety performance of nuclear power plants:

(12) The Energy Department will give a small company in Corvallis, Ore., up to $226 million to **advance the design of tiny nuclear reactors that would be installed under water**, making **meltdown far less likely** and opening the door to markets around the world where the reactors now on the market are too big for local power grids. […] On Tuesday, Sergey V. Kirienko, the director general of Rosatom, the Russian state atomic energy company, told a small group of reporters in Washington that **a floating nuclear power plant**, which could be moored near a load center, was "entering its finalization stage."

(NYT, 12.12.2013)

(13) Either the UK wants **new nuclear** at a sensible price or it decides that **other energy sources are safer and more affordable**.

(IN, 21.03.2013)

(14) *Стойнев: Няма* ***по-модерна*** *технология* ***от тази на 'Уестингхаус', а аз компромис с безопасността няма да правя*** /h/

[Stoynev: There isn't any technology **more modern than that of Westinghouse's and I would not compromise on safety** /h/]

(DN, 01.08.2013)

As the above examples suggest, safety goes hand-in-hand with innovation and modernity (cf. "advance the design", "tiny nuclear reactors […] installed under water", "meltdown far less likely", "a floating nuclear power plant" in example 12; "new nuclear" and "safer" in example 13; "more modern" and "safety" in example 14). At the same time, despite the innovations, few modern nuclear power stations are being built globally. That is why most of the articles speak about old or aging nuclear plants that are about to be closed down, or about such whose life cycle has been or is about to be extended. In some cases, this can lead to an absurd situation:

(15) The nuclear plants at Hinkley Point in Somerset are so old that the health & safety notice boards warn workers not to take snuff into a building that houses two uranium-fuelled reactors.

(IN, 28.03.2013)

However, innovation does not refer only to the changing the technology of the reactors inside the power plants but also to the technologies related to tracing radiation leaks (cf. the novel safety device described in example 16, the need for a new type of nuclear power plants mentioned in example 13) or technologies involved in issuing tsunami warnings (in example 17), which could have otherwise reduced or held back the Fukushima disaster:

(16) A decade from now his colleagues will go through the seemingly endless radiation clearance checks, such as **putting their arms in what look like Dyson Airblade hand dryers for six seconds**, for the last time when the reactors generate their final watts.

(IN, 28.03.2013)

(17) *Япония също така показа и* ***нова, подобрена система за предупреждение за цунами.***

[Japan also presented **a new improved tsunami warning system**.]

(DN, 11.03.2013)

The topic of nuclear power safety is also closely connected with risk management. This issue is raised in a number of articles discussing the process of fuel rods extraction from the affected Fukushima plant (see examples 19 and 20), or in articles describing the way a specific problem at a power station has been dealt with (see examples 18 and 19). The narrative of these articles invariably features assessment of the risk juxtaposed with the question of safety:

(18) *Скъсано уплътнение е причинило повредата в АЕЦ "Козлодуй"* /h/

[...] ***Не говорим изобщо за авария с радиационна заплаха, няма никаква опасност*** *за служителите на централата и за гражданите, коментира още Станимиров.*

[A torn insulation has caused the malfunction at NPP Kozloduy /h/

[...] It is **not an incident having to do with radiation threat, there is no danger** for the workers in the station or for the citizens, added Stanimirov]

(DN, 15.04.2013)

(19) But Japan's nuclear regulator has pointed out that the process also **poses some risks**. If damaged or left uncovered, the fuel assemblies **could overheat or emit large amounts of radiation**. [...] **Lake Barrett, a former United States nuclear regulator involved with the cleanup after the nuclear accident at Three Mile Island in 1979**, said he had been invited by Tepco to review its contingency plans and **found them thorough**.

(NYT, 18.11.2013)

(20) "Considering the equipment situation, we may be pushing a little too hard." [...] "In a sense, **we have put in place measures that leave no room for worry**," Suga told reporters in a regular press briefing

(IN, 19.03.2013)

References to fuel removal from Fukushima Daiichi, as stated above, are quite frequent in the corpus (more than 40 articles in total) and they all follow the same pattern: a detailed description of what is to be done, what risks there are, and what will happen afterwards (as in examples 19 and 20). The author's main goal is to make the general public aware of what is happening on site and of the risk involved. While, psychologically, being made aware of an imminent threat can have two opposing effects on people, namely either make them panic or make them feel calm, the articles analyzed perform the latter option. The use of positive assessments provided in the first person singular by local (as in examples 18 and 20) or foreign experts in the field (as in example 19) increases the truth value of the accounts given as well as brings relief.[8]

Another topic frequently employed in nuclear power discourse is financing, which, like risk management, is also viewed from different perspectives: on the one hand it concerns investment in research and development of new technologies and new reactors, and on the other hand it refers to investment in constructing new power plants. The latter is seen in example (21):

(21) **A pan-European group** including many **leading nuclear energy companies** has also called for the commission to provide public finance for **new nuclear power stations**. The group, called the European Nuclear Energy Forum, argued in 2011 for **"innovative financing" for new nuclear plants**, including direct loans and guarantee schemes.

(IN, 17.03.2013)

Building new nuclear power plants is an issue specific to the policy of a given country and the political agenda of each political party. This is particularly obvious in Bulgaria, where a referendum was held on the nuclear future of the country in

8 Ericson (1998, p. 85) states that the "[j]ournalists establish factuality by using credible sources who make statements that can be quoted as a fact without further investigation".

January 2013. The political turmoil that preceded and followed the referendum was due to the different opinions held by the main parties in Bulgaria on the topic of the development of a new nuclear power plant in the town of Belene. The Socialist Party's agenda was rife with examples of why Belene was a project that must be continued, while their opponents from the centre-right party GERB held the opposite opinion. Although the 60% threshold was not achieved and the referendum's result was non-binding, it marked an attempt to make the voice of common people heard. In general, as example (22) shows, the truth is that common people usually have little or no say on nuclear power plants in their region or country. This point is summarised in an example from the American daily:

(22) "This isn't a decision about the price for one power station," said Dieter Helm, a professor of energy policy at the University of Oxford. "This is about whether **we** want a nuclear industry or don't **we**. That is the question. **Only the politicians can decide**."
(NYT, 15.03.2013)

This stance is further supported by the associate business editor of *The Independent* Mark Leftly, who says:

(23) "Just look as objectively as possible over the negotiations between EDF and the Government on building the first civil nuclear plant since 1995 and the sole conclusion is that **politics, not concerns over the environment or energy, will decide whether or not £14bn will be spent at Hinkley Point**"
(IN, 21.03.2013)

In a way the message conveyed in examples (22) and (23) is that common people are in a way volitionless, despite the inclusive *we* used by the NYT's article's author, Dieter Helm, in example (22).

Yet another topic discussed in nuclear power discourse, especially in British and Bulgarian articles, is employment in the sector in general, and the development of new job opportunities through the construction of new nuclear plants, as can be seen in examples (24) and (25). The latter entails possible redistribution of energy production and in turn loss of jobs in some power plants (see example 25):

(24) Drawn-out negotiations '**put Hinkley Point jobs at risk**' /h/
(IN, 28.03.2013)

(25) *Работещите във въгледобива* ***се опасяват за работните си места,*** *ако от енергийния микс бъдат извадени топлоцентрали, които произвеждат по-скъп ток.*

[The workers in the coal production **are worried that they would have no job** if the heating plants, which produce more expensive electricity, are taken out of the energy mix.]
(DN, 14.03.2013)

The difference in the way British and Bulgarian media discourses view the issue is related to different realities in these countries: while in the UK the main problem is closing down of ineffective and old nuclear power stations, which would mean quite a few redundancies but greater safety, in Bulgaria it is the closing of heating plants (which are more numerous than nuclear power plants and the electricity they produce is more expensive than the one obtained in the latter), which would result in lower price of electricity.

The justification of the concerns of the miners, as discussed in example (25), is invariably bound up with the financial side of electricity production. This is again stated in example (26):

(26) *В този "микс"* ***най-скъпи са киловатите на когенерациите на топлофикациите*** [...], ***а най-евтин засега е токът от АЕЦ-Козлодуй.***

[In this "mix" **the most expensive energy comes from the kilowatts of the cogenerations of the heating plants** [...], **at this point the cheapest energy comes from NPP-Kozloduy**]

(DN, 23.03.2013)

The above examples also show the vicious circle in which people get trapped: if you want a low price for electricity, some plants have to be shut down, but then many employees there would lose jobs, and so they would not have money to pay even the lowest possible price this whole process might trigger.

Still, low electricity cost and employment opportunities are the top two reasons used by politicians in order to justify a nuclear project (explicitly stated in example 29). Only then come nuclear energy's environment-friendliness (mentioned in examples 27 and 28), possibilities for development of an area (discussed in example 28), etc.:

(27) While nuclear power comes with drawbacks like the possibility of major accidents and the still-unresolved issue of how to dispose of waste fuel, **it is a low emitter of carbon dioxide**.

(NYT, 02.12.2013)

(28) "This planned new nuclear power station in Somerset will generate **vast amounts of clean energy** and enhance our **energy security**. It will **benefit the local economy, through direct employment, the supply chain and the use of local services.**"

(IN, 19.03.2013)

(29) Earlier this month, *The Independent on Sunday* reported that **a strike price**, which is the guaranteed minimum that EDF will get for the electricity it generates at Hinkley, had been provisionally agreed at **£96–£97** per megawatt hour. That means that **producing electricity from nuclear will be a bit cheaper** than from windfarms, which

in turn means that the Government can claim **it was right to pursue a radioactive path**.

(IN, 21.03.2013)

All the expressions highlighted in examples (27–29) show politicians' ability to use people's fears in their favour, and thereby conform with the "public accountability package" (see Gamson & Modigliani, 1989, pp. 23–24), in which profit in general is juxtaposed with public safety.

At the same time, it is interesting to note another difference between discourse on nuclear power in British and American newspapers on the one hand, and the one found in the Bulgarian daily on the other. The former seems to focus more on the ecologically clean nature of nuclear energy, its low price and possible energy shortages in order to justify the development of new nuclear power plants. By contrast, the latter focuses on a different phenomenon specific to Bulgaria: the country has excessive production of electricity, which the local market alone cannot consume, so Bulgaria is actually exporting electricity to its neighbouring countries. These two factors make the need for a new nuclear power station in Bulgaria promoted by the Socialist Party sound absurd: there is no market demand for more energy and the cost of the new plant would be very high.

In addition, there are implications that the Belene project is actually a result of political backdoor games. The way this has been ingeniously presented in *Dnevnik* is through an intertextual reference to the *Aeneid* by Virgil or *Odyssey* by Homer:

(30) *Белене* – ***троянският кон на Москва?*** /h/
[…] "Изграждането на 'АЕЦ Белене' може да стане единствено на гърба на българските данъкоплатци – по простата причина, че никой частен инвеститор ***няма да се набута в изграждането на електроенергийна мощност, за чието производство няма пазар нито в България, нито извън нея.***

[Belene – **the Trojan horse of Moscow?** /h/
[…] The development of NPP Beleve could happen only at the expense of the Bulgarian tax payers – the reason for that is quite simple: **no private investor would let him/herself in the construction of an electrical plant whose production could be sold neither on the Bulgarian nor on the international market.**]

(DN, 09.06.2013)

The implications presented in example (30) are clear: references could be made between the policy followed by the Bulgarian Socialist Party, who are openly in favour of the development of a new nuclear plant and their alleged 'servitude' to Russia. The implication is also quite obvious: it is suggested that Russia wants to undermine Bulgarian economic stability by involving the country into a project which would be costly and eventually useless.

5. Conclusion

Despite the socio-political differences among the three countries concerned, the topics discussed in nuclear power discourse by the three analysed newspapers show much similarity. All three newspapers discuss the danger and fear that go hand-in-hand with the topic of nuclear power generation and the possible transfer from nuclear for non-military to nuclear for military purposes. Moreover, they all refer to fear: the evident fear of radiation, which could lead to terminable diseases, but also the fear of losing employment once old reactors or power stations are closed down.

At the same time, it is interesting to note two new phenomena present in the discourse on nuclear power. Firstly, in the articles presenting the disaster at Fukushima power plant, the media have adopted a new coinage to refer to people who had to flee from their places of birth – *nuclear refugees*, which marks a mapping between two different domains: the one of nuclear power generation, and the other of war or military conflicts as the most characteristic reasons for people to become refugees. Secondly, there is the phenomenon of *the fear of the dark*, which is new for contemporary Western societies. Here we can notice the cultural differences that exist between British and Bulgarian societies: the publications in *Dnevnik* do not so much focus on the fear of the dark probably due to the fact that in Bulgaria's socialist past power cuts and power shortages used to be part of everyone's reality. By contrast, the situation is different in the UK (and so it is in the USA), where such shortages are not so common and therefore an image of such an event can raise fear in the public.

All the three newspapers also present accounts of risk management, usually quoting the words of local or foreign experts who report on the issues in such a way so as to make the information clear to understand and at the same time bring comfort and reduce panic.

Closely connected to the texts on risk management are the publications on the investments made into research and development in order to assure better safety levels compared with older risk-prone plants. On the other hand, the topic of investments is invariably linked with the investments necessary for the completion of a new power plant and the ensuing reduction of the cost of the electricity generated.

The analysis has also shown references to Chernobyl mostly in relation to the effects radiation had and continues to have on the people who faced the nuclear disaster in Pripyat. These references seem like a bad omen for those who have lived through the most recent nuclear disaster, i.e. the one in Fukushima Daiichi, as they show the possible effects of radiation on people which could be expected in the span of the next few years.

Summing up, similarity rather than difference in the presentation of the above topics in discourse on nuclear power plants in British, American and Bulgarian newspapers indicates that the ways these three different nations perceive nuclear plants and nuclear power are comparable, which is all the more interesting given the apparent differences in political and economic development of the countries in question.

References

Allan, S., Adam, B., Carter, C., & Beck, U. (2000). *Environmental Risks and the Media*. London: Routledge.

Beck, U. (2001). *World Risk Society*. Cambridge: Polity.

Cottle, S. (Ed.) (2000). *Ethnic Minorities and the Media: Changing Cultural Boundaries*. Buckingham, Philadelphia: Open University Press.

Cottle, S. (2009). *Global Crisis Reporting: Journalism in the Global Age*. New York: OUP.

Cottle, S. (2006). *Mediatized Conflict: Developments in Media and Conflict Studies*. New York: Open University Press.

Ericson, Richard R. V. (1998). "How Journalists Visualize Fact." *The Annals of the American Academy of Political and Social Science*, vol. 560, 1998, pp. 83–95. www.jstor.org/stable/1048978.

Fairclough, Norman. (1993). *Critical Discourse and Social Change*. Cambridge: Polity Press.

Fairclough, Norman. (1995). *Critical Discourse Analysis: The Critical Study of Language*. London: Longman.

Fowler, R. (1991). *Language in the News: Discourse and Ideology in the Press*. London & New York: Routledge.

Galtung, J., & Ruge, M. H. (1965). The structure of foreign news. *Journal of Peace Research*, 2(1), 64–91.

Gamson, W. A., & Modigliani, A. (1989). Media Discourse and Public Opinion on Nuclear Power: A Constructionist Approach. *American Journal of Sociology*, 95(1), 1–37.

Huckin, T. N. (1997). Critical Discourse Analysis. In T. Miller (Ed.), *Functional Approaches to Written Text: Classroom Applications*. Washington: English Language Programs, 78–92.

Perko, T., Turcanu, C., Geenen, D., Mamane, N., & Van Rooy, L. (2011). Media content analysis of the Fukushima accident in two Belgian newspapers. *OPEN REPORT of the Belgian Nuclear Research Centrum SCK•CEN-BLG-1084*. Belgium:

Nuclear Science and Technology Studies (NST). Programme for Integration of Social Aspects into Nuclear Research (PISA).

Savada, A. M. (Ed.) (1993). *North Korea: A Country Study*. Washington: GPO for the Library of Congress. Retrieved from http://countrystudies.us/north-korea/. DOA: 16.06.2016.

Todorova, R. (2015). *Insights in Text Linguistics. From Theory to Practice*. 2nd ed. Shumen: Konstantin Preslavsky University Press.

Oleksandr Kapranov

University of Bergen, Norway

A diachronic corpus-assisted study of climate change discourse in annual reports by British Petroleum

Abstract: This article presents the results of a diachronic corpus-assisted study of climate change discourse in annual reports by British Petroleum (BP). It focuses on how the issue of climate change has been framed by BP in its annual reports (ARs) within the timeframe 2006–2015, and whether quantitative changes in word frequencies pertaining to the issue of climate change are reflected in this framing. The corpus used in the study involves ARs available online to the general public (at www.bp.com), with the following ARs' subsections selected for the analysis: "The Chairman's Letter", "The Chief Executive Officer's Letter" and the subsection "Climate Change". The quantitative analysis was executed by means of the computer program WordSmith (Scott, 2015) to identify word frequencies, which are further analyzed in the SPSS statistical package. The analysis reveals that BP's framing of the issue of climate change involves discursive constructions which are diachronically stable. The results of the statistical analysis indicate that whilst some variation in word frequencies is observed over time, it is not statistically significant. These results are indicative of BP's diachronic view of climate change as a topical issue which is constantly present in the corporation's ARs from 2006 onwards.

1. Introduction

Climate change is a global problem, which is represented in discourse by national and transnational actors (Fløttum & Dahl, 2012). British Petroleum (further referred to as BP), as a petroleum and gas supplier, is one of the transnational actors directly and indirectly involved in human activities which cause anthropogenic climate change (Lorenz, Rabinsky & Wurtzel, 2008). The aim of this paper is to analyze BP's climate change discourse by means of a corpus-assisted study. In particular, it focuses on how the issue of climate change has been framed by BP in its annual reports (further referred to as ARs) within the timeframe 2006–2015, and whether this framing is reflected in quantitative changes in word frequencies pertaining to the issue of climate change.

Whilst there is previous research involving a corpus-assisted approach to climate change (Etkin & Ho, 2007; Kirilenko & Stepchenkova, 2012; Schmidt,

Ivanova & Schäfer, 2013; Bevitori, 2015; see also section 2 below), a novel facet of this study consists in the application of the corpus-assisted methodology to climate change discourse in corporate ARs. Specifically, the study seeks to elucidate the diachronic aspect of BP's framing of climate change discourse in the corporation's ARs from 2006 until 2015.

Climate change is an important transnational challenge, which requires the cooperation of national states and transnational corporations to avert the imminent negative consequences associated with such phenomena as greenhouse gas emissions, industrial pollution, urbanisation and deforestation (Ansari, Wijen & Gray, 2013, p. 1015). Transnational fossil fuels corporations operating on international oil and gas markets, e.g. BP, Exxon, Shell, etc., are generally regarded as significant contributors to the greenhouse effect and global warming. Having said that, previous research indicates that major transnational fossil fuels corporations exhibit awareness of the issue of climate change and reflect upon relevant measures to mitigate and reduce its negative consequences (Spence & Pidgeon, 2010, p. 656).

It has also been suggested (e.g. Lorenzoni & Pidgeon, 2006) that fossil fuels corporations' impact on economy and politics in terms of climate change is manifested in corporate discourse, specifically in corporate narratives associated with climate change. Researchers have also observed that the stance presented in these narratives can differ from the view of climate change as shared in the scientific community and/or the general public's perceptions thereof (Etkin & Ho, 2007, p. 624). In yet another study (Holzer, 2007) an argument is made that climate change is an important issue for transnational corporations, which is framed, represented and structured according to their specific needs. BP, as a leading fossil fuels corporation whose assets and annual sales exceed the gross national products of some of the developed nations (Robbins, 2003, p. 1074), frames the issue of climate change as an integral part of its corporate discourse (Cox, 2008).

Currently, however, little research has been done on BP's framing of climate change in its ARs. Whilst there is a growing body of literature involving BP's environmental discourse in general, especially following the aftermath of the Gulf of Mexico oil spill (e.g. Breeze, 2012; Choi, 2012; Hall, Kice & Choi, 2012), there is still a range of open questions regarding BP's climate change discourse. In particular, little is known about how BP's climate change discourse has been changing diachronically. This question is addressed in this paper; for this purpose I examine how word frequencies for lexical items pertaining to the issue of climate change in BP's ARs have changed from 2006 until 2015.

The article is structured as follows. Firstly, an overview of previous corpus-assisted studies of climate change discourse are presented (section 2). Secondly, a similar overview of corpus-assisted studies of corporate discourse in ARs is made (section 3). Thirdly, I introduce and discuss my own diachronic corpus-assisted study of climate change discourse in BP's ARs from 2006 until 2015 (section 4).

2. Previous corpus-assisted studies of climate change discourse – an overview

Discourse concerning the issue of global climate change is extensively studied in linguistics from a variety of linguistic subfields (e.g. Livesey, 2002; Fløttum, 2010; Nerlich & Koteyko, 2010; Garcia, 2011; Dahl & Fløttum, 2014), and in particular from the vantage point of corpus-assisted studies (Boykoff, 2007; Etkin & Ho, 2007; Grundman & Krishnamurty, 2010; Kirilenko & Stepchenkova, 2012; Koteyko, Jaspal & Nerlich, 2013; Schmidt et al., 2013; Bevitori, 2015). Corpus-assisted studies are a relatively recent area of corpus linguistics, which aims at identifying changes in modern language usage, as well in social, cultural and political changes reflected in language (Partington, 2010, p. 83). Baker, Gabrielatos, Khosravinik, Krzyżanowski, McEnery and Wodak (2008, p. 273) indicate that methods typically associated with corpus linguistics can be successfully applied to discourse studies. In particular, diachronic corpus-assisted discourse studies, of which this paper is an example, employ key word analysis to facilitate the identification of possible changes of language items and discourse categories over a brief period of contemporary time (Partington, 2010). Diachronic corpora are employed to monitor lexical, grammatical and discursive developments of the language. Also, corpus-assisted discourse studies are "characterised by the compilation of ad hoc specialised corpora, since, very frequently, there is no existing collection of the discourse type that is under investigation" (Partington, 2010, p. 90).

A typical research methodology applicable to diachronic corpora involves the comparison of most frequent words in parallel corpora, the dynamics of frequent words and constructions over time, the investigation of the keywords, etc. (Baker, 2009; Mair, Hundt, Leech & Smith, 2002). Corpus-assisted studies aim at revealing possible aspects of the given discourse types, an example being corporate discourse on the topic of climate change as discussed in this paper.

As for their topics of earlier contributions to the field, recent corpus-assisted studies of climate change discourse focus on a diachronic investigation of discursive constructions of the environment and climate change in American presidential speeches 1960–2013 (Bevitori, 2015), the public's perception of this issue (Etkin & Ho, 2007), newspaper coverage of anthropogenic climate change in the United States and United Kingdom from 2003 to 2006 (Boykoff, 2007), a diachronic study of discursive representations of climate change in the media (Kirilenko & Stepchenkova, 2012), media's coverage of the topic of climate change (Koteyko et al., 2013; Schmidt et al., 2013), the framing of climate change discourse (Grundmann & Krishnamurthy, 2010), and the issue of climate change in online readers' comments in the UK (Koteyko et al., 2013), to mention just the few.

Amongst the studies outlined above, the diachronic corpus-assisted analysis of discursive constructions by Bevitori (2015) examines climate change discourse as a part of the more general environmental agenda of American presidents. In other words, Bevitori (2015) embeds climate change discourse within a broader spectrum of environmental issues addressed by US presidents in the period 1960–2013. The methodological approach of the study involves a diachronic quantitative analysis of frequency counts and key words of relevant items (Bevitori, 2015, p. 113). The results of the analysis show that the meanings of *climate* and *environment* vary over time due to the shifts in political priorities and world views (Bevitori, 2015, p. 129). Bevitori (2015) concludes that in the US presidential speeches analyzed there is a marked preference for concrete over abstract lexis, this tendency being on the increase in the diachronic perspective.

By contrast, in their corpus-assisted study Etkin and Ho (2007) analyze a corpus of the general public's perceptions of climate change. Etkin and Ho's (2007) investigation involves the identification of key word frequencies, which are further employed by the authors to identify discourse themes associated with the issue of climate change (Etkin & Ho, 2007, p. 179). Etkin and Ho (2007) report the identification of several discourse themes related to climate change, e.g. 'polar regions', 'physics of climate', 'coastal erosion and floods', 'scientific debates', 'politics', 'food and poverty', 'air pollution', 'biodiversity', 'religion', etc. It is suggested that these themes are dynamic and change over time, as the public's perception of climate change is subject to focus shifts (Etkin & Ho, 2007).

A corpus of newspaper texts on anthropogenic climate change in the UK and the USA was analyzed by Boykoff (2007) in a diachronic corpus-assisted study by means of coding through word and phrase frequencies. Boykoff (2007) posits that the results of his study reveal "a dramatic increase in the quantity of newspaper coverage of the anthropogenic climate change in both the UK and the US over the study period" (Boykoff, 2007, p. 475). Additionally, this diachronic corpus-assisted study suggests a shift in the US newspapers' accounts of climate change from a balanced towards a more scientific view of the issue. Boykoff's (2007) approach is extended in a diachronic study by Kirilenko and Stepchenkova (2012), who report a decrease in the framing of climate change discourse as a phenomenon of science and a concurrent increase of the discourse on climate change represented as a political issue.

Boykoff's (2007) findings are, in turn, echoed in a corpus-assisted study by Schmidt et al. (2013), who conducted a comparative analysis of media coverage of the issue of climate change. The authors compiled a corpus of media articles from 27 countries, and analyzed them by means of relevant key words (e.g. 'climate', 'greenhouse effect', 'global warming'). Schmidt et al. (2013) indicate that climate change discourse from 1997 till 2009 appears to be a topical issue in the mass media.

Similarly to Boykoff (2007) and Schmidt et al. (2013), Koteyko et al. (2013) employ the corpus-research tools of relative word frequency, key words and collocations in their corpus study of online readers' comments on the issue of climate change, the aim being to compare discursive patterns in the readers' comments during two different time periods, i.e. before November 2009 and in 2010. The study reveals, among others, that references to climate scientists are accompanied with negatively connoted lexis in the readers' comments on the issue of global climate change.

Whilst Koteyko et al. (2013) examine texts from UK sources, Grundman and Krishnamurty (2010) use a corpus of news articles from the USA, the UK, France and Germany in their corpus-assisted study of the discourse of climate change. The corpus is analyzed to reveal significant differences in the framing of climate change discourse in these countries. Grundman and Krishnamurty (2010) use research methodology identical to the one applied in Koteyko et al. (2013), with a focus on word frequency lists and collocation lists compiled by means of the WordSmith (Scott, 2015) software.

3. Previous corpus-assisted studies of corporate discourse in ARs – an overview

Discourse in general is regarded as "a cluster of context-dependent semiotic practices that are situated within specific fields of social action" (Reisigl & Wodak, 2009, p. 89). Corporate discourse, as a subgenre of discourse, involves "how people communicate using talk or writing in commercial organizations in order to get their work done" (Bargiela-Chiappini, Nickerson & Planken, 2013, p. 3). Corporate discourse involves such social actors as transnational corporations, small- and medium-sized national enterprises, regulatory bodies, government organizations, shareholders, consumers and other socio-economic actors (Christensen, 2002).

As a genre of corporate discourse corporate ARs involve a class of communicative events with certain structural characteristics that serve a well-defined purpose: to meet the expectations of shareholders and other actors in terms of both content and form (Upton & Connor, 2001, p. 316). It is thus indicated that ARs are "composed and read within a dense and complex web of stakeholder communication, which includes interim reports, preliminary announcements, analyst presentations, corporate Web sites, media releases, direct contact with large investors" (Rutherford, 2005, p. 249). The purpose of corporate ARs is to provide measurable and comparable data of the corporation's performance to inform the shareholders, investors, employees, as well as public and government actors of corporate gains, losses and strategies in a given fiscal or calendar year (Boiral & Henri, 2015, p. 3).

Corporate ARs reflect corporate law, the interest of the management, creditors, shareholders and employees (Spencer & Fitzgerald, 2013, p. 215). However, transnational corporations regard their ARs not only as fiscal documents aimed at shareholders and/or government bodies, but as a facet of the corporate image and reputation (Bebbington, Larrinaga & Moneva, 2008). For this reason, fossil fuels corporations, e.g. BP, Shell, etc., include specific sections into their ARs to present the corporation in a favorable light and to indirectly manage their public image in the areas of environmental sustainability (Cox, 2008, p. 33), human rights record (Livesey, 2002) and climate change agenda (Fløttum, 2010). Specifically, in addition to the obligatory statements by the chairperson (often referred to in BP's discourse as "The Chairman's Letter") and the Chief Executive Officer's annual address, commonly referred to as "The Chief Executive Officer's Letter", there are AR subsections which address corporate social responsibility, the protection of the environment, human rights, etc. In ARs by BP these sections are presented in the main body of the AR, thus creating a complex and polyphonic discursive space.

In a corpus-assisted study of corporate ARs, and chairpersons' statements in particular, Smith and Taffler (2000) propose a model that is able to predict corporate performance. The model is based upon word and theme counts in corporate ARs. It should be noted that word frequencies have been successfully applied to AR discourse to reveal that those corporations which experience financial difficulties refer to profits more frequently than losses (Smith & Taffler, 2000). Following these findings, it could be assumed that transnational fossil fuels corporations would refer to the issue of climate change and greenhouse gasses frequently, striving to create an impression of corporations which are concerned with the environmental and climate change-related issues.

In another corpus-assisted study, Rutherford (2005) reports that word frequencies identified in ARs are relatively stable over time. Stability in word usage and word frequencies is explained by the context in which ARs are written. According to Rutherford (2005, p. 372), the corporate context of ARs is stable due to the "influence of authoritative guidance", i.e. the corporation strives to maintain a stable and positive image in the eyes of the consumers and the stakeholders. Maintaining a positive image results, in turn, in a relatively stable discursive representation of the corporation in the AR.

All in all, it should be noted that whilst there exist a number of studies involving corpus-assisted methods to analyze climate change discourse (see section 2) and equally many corpus-assisted studies of corporate discourse in ARs (this section), there are few corpus-assisted studies of corporate discourse in ARs related to the issue of climate change. The latter is the topic of this paper.

4. A diachronic corpus-assisted analysis of climate change discourse in BP's ARs from 2006 until 2015

The study whose results are further presented in this article aims at identifying the discursive representations of climate change in BP's ARs over a ten-year period (2006–2015). The quantitative analysis is concerned with the diachronic aspects of BP's climate change discourse (see section 4.4). Additionally, I contrast separate voices in BP's corporate discourse on climate change, as represented by the Chairman and the Chief Executive Officer (see section 4.4). For this purpose, two specific AR subsections, i.e. "the Chairman's Letter" and the "Chief Executive Officer's Letter", respectively, are examined diachronically to identify the polyphonic discursive space of BP's discourse involving climate change.

4.1. Hypothesis and Research Questions

The hypothesis of the present study is based upon the assumption that transnational corporations manage their corporate narratives strategically (Rutherford, 2005, p. 350), and exhibit a tendency to frame the issue of climate change discourse via diachronically stable discursive representations (Kapranov, forthcoming). Specifically, it has been found that BP and Shell frame their climate discourses with the use of similar conceptual metaphors, which are stable over the period of five years. Following these findings, it is hypothesized in this study that BP's climate change discourse is characterized by diachronically stable discursive representations of climate change; to prove this thesis I will examine the distribution of key words in word frequency lists.

Following the above hypothesis, the specific research questions involve three considerations: (1) how the word frequencies of the key words ('climate change', 'emission(s)', 'greenhouse gas(ses)', 'low carbon', 'solar', and 'wind') change over time in BP's ARs from 2006 until 2015; (2) are there quantitatively significant differences in the distribution of the aforementioned key words in the subsections "The Chairman's Letter" and "The Chief Executive Officer's Letter" in the course of time?; (3) what voices can be identified in the two specific AR subsections, i.e. "the Chairman's Letter" and the "Chief Executive Officer's Letter", and how they contribute to creating the polyphonic discursive space of BP's discourse involving climate change in a diachronic perspective.

4.2. Materials

Materials selected for the study involve a corpus of ten ARs available to the general public online at www.bp.com, with the following subsections selected for the analysis: "The Chairman's Letter" (the whole section in each AR, total number of words = 6549), "The Chief Executive's Letter" (the whole section in each AR, total number of words = 6989), and "Climate Change" (the whole section in each AR, total number of words = 4142). The timeframe of the analysis involves a ten-year period from 2006 until 2015 (including the 2015 AR). Following Bargiela-Chiappini et al. (2013), all three sections of the ARs selected for the analysis are deemed to adhere to the subgenre of corporate annual reporting within the general genre of business communication.

4.3. Methodology

The quantitative corpus-assisted methodology is employed in the present study. Following Partington's (2010) definition, *corpus-assisted methodology* in relation to the present work involves a diachronic comparison of subsections of the corpus against other subsections from different periods of time. In terms of the procedure and data analysis, the present study is designed in accordance with the corpus-assisted investigation outlined in Bevitori (2015), where the key words are selected and examined against the word frequencies in a diachronic corpus. The following key words have been selected in the present study: 'climate change', 'emission(s)', 'greenhouse gas(ses)', 'low carbon', 'solar', and 'wind'. These key words were examined in the software program WordSmith (Scott, 2015).

4.4. Results and Discussion

Overall statistics of the total word count are given in Table 1.

Table 1. Statistics of the word count in BP's AR corpus

Subsection/Year	2006	2007	2008	2009	2010	2011	2012	2013	2014	2015
Climate Change	193	481	884	241	241	530	482	360	291	438
Chairman's Letter	564	423	599	659	836	865	630	628	587	558
Chief Executive Officer's Letter	638	498	880	949	683	1062	726	642	674	337

The results of the quantitative corpus-assisted data analysis are summarized in Tables 2–4 below. Table 2 presents the data elicited from the "Climate Change" subsections of BP's ARs from 2006 until 2015:

Table 2. Key word frequency per 1000 words in "Climate Change" subsections

Subsection/Year	2006	2007	2008	2009	2010	2011	2012	2013	2014	2015
climate change	2.1	1	0.8	4.1	1.5	2.5	2.1	1.4	1.1	1.4
emission(s)	1.6	2.3	2.5	2.5	1.3	1.7	3.9	5.5	4.6	1
greenhouse gasses	1	1.5	1.5	1.2	1.2	0.8	0.4	1.3	2.1	1.8
low carbon	0.2	0.2	0.2	0.1	0	0.7	0.3	1.4	1.4	0.3
solar	0	0	0	0	0	0	0	0	0	0
wind	0.1	0.2	0.1	0	0	0	0	0	0	0

Table 3. Key word frequency in the "Chairman's Letter" subsection

Key words/Year	2006	2007	2008	2009	2010	2011	2012	2013	2014	2015
climate change	0	0	0.1	0.1	0.1	0	0	0	0	0.2
emission(s)	0	0	0	0	0	0.1	0	0	0	0
greenhouse gasses	1	1.5	1.5	1.2	1.2	0.8	0.4	1.3	2.1	1.8
low carbon	0.2	0.2	0.2	0.1	0	0.7	0.3	1.4	1.4	0.3
solar	0	0	0	0	0	0	0	0	0	0
wind	0.1	0.2	0.1	0	0	0	0	0	0	0

Table 4. Key word frequency in the "Chief Executive Officer's Letter" subsection

Key words/Year	2006	2007	2008	2009	2010	2011	2012	2013	2014	2015
climate change	0	0	0.1	0	0	0	0	0	0	0
emission(s)	0	0	0.3	0	0	0	0	0	0	0
greenhouse gasses	0	0	0.1	0	0	0	0	0	0	0
low carbon	0.4	0.2	0.3	0.3	0	0.1	0	0	0	0
solar	0.3	0	0.2	0	0	0	0	0	0	0
wind	0	0	0	0.1	0	0	0	0	0	0

It was assumed in the hypothesis (see section 4.1) that corporate discourse exhibits a tendency to be diachronically stable. Statistical data analysis in software package SPSS indeed reveals no statistically significant differences in key word frequency in diachrony. In particular, a paired-samples t-test was conducted to compare the distribution of the aforementioned key words in the subsections "The Chairman's Letter" and "The Chief Executive Officer's Letter".

A possible explanation as to why there are no statistically significant results in terms of the key words change in diachrony might in fact be the specifics of corporate communications. According to Christensen (2002, p. 162), corporate communicators "hope to project one uniform and unambiguous image of what the organization is and stands for". Since corporations nowadays are expected to be socially and environmentally committed (Scherer & Palazzo, 2007, p. 1096), BP also projects a stable image of an environmentally conscious corporation. This finding supports previous research (Boiral & Henri, 2015; Lyon & Montgomery, 2015), which emphasizes the increased role of environmental and climate change-related discourse in corporate communication. Hence BP's climate change discourse can be regarded as conforming to the global trend of environmental reporting and commitment to the issue of climate change.

Whilst variation in key word frequency does take place, it is not statistically significant. Arguably, BP's climate change discourse exhibits a tendency to be framed by diachronically stable discursive representations. Specifically, the data analysis reveals that 'greenhouse gases' and 'low carbon' are diachronically stable key words by which BP frames its climate change discourse in the "Climate Change" subsections of all the examined ARs from 2006 until 2015. To illustrate, the frequency of the key word 'low carbon' in the corpus is as follows: 0.2 (2006), 0.2 (2007), 0.2 (2008), 0.1 (2009), 0 (2010), 0.7 (2011), 0.3 (2012), 1.4 (2013), 1.4 (2014), and 0.3 in 2015. Similar statistics are observed in "The Chief Executive Officer's Letter" in 2006–2009, e.g. the frequency of the key word 'low carbon' exhibits the following dynamics: 0.4 (2006), 0.2 (2007), 0.3(2008), 0.3 (2009), 0 (2010), 0.1 (2011), and 0 in 2012–2015.

Additionally, it was found in the present study that renewable energy sources such as solar and wind energy have been consistently framed as epiphenomenal in BP's climate change discourse from 2006 onwards. For instance, solar energy is mentioned in "The Chief Executive Officer's Letter" in 2006 and 2008, whilst in the "Climate Change" subsection there is no reference to it within the context of climate change in the period under scrutiny. The same situation concerns wind energy, referred to in 2009 in "The Chief Executive Officer's Letter" and mentioned in the "Climate Change" subsection only in the period 2006–2008, but not later.

As far as the third research question is concerned, i.e. what voices can be identified in two specific AR subsections, i.e. "the Chairman's Letter" and the "Chief Executive Officer's Letter", and how they contribute to the creation of a polyphonic discursive space of BP's discourse involving climate change in a diachronic perspective, the present data show a polyphony of corporate voices in BP's framing of its climate change discourse. For instance, whilst the key words 'greenhouse gasses', 'solar' and 'wind' are not mentioned in "The Chairman's Letter" sections in the ARs 2006–2015, these key words were identified in "The Chief Executive Officer's Letter" sections in the period 2006–2009, though they are absent from 2010 onwards. The discursive voices of both the chief executive officer and the chairman appear to concur on the matter after the 2010 ecological disaster in the Gulf of Mexico. Presumably, the 2010 oil spill in the Gulf has such serious repercussions for BP that its senior management focused on financial, risk-related and spill-related matters, completely relegating the issue of climate change to the background.

It should be observed that whilst media representations of climate change usually refer to global warming as a multi-faceted threat (Jaspal & Nerlich, 2012), BP does not mention global warming in any of its ARs in 2006–2015. In contrast with media discourse, BP appears to frame the issue of climate change through the lenses of 'emissions', 'greenhouse gases' and 'low carbon' to communicate the company's environmental performance, its attempts at sustainable development and climate change mitigation. These findings are in concert with the contention that fossil fuels corporations frame their climate change agendas in environmental and economic terms (de Vries, Terwel & Ellemers, 2015, p. 16). From both the environmental and economic perspectives, the analysis of BP's ARs from the period 2006–2015 indicates that BP considers climate change in conjunction with the measures to address and mitigate the process, as can be implied from the presence of key words 'emissions', 'greenhouse gasses' and 'low carbon'.

5. Conclusions

The present article involved a diachronic corpus-assisted analysis of climate change discourse in Annual Reports published by British Petroleum in the period 2006–2015. The main aim of the analysis was to investigate the distribution of references to climate change in British Petroleum's Annual Reports within the said time frame. Specifically, it was investigated how the framing of climate change was reflected in quantitative changes in word frequencies. Such sections of the Annual Reports as "The Chairman's Letter", "The Chief Executive's Letter", and "Climate Change", respectively, were analyzed in terms of word frequencies. The results revealed that BP's framing of climate change involved diachronically stable discursive constructions, illustrated by the frequency of the key words. In particular, statistical data analysis revealed no statistically significant differences in key word frequencies across time in the sections "The Chairman's Letter" and "The Chief Executive's Letter".

Acknowledgements

The author wants to acknowledge research funding from the Norwegian Research Council and the University of Bergen (Norway), which enabled the writing of this article and presenting it at the GlobE international conference in Warsaw in May 2015.

References

Ansari, S., Wijen, F., & Gray, B. B. (2013). Constructing a Climate Change Logic: An Institutional Perspective on the 'Tragedy of Commons'. *Organization Science*, 24(4), 1014–1040.

Baker, P. (2009). The BE06 Corpus of British English and recent language change. *International Journal of Corpus Linguistics*, 14(3), 312–337.

Baker, P., Gabrielatos, C., Khosravinik, M., Krzyżanowski, M., McEnery T., & Wodak, R. (2008). A useful methodological synergy? Combining critical discourse analysis and corpus linguistics to examine discourses of refugees and asylum seekers in the UK press. *Discourse and Society*, 19(3), 273–306.

Bargiela-Chiappini, F., Nickerson, C., & Planken, B. (2013). *What is Business Discourse*? Basingstoke: Palgrave Macmillan UK.

Bebbington, J., Larrinaga, C., & Moneva, J. (2008). Corporate social reporting and reputation risk management. *Accounting, Auditing & Accountability Journal*, 21(3), 337–361.

Bevitori, C. (2015). Discursive Constructions of the Environment in American Presidential Speeches 1960–2013: A Diachronic Corpus-Assisted Study. In P. Baker (Ed.), *Corpora and Discourse Studies*. Basingstoke: Palgrave Macmillan UK, 110–133.

Boiral, O., & Henri, J. F. (2015). Is Sustainability Performance Comparable? A Study of GRI Reports of Mining Organizations. *Business & Society*, 56(2), 283–317.

Boykoff, M. (2007). Flogging a dead norm? Newspaper coverage of anthropogenic climate change in the United States and United Kingdom from 2003 to 2006. *Area*, 39(4), 470–481.

Breeze, R. (2012). Legitimation in corporate discourse: Oil corporations after Deepwater Horizon. *Discourse and Society*, 23(1), 3–18.

Choi, J. (2012). A content analysis of BP's press releases dealing with crisis. *Public Relations Review*, 38, 422–429.

Christensen, L. T. (2002). Corporate communication: the challenge of transparency. *Corporate Communications: An International Journal*, 7(3), 162–168.

Cox, M. J. (2008). Sustainable Communication: A Study of Green Advertising and Audience Reception within the Growing Arena of Corporate Social Responsibility. Case Study: British Petroleum. *Earth & Environment*, 3, 32–51.

Dahl, T., & Fløttum, K. (2014). A linguistic framework for studying voices and positions in the climate debate. *Text & Talk*, 34(4), 401–420.

de Vries, G., Terwel, B., & Ellemers, N. (2015). Perceptions of Manipulation and Judgement of Illegitimacy: Pitfalls in the Use of Emphasis in Framing when Communicating about CO2 Capture and Storage. *Environmental Communication*, 10(2), 206–226.

Etkin, D., & Ho, E. (2007). Climate Change: Perceptions and Discourse of Risk. *Journal of Risk Research*, 10(5), 623–641.

Fløttum, K. (2010). A linguistic and discursive view on climate change discourse. *ASP*, 58, 19–37.

Fløttum, K., & Dahl, T. (2012). Different contexts, different 'stories'? A linguistic comparison of two development reports on climate change. *Language and Communication*, 32, 14–23.

Garcia, M. M. (2011). Perception is truth: How US newspapers framed the 'go green' conflict between BP and Greenpeace. *Public Relations Review*, 37, 57–59.

Grundmann, R., & Krishnamurthy, R. (2010). The Discourse of Climate Change: A Corpus-based Approach. *Critical Approaches to Discourse Analysis across Disciplines*, 4(2), 113–133.

Hall, Z., Kice, B., & Choi, J. (2012). Damage Control: Rhetoric and New Media Technologies in the Aftermath of the BP Oil Spill. *Poroi. An Interdisciplinary Journal of Rhetorical Analysis and Invention*, 8(1), 1–7.

Holzer, B. (2007). Framing the corporation: Royal Dutch/Shell and human rights woes in Nigeria. *Journal of Consumer Policy*, 30(3), 281–301.

Jaspal, R., & Nerlich, B. (2012). When climate science became politics: British media representations of climate change in 1988. *Public Understanding of Science*, 23(2), 122–141.

Kapranov, O. (forthcoming). Do International Corporations Speak in One Voice on the Issue of Global Climate Change: The Case of British Petroleum and The Royal Dutch Shell Group. In C. Cem & K. Papaja (Eds.), *Global Perspectives on Social Sciences and Humanities – Theory and Practice*. Warszawa: LiF.

Kirilenko, A., & Stepchenkova, S. (2012). Climate change discourse in mass media: application of computer-assisted content analysis. *Journal of Environmental Studies*, 2, 178–191.

Koteyko, N., Jaspal, R., & Nerlich, B. (2013). Climate change and 'climategate' in online reader comments: a mixed methods study. *The Geographical Journal*, 179(1), 74–86.

Livesey, S. M. (2002). Global Warming Wars: Rhetorical and Discourse Analytic Approaches to Exxonmobil's Corporate Public Discourse. *Journal of Business Communication*, 39, 117–146.

Lorenz S., Rabinsky M., & Wurtzel, J. (2008). Exxon Mobile and British Petroleum: A tale of two companies or just business as usual? *Natural Resources and Environment*, 501, 1–22.

Lorenzoni, I., & Pidgeon, N. F. (2006). Public views on climate change: European and USA perspectives. *Climate Change*, 77, 73–95.

Lyon, T., & Montgomery, W. (2015). The Means and End of Greenwash. *Organization and Environment*, 28(2), 223–249.

Mair, C., M. Hundt, M., Leech, G., & Smith, N. (2002). Short term diachronic shifts in part-of-speech frequencies: a comparison of the tagged LOB and F-LOB corpora. *International Journal of Corpus Linguistics*, 7(2), 245–264.

Nerlich, B., & Koteyko, N. (2010). Carbon gold rush and carbon cowboys: a new chapter in green mythology? *Environmental Communication*, 4(1), 37–53.

Partington, A. (2010). Modern Diachronic Corpus-Assisted Discourse Studies (MD-CADS) on UK newspapers: an overview of the project. *Corpora*, 5(2), 83–108.

Reisigl, M., & Wodak, R. (2009). The discourse-historical approach (DHA). *Methods of critical discourse analysis*, 2, 87–121.

Robbins, P. (2003). Transnational corporations and the discourse of water privatization. *Journal of International Development*, 15, 1073–1082.

Rutherford, B. (2005). Genre analysis of corporate annual report narratives. A corpus-linguistics-based approach. *Journal of Business Communication*, 42(4), 349–378.

Scherer, A., & Palazzo, G. (2007). Toward a Political Conception of Corporate Responsibility: Business and Society Seen from a Habermasian Perspective. *Academy of Management Review*, 32(4), 1096–1120.

Schmidt, A., Ivanova, A., & Schäfer, M. (2013). Media attention for climate change around the world: A comparative analysis of newspaper coverage in 27 Countries. *Global Environmental Change*, 23(5), 1233–1248.

Scott, M. (2015). *WordSmith*. Software program.

Smith, M., & Taffler, R. J. (2000). The chairman's statement: A content analysis of discretionary disclosures. *Accounting, Auditing and Accountability Journal*, 13(5), 624–646.

Spence, A., & Pidgeon, N. (2010). Framing and communicating climate change: The effects of distance and outcome. *Global Environmental Change*, 20, 656–667.

Spencer D., & Fitzgerald, A. (2013). Three ecologies, transversality and victimization: the case of the British Petroleum oil spill. *Crime Law Social Change*, 59, 209–223.

Upton, T., & Connor, U. (2001). Using computerized corpus analysis to investigate the textlinguistic discourse moves of a genre. *English for Specific Purposes*, 20, 313–329.

Part 3.
Discourse in professional domains

Britt-Louise Gunnarsson

Uppsala University, Sweden

Discourses in organizations and workplaces in the globalized economy

Abstract: The conditions for professional discourse have been influenced by a series of changes taking place in recent decades. One striking feature is the increased reliance on the Internet for internal and external communication, another one the ongoing globalization of the business world and the job market. Multilingual companies use English as their corporate language, and the globalized job market bring issues of multilingualism and multiculturalism to the surface, both in relation to the organization as a whole and to workplace practices.

This paper summarizes the results of studies exploring discourses in organizations and workplaces in the globalized economy. It (1) analyzes staff policy documents and career stories from nine multinationals' websites, with a focus on the images of the company and its culture which they reveal. It also (2) explores multinationals' language policy through an analysis of explicit language requirements in advertisements for jobs in Swedish branches of multinationals. Finally, it (3) looks at multilingualism at work from a workfloor perspective, then focusing on the communicative situation of immigrants in a Swedish hospital and a transnational company. In the Discussion (section 5), the results are viewed in a broader perspective and related to a model for the analysis of the contextual construction of professional discourse.

1. Introduction

The conditions for professional discourse have been influenced by a series of changes taking place in recent decades. In organizations throughout the world we find a widespread use of technology and increased reliance on the Internet for internal and external communication. Another striking feature is the globalization of the business world and the job market. Throughout the world we find multinational companies which use English as their corporate language and employ multilingual people who can move between jobs, between branches and between countries. Workforce mobility and workplace diversity which characterize the globalized economy also bring issues of multilingualism and multiculturalism to the foreground, both in relation to the organization as a whole and to workplace practices.

In this paper I discuss the results of studies which explore the complexity and diversity of communication in organizations and workplaces in the globalized economy. Firstly, I explore the images of the company and its culture as are presented on multinationals' websites (section 2). Secondly, I focus on multilinguals' language policy as is revealed in job advertisements (section 3). Thirdly, I discuss multilingual workplaces with workforce diversity (section 4). In the final part of this paper I assume a broader perspective in order to relate the studied discourses in organizations and workplaces to their various contextual frameworks (section 5). Conclusions of my research are presented at the end of the paper.

2. Images of the company and its culture on multinationals' websites

Global accessibility – and simultaneous access by different reader groups – is a reality for texts published on websites. For multinational companies this means a shift from once specific and limited-access documents to inter-related texts on various subpages of the company website (Castells, 1999; Lemke, 2002; Qvortrup, 2002). In consequence, texts on websites necessitate a new type of writing and reading (Herring, 2001; Kress & van Leeuwen, 2001; Ylönen, 2007), and also a new and challenging way of handling the complex interweaving of texts on the Internet (LeVine & Scollon, 2004; Norris & Jones, 2005).

In this section I discuss the images of staff policy and company culture which are constructed in texts found on the career-oriented subpages of nine multinationals' websites. Here I refer to my earlier study (Gunnarsson, 2014a), where I explored these websites focusing on staff policy documents and on career stories. The studied multinationals are Nokia, AstraZeneca, Ericsson, Electrolux, Bosch, Siemens, ABB, McDonald's and Ikea. The texts analysed were published on the career-oriented subpages of the respective multinationals' global websites, including www.nokia.com/global, www.astrazeneca.com/careers, www.ericsson.com/careers, http://group.electrolux.com/en/, www.bosch-carreer.com/home/, www.siemens,com/jobs/en, www.abb.com/seabb361/, www.mcdonalds.com/us/careers, www.ikea.com/co_worker_stories. The corpus was collected in July-August 2011 and in September-October 2012.

2.1. Staff policy documents on multinational companies' websites

All nine multinationals have texts on their websites which could be labeled 'staff policy documents'. In these documents a number of 'core values' are presented and highlighted. The results of the analysis show that the following five values are stressed in all staff policy documents studied: (1) 'diversity', (2) 'respect',

(3) 'development', (4) 'openness' and (5) 'creativity'. Nokia's website is here used as an example; references to these core values are bold-typed:

Example (1)

Our people & culture

Let's agree to disagree

At the last count, the Nokia Group employed approximately 139,000 people around the world: not bad for a company that started life as a small riverside paper mill in Finland.

In 2010, the devices and services business alone employed approximately 60,000 people from around 115 **different nationalities**. And approximately 41% of them were women. Such diversity is crucial to our success so far – and to our continued success in the future. We're operating in more markets than ever before, and employees from **diverse backgrounds** can give us invaluable insights into our customer bases. Just as important, a **mix of cultures**, genders, age groups, beliefs, interests and opinions in the workplace helps foster **debate, discussion, ideas and innovation**. Not to mention making Nokia a more enjoyable, stimulating and **rewarding** place to spend your working day.

Doing things the Nokia Way

Commitment to **diversity** is just part of what we call the Nokia Way – the core values and shared philosophy that make our company tick. **Creativity, empowerment, openness, collaboration**, and **consideration for people** and the environment – these are all integral to the way we do business. But above all, it's about **being human** in everything we do – **respecting and caring**, even in tough business situations.

(www.nokia.com/global/about_nokia; emphasis mine)

In staff policy documents the concept (1) 'diversity' is a core value which multinationals claim to be important in relation to the composition of their staff. In the Nokia text (Example 1), the expressions *different nationalities*, *diverse backgrounds* and *mix of cultures* make this core value concrete.

In relation to the treatment of their employees, multinational companies stress (2) 'respect'; again, in the Nokia text (Example 1), this value is expressed as *consideration for people*, *being human* and *respecting and caring*.

Many staff documents also describe an interest in the (3) 'development' of their staff, and in Example (1) we find that working for Nokia is stimulating and *rewarding*, and combined with *empowerment*.

Claims in relation to the workplace culture are also frequent in staff policy documents; among them one workplace value which is stressed is (4) 'openness'. In the Nokia text (Example 1) we find such key terms related to this value as *debate*, *discussion*, *openness* and *collaboration*.

The final workplace value frequently cited in multinationals' staff policy documents is (5) 'creativity', which in the Nokia text (Example 1) appears as *ideas and innovation* and *creativity*.

2.2. Career stories on multinational companies' websites

The texts representing the 'career story' genre were found on subpages entitled for instance "Nokia people" (Nokia), "Our people" (Ericsson), "Our employees" (McDonald), "Working with Bosch" (Bosch), "People on the move" (Electrolux), etc. In total more than 100 career stories were found on the nine multinationals' webpages analyzed. The career stories were structured similarly: all of them comprised a photo of the featured employee, his/her first or full name, some facts relating to his/her position in the company, and a narrative presenting this employee.

Firstly, I will illustrate what I mean by a *career story*, using a story at Nokia's website as an example. Below the staff policy document (see Example 1 above) we find the subheading "Nokia People", with names of six employees, who work in Beijing (China), Burlington (Massachusetts, USA), London (UK), Gurgaon (India), and two persons in Espoo (Finland). Each entry features the name of the employee in bold type, an introductory description, and a "Read more" link.

At the time of my study one of the featured Nokia employees was Carol Soriano. When the "Read more" link is opened, we find her full name and her picture. These are followed with a brief introduction and then a story featuring this employee. The story is based on a question-answer pattern; a set of questions, marked in bold, structures Carol's story, which moves from a description of her job at Nokia (*What do you do?*) to her career (*How's your career progressed?*), then her views on her job (*What do you like about your job?*) and on the company (*What do you like about Nokia?*). The next two questions concern her role in the company (*How do you help Nokia?*) and how Nokia as an employer has made her develop (*How has Nokia helped you?*). The last question then concerns her private life (*When you're not working, what are you doing?*).[1]

We do not know who is posing these questions, nor who has written the text. In the answers, however, the voice of the employee, Carol Soriano, is made explicit by the use of *I*, *me* and *my* throughout the story, as in e.g. "*I* head up the Consumer Communications team", "*My* team's …", "*I* trained to be a lawyer", "*I* decided to work" etc. (italics added)

It should be noted that all six career stories on Nokia's website are structured in the same way as Carol Soriano's story, with a brief introduction and the main text organized following a question-answer pattern. Also, the majority of the stories presented in the nine multinationals' websites analyzed in my corpus follow a similar pattern. They all have a heading and a brief introduction, either summarizing, or asking a question, or giving a perspective, or quoting what the

---

1 The whole career story featuring Carol is presented in Gunnarsson (2014a, pp. 99–100).

employee said. What is worth noting, however, is that none of them provides any cues as to who in fact has posed the questions, answered them or provided the employee's statements. The interviewer is unknown to the reader, and so is the author of the stories.

2.2.1. *Career stories – analysis*

For a detailed analysis which concerned 27 career stories (three on each website of the nine companies) I used a methodological framework which combines textlinguistics (aspects of *macro structure*, *foregrounding* and *salience*, Gunnarsson, 2009) with narratology (*voice*, Vološinov, 1973; Mishler, 1987; and *model reader*, Eco, 1984; Bakhtin, 1986; Nord, 2011). Due to space limitations of this paper my summary below concerns only the analysis of foregrounded content and voice (section 2.2.1.1), and salient elements (sections 2.2.1.2 and 2.2.1.3).[2]

2.2.1.1. *Foregrounded content and voice*

In my analysis of the career stories I have explored how the career stories balance between the presentation of the company and the employee, and also whose voice is heard in the different parts of the story. Let us look at some extracts which illustrate these aspects.

The first excerpt (Examples 2a and 2b) is extracted from a career story on AstraZeneca's website. It illustrates how a 'neutral' voice, 'the voice of the company', is used both in parts foregrounding the company and in parts foregrounding the employee.

The voice of the company
Foregrounding the company

Example (2a)
Personnel at the Regulatory Affairs department work together with scientists and commercial colleagues to support the development of new drugs and to maintain marketing licenses worldwide. …

Foregrounding the employee

Example (2b)
Britt-Marie Stålbom has a broad experience within the regulatory field and has worked for AstraZeneca over 10 years, in a number of different positions within Regulatory Affairs. Today Britt-Marie is working with knowledge transfer and internal trainings for her co-workers at Regulatory Affairs.

(www.astrazeneca.com/careers)

2 For a more detailed analysis, see Gunnarsson (2014a).

Without references to any source, the reader gets to know that the AstraZeneca's department's personnel collaborate with scientists and commercial colleagues globally (Example 2a). Also the second paragraph, which foregrounds the employee, is written in a 'quasi-neutral' way (Example 2b). Britt-Marie Stålbom's "broad experience within the […] field", her years with the company and her career are summarized without any direct quotations from her or any other references. All career stories in my corpus contain similarly short passages presented in a neutral voice, for instance in their introductory parts.

Let us now turn to some passages where the 'voice of the employee' is explicitly heard. Here the relationship between content and voice is more complex, as illustrate the following passages from a career story published on Ericsson's website. The career story has the heading "Meet Yu who joined Ericsson in 2007". The full name of Yu is not revealed; there is only a photo attached to the story on which we see a young man.

The voice of the employee
Foregrounding the company and the employee

Example (3a)
Ericsson does not only provide world-class products to the customers but also world-class services. As an instructor, the customer-first aspect is always the most important thing but also the greatest challenge in my job. […]

I have always considered respect as Ericsson's most attractive characteristics. The respect permeates the whole organization as well as respect towards our customers. My managers always delegates [sic] me the jobs I am competent for, and coach me on the jobs I am not that familiar with. The fact that we respect our customers from our hearts is the foundation for them trusting us as a supplier.

Foregrounding the employee and the company

Example (3b)
During that time I realized that influencing people is what I really like and something I am good at as well, so I applied for an internal job as an instructor and got it. Ericsson really encourages all employees to constantly look for new challenges and new positions in the organization to enable each person to develop his/her talent.
(www.ericsson.com/careers/ourpeople/yu)

The use of first-person pronouns in Examples (3a) and (3b) indicates that the voice heard is that of the employee Yu. He constructs a positive image of the company, and at the same time he is presenting himself as a professional. We can therefore note here the intertwinement of (1) a description of the company and its products (Example 3a), and (2) Yu's self-presentation as a professional, that is in his role as an instructor (Example 3a), but also of (3) his possibility to advance (Example 3b), and (4) the company's general treatment of its staff (Example 3a).

Through Yu's story we are informed that Ericsson delegates and coaches its staff, and shows them respect, and also that Ericsson encourages their employees to look for new challenges and positions.

While the career story on Ericsson's website gives an impression that we hear Yu's own voice, we are not told anything about his family and private life. However, in other stories included in my corpus, such information is sometimes provided, although usually we only get glimpses from the featured employee's life outside the job.

2.2.1.2. Salient elements in the construction of the company and its workplace culture

My next research question concerns salient elements in the career stories. I will first summarize my results, focusing on how the company and its workplace culture are constructed in these texts. In particular I draw attention to elements which reveal how the company's policy balances between global and local concerns, and between economic concerns and social values.

As for *global concerns*, all nine multinational companies are constructed as *global companies* in the career stories published on their websites. For instance, in the story featuring Carol, she mentions among the things which she likes about Nokia that "it is a truly global company. You work with people from all over the world, and you get to hear – and appreciate – many different points of view". Similarly, Yu highlights the global character of the company: "Ericsson is a truly global company with presence in 175 countries which gives me as an employee a lot of opportunities to work with people from all over the world".

By contrast, the company's *local concerns* are stressed in some stories but not in all. In Carol's story, for instance, Nokia is constructed as a company that makes a difference for people in the Philippines, where she has worked: "I have witnessed first hand how mobile phones (the ones that Nokia has developed and brought to market) can make a real difference in people's lives. Whole villages and industries are transformed as a result of connectivity."

As far as *economic concerns* are concerned, the key one is *excellence*: the companies' *excellent* products, *excellent* services and economic *success* are highlighted in one way or another in all the career stories analyzed. For instance, Nokia is said to be "one of the top 10 brands in the world [...] with the latest and greatest devices and services". Similarly, Ericsson is described, through the voice of Yu, as a company which "not only provide world-class products to the customers but also world-class services".

As for *social values*, they are stressed in many of the stories but, as in the case of local concerns, not in all. In this respect the companies are described as employers which give their staff training and support. For instance, on Ericsson's website, we hear Yu's voice saying: "Ericsson really encourages all employees to constantly look for new challenges and new positions in the organization to enable each person to develop his/her talent". Yu also notes that "[m]y managers delegate me the jobs I am competent for, and coach me on jobs I am not familiar with." Similarly, Nokia is constructed as an employer which gives its staff a possibility to develop; as Carol in her career story notes, "[f]rom a career perspective, Nokia has allowed me to experience different aspects of marketing (from creative development to implementation) in different locations (from local to global)."

2.2.1.3. Salient elements in the presentation of the employee and his/her career

I will now turn to salient elements in the presentation of the employee and his/her career in the career stories. Many of the career stories analyzed include background details about the employee's education and earlier jobs. Age is seldom mentioned explicitly, but as all career stories include a picture, the readers get a general idea of the individual's age. However, I will leave these background data aside, and instead focus on what is highlighted in relation to the employee's career and his/her profile.

The key salient elements in the construction of all the featured employees are *open-mindedness* and *flexibility*; they are described as people open to new challenges, new responsibilities and international experience. Most employees are also presented as *ambitious*, by which it is meant a wish to develop and grow as professionals and as individuals. Many stories further stress the employees' *interest in other people*: they are educators or leaders of teams, and are in frequent contact with customers and colleagues. Another element which is highlighted in the presentation of the employee is *loyalty with the company*; we are informed when the employee joined the company or how many years he or she has been employed there.

A difference can, however, be drawn between stories where the model reader[3] is a well-educated and skilled person, and those where the model reader is an unskilled person, possibly a would-be applicant for the company's educational program.[4]

---

3 For a definition of *model reader*, see Eco (1984) and Nord (2011).

4 For details, see Gunnarsson (2014a).

Another difference is found between stories which include information about the employee as a private person, that is to say a person with a family and children to take care of, a and/or a person with hobbies, or with interest in new cities, etc., and the stories which only present a skilful, professional person, with no personal details provided.[5]

2.3. Company image(s) on multinationals' websites

One aim of the staff policy documents and career stories found on the nine multinationals' websites is to give a positive image of the company, its staff and its workplace culture. As texts on websites are globally accessible, and hence available for large, anonymous reader groups, the company's *image work* takes place in a new complex context, compared to similar work performed in the 'paper era', where most documents had a specified reader group and were not generally accessible to such large audiences.

In Gunnarsson (2009, pp. 208–209) I discuss how company images in general are constructed. I claim that the creation of an image of the corporate culture is part of the construction of an 'organizational self' in large organizations. What follows is that the company image depicts the company's common values, and shows the company's culture and its value system both to the staff and to outsiders.

Different kinds of images exist within a company: (1) There are *internal images*, relating to the perception of a corporate identity, a corporate self. Such images appear in presentations of the company to prospective and new employees, in staff magazines, in course materials, in letters and notes to staff etc. They can also be part and parcel of the internal discourse. (2) There are *externally addressed images*, relating to the outward presentation of the corporate culture. These images appear in texts and discourse aimed at customers, owners and the general public, i.e. letters, brochures, advertisements, annual reports, press releases, general information leaflets, books about the company etc. They not only depict the company as a corporate unit, but also its relationship to the buyers' market, the stock market, the labour market and society in general (Gunnarsson, 2009, pp. 208–209).

The company images presented in the texts on the multinationals' websites studied here, in both staff policy documents and career stories, must be considered to be mainly externally addressed. However, reliance on the Internet for disseminating company images entails a complexity. As the image of the company's organizational policy and practices becomes visible to both "outsiders", that is prospective employees and other readers outside the organization, and "insiders",

5 For details, see Gunnarsson (2014a).

that is its managers and employees, the external marketing of the company is often intertwined with its internal marketing. Therefore the border between externally addressed images and internal images is not always clear.

3. Multinational's language policy as revealed in job advertisements

For practical and ideological reasons large organizations often choose one official, corporate language. This language is used as a *lingua franca* in meetings and written communication; it also functions as a symbolic expression of organizational unity. In many cases the official/corporate language penetrates the whole organization, which means that all employees are assumed to master this language at sufficient level. In other cases, however, the official language is an elite language used at top level meetings and for external, international contacts, while other languages are used in daily interaction at work. The organizational language policy is, for instance, revealed in the language of major documents such as annual reports, contracts, company presentations, messages to top level staff, etc. Other genres which reveal the language policy of a company are statements in press releases, surveys directed to managers and staff (e.g. Day & Wagner, 2007, p. 395), and job advertisements, which I examine in this section.

In order to get a picture of a multinational's language policy I studied language requirements in job advertisements posted on nine large companies' websites. I focused on the Swedish job market and analysed the explicitly stated language requirements in advertisements for jobs in Swedish branches of these companies published on their websites in April 2015; the total number of advertisements was 101. The studied multinationals are ABB, AstraZeneca, Electrolux, Ericsson, Scania, Bosch, Siemens, Ikea and McDonalds[6] (Gunnarsson, 2015).

Below I briefly summarize the results of this analysis. As concerns the language of the advertisements, 68% of the ads are written in Swedish, and 32% in English. Since Swedish is the main official language in Sweden, the fact that two thirds of the advertisements for job ads are in Swedish is therefore not surprising. However, if we look at the explicit language requirements, we find that 68% of the job advertisements mention Swedish as a requirement for the job, and 84% of the ads mention English. Both Swedish and English are mentioned as a requirement in 55% of the ads, whereas only English in 29%, and only Swedish in 13%. Other languages than Swedish and English are mentioned as requirements in only 10%

6 Nokia was not included in this study, as their website did not include jobs available in Sweden.

of the jobs, and even then always in combination with Swedish and English. There are also ads which do not have any language requirements (13% in total).

In Gunnarsson (2015) I also proposed a categorization of the type of jobs in the ads based on the stated background requirements. The classification distinguishes into advertisements requiring (1) university education, (2) college education, (3) 12 years' of school (i.e. primary and secondary education), (4) leadership and work experience, and (5) no specification of background. For jobs which require university education or college education (categories 1 and 2), English is mentioned as a requirement for the majority of the ads: 91% in category 1 and 95% in category 2, while Swedish is mentioned less often: in 55% of the ads which require university education and 63% with college education. There is thus a considerably lower proportion of ads which require Swedish than those requiring English for applicants with higher or college education.

In the ads which concern applicants with 12 years of school or leadership and work experience (category 3 and category 4, respectively), English and Swedish are required in similar proportion of the ads (approximately 60 % in each case).

Another interesting result is that in ads which do not specify anything about the applicant's background (category 5), there are also explicit language requirements: in 38% of these ads English is required, whereas Swedish in 25% of them.

In sum, the results point to an ongoing globalization of multinational companies, and to the important role of English as corporate language in the studied multinationals.[7] It is also of interest to note that a considerable proportion of the ads targeted at Swedish readers mention Swedish as a requirement for the jobs, indicating that nowadays it is relevant to mention good knowledge of Swedish, both in written and spoken discourse. The reason is that the current demographic situation of Sweden includes an increasing number of immigrants: in 2014 this percentage was over 16%. As statistics for 2012 show, 39% of Swedish citizens born outside Sweden belong to the group between 25 and 44 years old, compared with only 23% of Swedish born people in this age group.[8] Assuming that this range

7 In an earlier study, carried out in 2006, I analysed language requirements in 100 ads for jobs in Sweden posted on the websites of five companies: ABB, AstraZeneca, Electrolux, Ericsson and Scania (see Gunnarsson, 2009, pp. 227–230, 2014b, p. 15). A comparison of the language requirements in the ads presented in this earlier study and the present paper for the same five companies reveals a considerable increase in the proportion of ads mentioning Swedish as a requirement (34% in 2006 and 68% in 2015) and an increase in the proportion of ads mentioning English as a requirement (70% in 2006 as compared to 84% in 2015).

8 These data are gathered from www.migrationsinfo.se/migration/Sverige.

covers the most common job seeking ages, there can be expected a greater proportion of immigrants among possible applicants than people from other groups in the total population. I would assume that this fact is reflected in the increased mentioning of Swedish as a requirement in Swedish job advertisements.

Finally, it is also noteworthy that languages other than Swedish and English are mentioned in some (though only in 10%), but, as has been noted above, always in combination with English and Swedish. This focus on bi- and multilingualism is representative of the modern European company culture (for current overviews, see Gunnarsson, 2013, 2014b).

4. Multilingual workplaces with a workforce diversity

All over the world there are workplaces where some employees, mostly minorities, migrants or unskilled guest workers, have to use their second, third or fourth language at work. From the perspective of language users, there is indeed a difference between regions where the majority language is a global language and those where the majority speaks a less widely spoken language. For instance, individuals who migrate to English-speaking countries have often learnt English at school in their countries of origin. At the same time, however, in parts of the world where less widely known languages are used, immigrants meet both a new country and a new language. For them learning the majority language becomes a part of their adjustment to a new country and culture. This is also the case of certain Swedish workplaces, to which I will now turn.

Here I would like to present some results of a research project which focused on immigrants at two Swedish workplaces: a hospital and a large company (Gunnarsson, 2009, pp. 173–191). A fairly large proportion of the population in Sweden are first generation immigrants, currently more than 16%. Though many of them are found in low paid jobs, e.g. cleaners and factory floor workers, many immigrants also have high-status jobs such as doctors and skilled nurses in hospitals, or researchers, engineers and computer experts in large companies.

In a recent research project, KINSA, which I directed at Uppsala University, we studied the communicative situation of immigrants at two Swedish workplaces: a large hospital and a major Swedish company.[9] Using a similar design based in interactional sociolinguistics, Andersson (2010) studied the former, and Nelson (2010) the latter. The first phase involved interviews with immigrants, 18 at each workplace. The immigrants came from different parts of the world and had

9 The KINSA-project was financed by Vetenskapsrådet, The Swedish Research Council.

migrated to Sweden as adults. They had permanent jobs though in different positions: at the hospital the study included doctors, nurses, midwives and cleaners, while at the company it involved office staff and factory floor workers. The employees were all second-language users at work, i.e. both Swedish and English were foreign languages for them. The second phase involved case studies, five at each workplace. The employees were shadowed during a week, and the data related to their workplace communication were collected (Gunnarsson, 2009, pp. 177–191; Andersson, 2010; Nelson, 2010).

4.1. Language situation at two Swedish workplaces

The results of the research at the hospital (see Andersson, 2010) show that communication with lay people – patients and relatives – forms an important part of the daily work of the medically trained staff, i.e. doctors, nurses and midwives. This means that the majority language of the local community, i.e. Swedish, is the dominant language in their work. As for other languages, the doctors interviewed reported that they use English in their research and in writing articles for publication. Also, some of the nurses said that they every now and then they use their mother tongue, i.e. neither Swedish nor English, which they use in communication with patients who come from their countries of origin. Then they find themselves in the role of interpreter between patient and doctor.

By contrast, the communicative situation for the cleaners at the hospital is very different from that of the medically skilled staff. When interviewed, the cleaners said that Swedish is used when they speak to their managers, to hospital staff whom they meet when cleaning their areas, and to other cleaners if they do not have a common mother tongue. Many of the cleaners have very poor skills in Swedish, and since they mainly interact with others from the same countries, they do not get much practice in Swedish so their proficiency hardly improves. This observation was confirmed by the managers who were interviewed.

As for the company, communication is mainly directed to professionals, i.e. to colleagues in the same workplace or within the same organization, or to other professionals. As the workplace studied belongs to a large, transnational company for which English is the corporate language, its language practices are of a *diglossic* nature. In other words, English is used as a *lingua franca* for external purposes, e.g. in written correspondence with colleagues in other countries and in meetings with external professionals, while the local majority language, i.e. Swedish, is used for internal purposes and in the daily spoken interaction with colleagues.

From the point of view of language use, a clear division exists between office staff and factory floor workers. When the office staff were asked about the languages they used at work, three of nine said that they mainly use Swedish, three that they mainly use English, and three that they use English and Swedish to an equal extent. All claimed that they write in English more often than they speak it. Six respondents of the office staff also said that they have used their mother tongues at work.

By contrast, all factory floor workers interviewed said that Swedish is the language they use at work. Although they said that they have contact with English texts, they did not claim to read them. Only three out of nine immigrant factory workers said that they have used their mother tongues at the workplace, compared with six out of nine in the case of the office staff (see above). The office staff thus seem to use languages other than Swedish and English to a greater extent than factory floor workers. One of the reasons is that the office staff are responsible for e.g. guiding or taking care of groups and representatives from foreign countries, whereas factory employees are not.

4.2. Workplace interaction from a diversity perspective

The communicative situations for the employees interviewed are thus different at the hospital and at the company, and also within each environment. As I mentioned above, all informants have permanent jobs and they also seem to be able to perform the tasks they are assigned. Their position at work (e.g. doctor, nurse or cleaner; engineer or factory floor worker) and the tasks they are given correspond to their linguistic competence and communicative skills. Also, lack of language skills hinders promotion in both environments: at the hospital good Swedish is necessary for further career opportunities, and at the company both English and Swedish are required for this purpose. In the company good writing skills are also important for promotion. We thus find that language proficiency creates a divide between those who master the corporate language and those who do not, and also between those who master the majority language and those who do not.

5. Discussion: Professional discourse and its contextual frames

In this section I take a more general perspective and discuss discourses in organizations and workplaces with a focus on their contextual frames. In Gunnarsson (2009, pp. 16–27) I have introduced a model whose aim is to grasp the complex and dynamic interplay between professional discourse and its various contextual frames in a general way. I will use this model now to summarize my reflections presented in earlier studies on organizations and workplaces.

5.1. The environmental framework

At a micro level, written and spoken discourses at work could be described as related to different situated *communicative events*. An in-depth analysis, however, must also include the macro level, that is the *environmental framework* in which the communicative events, or chain of events, occur (Figure 1). Text and talk in a small, close-knit working group form part of traditions that evolve within an environmental structure, that is a small *working group* is included in a larger unit such as a *workplace*, which in its turn belongs to *a local branch* of a large *organization*. In many cases we further find additional *organizational levels*, which means that the organization belongs to a *corporation*, which might also have its partners etc.

Figure 1. Model of professional discourse and its contextual frames (after Gunnarsson, 2009)

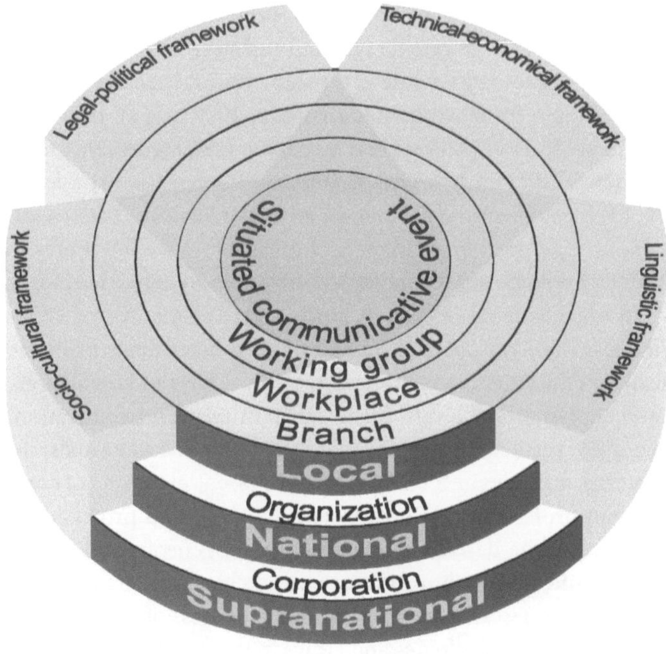

The studies of multinational companies discussed in this paper and presented in sections 2 and 3 focused on communication in large private companies with an organizational language policy affecting workplace interaction at different levels.

The multinational environmental frame with English as a corporate language and a need for employees to master this language have been shown to be reflected in job advertisements (Gunnarsson, 2015; see also section 3), and in the diglossic situation found among employees in the technical, transnational company studied in the KINSA-project (Nelson, 2010; see also section 4). The conditions framing workplace interaction in environments which serve the local public, such as hospitals, shops, food stores or restaurants, are made salient in advertisements for jobs in McDonalds and Ikea (Gunnarsson, 2015), and in the study of the hospital workplace (Andersson, 2010; see also section 4). In these contexts the close working group and local customers (or patients, in the case of the hospital) become important in the daily work-related interaction.

5.2. The societal framework systems

What also characterizes discourse in organizations and workplaces is its dependence on various *societal framework systems.* Professional discourse in the globalized economy is to a large extent regulated and steered from the 'outside', from different societal frameworks, while at the same time it is an essential part of the construction of these frameworks (Gunnarsson, 2009, p. 24). In the theoretical model for the analysis of professional discourse (see Figure 2), I discern four societal frameworks: (1) a *technical-economical framework*, (2) a *legal-political framework*, (3) a *socio-cultural framework* and (4) a *linguistic framework.*

The *technical-economic framework* is of great relevance for professional discourse. Both technology and technological advances are important for the dynamism within organizations of various kinds, as are economy and economically driven changes. The *legal-political framework* also determines professional discourse, insofar as the latter is constrained by politics, laws and regulations at local, national and supranational levels, for instance in relation to education. Professional discourse is further constrained by a *socio-cultural framework* system, since cultural patterns, attitudes and social values are essential aspects of communication in different professions. Although we might still find professional organizations which could be described as socially homogeneous and monocultural, social diversity and multiculturalism are more characteristic of organizations today. The ethical codes adopted in a particular professional environment thus reflect, to a large extent, ideologies and ethics in this framework. Finally, professional discourse is also dependent on the *linguistic framework.* The local language community, the national language community, and the supranational language community establish and follow language laws and policies which directly or indirectly influence text and talk use at work. Policies and practices related to the use of the dominant language, formed within the various levels of the linguistic framework, also influence communicative events for professional purposes in terms of language choice and practice.

Figure 2. The societal framework systems.

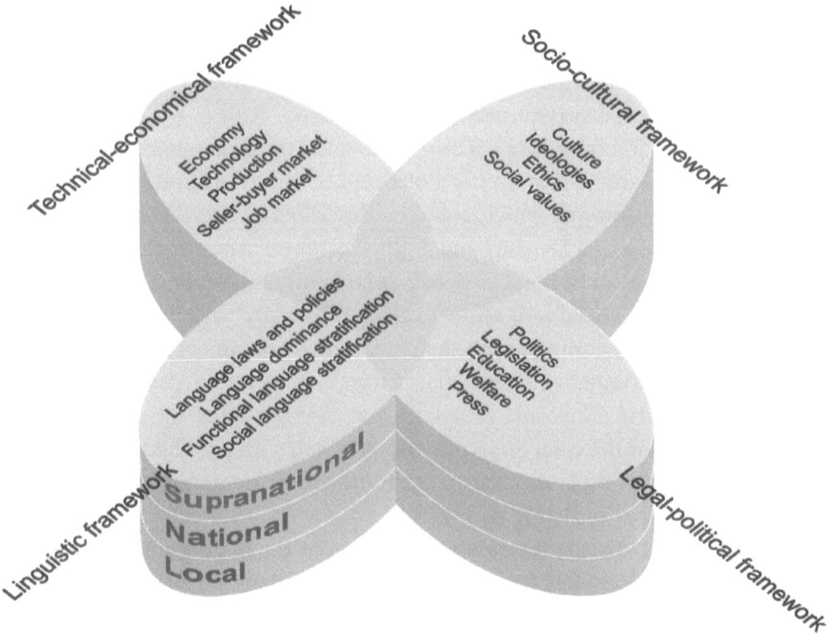

If these four societal framework systems are applied to the contexts presented in this paper, it is the technical-economic framework that is reflected in all of them, in one way or another. In the expanding global business world, many workplaces are found in trans- and multinational companies, which operate in different countries, and the fact that workforces move from one country to another is, at least to some extent, dependent on economy. Skilled and unskilled workers move to wealthier regions in order to seek employment, which also means that immigrants are found both in high and low status jobs (Gunnarsson, 2009, 2013, 2014b).

Turning next to the legal-political framework, there are of course a number of legal and political constraints on business discourse both globally and locally. What my data reflect is a concern for – or an awareness of – the so called 'corporate social responsibility'. In their staff policy documents, the companies make claims which show that they wish to create an image of their company culture which allows for diversity instead of social discrimination and marginalization.

Of great importance for workforce mobility is of course the education system in different countries, in particular in relation to the teaching of languages. Although English is taught as a first foreign language in many parts of the world, there are many regions where language education does not involve English. Earlier studies of immigrants in Swedish workplaces, for instance, showed that the lack of language skills in English created a divide between skilled and unskilled staff in a transnational company (Gunnarsson, 2009; Nelson, 2010).

The socio-cultural framework is also reflected in the professional discourse of organizations and workplaces in the globalized economy. Although we still find professional organizations which could be described as socially homogeneous and monocultural, social diversity and multiculturalism are more characteristic of organizations today. Both the staff policy documents and career stories analyzed explicitly highlight social and ethical values. 'Diversity' and 'respect' are core values claimed by all companies in their staff policy documents, whereas in the description of the company culture, social values like 'openness', 'development' and 'creativity' are found. The same values are also highlighted in the career stories, which describe how the companies provide their staff with possibilities to develop and grow, that the workplace culture is open and team-oriented, and that working for the company is stimulating and varied.

Lastly, I wish to discuss my results in relation to the linguistic framework. In the study of advertisements for jobs in Sweden (Gunnarsson, 2015; see also section 3), and the two studies of immigrants at Swedish workplaces (Andersson, 2010; Nelson, 2010; see also section 4), the issues of language dominance are central. The balance between the local majority language, i.e. Swedish, and the global language par preference, i.e. English, is made salient in these studies. The organizations and workplaces analyzed are to a large extent bilingual; at the same time there exists a divide between those who are proficient English users and those who are not.

6. Conclusion

The conditions for professional discourse have been influenced by a series of changes taking place in recent decades. New technology, workforce mobility and a globalized job market have transformed many workplaces to bilingual and multicultural settings. Lifelong learning, flexibility, mobility and diversity have come to be key values in the global economy.

As for communication practices in multinational companies, the paper has shown that they rely on the Internet for their presentation of staff policy and company culture, for their featuring of successful employees in career stories, and for advertisements of available jobs. All the companies analyzed operate globally and employ people in different countries and different parts of the world. The texts published on the career-oriented subpages reflect this global orientation. Similarly, in their staff policy documents, the companies present themselves as global ones, and stress the fact that they employ people all over the world. Also, the career stories reflect this global orientation, and the employees featured have different backgrounds and work in different regions. Mobility, flexibility and the employees' interest in international experience are also found among the elements highlighted in the construction of the employees featured in the stories.

Multilingual companies use English as their corporate language, and the globalized job market bring issues of multilingualism and multiculturalism to the surface, both in relation to the organization as a whole and to workplace practices. In the study of multinationals' career-oriented websites (Gunnarsson, 2014a), the language issue is strikingly absent. Although diversified background, different nationalities and mix of cultures are highlighted in company documents and stories, multilingualism or bilingualism are not mentioned there at all. None of the staff policy documents in question mentions languages; in other words, the companies' concept of diversity includes diversified cultures, nationalities and backgrounds, but not different languages. And although it is obvious that English must be a second language to several of the employees, the language issue is not brought up as a topic in the career stories. Also, we are not informed if employees who have held positions in different countries, e.g. in Germany, France, or Italy, have had to make efforts to learn the local majority language. Briefly, for the multinationals studied in this paper the language issue does not seem to be important for the image they wish to transmit to prospective employees. For a linguist, this fact is of course worth noticing.

References

Andersson, H. (2010). *Interkulturell kommunikation på ett svenskt sjukhus. Fallstudier av andraspråkstalare i arbetslivet.* (Digitala skrifter från Nordiska språk 2). Uppsala: Uppsala University.

Bakhtin, M. M. (1986). The problem of speech genres. In *Speech Genres and Other Late Essays*. Austin: University of Texas Press, 60–102.

Castells, M., 1999. *The information age. Economy, society and culture.* Vol. 1–3. Oxford: Blackwell Publishers.

Day, D., & Wagner, J. (2007). Bilingual professionals. In P. Auer & L. Wei (Eds.), *Handbook of multilingualism and multilingual communication*. Berlin: De Gruyter, 391–404.

Eco, U. (1984). *The role of the reader. Explorations in the semiotics of text.* Bloomington: Indiana University.

Gunnarsson, B.-L. (2009). *Professional discourse.* (Continuum Discourse Series.) London & New York: Continuum.

Gunnarsson, B.-L. (2013). Multilingualism in the Workplace. *Annual Review of Applied Linguistics*, 33, 1–28.

Gunnarsson, B.-L. (2014a). Business discourse in the globalized economy: The construction of an attractive workplace culture on the Internet. In J. Flowerdew (Ed.) *Discourse in Context, Contemporary Applied Linguistics*, Volume 3. London, New Delhi, New York & Sydney: Bloomsbury, 91–112.

Gunnarsson, B.-L. (2014b). Multilingualism in European workplaces. *Multilingua. Journal of Cross-Cultural and Interlanguage Communication*, 33(1–2), 11–33.

Gunnarsson, B.-L. (2015). Transnational companies and their language requirements for jobs in Sweden. Paper presented at The Sociolinguistics of Globalization. (De)centring and (de)standardization, The University of Hong Kong, 3–6 June, 2015.

Herring, S. C. (2001). Computer-mediated discourse. In D. Schiffrin, D. Tannen & H. Hamilton (Eds.), *The handbook of discourse analysis*. Oxford: Blackwell Publishers, 612–634.

Kress, G., & van Leeuwen, T. (2001). *Multimodal discourse. The modes and media of contemporary communication.* London: Arnold.

Lemke, J. L. (2002). Travels in hypermodality. *Visual Communication*, 3, 299–325.

LeVine, P., & Scollon, R. (Eds.) (2004). *Discourse and Technology. Multimodal Discourse Analysis.* Washington DC: Georgetown University Press.

Mishler, E. G. (1987). The interactional construction of narratives in medical and life-history interviews. In B.-L. Gunnarsson, P. Linell & B. Nordberg (Eds.) *The Construction of Professional Discourse.* London & New York: Longman, 223–244.

Nelson, M. (2010). *Andraspråkstalare i arbete. En språkvetenskaplig studie av kommunikation vid ett svenskt storföretag.* (Skrifter utgivna av Institutionen för nordiska språk, 82.) Uppsala: Swedish Science Press.

Nord, A. (2011). The reflective cultivator? Model readers in eighteenth century Swedish garden literature. In B.-L. Gunnarsson (Ed.) *Languages of Science in the Eighteenth Century.* Berlin & New York: De Gruyter Mouton, 279–301.

Norris, S., & Jones, R. H. (2005). *Discourse in Action. Introducing mediated discourse analysis.* London & New York: Routledge.

Qvortrup, L. (2002). *The hypercomplex society*. New York: P. Lang Publishing Co.

Vološinov, V. N. (1973). *Marxism and the philosophy of language*. New York & London: Seminar press.

Ylönen, S. (2007). Culture Specific Differences in Business Communication with New Media? In J. Murath & A. Olàh-Hubai (Eds.), *Interdisciplinary Aspects of Translation and Interpreting*. Wien: Praesens Verlag, 337–366.

Catharina Nyström Höög

Uppsala University, Sweden

Texts at work: The construction of an ideal workplace in 'platforms of values'

Abstract: Changing communicative patterns within the Swedish public sector have given rise to new types of texts, which serve the purpose of managing through visions and ideals rather than by means of direct orders. This paper presents one such new text type, the 'platform of values', which uses visual resources as well as verbal descriptions of core values as part of a practice which might be described as 'soft steering'. Using theoretical concepts from CDA as a starting point, and methods of textual and multimodal analysis based on systemic functional linguistics, three common features of the platforms of values are presented: visual resources, mood metaphors and noun phrases describing positive qualities. The paper concludes that all three features contribute to a non-authoritative managerial ideal where responsibility is open for negotiation.

1. Introduction

In Sweden, communication in the public sector has been changing rapidly during the beginning of the new century. Printed texts have been replaced with digital ones, pamphlets are no longer distributed at public places, but can be downloaded from the website, telephone calls are discouraged while self-service encounters with the authorities' websites are encouraged. This process of restructuring of communication affects the textual repertoire in several ways. It influences the design and development of existing genres. It also affects the way management is carried out through texts within the public sector. This paper focuses on one particular new genre, closely connected to changing management practices: the 'platform of values'.

The change of communicative patterns is part of a more general process of society transformation in the western world. Different expressions have been used to capture these changes, such as *commercialization*, *informalization* and *individualization* (Rehnberg, 2014, p. 24), among others. Fairclough (2003, p. 4) uses the term *new capitalism*. Changes in public administration are part of the transformation of our societies. Pollitt and Bouckert (2011), who relate the changes in Swedish public administration to the rise of New Public Management, identify the regulation of staff behavior as a central part of changes in public administration.

In the words of Rehnberg (2014, p. 243, my translation) "in the new work order, managers who give direct orders are obsolete, and will be replaced by leaders who strive to influence the attitudes of their employees". I see the 'platform of values' as a potential tool to be used in such leadership, and the emergence of the genre as an effect of the transformation of society into a new work order.

Prior to 2005, hardly any public authority in Sweden published 'platforms of values' (PV). Today, they frequently appear on the websites of public authorities. Typically, PV is a multimodal text, often including a bullet point list presenting core values in single words or short phrases. Although the design may vary from quite long and elaborated multi-colored documents to extremely minimalistic texts consisting only of three noun phrases published on a website, there are some features that almost all PV texts have in common. PV texts present a public authority in a positive manner, which clearly relates PV texts to marketing materials, and to the ideal of commercialization. This feature is manifested in the texts for instance by the use of visual resources in a way which makes them stand out from most texts written by public authorities, which rely heavily on written text in a more or less monomodal design (Nyström Höög, Söderlundh & Sörlin, 2012).

Besides presenting a positive picture of a public authority, PV texts articulate expected codes of behavior for the authority in question. In this respect, PV texts bear resemblance of the texts used as tools of 'soft power' in Mulderrig's (2011) study of education policy documents in the UK. Mulderrig argues that policy discourse, to which both education policy documents and PV texts clearly belong, is 'intrinsically hortatory' (2011, p. 53). The texts are designed to make someone *do* something. This can be done by directing someone towards specific actions, or, in the case of policy texts using soft power, by 'assuming, rather than winning compliance' (2011, p. 45). Further, Mulderrig states that soft power, as it is articulated in the texts in her study, operates through 'attraction and persuasion' (2011, p. 52).

My starting point in understanding PV texts is that it is a genre intrinsic to the purpose of shaping a common ground and communicating core values within and outside a public authority. *Genre*, here, is not primarily perceived as a unity of form, but as a means of typifying social practice. It is a view on genre closely related to that of Miller (1984, p. 151), who puts emphasis on the action a genre is used to accomplish, and the text analyses provided in this paper are a step towards describing what type of action PV texts are involved in. By analogy to Mulderrig's (2011) 'soft power', I will use the term *soft steering*, for the type of managerial ideal that I assume to be connected with PV texts.

My aim in this paper is to focus specifically on three common features of PV-texts: (1) the high frequency of nouns and noun phrases describing qualities;

(2) the lack of personal agents; and (3) the use of visual resources. I exemplify these features with two different PV texts. My ambition is not to undertake a detailed analysis of either of these texts, but rather to present them as typical examples of the genre. PV texts seem to be used to shape values, so one might conclude that their design is oriented towards those goals. One important question, then, is how different features of text design serve that purpose.

The structure of the paper is organized around two different examples of PV texts. After a brief presentation of the text corpus and my theoretical framework in section 2, I give a general presentation of the genre in section 3, followed by three different sections focusing on noun phrases, mood metaphors and visual resources in sections 4, 5 and 6, respectively.

2. The corpus and the theoretical starting point

The presentation of PV texts in this paper is based upon a corpus of approximately 230 PV, vision and strategy texts from 154 different Swedish authorities. The corpus is part of an ongoing research project: *The archaeology of a new genre: Platforms of values texts of public authorities in Sweden.*[1] In collecting the texts for the corpus, we have visited the website of and/or contacted all the authorities listed as administrative authorities at Statistics Sweden, a list which includes 240 different entities.[2] In addition to collecting texts, we build our understanding of managerial texts on focus group discussions and on questionnaire surveys (cf. Björkvall, forthcoming). In this paper, however, the data is limited to the corpus of texts.

My point of departure in this textual analysis is critical. The emergence of PV texts changes the *order of discourse* – the network of social practices in its language aspect (Fairclough, 2003, p. 24) – within the public sector, which used to be a relatively stable system. In such a change, at least one critical question seems relevant to ask: why are PV texts gaining ground in the order of discourse within the public sector? In the framework of Critical Discourse Analysis, in which I want to place this study, I want to challenge the object of study rather than take it for granted.

---

1 *The archaeology of a new genre: 'Platforms of Values' texts of public authorities in Sweden.* A. Björkvall & C. Nyström Höög 2015. Financed by Riksbankens Jubileumsfond: The Swedish Foundation for Humanities and Social Sciences 2016–2018.

2 Since the concept 'public authority' may differ from one country to another, it may be worth pointing out that universities and university colleges are considered public authorities according to Statistics Sweden.

The emergence of new genres is an indication that the order of discourse is unstable, or in motion. In Fairclough's understanding, language figures in social practice as *genres*, *discourses* and *styles* (2003, p. 26). My focus of interest here is *genre* as a way of acting. I am interested in the defining features of PV texts, and how they – one by one or altogether – function in the social practice of soft steering. Following Fairclough (2003), I see texts as action, and I use methods from the framework of systemic functional linguistics (Halliday & Matthiessen, 2004) in text analysis. Since many of PV texts are multimodal in design, I also use multimodal analysis, relying on the social semiotic understanding of visual design presented in Kress and van Leeuwen (1996).

3. 'Platforms of values' – a brief presentation of the genre

The PV texts collected in the aforementioned corpus vary as regards design and content, but also – and perhaps more importantly – as regards labelling. Depending on the authority, the texts may be labelled *key words*, *words denoting values*, *values*, *vision* or *platform of values*.[3] This diversity of labelling may be related to the genre's rapid establishment in the Swedish society. If PV texts remain essential to public administration in Sweden, they will most likely be consolidated with regards to form and shape. If that happens, the number of labels used by different authorities to name such texts may also decrease.

Some common features of these texts, regardless of how they are labelled, include: (1) core values, often presented in bullet point lists; (2) mood metaphors, where directives are presented in the form of statements; and (3) careful design using colors, information graphics and images. The text presented in Figure 1, which is a document from a university college in southern Sweden, can serve as an example of these features.

3 Swedish terms: *nyckelord, värdeord, värden, vision and värdegrund*, respectively.

Figure 1. Core values and platform of values. Malmö University College. Published with permission from Malmö University College.

Figure 1 represents a type of PV text where visual and verbal elements are separated. The picture shows a young man on a skateboard, which might be interpreted as highlighting youth and activity, possibly important ideals for a university college and its students, and aimed at attracting young people. This is a summer picture, which may not be incidental since – as I show below – the quality of 'warmth' recurs in the visual material of PV texts. Following Kress and van Leeuwen's (2006) analytical framework for visual design, we can note that the picture realizes a narrative process, one of a *non-transactional action*, which means that a vector (formed by the movement of the skateboard, in this case) emanates from a participant, but does not point at any other participant (Kress and van Leeuwen, 2006, p. 74). This makes this picture a variation of the visual theme in the material collected for our project. Most of the pictures include people, typically involved in activities signaling a sense of community.

The text of the document presented in Figure 1 represents a typical 'double labelling' of the genre: the document is entitled 'core values and platform of values', thus featuring two synonymous expressions. Colors are used here to highlight the most important features of the text: the title of the document and the core values supported by the university. In this case, there are four: *mångfald* 'diversity', *kreativitet* 'creativity', *kvalitet* 'quality' and *samhälls-engagemang* 'commitment to the community'.[4] In relation to the picture depicting the skateboarder, it can be noted that core values are relatively independent of it. Possibly the values of *creativity* and *quality* might be somehow related to the picture if skateboarding is regarded as a creative activity and one involving a certain quality; by contrast, the values of *diversity* and *commitment to the community* are more difficult to read into the picture. As a whole, the written mode in this PV text seems separated from the visual mode. Nothing in the written text repeats or interprets the visual. This type of complementarity between visual and verbal elements is frequent in the corpus.

The rest of the text consists of seven paragraphs. The first simply frames the rest of the text, stating that "Malmö University bases its work on the following values". The next four paragraphs elaborate on the core values, placing each of them in context. The final two paragraphs add other values, namely *delaktighet* 'participation', *öppenhet* 'openness' and *nyfikenhet* 'curiosity', and then employs additional noun phrases to describe possible desirable values for the university college. The final paragraph states how the goals are to be achieved: "[i]n order to achieve our objectives, we work in a resource-efficient manner whilst striving towards increased systematics and quality-assured processes". As a whole, the text displays all the common features of a PV text: core values are clearly emphasized in the text, the visual element has a positive 'vibe', the most frequent human actor is a 'we' with an unclear reference, and many of the noun phrases refer to positive values.

4. Core values and other quality-related noun phrases

The core values of Malmö University College (Figure 1) are, as already mentioned, introduced at the beginning of the text and then further explained in four paragraphs. They are, however, not the only values articulated in the text. This makes the document in Figure 1 a typical PV text – it is densely packed with abstract noun phrases and articulates values that might be hard to relate to tangible action. One of them is *öppenhet* 'openness', which has also been proven to be one of the most popular nouns in PV texts produced by Swedish public authorities (Nyström Höög, 2015). Even though it is not highlighted as one of the four core values of the university at the beginning of the text, the quality of being *open* or *openness* are mentioned three times in this short text.

4 English translations of the text in Figure 1 come from the English version of the document, published on the website www.mah.se.

The core values are contextualized in the aforementioned four paragraphs (paragraphs 2–5 in Figure 1). The first of them refers to *diversity*, as mentioned in the final sentence of the text: "We take an open, inclusive approach built on diversity and widening participation, which is a necessary requirement for a successful university". In this case, the quality of being *open* (cf. 'take an open [...] approach') plays a role as a prerequisite for success and as a kind of synonym of *inclusive* (cf. 'an open, inclusive approach'), which in current political discourse in Sweden often alternates with *diversity*.

By contrast, the third paragraph contextualizes *creativity* and *quality*. In sum, the argument is that each person's skills, experience and desire to change must be utilized. Only then can the best conditions be created for "a good working environment, an open and creative learning environment and a high quality of work". In this last quoted sentence, the word *open* appears again, now with a slightly different meaning, as something like a synonym of 'creative'. This semantic vagueness might in fact be one of the explanations for *open* being such a frequent word in strategic and visionary texts.

Finally, the fourth paragraph, referring to the core value of *commitment to the community*, consists of only one sentence: "A scientific basis, academic integrity, critical thinking and commitment to our community create the foundation of our university".

The core values of Malmö University College (i.e. *diversity*, *creativity*, *quality* and *commitment to the community*) are not the only qualities described in the text. Rather, the PV text offers a list of desirable values. In this wording of the college's core values, it can be noted that they differ very little from values presented by other public authorities. They are all hard to dispute – which enterprise does not want to achieve quality? And they are likewise difficult to pinpoint and convert into action: what does it mean to be 'creative' and 'committed to the community' in daily practice?

As can be concluded from my argument on Figure 1, an abundance of positive qualities is articulated in the text. This is a distinctive feature of PV texts. Since most of the texts, such as the one from Malmö University College, are published on public websites, they may be regarded as part of a commercial façade which constructs a positive image for the authority in the public context.

There is also another side to the texts in question, however: they are aimed at the employees of the authorities and inform them of the desired qualities of staff members. The number of positive qualities in the texts is often overwhelming. In this case (Figure 1), the text consists of 178 words (excluding headings).[5] Of these words, 98 are included in noun phrases, giving the text a heavily nominalized character. Although not all of the noun phrases exemplify qualities, many obviously do. Here we find, for example, *ansvar* 'responsibility', *mångfald* 'diversity', *framförhållning* 'clear long-term approach', *ömsesidig nytta* 'mutual benefits' and *fungerande samverkan* 'functioning collaboration'.

While the Malmö University College text is designed as a running text, it is common for PV texts to be designed in the form of bullet point lists. In such cases, noun phrases are listed, leaving the reader to construe the intended processes in which the nouns act as participants.

The preferred design of bullet point lists exemplifies how PV texts are part of a dominant trend in Swedish – or possibly Western – text design, that of decreasing discursivity (Svensson, 2005). An increasing number of texts in public administration as well as in news media rely on predesigned formats or document designs, where frames, bullet points or figurative patterns carry textual cohesion while running text continually loses ground. For texts, the consequence of this process is that they become more nominalized and rely on lists or groups of noun phrases. For readers, the texts can become more demanding (possibly contrary to the authors' and/or editors' expectations), leaving the reader to determine how the noun phrases are related and, more importantly, who actually is the intended agent behind all the work leading to the desired goals articulated in the core values.

5. Mood metaphors – a subtle way of steering

A closer look at the core values and platform of values from Malmö University College reveals yet another feature typical of PV texts, apart from the abundance of quality-related nouns: the tendency to write directives in the form of statements. The first paragraph under the core values reads as follows:

(1) *På Malmö högskola tar var och en ansvar för det gemensamma. En helhetssyn på vårt uppdrag bildar grunden i vår verksamhet. Vi har ett öppet och inkluderande förhållningssätt som bygger på mångfald, vilket är grunden för en framgångsrik verksamhet.*

[At Malmö University, each person has both an individual and a mutual responsibility. The university is founded on a holistic view of our objective. We take an open, inclusive approach built on diversity and widening participation, which is a necessary requirement for a successful university.]

5 Quantifications are based on the Swedish text version.

What is striking about this passage is the absence of specified human actors. The grammatical subjects here are 'each person', 'the university' and 'we', respectively. Of these, *we* is a subject typical of PV texts. It refers, in a vague sense, to the public authority as a whole, where staff members are part of a collective identity. The same generic *we* can be read as the referent of 'each person'. It is the university college as a whole that takes on the obligation of fulfilling the core values stated in the document.

The second sentence in paragraph 2 contains a typical example of an *ideational metaphor* (Halliday & Mathiessen, 2004, pp. 636–637), where a mental process is packed into a noun phrase, here *helhetssyn* 'a holistic view'. This metaphor makes it possible to omit any (human) actor who could view the mission of the university college in a holistic way.

The first and third sentences in Example (1) describe an existing situation, attested by the use of the present tense and the indicative mode: ***tar*** *var och en ansvar* [each person **has** ... a responsibility], *vi* ***har*** *ett öppet och inkluderande förhållningssätt* [we **take** an open, inclusive approach].[6] The question of *how* to achieve a situation where everyone takes responsibility is left unanswered. Grammatically, this type of writing can be described as a *mood metaphor* (Halliday & Mathiessen, 2004, pp. 626–627). The actual grammatical mood is indicative, but the assumed mood is directive; therefore the sentence "We take an open, inclusive approach" may be interpreted as "If you are an employee of this authority, you are obliged to have an open, inclusive approach".

The use of the mood metaphor makes this text a clear example of a text with a double addressee. The first addressee is the public. For them, the said sentence is first and foremost a declarative sentence, stating the quality of the authority. Perhaps it might be interpreted as a kind of promise: the public can rely on the authority being open and inclusive. The second intended addressee may be the employees. For them, the sentence is – or at least could be read as – a demand. This type of double addressee has been discussed in relation to working plans in schools (Hamberg, 2011), another type of document that represents a similar type of policy text to PV texts. Hamberg (2011) points out that this type of writing makes the text difficult to interpret; readings and interpretations will differ based on the reader's relationship with the authority.

---

6 English translations here, again, from the website of Malmö university college. Verbatim, the translation would be 'everyone takes responsibility' and 'we have an open, inclusive approach', respectively. This more direct translation gives better justice to the Swedish text, where the interpretation can only be that these are already existing conditions.

The strategy of using mood metaphors in a policy document leaves the text open for interpretation. A more severe effect of this style of writing has been pointed out by Ahmed (2007), in her study of anti-discrimination policies at universities. Policy documents have a tendency to gloss over possibly problematic situations since they focus on ideal situations. Should an employee wish to debate a situation at his or her workplace, a policy document with mood metaphors lends little support since it describes an existing situation in a positive manner rather than an ambition to reach a certain state of working conditions. Therein lie the advantages of the mood metaphor, if you look at it from the perspective of the sender of the document. Mood metaphors make it possible to impose an ideal, or a demand, on the addressee without using direct instructions. In today's workplace environment, in Sweden at least, it is almost impossible to use an authoritative voice when promoting ideals or a sense of responsibility among staff (cf. Rehnberg, 2014, p. 243). The mood metaphors of PV texts offer a softer way of steering towards a common goal.

6. Visual resources – warmth and participation

Visual elements in PV texts come in many forms. There are several examples of organization schemes and graphic elements which intend to show the authority's decision-making processes or activities in a systematic and technical manner. However, it is no doubt photographs of people that dominate the visual material of the text corpus. In Figure 1, the example showed that visual and verbal elements were separated from each other. In other cases, those elements may reinforce each other. I have chosen one such example from a PV text in Figure 2. The photograph is reproduced from the 'platform of values' of the National Board of Health and Welfare, which was published in 2014.

The document as a whole consists of 12 pages, and four of these contain photographs of the same group of people. In the first photograph, we can see a group of people at a meeting, possibly in the foyer of their workplace. In the second, they remain in the same place but have books and papers open and appear to be involved in a discussion. In the third picture, which is presented in Figure 2, they are working, and in the last picture they are taking leave of each other. There is also a speech bubble featured in the last picture, clarifying that this is indeed a good-bye scene. Thus, there is a clear narrative progression in the pictures as a series, possibly illustrating a day at work.

Figure 2. Group of workers. The National Board of Health and Welfare. Photo Rikard Westman. Published with permission of The National Board of Health and Welfare.

The picture in Figure 2 shows two women and a man discussing a text. The text appears to be a sort of mind-map of the type that is commonly used in group discussions in the workplace. A closer look reveals the word *vision* written in the middle of the paper. The woman standing between the seated figures is pointing at the document on the table; her arm creates a vector, directing our (the viewer's) gaze towards the paper. The arms of the other two participants are also important here. They both have their outer arms stretched out towards the paper, with the woman on the left holding a pen as if caught in the act of writing on it. The effect is that the arms of the sitting participants almost embrace the paper. It is obvious that the paper is the center of interest in this picture. The picture, as well as the PV text as a whole, has some sort of a 'double addressee'. The fact that the three employees gather around the text means that it is important to their work, and since they embrace it, point at it and have their heads bent over it, their gestures draw the attention of the bystander to the text. The fact that we can only make out the word 'vision' can also be relevant here. The document, more than the actual content, is what matters in the social practice.

Again, the participants in the picture do not look straight at us, readers/viewers of this PV text. This picture makes not a demand but an offer (Kress & van Leeuwen, 2006, pp. 116–117): we are invited to observe the participants in the picture as they occupy themselves with some 'vision', as highlighted in the text in front of them. The participants are smiling, not at one another, but the clear smiles on all of their faces indicate their happiness with the situation. This type of an inward smile is very common in the photographic material of PV texts as it brings warmth into the image material. In other words, people portrayed in work situations are shown to enjoy what they are doing. In the case of the National Board of Health and Welfare, the atmosphere in the picture is a kind of visual parallel to one of the points in the bullet point list which verbalizes the authority's 'platform of values': "We work together and use the knowledge of both each other and others for the best results".

A final observation on the picture concerns the color scheme. The women in the picture are both wearing navy blue clothes, and the man – a paler shade of blue. Although it is contentious to claim that a certain color signifies a certain thought or message, it can be noted that navy blue is a very common color in the picture gallery of PV texts. In the case of this particular PV text, the navy blue color dominates the document, possibly to connote seriousness or reliability. This feature of the picture series accompanies the verbal message "we are trustworthy"[7], which is a core value of this particular public authority. The pictures amplify some aspects of the bullet point list.

The meaning-making potential of the visual serves the non-authoritative ideals of PV texts well since pictures allow for the visualization of a desired situation without accepting responsibility for directing employees toward certain codes of behavior.

---

7 Kress and van Leeuwen (2002) would argue, and I agree, that color is metafunctional. The association from navy blue to trustworthiness applies only within a limited socio-cultural group. One could, however, argue that the Swedish public sector is just an example of such a limited group.

7. Conclusion: responsibility and authority at stake

When the distinctive features of PV texts are grouped together it is possible to draw the conclusion that these texts negotiate responsibility. The PV text's initiator, i.e. the management of a public authority, presents a vision of an ideal authority and workplace using different discursive means, of which noun phrases have been shown here as one of the most important. At the same time, the initiator avoids taking responsibility for the work required to reach the ideal state by using mood metaphors. Instead, the employees, individually and collectively, are invited to take responsibility for their work. Both the visual resources and the absence of tangible human actors in verbal texts contribute to this invitation, and can be seen as features of a leadership which works through *attraction* rather than *coercion* (cf. Mulderrig, 2011, p. 52). Obviously, every text needs to be interpreted in relation to context, but findings in this paper support the assumption that the genre 'platform of values' is involved in actions of soft power.

It is clear that PV texts are a type of text into which public authorities invest a great deal of energy and ambition. There is no other explanation for the fact that the genre has established itself so rapidly, not only in the Swedish society as discussed in this paper, but arguably in other societies as well. Nor is there another explanation for the elaborate document design of most PV texts. One possible explanation of this interest is that PV texts are considered powerful tools in managing public administration. In the previously mentioned PV text from The National Board of Health and Welfare, there is a sort of flow chart which places the 'platform of values' as the foundation of strategic planning. This feature of the text might be described as *self-authorization*, a term used in a Finnish study of public visions (Vaara, Sorsa & Pälli, 2010) to describe the fact that texts communicate their own importance. The feature *self-authorization* articulates a view on PV texts as (non-human) agents which initiate change and movement towards better public administration. This type of trust in a written document might signify a move towards a more disclosed power of authority.

The establishment of PV texts as part of public administration is part of a larger process of transformation. As Sarangi and Slembrouck (1996) observe, there is a trend towards debureaucratization occurring in public administration, and PV texts are good examples of that trend. PV texts use un-bureaucratic language and pictures showing relaxed employees. Borrowing a term from Fairclough (1993), one might also identify here the *appropriation of private domain practices*. This appropriation manifests itself not only in PV texts, but also in practices such as corporate storytelling, which also aim to construct a collective identity in a workplace or an enterprise, and are now entering the realm of public administration

(Rehnberg, 2014). The use of private practice features is effective in steering a public authority without recourse to authority.

Finally, PV texts are only one side of soft steering towards a common goal. An equally important side lies in the work based around the document: how it is produced and received, how it is valued and used as a basis for action in daily work practices. We know little about the processes that anchor platforms of values texts into the practices of public administration. There is, however, every reason to further investigate these; public authorities ought not only to be *open* in the general sense communicated in their own positive presentations, but also open to public scrutiny by researchers and citizens.

References

Ahmed, S. (2007). 'You end up doing the document rather than doing the doing': Diversity, race equality and the politics of documentation. *Ethnic and Racial Studies*, 40(3), 590–609.

Björkvall, A. (forthcoming). Critical genre analysis of management texts in the public sector. Toward a theoretical and methodological framework.

Björkvall, A., & Nyström Höög, C. (2015). *The archaeology of a new genre. 'Platforms of values' texts of public authorities in Sweden*. Research proposal. Retrieved from anslag.rj.se/en/fund/49905. DOA: 14.03.2017.

Fairclough, N. (1993). Critical discourse analysis and the marketization of public discourse: The universities. *Discourse & Society*, 4(2), 133–168.

Fairclough, N. (2003). *Analysing Discourse. Textual Analysis for Social Research*. London: Routledge.

Halliday, M. A. K., & Matthiessen, C. (2004). *An Introduction to Functional Grammar*. 3rd ed. London: Hodder Education.

Hamberg, L. (2011). Alternativa läsarroller i en arbetsplan. Språkhandlingar ur läsarperspektiv. In P. Holmberg, A-M Karlsson & A. Nord (Eds.), *Funktionell textanalys*. Stockholm: Norstedts, 97–113.

Kress, G., & van Leeuwen, T. (1996). *Reading Images: The Grammar of Visual Design*. London: Routledge.

Kress, G., & van Leeuwen, T. (2002). Colour as a semiotic mode: notes for a grammar of colour. *Visual Communication*, 1(3), 343–368.

Kress, G., & van Leeuwen, T. (2006). *Reading Images. The Grammar of Visual Design*. 2nd ed. London: Routledge.

Miller, C. R. (1984). Genre as Social Action. *Quarterly Journal of Speech*, 70, 151–167.

Mulderrig, J. (2011). The grammar of governance. *Critical Discourse Studies*, 8(1), 45–67.

Nyström Höög, C. (2015). Värdegrundstexter – ett nytt uppdrag för klarspråksarbetet? *Sakprosa*, 7(2), Paper 6.

Nyström Höög, C., Söderlundh, H., & Sörlin, M. (2012). *Myndigheterna har ordet. Om kommunikation i skrift*. Stockholm: Språkrådet and Norstedts.

Pollitt, C., & Bouckaert, G. (2011). *Public Management Reform. A Comparative Analysis: New Public Management, Governance and the New-Weberian State*. Oxford: Oxford University Press.

Rehnberg, H-S. (2014). *Organisationer berättar. Narrativitet som resurs i strategisk kommunikation*. Uppsala: Department of Scandinavian Languages, Uppsala university.

Sarangi, S., & Slembrouck, S. (1996). *Language, Bureaucracy and Social Control*. London: Longman.

Svensson, J. (2005). Det offentliga samtalet. Några utvecklingslinjer mot slutet av det 20:e århundradet. In L. Moberg & M. Westman (Eds.), *Svenskan i tusen år. Glimtar ur svenska språkets utveckling*. Stockholm: Norstedts Ordbok AB, 142–162.

Vaara, E., Sorsa, V., & Pälli, P. (2010). On the force potential of strategy texts: a critical discourse analysis of a strategic plan and its power effects in a city organization. *Organization*, 17(6), 685–702.

Agnieszka Kiełkiewicz-Janowiak & Magdalena Zabielska

Adam Mickiewicz University, Poznań, Poland

Healthcare communication in transition: A cross-cultural study of migrant patients and doctors

Abstract: Poland's admission to the EU and, more specifically, the opening of the labour market has triggered a major wave of Polish immigrants into the UK, including a significant migration of Polish medical professionals. The aim of this paper is to explore the communication cultures of Polish and English healthcare encounters on the basis of patients' and doctors' accounts elicited through narrative interviews. The accounts were complemented by ethnographic interviews with doctors who have cross-cultural professional experience and by comments from Polish internet forums and blogs on the quality of healthcare in Poland and England. A qualitative analysis of the data uncovers the ways participants discursively construct their identities and position themselves (and others) in relation to health-care but outside the axiomatically asymmetrical doctor – patient interaction and apart from their institutional roles. The status of observer-commentators allows them to reflect on their experience and evaluate it. We also point to the need for professional medical training to be informed by linguistic research, which calls for an interdisciplinary outlook on both sides.

1. Introduction

The discursive turn in social studies has highlighted the significance of language in the construction of social reality. Ever since the beginnings of discourse analysis as an approach to language in relation to social phenomena and speakers' socio-psychological characteristics, scholars have addressed discourses on numerous social and political problems in the world.

Nowadays, one of the key processes in Europe and beyond is the existence of major population movements and their consequences for the well-being of communities in contact. In the current paper we focus on one of the more recent demographic shifts in Europe, namely the migration of Poles to the UK and Ireland, accelerated by EU regulations giving Polish people access to western European labour markets. In view of the significant mobility of Polish patients (as well as Polish healthcare professionals), we investigate the contact of two different healthcare communication cultures, specifically the discursive aspects of

Polish patients' and doctors' transnational movements between the two healthcare systems and their adaptation in a new context as revealed in the relevant discourse data. Theoretical concepts and methodological reflections, along with some early results are reported on at this preliminary stage of a project on cross-cultural healthcare communication.

2. Migration and healthcare

This section provides the background for the analysis of the communication cultures of Polish and English healthcare encounters. Specifically, it discusses the migration of Polish patients and doctors after Poland's admission to the European Union (section 2.1) and the accompanying problems (section 2.2) as well as the character of the healthcare system in Poland (section 2.3).

2.1. Migration of Poles – patients and doctors

As discourse studies have become methodologically consistent and well-established, the research contexts are becoming increasingly specialised (in focusing on restricted contexts) and, at the same time, extended (with and to interdisciplinary approaches). One opportunity for such research specialisation and extension may be provided by major demographic shifts in Europe. One of them has resulted from Poland's admission to the European Union in 2004 and the opening of the EU labour market, which has triggered a significant wave of Polish migration, in particular into the UK. Figure 1 shows the countries to which Poles began emigrating after the 2004 EU accession, with the UK being the most frequently chosen destination.

Figure 1. Migration outflows from Poland (Kaczmarczyk, 2014)

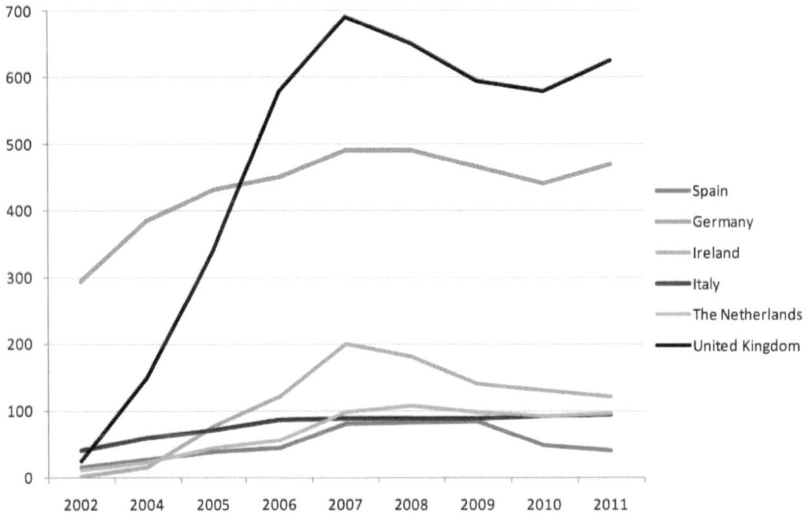

Table 1 below represents the overall fluctuations in Polish migration outflow to the UK and Ireland across the 2004–2014 decade, with a decrease between 2008–2010, and a constant, if small, increase starting in 2011. The two receiving countries in focus here differ in that Polish immigration to the UK follows the general pattern, while Ireland has received systematically fewer Polish migrants since the peak in 2007. As a result, in 2014 Poland was the country of birth of the second biggest group of foreign-born inhabitants in the UK, and the country of citizenship of the biggest group of foreign citizens in the UK (Rienzo & Vargas-Silva, 2014, p. 6).

Table 1. Estimated numbers of Polish immigrants in the UK and Ireland over 2004–2014 (in thousands)[1]

	2004	2005	2006	2007	2008	2009	2010	2011	2012	2013	2014
All	1000	1450	1950	2270	2210	2100	2000	2060	2130	2196	2320
UK	150	340	580	690	650	595	580	625	637	642	685
Ireland	15	76	120	200	180	140	133	120	118	115	113

1 "Informacja o rozmiarach i kierunkach czasowej emigracji z Polski w latach 2004–2014", GŁÓWNY URZĄD STATYSTYCZNY, Notatka informacyjna, Warszawa 5.10.2015. Retrieved from http://docplayer.pl/6561882-Informacja-o-rozmiarach-i-kierunkach-czasowej-emigracji-z-polski-w-latach-2004–2013.html. DOA: 01.03.2017

The large numbers of incoming (potential) patients were followed by a significant migration of Polish medical professionals (Brink-Muinen, Verhaak, Bensing, Bahrs, Deveugele, Gask, Mead, Leiva-Fernandez, Messerli-Rohrbach, Oppizzi, Peltenburg & Perez, 2003; see also the *brain drain*, Commander, Kangasniemi & Winters, 2003; Leśniowska, 2008).[2] The migration of this particular group was motivated by better-paid jobs and better working conditions (Wyrozębska, Wyrozębski & Dmoch-Gajzlerska, 2013), but was possibly also triggered by population changes in the British Isles, i.e. a major influx of (Polish) migrant patients.

As a result of these population movements of both patients and healthcare workers, the two groups have found themselves in a new healthcare environment, with an urgent need to adapt to their new circumstances. One of the challenges which they face is being confronted by a different communication culture (see also *health acculturation* discussed by Ronellenfitsch and Razum, 2004, as cited in Sime, 2014, p. 86). In this study we hope to uncover these processes of adaptation as they are reflected in discourse.

2.2. Mobility, diversity and associated problems

While cultural diversification of the EU region (Ognyanova, Maierb, Wismarb, Girasekc & Bussea, 2012) is widely acknowledged, the lack of cultural knowledge among medical practitioners (Dias, Gama, Cargaleiro & Martins, 2012) may not be all that apparent. This seems to be, however, an issue of concern, since migrants' cultural beliefs about the role of health services are brought by them to the host country, thereby affecting the character of doctor – patient communication. Moreover, when seeking medical advice, immigrants have a number of options. They can use the host country's health service or they can travel and use the system in their country of origin. The first option additionally allows them to choose between local doctors (who may be of different ethnicities as well, as in the UK context), or so called *ethnic niche doctors* (Osipovič, 2013), i.e. doctors from their country of origin. This choice may be dictated by geographical distance, service availability (insurance) and/or expenses, but also patients' preferences with respect to language/culture (see Glinos, Baeten, Helble & Maarse, 2010, p. 1147; Migge & Gilmartin, 2011, p. 1148; Goodwin, Polek & Goodwin, 2012; Osipovič, 2013; see also various press features confirming the popularity

2 According to Leśniowska (2007, p. 8), the number of Polish doctors registered in the UK rose considerably between 2004 and 2007 (by over 3000% in comparison with the period between 2000 and 2003).

of this conviction – Młynarski, 2007; PEO, 2015; Różalski, 2015). The last aspect concerns "feeling at ease with a system, trusting its providers and being able to speak one's language [, which] is important in situations of illness and vulnerability" (Glinos et al., 2010, p. 1147). This problem of trust and familiarity with the system will also be dealt with in the present paper.

Consequently, migration is a dynamic context, inviting change, in which routine behaviours are questioned. It is also an area of constant comparison between the two healthcare systems, their respective procedures and their participants (both patients and medical practitioners) (see Migge & Gilmartin, 2011; Goodwin et al., 2012; Osipovič, 2013; also Sime, 2014 below).

2.3. Healthcare system in Poland

The healthcare system in Poland has evolved quickly since the political changes at the end of the 1980s (Coulter & Jenkinson, 2005, p. 360). Similarly to Estonian and Romanian doctors, Polish medical professionals now act as gate-keepers and simultaneously many of them are self-employed. The former means that as part of the state healthcare system they are entitled to issue referrals to specialists; the latter entails that they can also run their own businesses as medical professionals. Additionally, a new health insurance scheme was introduced in Poland in 1999 and doctors are now paid by capitation fee (Meeuwesen, Brink-Muinen & Hofstede, 2009). Yet, the healthcare system in Poland is still in transition from a centralised state system to a Western model (Meeuwesen et al., 2009) and, as Coulter and Jenkinson (2005, p. 360) observe, it has not reached the standards of responsiveness achieved in other countries (see Gromulska, Goryński, Supranowicz & Wysocki, 2014). It needs to be noted, however, that most of the differences between the old and new EU countries (with regard to the 2004 wave of enlargement of the EU) concern not so much their status as old/new members (western European/central-eastern European) of the Union, but rather differences in their cultures (Brink-Muinen, Maaroos & Tahepold, 2008).

3. Theoretical background

For the purpose of this paper, we will now present selected models of the doctor – patient relationship as described in available literature in the field. As regards studies of healthcare communication styles in Europe, in general they have focused either on patients' preferences or their actual behaviour. Communication styles have been divided into the *affective* and the *instrumental*, with the latter further divided into *biomedical* and *psychological* models. In both types of study, communication styles may be considered with or without reference to cultural dimensions. The cultural dimensions discussed here are *power distance* and *uncertainty avoidance.*

3.1. Models of doctor – patient relationship

The conceptualization of the doctor – patient relationship in terms of autonomy and paternalism has been present in the literature for over fifty years (President's Commission, 1982). This relationship has been conceptualized in many different ways (Parson, 1951; Szasz & Hollender, 1956; Byrne & Long, 1976; Roter & Stewart, 1989; Emanuel & Emanuel, 1992), of which two approaches are relevant for the purpose of the present study.

Roter and Stewart (1989) identify four different models of doctor – patient relationship: *paternalism*, *consumerism*, *mutuality* and *default* (cf. Beisecker & Beisecker, 1993). The difference between them lies in the doctor's and patient's aims, the acknowledgement of the patient's values and autonomy as well as the assumed doctor's duties towards the patient (Roter et al., 1997). Briefly, in the *default* model both participants lack control over each other, which may result in the patient giving up treatment. In contrast, in *paternalism* the doctor is viewed as an authority and a guardian, while the patient's main role is to cooperate in an informed way. *Consumerism* views the said relationship in terms of marketplace economics, where doctors are seen primarily as service providers to patients-clients, with a strongly emphasized financial aspect of the relation. An alternative to consumerism and paternalism is *mutuality*, where both parties are seen as valid participants and contributors who share power by negotiating solutions. This model is the least preferred by Polish patients when decisions on treatment are being made (Coulter & Jenkinson, 2005, p. 359). As Roter and colleagues (1997) point out, these four models are important since they have a bearing on the perception of and attitudes to doctor – patient communication as well as on standards regarding medical practice.

Additionally, of relevance for this study are also the models identified by Emanuel and Emanuel (1992), who focus specifically on how information is conveyed to patients. In the *information* model the doctor is viewed as an expert who provides relevant facts to the patient. However, it is the patient who makes decisions based on his/her preferences. By contrast, in the *interpretative* model the doctor's role is greater as he/she is supposed to attempt to understand the patient's needs and choose the most optimal treatment solution. The *deliberative* model assumes that the doctor becomes a mentor who guides the patient in their choice of treatment. The final model, the *paternalistic* one, follows Roter and Stewart's (1989) conceptualization. Both Emanuel and Emanuel's (1992) and Roter and Stewart's (1989) models provide a conceptual grounding for the comparison of Polish and English communication styles in healthcare.[3]

3.2. Communication styles in healthcare

Typically, a health encounter has two primary aims: to provide expertise to manage a medical problem (instrumental) and to build a relationship supporting the treatment (affective). Assuming the patient's perspective, Engel (1988) refers to them as

> 'the need to know and understand' (to know what is the matter with him or her, what causes the pain, and how this can be stilled) and the 'the need to feel known and understood' (to know that he/she is accepted by the doctor as a person and is not seen as a malingerer)
>
> (Engel, 1988, as quoted in Bensing & Dronkers, 1992, p. 283).

Similarly, in medical practice in general, two communicative behaviours are identified, i.e. *instrumental* (task-focused) vs. *affective* (socio-psychological), which correspond to the two aims of a healthcare encounter identified by Engel (1988): providing knowledge necessary for the success of treatment and the healing potential of the encounter, i.e. managing its socio-psychological aspects (see also Desjarlais-deKlerk & Wallace, 2013). In particular, the instrumental behaviour is further divided into *psychological talk*, addressing aspects of the patient's everyday life, his/her mental state as well as the relationship with others; and *biomedical talk*, when the patient is questioned and instructed about his/her condition and therapy (Brink-Muinen et al., 2008). By contrast, affective behaviour includes personal comments, manifestations of agreement or understanding as well as disagreement and criticism, and attempts at streamlining the communication process. The two types of behaviour are discussed in the literature also as: *technical* vs. *interpersonal* (Cheraghi-Sohi et al., 2008), *cure-* vs. *care-oriented*; *scientific-technical* vs. *socio-emotional* (Carmel & Glick, 1996) and *physician-* vs. *patient-centred approach* (Hall, Roter & Katz, 1987).

As regards patients' views on these behaviours in Western countries, in general, the technical aspect of care is clearly favoured but not to the exclusion of the interpersonal quality (Cheraghi-Sohi et al., 2008; see also Segall & Burnett, 1980; Fletcher et al., 1983; Vick & Scott, 1998; Campbell, Roland & Buetow, 2000; Fung et al., 2005; Espinel, Shah, McCormick, Krakovitz & Boss, 2014). Comparing the communicational styles in old and new EU countries (with regard to the 2004 wave

3 See Rees, Monrouxe and Wilkinson (2007) for a study of metaphors used by patients and medical students which reflect these models.

of enlargement of the EU), Brink-Muinen and colleagues (2008) found that in Poland instrumental behaviour is more common, and more specifically the biomedical talk in the doctor – patient communication, with less eye contact and less room for discussion offered to patients. In the UK, by contrast, the communication style tends to be more of the affective type, with more "signs of agreement" by doctors. The authors conclude that "the GPs in the new EU countries [take] more speaking time than their colleagues of the old EU countries. Therefore, their patient [gets (or takes)] less time to tell their story" (Brink-Muinen et al., 2008).

3.3. Cross-cultural healthcare communication: literature review

In this section we discuss the results of the studies of cross-cultural healthcare communication, adopting the distinctions presented in sections 3.1 and 3.2 as well as introducing selected cultural dimensions. We also point to particular problems which may arise in such healthcare encounters and illustrate them with relevant examples from the available literature.

3.3.1. Patients' views on the responsiveness of healthcare systems and providers

Regarding patients' preferences, Brink-Muinen and colleagues (2008) view the doctor – patient relation as "possibly more hierarchical (…) in Eastern European countries as opposed to Western European countries". According to Coulter and Jenkinson's (2005, p. 359) study, in Poland more patients felt the doctor (rather than the patient) should be the primary decision-maker. Yet significant numbers of people in Poland were dissatisfied with the paternalistic approach of doctors. It is possible that the Polish patient expects medical expertise but, at the same time, does not want to be treated in a patronising way. More specifically, Polish patients value the "opportunity to ask questions, receipt of information [and] being taken seriously" (Marcinowicz, Chlabicz & Grebowski, 2010, p. 713). They also emphasise the doctor's expertise as contributing to their satisfaction with the healthcare provided (Marcinowicz et al., 2010, p. 713; see also Marcinowicz, Chlabicz & Grebowski, 2009). The researchers note as well that patients' preferences and views may stem from their previous experience with particular medical systems (Marcinowicz et al., 2010, p. 714), i.e. "knowledge from back home" based on "pre-migration experiences" (Goodwin et al., 2012, p. 153), which is also confirmed in English medical practitioners' accounts on Polish migrants' health-seeking behaviours (Sime, 2014, p. 90; see also section 3.3.3 below). This is an important observation in the context of the present study (cf. sections 4.3.2–4.3.5).

3.3.2. Cultural dimensions of healthcare

While the above-discussed studies of communication styles in healthcare referred primarily to content, the current study takes into consideration cultural dimensions of *power distance* and *uncertainty avoidance* (Hofstede & Hofstede, 2005) that may affect doctor – patient communication. Comparing the two contexts under consideration, Poland is seen as a high power distance culture, where the roles of the physician and the patient are fixed and hierarchical. Generally, Polish doctors are believed to be "directive and verbally dominant", but, at the same time, "warmer by expressing positive feelings toward patients" (Heszen-Klemens & Łapińska, 1984) (cf. 'warm autocrats' vs. North American 'cold experts', Meeuwesen et al., 2009, p. 60). High power distance cultures also tend to have shorter consultation time.

Polish culture is also viewed as having a preference for avoiding uncertainty, which, in the context of healthcare communication, means relatively low priority for rapport building. In comparison to the UK, which is described as low on power distance and uncertainty avoidance, Poland can be therefore characterised as paying less attention to rapport building and having shorter consultation time (Meeuwesen et al., 2009, pp. 60, 64). In other words, the doctor – patient relationship in the Polish context is one where partnerships and joint decisions between doctors and patients are neither sought nor required.

The discussion of the above-presented research has allowed us to subscribe to the view that "cultural norms, values, beliefs and attitudes towards health and healthcare may influence the communication between doctors and their patients too and, therefore, the quality of healthcare and the patients' health" (Meeuwesen et al., 2009, p. 64). Consequently, we call for a general greater recognition of the migrant patients' cultural background with which they come to host countries, which would in turn result in "culturally responsive health care" (Durieux-Paillard, 2007, p. 203; Migge & Gilmartin, 2011, p. 1144). Thus, in empirical research, we suggest that data should be considered on the behaviour of individual physicians and/or patients in microscale and from a qualitative perspective. Micronarratives in accounts of personal experience and in opinions evaluating the systems seem to lend themselves to this type of analysis. This way, the focus of the study is shifted from the widely-studied doctor – patient communication to these interactants' individual accounts, thereby combining the "institutional and the personal" and leading to analytical "hybridity" (Sarangi & Roberts, 1999, p. 12).

In order to illustrate the problems an immigrant patient may experience in the receiving country when consulting a doctor, a number of exemplary accounts will be presented. They are derived not only from existing scholarly (empirical) work but also from the local daily press as well as Internet forums for migrants (Forum 1, Forum 2 – see References for details). As far as newspapers are concerned, patients' accounts are keenly used by journalists to authenticate their representations of migrants' situations; as for Internet forums, migrants themselves seek out opportunities to share their experiences with other members of the community.

3.3.3. Problems of intercultural communication in healthcare: selected studies

Migrants' problems related to using healthcare in their host countries and their reasons for doing so have been referred to in a number of studies. For instance, in their paper on Korean immigrants in New Zealand, Lee and colleagues (2010) point to cultural and linguistic misunderstandings during healthcare encounters that make Koreans choose to travel to their homeland to seek medical advice (2010, p. 214). As Nielsen, Yazici, Petersen, Blaakilde and Krasnik (2010) show, for Turkish immigrants in Denmark similarly problematic is the different character of the doctor – patient communication as well as "different patient preferences, and health-seeking behaviours" (2010, p. 390).

As regards cross-cultural and intercultural healthcare communication of Polish migrants in the British Isles (Brink-Muinen et al., 2008; Meeuwesen et al., 2009; Migge & Gilmartin, 2011; Goodwin et al., 2012; Osipovič, 2013; Main, 2014; Sime, 2014; Ślęzak, 2014, 2016), the studies report on more talk delivered by the doctor and its biomedical and instrumental nature. The verbal contribution of the GPs in the new EU countries is greater than in the old EU countries (with regard to the 2004 wave of enlargement of the EU).

Differences can also be seen between new EU countries, for instance Poland, Romania and Estonia as investigated by Brink-Muinen and colleagues (2008). In the study it has been found that in Poland and Estonia there was more biomedical talk than in Romania. Also, Estonian doctor – patient communication was more affective whereas in Poland and Romania it was more instrumental.

Finally, it should also be noted that, as Sime (2014) reports, Poles arrive in the host country with a certain idea of healthcare services and, when faced with the local system, make countless comparisons with the home system (see Marcinowicz et al., 2010, p. 714; Migge & Gilmartin, 2011; Goodwin et al., 2012; Osipovič, 2013).

3.3.4. *Examples of patients' and doctors' accounts*

The following examples[4] of patients' and doctors' accounts are drawn from the existing research discussed in section 3.3.3. For instance, excerpt (1) comes from Lee and colleagues' (2010) study of Korean immigrants in New Zealand. The problem, as perceived by the patient (Mrs. Lee), does not concern language proficiency but rather a cultural mismatch with regards to the way certain medical issues are communicated to the patient.

(1)
Well… there was no English problem for me. However, yes I did have a communication problem. I was so shocked when my doctor told me that I could have cancer (…) Cancer means death for me. (…) In Korea, if this is the case, they usually only communicate to the patient's family and wait until the surgery so that there can be no stress for the ill patient.
(Mrs Lee)

(Lee, Kearns & Friesen, 2010, p. 112)

Lee and colleagues' (2010) study attempts to emphasise the growing importance of cultural competence in the context of cross-cultural healthcare communication (Betancourt, Green, Carillo & Park, 2005). The relevance of the perceived differences in the patients' socio-cultural background is sometimes part of the patients' own diagnosis of communication problems. This happens more often in the case of non-European migrants in Europe (Migge & Gilmartin, 2011, p. 1148), but the following two examples illustrate (implicit or explicit) cultural references by Polish migrants' diagnostic comments on primary healthcare in the UK and Ireland (respectively). In example (2) a Polish immigrant patient's wife in the UK comments on the inappropriateness of the doctor's reaction to the message communicated by her husband.

(2)
my impression is that the GP is like a shield to defend the specialist … he has to treat everything: my gynaecological problems and my husband's psychiatric problems … It frustrates me a lot … when my husband mentioned his [psychiatric] problems to the GP, the GP asked him about our financial situation. It took my husband more than two weeks to get over it.
(Zofia, 30 years old, 4 years in London)

(Main, 2014, p. 904)

In example (3), the patient comments on an Irish doctor's approach to the patient who provided ample information about her medical history, which the doctor treated as superfluous and oversensitive.

---

4 Transcription conventions are provided at the end of the paper.

(3)

Well I think doctors here and in general the medical services people, they don't take into account that **when foreign people come they have a different culture** and they don't know how to deal with it or they don't want to. Because I can tell you I wasn't the first person and I won't be the last person who had that.

(2004POL04)

(Migge & Gilmartin, 2011, p. 1148; emphasis added)

The following two extracts are also accounts of the experience of using the receiving country's healthcare system. Here the manner in which the 'local' medical practices are discussed implies that a Polish doctor would behave differently.

(4)

W moim moczu pojawiła się krew, poczułam też silne kłucie w podbrzuszu. Do angielskiego lekarza nie poszłam, bo jak bywałam wcześniej z czymkolwiek innym, to słyszałam: „przyczyna nieznana". Z tym pęcherzem jednak było coraz gorzej i sytuacja zmusiła mnie do skorzystania z usług angielskiego lekarza. Powiedział mi, że mam dbać o higienę. Zaznaczam, że o higienę dbałam i dbam wręcz przesadnie. Pojechałam do Polski, przepisano mi furagin i wszystko jest ok."– mówi Majka, kelnerka z baru kawowego na Highgate.

["I noticed blood in my urine, I also felt a strong prickling in my underbelly. I did not visit an English doctor because when I had done so previously with any other problems, I heard 'cause unknown'. But my bladder was getting worse and the situation forced me to visit an English doctor. He told me to take better care of my hygiene. In fact I do that, even excessively so. I went to Poland, I was prescribed Furagin and now everything is okay", says Majka, a waiteress from a coffee bar on Highgate.]

(Młynarski, 2007)

In another account the patient describes her experience of a night visit to a hospital in the UK, due to her child's medical emergency. The parent's disdainful attitude is visible in the negative evaluation of the health professionals involved.

(5)

*Przed ostatnimi świętami Bożego Narodzenia dwuletni syn Jagody dostał bardzo wysokiej gorączki. […] Jagoda z mężem i dwuletnim Dawidem od siedmiu lat mieszka pod Londynem. Mimo że był środek nocy, zdecydowali się jechać do szpitala w swoim angielskim miasteczku Reading. Zastaliśmy tłum ludzi. […] Na wizytę czekaliśmy dwie godziny. Tłumaczenia, że dziecko ma prawie 40 stopni gorączki, w ogóle **nie poruszyły pań w rejestracji**. - Gdy w końcu udało się dostać do lekarza, **konował** spojrzał jedynie na syna i zawyrokował, że to przeziębienie. Zalecił podawanie paracetamolu. **Nawet nie zbadał** syna stetoskopem. […]*

[Before last Christmas Jagoda's two-year-old son had a high fever. (…) Jagoda, her husband and her son had lived near London for seven years. Although it was in the middle of the night, they decided to visit the hospital in the English town of Reading. We found crowds there. (…) We waited 2 hours to be seen. We explained to the women at the reception desk that our son had a 40 degree fever but **they showed no sympathy**.

When we finally got to see the doctor, the **quack** merely looked at our son and announced that it was just a cold. He prescribed paracetamol. **He didn't even bother to check** him with a stethoscope. (…)]

(Różalski, 2015; emphasis added)

Example (5) comes from a short piece from a Polish daily, *Gazeta Wyborcza*, addressing the issue of an increase in "medical tourism" (Connell, 2006) to Poland (and not only by Polish immigrants). In fact both accounts above reveal the patients' frustration and their possible motivation in turning to healthcare back in their country of origin.

Finally, scholarly and popular sources alike present accounts in which medical professionals comment on some cultural specificity of Polish patients in their health-seeking behaviours (see examples 6–8 taken from Sime, 2014, p. 90):

(6)
The thing with Eastern Europeans – their perception of illness and health is different and what they want from us. Sometimes, they see their doctor in Poland and come to us for a second opinion, so there is a clash of cultures.

(GP, Rural area)

(7)
Culturally, back home they will just go wait for the GP, and they will just sit until they are seen, and that doesn't go well here, when we say, come back next week, with an appointment.

(Regional Health Manager, Urban Area)

(8)
Sometimes, they come and say 'I want a referral to the allergy specialist' or whatever, and it just isn't clinically indicated, well not here [in the UK].

(GP, Urban area)

4. The current project

4.1. Aims and assumptions

The current study has the following aims: (1) to explore the communication cultures of Polish and British/Irish healthcare encounters; (2) to study Polish migrant patients as participants in British and Irish healthcare cultures; and (3) to find a discursive representation of this participation in the patients' narratives. Importantly, healthcare communication has been studied here from outside the healthcare encounter, i.e. on the basis of patients' reflections on their experience.

Our assumption is that migrants bring their culture-specific discursive competence into the receiving country and adapt to the new healthcare context. In this respect Polish patients' accounts of healthcare encounters in the UK and Ireland give an insight into this process of adaptation and, when analysed discursively, reveal the patients' acts of evaluating communication and comparing the efficiency of the two healthcare systems.

4.2. Data and methodology

The data in the present study include patients' and doctors' accounts elicited through narrative interviews (Flick, 1998, 2000; Jovchelovitch & Bauer, 2000). The format of the interviews was very open and the interviewer's role relatively flexible, with the major aim of allowing the interviewees to introduce and discuss the topics which they themselves considered relevant in their experience of healthcare. The focus has been specifically on the migrant patients' accounts of contact with healthcare professionals and treatment as well as the strategies of coping with a foreign healthcare system. These narratives were complemented with the data obtained in ethnographic interviews with doctors who have cross-cultural professional experience. In this case the focus of attention was their references to intra-professional rules, codes of conduct and system evaluations. In this way, we juxtapose the personal accounts of lived experience with surveys or recordings of actual healthcare encounters, and point to the former as being an important and valuable source of information, a means to capture unique and intimate understandings of concepts related to individual well-being.

Some research suggests that the use of exclusively quantitative methodology is not adequate in the healthcare context; many concepts and problems studied are very complex and require the use of more flexible tools, such as open questions, to elicit responses not initially assumed by the researchers (see, for example, Marcinowicz et al., 2009).

When considering the data collection process, two issues need to be reflected upon. Firstly, the sensitivity of the research context under consideration (Alty & Rodham, 1998; Sarangi & Roberts, 1999; Watts, 2008, 2010; Pawelczyk, 2011) should be emphasized, since the matters discussed concern the patient's well-being, oftentimes touching upon deeply intimate issues and topics (Watts, 2010). Secondly, the focus here is on the special character of the relationship between the interview participants (i.e. interviewer and interviewee), where patients' accounts about the medical encounter are elicited outside the power-based doctor – patient interaction. The consequence of this shift in perspective is an opportunity for the speakers to reflect and comment on their experiences of cross-cultural healthcare communication, and to share their perceptions and observations that could hardly be possible (and usually irrelevant) in regular doctor – patient interactions. In other words, in such an approach the participants have the freedom to construct their identities and positions, unconstrained by their institutional roles. Following this line of reasoning, both Polish patients and Polish medical professionals may compare and evaluate Polish and British/Irish healthcare communication styles and the strategies of adaptation and acculturation.

At this preliminary stage of the proposed project, we chose to report on four interviews with migrant patients and doctors, collected through a convenience sample. The interviews were recorded, transcribed and analysed for themes and discourse structure. In particular, the patients' small narratives were examined for the way they represented their understanding of the key concepts of healthcare and the processes of adaptation in a new environment. It was assumed that a close analysis of the discursive features would capture the views and attitudes emergent in narration. For example, shifting the narrator's perspective (see Labov, 2013) by the use of deictic expressions may mark positioning oneself as belonging to geographical and/or identity spaces. Expressing emotions and attitudes would be implemented through noun phrases (e.g. *ogromny szok* 'big shock'), adjectives/adverbs (*miłe* 'nice', *bardziej twarde* 'stricter', *zbywczo* 'dismissively') and other evaluative statements (*mam w stymie* 'I hold it in high esteem', *pomyłka z tym lekarzem* 'this doctor is a mistake').

4.3. Results: themes in patients' narratives

This section presents the results of the analysis in the following order. First, discursively constructed migrant patients' identity and cultures are shown as undergoing transition. Secondly, Polish patients' opinions and attitudes are discussed, presenting the UK healthcare system as patient-centred and more friendly than in Poland. Thirdly, the portrayal of the interviewed patients is inferred on the basis of their accounts. Finally, their strategies of adaptation in a new context are traced.

4.3.1. Migrants: identity in transition

The migration situation is, for obvious reasons, a challenge to identity. Specifically, the need to adapt to a new environment always destabilises one's identity and calls for identity transformation. Migration processes are therefore a prototypical context of (re)construction and negotiation of identity (see La Barbera, 2015). The transformation of identity takes place in interaction, in which speakers relate to others, but also struggle to achieve personal, social and economic ends.

The context of healthcare is a sensitive one, in which patients' health is at stake and their adaptation to a new system will thus be guided by the aim to restore health. Therefore, the interplay between migrants' allegiance to their former or original identity and the adoption of a new identity may be acute when participants strive for their well-being.

The process of identity shift is predictably testified in records of communication and is visible in how identity is marked deictically (see *personal* and *spatial reference*, Farrell, 2008). The main distinction between 'us' and 'them' will be used when migrants make constant comparisons between the home and the host country healthcare systems and align with either. In particular, the way patients' affilitation is marked by personal and spatial deixis will depend on

- geo-demography (Which country do I live in permanently?), e.g. *w Polsce* ('in Poland')
- place of current position (Where do I currently live? Where am I now? Where is the interview conducted?), e.g. *tutaj* ('here'), *tam* ('there')
- affinity for one's country, feeling of personal belonging, e.g. *u nas* ('with us', 'at our place'), *u nas w Polsce* ('back home in Poland') (cf. Wodak, de Cillia, Reisigl & Liebhart, 1999, p. 35; Petersoo, 2007)

The data in the interviews show how these various dimensions of belonging interact. In example (9) the speaker straightforwardly uses the deictic adverbs of 'here' (*tutaj*) and 'there' (*tam*) to refer to where she lives now (in migration) and her country of origin.

(9)
no ***tam*** *gdzie my jeździliśmy do tego lekarza on nam wiesz no nam bardzo dużo no tam nie wiem tłumaczył opowiadał mówił,* ***tutaj*** *było inaczej* [...]

[**the place** where we used to go, to this doctor, he, you know, he would [tell] us a lot I don't know, explained, told, said, **here** it was different (...)]

(P2)

In example (10) the interviewee uses *w Polsce* 'in Poland' and *tam* 'there' to refer to her country of origin and the host country. Significantly, even though at the time of the interview the speaker was physically in Poland, she refers to her country of origin by explicitly naming it rather than using the deictic adverb of place, which she does use to refer only to the host country. Additionally, the adjective *ichniejszy* 'theirs; not ours' modifies the indirect reference to the English health service system. Thus, she seems to be demonstrating some level of distance from the host country.

(10)
jeśli chodzi o dziecko to [...] *mimo wszystko* ***w Polsce*** *jest podejście jakoś takie* [...] *nie zbywają cię z dzieckiem w tym sensie że no tak mi się wydaje że jeśli chodzi zwłaszcza o dzieci to* ***w Polsce*** *jednak wiesz rzadko kto by tobie odmówił wizyty na przykład bo od*

razu też no ta odpowiedzialność [...] *czy to ryzyko jest chyba że lekarze pielęgniarki czy rejestratorki czują że jest większe, że dziecko jest bardziej nieprzewidywalne że dla swojego spokoju wolą jednak obejrzeć osłuchać i żeby nie było jakiś tam problemów tak mi się wydaje, natomiast* ***tam*** *tak jak mówię telefon jest infolinia* ***ichniejszego*** *NFZ-u na którą dzwonisz i mogą ci dać jakieś tam wskazówki*

[when it comes to a baby (...) **in Poland** the approach is somewhat (...) they do not treat you dismissively when you come with a child in the sense that, well, I think that when it comes specifically to children, **in Poland** you know hardly anyone would refuse you a visit for example because immediately there is this responsibility (...) or maybe there is this risk that doctors, nurses or receptionists feel that there is this bigger, that a child is more unpredictable, that for their own safety they still prefer to examine and use a stethoscope and that there are no problems I think but **there**, like I said, a telephone line, there is that NHS helpline of **theirs** which you call and they can give you some guidelines]

(P1)

On the other hand, in example (11) the interviewee, a Polish migrant from Ireland, uses a double marking in referring to the host country – *tutaj w Irlandii* 'here in Ireland' – by both a deictic adverb and the country name.

(11)
ale jak chodziłam na wizyty no to często się tam pytali właśnie skąd jestem ile jestem już ***tutaj w Irlandii*** *i raczej tak troszkę bardziej chcieli się dowiedzieć o pacjencie to na pewno ci GP to na pewno bardziej niż ci polscy*

[but when I visited doctors they asked me very often where I was from, how long I had been **here in Ireland** and rather they wanted to learn a little bit more about the patient, for sure, these GPs, for sure, more that these Polish ones]

(P3)

Finally, another interviewee juxtaposes *tam* 'there' with *u nas* 'here; with us', a prepositional phrase which combines personal and spatial reference (cf. German *bei uns*).

(12)
mi się wydaje że ***tam*** *na przykład nie wiem czy* ***u nas*** *jest podobnie czy nie bo mówię trudno mi jest to porównywać*

[it seems to me that **there**, for instance, I don't know if it's the same **with us** or not because as I say it is difficult for me to compare]

(P1)

To conclude, the examples above show an array of discursive choices made by the migrants to claim their national identity and to refer to their location/residence. It seems that the use of locational reference is context sensitive in that the choice depends on where the interview is conducted; certainly, the interviewer's identity may also be relevant to the speaker (for example, is the interviewer also Polish?). It is possible that by naming the country of reference (and especially by double marking the reference as in 'here in Ireland', see example 11) the speakers aim at avoiding an ambiguity of their own position. By combining the personal and spatial references migrants work out a hybrid third space (see Bhabha, [1994] 2007), which affords a way of placing one's identity in a space in-between: "[p]articipants move *across* cultures, inhabit places *in-between*" (Farrell, 2008, p. 182).

4.3.2. Migration: cultures in transition

Next to identifying themselves as belonging to an in-group and/or an out-group, migrants align with cultural values and behaviours. This is done discursively by using a variety of evaluative forms (adjectives, verbs, complex phrases) to describe one of the cultures and thereby compare it with the other.

In the following excerpt the speaker clearly distinguishes between herself and the out-group by means of deictic pronouns (*ja* 'I' vs. *oni* 'they'), and she also positions herself in the space in-between (see subsection 4.3.1) by marking her movement as outward (*ja przyjechałam* 'I went there' and *jestem tam* 'I am there'). Yet, she particularly forcefully juxtaposes two sets of cultural values in terms of experience, cultural truths, folk wisdom, medical truths and attitudes (see also Osipovič, 2013). She respects the other, but suggests she cannot help aligning with her (original) culture (*jestem tym bardzo przesiąknięta* 'I am steeped in that').

(13)
ja przyjechałam czy jestem ***tam*** *z całym* ***bagażem doświadczeń*** *i takich wiesz* ***prawd ludowych*** [...] *ja się z tego nie śmieję tak ale to są czasami takie no trochę prawdy ludowe trochę medyczne jestem tym te* ***bardzo przesiąknięta*** *tym polskim podejściem i do dziecka i do samego rozwoju natomiast* ***oni*** *maja swoje podejście tak może* ***bardziej twarde*** *może* ***bardziej chłodne***

[I went **there** or I am **there** with all this **baggage of experience** and of you know **cultural truths** [...] I'm not laughing at it no but these are sometimes some kind of folk wisdom or medical truths I am **steeped in** that this Polish attitude both toward children and their development and **they** have their own attitude, right, maybe **stricter**, maybe **colder**]

(P1)

Throughout the narrative, the speaker basically abstains from making evaluative comments. She shows an attitude of tolerance towards the other but, at the same time, one that affirms the migrants' right to adhere to the home culture.

4.3.3. *Awareness of cultural differences*

The same participant whose utterance has been quoted in example (13) recounts her encounter with a doctor from Bangladesh: she interprets the doctor's behaviour implying a difference in attitude (from indigenous doctors) (*bardziej chciała współpracować* 'more willing to cooperate') and shares her impression of the doctor not having (*jeszcze* 'yet') internalised the host country's understanding of social hierarchy (*sztywnej struktury kontaktów* 'rigid structure of relations'). The speaker seems to project a solidary perception of the doctor as a fellow migrant.

(14)
[lekarka] z Bangladeszu [...] co zauważyłam że ona na przykład była dużo bardziej skłon- znaczy jakoś ten ***kontakt z nią*** *widziałam że [...]* ***bardziej chciała współpracować*** *[...] wydawało mi się że ona przez to że też nie była* ***jeszcze tak przesiąknięta takim*** *taką trzymaniem takiej* ***sztywnej struktury kontaktów*** *między pacjentem i postępowaniem takim jakby niektórzy powiedzieli* ***bardziej ludzka*** *[...]*

[[a doctor] from Bangladesh [...] what I noticed, she for instance, was far more like- this **contact with her**, I mean somehow, we had, I saw that [...] **she was more willing to cooperate**, I had the impression that that was because **she was not yet steeped in this** this **rigid structure of relations** between the patient and rules, this, some would say was **more humane**]

(P2)

Another patient explicitly, however unclearly, talks about her feelings of being patronised by means of a generic reference to a doctor who is not at all interested in the migrant patient as a human being, possibly a respectable member of society.

(15)
[...] że człowiek, nie ma człowieka, nie wie czym się zajmuje ani (.) ***ale on pokazuje swoją taką jakąś wyższość na tobą****, nie wiem, jak tak odczuwam*

[[...] that one, that there is no human being there, [the doctor] does not know what you do or (.) **but he** [the doctor] **demonstrates some kind of superiority**, I do not know, this is what I sense]

(P3)

4.3.4. *UK healthcare system – patient-centred/friendly*

In the specific context of healthcare encounters recounted here, migrants operationalise their awareness of cultural differences to spell out the manifestations of culture-specific attitudes to patients. They do not exactly use the phrase 'patient-friendly', which they may have internalised from media messages, yet they have been able to supply examples of health professionals' empathetic behaviour which, according to the participant in examples (16) and (17), was 'nice' and which she 'liked', in contrast with what she feels is common in her country of origin:

(16)
to są różnice na przykład pacjent jest proszony do gabinetu imiennie tak ***to nie jest coś takiego jak u nas****, znaczy to mi się bardzo* ***podoba*** *bo pacjent jest zapraszany tak do gabinetu, jest Pani X Pan Y, co wydaje mi się że jest* ***sympatyczne*** [...]

[there are differences, for instance, when a patient is invited to a surgery by name, right, **it is not like with us**, I mean I **like** it very much because the patient is invited, right, surgery, there is a Ms. X, Mr. Y which seems **nice** to me [...]]

(P2)

(17)
to mi się bardzo to ***podobało*** *dlatego że położna zawsze po mnie wychodziła i było to takie* ***miłe***

[**I really liked** it because the midwife always came out to meet me and that was very **nice**]

(P2)

This observation was also confirmed by Goodwin and colleagues (2012) in their study of Polish migrants. Osipovič (2013) reports that her respondents were actually "baffled" by the patient-centred way in which they were addressed by local doctors.

4.3.5. Migrant doctors and patients

The participants often conceive of themselves as entitled to compare and evaluate realities of health service in Poland and the UK/Ireland because of them being familiar with both healthcare systems. Thus, perceptions of migrant patients' attitudes and behaviour are spelled out as implicitly resulting from their cultural background. In particular, Polish patients in the UK and Ireland have been commented on as being more demanding and determined to claim their rights as patients.

In previous research on patient satisfaction conducted in Poland (Marcinowicz et al., 2009), patients showed greatest concern for their interpersonal relations with (family) doctors (whether positively or negatively evaluated), and in the second place for the conditions of medical treatment. Interestingly, evaluations of doctors' competence and their personal qualities were not commonly expressed. In the current study, doctors' perceptions of patients or patients' opinions of other patients do not paint a portrait of a Polish migrant patient who refrains from evaluating the medical professional's expertise. Rather, Polish migrant patients are represented as people who demand adequate professional expertise (see also Osipovič, 2013), and expect of the doctor an authoritative stance (Coulter & Jenkinson, 2005, p. 359) as well as a justification of treatment decisions (see also Marcinowicz et al., 2010, p. 713). It is possible that migrant patients are accustomed to struggling through their new environment in all walks of life – and healthcare is no exception. Additionally, if not satisfied with the service or the treatment they receive, they may often fall back on the option of going back to Poland for a second opinion or alternative treatment (see also Osipovič, 2013).

The reason for dissatisfaction that recurs in the interviews is having to wait too long for an appointment. The following is a blunt way of describing the inconvenience:

(18)
generalnie [jest] *tak, umówić się do lekarza to jest* ***koszmar****, jeśli ja idę dzisiaj to wcześniej niż za tydzień to nikt mnie nie przyjmie, to jest pewne*

[in general [it's] like this, to get an appointment with a doctor is a **nightmare**, if I go today no one will see me any earlier than in a week, that's for sure]

(P4)

However, the interviewees have suggested that this is not acceptable to Polish patients, who would 'rebel' (*byłby bunt pacjenta*), and maybe they would even get the media involved, while "there people do wait" (*tam ludzie czekają*):

(19)
fakt że musisz czekać tydzień czy nawet dni na wizytę no to to u nas by to nie przeszło z tego względu że ***byłby bunt pacjenta*** *byłyby zaraz media w to włączone natomiast no* ***tam ludzie czekają*** *nie*

[the fact that you have to wait a week or even two weeks for a visit well here [in Poland] it would be unacceptable because **patients would rebel** immediately, the media would be involved, and **there people do wait**]

(P1)

A contrast is made with local patients, who obligingly accept the situation rather than protest. The benevolent behaviour of the locals is thus described with some measure of astonishment in example (20) or scorn in example (21):

(20)
mi się wydaje też że oni w ogóle nie dyskutują faktycznie z tym to co lekarz powie to oni to przyjmują za, nie zastanawiają się czy on ma rację czy może warto to by było sprawdzić u kogoś innego, raczej to przyjmują na zasadzie że no ok byłam u lekarza i zrobiłam to co mogłam to on musi mieć rację [...]

[I think as well that they in general indeed do not question what the doctor will say, they take it as, they do not wonder whether the doctor is right or maybe it is worth getting a second opinion, they rather take it as, well okay I visited the doctor and did what I could then he must be right [...]]

(P1)

(21)
[Anglicy] *oni po prostu pójdą, co im przepiszą to oni będą brali i tak właśnie to wygląda*
[[the English] they will just go, they will take what they are prescribed and that's it]
(P4)

A question about the healthcare experience is primarily discussed with reference to the behaviour of the doctors. The contrast between two healthcare contexts is again heavily exploited to imply an argument. In (22) below, an example of a single consultation in England (*ta lekarka* 'this doctor') is used as the basis for generalizing the conclusions about English doctors (*ta wiedza ich* 'that knowledge of theirs') and Polish doctors (*ja szanuję polskich lekarzy i szanuję ich wiedzę i kompetencje* 'I respect Polish doctors and I respect their knowledge and expertise').

(22)
przy jakimś tam badaniu była trochę powyżej normy i na przykład ***ta lekarka już mi nie potrafiła odpowiedzieć*** *co to oznacza mówi że to będzie musiała skonsultować z pediatrą i tak dalej [...] ta wiedza* ***ich*** *jest bardzo taka taka mi się wydaje podstawowa nie [...] to znaczy* ***ja szanuję polskich lekarzy tak ja szanuję polskich lekarzy i szanuję ich wiedzę i kompetencje***

[a test was done [one parameter] was above the norm and for instance **this doctor was not able to tell me** what that meant, she said she would have to consult a paediatrician [...] that knowledge of **theirs** is, I think, basic, right? [...] what I mean is I respect Polish doctors, right, **I respect Polish doctors and I respect their knowledge and expertise**]
(P1)

(23)
tu podejście lekarza polskiego mi się bardziej podobało niż tego angielskiego bo on po prostu konkretnie pow- znaczy konkretnie tamten konkretnie podszedł do sytuacji a ten mi po prostu tak trochę no zbywczo powiedział że no nie, że to jest wiesz że to jest taka sytuacja że dzieci chorują i nie ma takiej potrzeby

[in this case I liked the Polish's doctor's approach more that that of the English one, as he simply sai-, in concrete terms, I mean concrete terms, that doctor approached the situation in an concrete way while this [doctor] just a little, well, dismissively told me that well no, that this is, you know, that it is normal that children get sick and that there is no need]
(P2)

Similarly, one of Goodwin and colleagues' (2012) respondents noted that GPs in the UK "are not very competent, but nice" (2012, p. 164, cf. section 4.3.4 above).

The above-given examples illustrate also the paternalistic (Roter & Stewart, 1989) or deliberative model (Emanuel & Emanuel, 1992; see subsection 3.1 above) of the relation between the doctor and the patient. Here the participants appear to be dissatisfied with the medical professionals, who are unable to see (cf. example 22) – or seem not to see – any reason to provide further information and treat the patient 'dismissively' (*zbywczo*, cf. example 23). In their view this additional detail of service is crucial.

4.3.6. *Strategies of adaptation*

The migration situation gives rise to an expected need of the migrants to adapt to a new context with a view of improving their opportunities and prospects. In the case of voluntary migrants, the natural result of finding oneself in an environment of cultural transition involves working out strategies of acculturation (see Berry, 1997). After all, these people represent a part of the population who have already decided to risk life-changing steps.

One obvious route towards success would be to attain better communicative power. The patient in example (24) was very precautious in preparing for delivery at an English hospital in that she studied the English vocabulary related to childbearing:

(24)

starałam się [...] *kiedy wiedzieliśmy* [...] *że Tomek będzie się tam rodził zaczęłam sobie czytać w języku angielskim pewne opracowania związane z samym porodem czyli zamiast przygotowywać się po polsku* ***starałam się przygotowywać się po angielsku*** [...] ***a po drugie żeby mieć też kontakt językowy*** [...] ***z obsługą, że tak powiem tutaj oddziału,*** *to nie było od razu wszystko takie dla mnie oczywiste jeśli chodzi o słownictwo* [...]

[I tried [...] when we knew that I would give birth in the UK I started reading some English materials about being in labour, in other words, instead of preparing myself in Polish **I tried to do it in English** [...] **and secondly in order to communicate** [...] **with hospital staff, or how shall I put it, the ward staff here**, not everything was obvious to me immediately when it came to vocabulary [...]]

(P1)

Interestingly, in the small sample of the data analyzed here, migrants rarely considered their insufficient language skills as the cause of poor communication. Rather, the participants focused on otherwise dealing with the failings of the local healthcare system and shared with the interviewers their strategies of adaptation. Among them were bending the rules, manipulating information (e.g. exaggerating the graveness of the health problem), threatening the care providers, using connections, double-checking the diagnosis and/or seeking second opinions (cf. Migge & Gilmartin, 2011, pp. 1147–1148). For example, in contrast with the attitude of the local patients, who obediently wait for an appointment, in example (25) the participant admits to 'stretching the truth' in order to get a consultation:

(25)
czego się nauczyłam no to jest może że na przykład jak mi ***bardzo zależy*** *na wizycie i uważam że* [imię] *powinien być zobaczony przez lekarza to po prostu w momencie kiedy dzwonię do poradni* ***wyolbrzymiam pewne****, to znaczy mówię że to* ***znaczy nie chcę powiedzieć że kłamię ale mówię że jest to poważniejsze niż faktycznie to jest***

[what I learned well maybe that for instance if I am really **determined** to get an appointment and I feel that [first name] should be seen by the doctor, then simply when I call the outpatient clinic **I exaggerate somewhat**, I mean, I say, **well, I do not want to say that I lie but I say that it is more serious than it really is**]

(P1)

Another patient suggests that seeking a second opinion is a culture-specific behaviour of migrant Polish patients. In the excerpt below she systematically distinguishes between the 'here' and 'there' of the migration situation and the 'us' and 'them' as the two parties involved:

(26)
jest coś takiego ***u nas kulturowego*** *że że ja na przykład wiesz cokolwiek mi* ***tam*** *było powiedziane to przyjeżdżam* ***tutaj*** *i idę do* ***swoich*** *lekarzy tak bo chcę sprawdzić czy* ***oni*** *mają rację*

[there is something **culture-specific in us** that, that, I for instance, you know, whatever I was told **there** I come **here** and go to **my own** doctors, right, because I want to check whether **they** are right]

(P1)

In fact, some patients may believe that they are better off taking the opportunity to be double-checked by a doctor in their home country, even if it is a payable consultation, as in examples (27) and (28) below.

(27)
rzeczywiście pojechaliśmy na tą pierwszą wizytę do polskiego ginekologa żeby po prostu upewnić się że jest wszystko ok [...] *że ten lekarz polski jest, że mnie zbada że jest wszystko w porządku i powie że że wiesz i da mi taką większą gwarancję niż tu, ja dochodziłam do wniosku że chyba jest to gra warta świeczki*

[indeed for a first visit we went to a Polish gynecologist just to make sure that everything was okay [...] that this Polish doctor is [available], that he would examine me, that everything was okay and he would say that you know and would guarantee me more than [is guaranteed] here, I concluded that the game was maybe worth the candle]

(P2)

(28)
[...] *ja takie badanie wykonałam sobie prywatnie będąc w Polsce, zrobiłam usg po prostu chciałam wiedzieć co to jest, diagnoza tak jakby została jeszcze wsparta, no nie wiem, wizytą u lekarza gdzie lekarz też to pooglądał no i stwierdził że taaak to pewnie jest to*

[[…] I did this test and paid for it when I was in Poland, I did USG, I simply wanted to know what that was, the diagnosis was somewhat confirmed, I do not know, with a visit to the doctor where the doctor also looked at that and concluded that ye:s, that was that]

(P2)

In extreme cases, a patient does not hesitate to threaten the care provider. In example (29) she systematically refers to the healthcare institution (*poradnia* 'clinic') in the third-person plural when she emotionally recounts her unmitigated confrontation with it:

(29)

Ja pamiętam w zeszłym roku był taki przypadek że [imię] *chwycił bardzo przykrego wirusa żołądkowego który się rozprzestrzenił na mnie na mojego męża po prostu na całą naszą rodzinę, to było fatalne nie, i ja przez tydzień co drugi dzień dzwoniłam do* ***poradni*** *z prośbą żeby dziecko obejrzeli bo on bardzo schudł, nie chciał jeść i się zaczęłam bać czy jakieś odwodnienie nie przychodzi i właśnie w momencie kiedy po prostu powiedziałam że zaczęłam już być bardzo taka konkretna, powiedziałam że w takim razie ja przyjdę po oświadczenie od* ***nich*** *że* ***oni*** *mi gwarantują że z dzieckiem jest wszystko ok i tak dalej to wtenczas mi* ***oddzwonili*** *i* ***powiedzieli*** *że mam przyjść na wizytę wieczorem*

[I remember last year there was this situation that [first name] caught a really nasty stomach bug which spread to me and my husband, simply to all our family, it was a disaster, right, and I called the **clinic** every other day for a week asking them to examine my child because he had lost a lot of weight, he was off his food and I began to be scared whether some dehydration occurred and just right then when I simply said, I started to be very, well, specific, I said that in that case I would come to them for a declaration from **them** that **they** guaranteed me that everything was okay with the child et cetera, then **they** called me back and told me to come for a consultation in the evening]

(P1)

Ultimately, when migrant patients feel helpless in front of the healthcare system, they realise the only way out is to make the best of what is available:

(30)

no bo ja mam świadomość że ***tego nie przeskoczę****, że tak na dobrą sprawę albo mi zostaje ten lekarz rodzinny i biorę to co jest, no mogę próbować jechać na ostry dyżur do szpitala* […] *tak zrobiliśmy dwa razy z dzieckiem* […] *ale tak na dobrą sprawę nie masz alternatywy*

[well I am aware that these **things are beyond me**, that in fact either I resort to this GP and I take what is available, well, I can seek emergency help in hospital […] we did it twice with our child […] but in fact you have no other option]

(P1)

It is reasonable to claim that migrants form a minority community which is, by definition, vulnerable: if they are not struggling to survive on an unknown territory, then they are at least accustomed to having to protect their rights and interests. Faced with the gradually weakening transnational ties with family and friends, migrants increasingly integrate into local networks and assimilate with the local culture. The process has been hinted at by one participant, who remarked that she moved from doctors from her home community to local (Irish) doctors as she became linguistically more confident and 'institutionally' adept.

5. Conclusion

This paper has reported on a study of the discourse of "patients in transition", which attempts to capture the realities of migrants approaching the healthcare system in the host country. The case of Polish migrants in the UK and Ireland illustrates a major inflow of patients to the host country healthcare systems. The patients, interviewed outside the healthcare context, reveal their experience of healthcare: their emotions, their critical views, and their strategies of coping.

Their attitudes are fed by evaluations of the host country healthcare system, which is constantly compared with that of the home country. Thanks to the open character of the interview process, numerous narratives have been retrieved about migrants' learning to cope in the new cultural, social and institutional contexts. The ultimate success for the integration process depends on overcoming the language barrier and understanding the new healthcare system. The length of residence and degree of adaptation are both significant factors in the transition process.

The potential implications of the extension of this pilot study into a wider project would be to support patient-centred care by informing local policies and practices referring to migrant communities ("health acculturation" of migrants, see Ronellenfitsch & Razum, 2004, as cited in Sime, 2014). Additionally, the conclusions might inform the professional education of healthcare workers in recognition of "the need for greater levels of awareness of culture specificity on the part of both migrants and healthcare providers" (Migge & Gilmartin, 2011, p. 1144) and "culturally responsive health care" (Durieux-Paillard, 2007, p. 203) offering "culturally familiar service" (Osipovič, 2013). All in all, we postulate that professional medical training should be informed by linguistic research, which calls for an interdisciplinary outlook on the part of both linguists and medical education experts.

References

Alty, A., & Rodham, K. (1998). The ouch! Factor: Problems in conducting sensitive research. *Qualitative Health Research*, 8(2), 275–282.

Beisecker, A. E., & Beisecker, T. D. (1993). Using metaphors to characterize doctor – patient relationships: Paternalism versus consumerism. *Health Communication*, 5(1), 41–58.

Bensing, J. M., & Dronkers, J. (1992). Instrumental and affective aspects of physician behavior. *Medical Care*, 30(4), 283–298.

Berry, J. W. (1997). Immigration, acculturation, and adaptation. *Applied Psychology: An International Review*, 46(1), 5–68.

Betancourt, J. R., Green, A. R., Carillo, E. J., & Park, E. R. (2005). Cultural competence and health care disparities: Key perspectives and trends. *Health Affairs*, 24, 499–505.

Bhabha, H.K. ([1994] 2007). *The location of culture*. New York: Routledge.

Brink-Muinen, A. van den, Verhaak, P. F. M., Bensing, J.M., Bahrs, O., Deveugele, M., Gask, L., Mead, N., Leiva-Fernandez, F., Messerli-Rohrbach, V., Oppizzi, L., Peltenburg, M., & Perez, A. (2003). Communication in general practice: Differences between European countries. *Family Practice*, 20, 478–485.

Brink-Muinen, A. van den, Maaroos, H.-I., & Tähepöld, H. (2008). Communication style in primary healthcare in Europe. *Health Education*, 108(5), 384–439. doi: 10.1108/09654280810900008

Byrne, P. S., & Long, B. E. L. (1976). *Doctors talking to patients*. HMSO: London.

Campbell, S. M., Roland, M. O., & Buetow, S.A. (2000). Defining quality of care. *Social Science & Medicine*, 51(11), 1611–1625.

Carmel, S., & Glick, S. M. (1996). Compassionate-empathic physicians: Personality traits and social-organizational factors that enhance or inhibit this behavior pattern. *Social Science & Medicine*, 43(8), 1253–1261.

Cheraghi-Sohi, S., Hole, A. R., Mead, N., McDonald, R., Whalley, D., Bower, P., & Roland, M. (2008). What patients want from primary care consultations: A discrete choice experiment to identify patients' priorities. *Annals of Family Medicine*, 6(2), 107–115.

Commander, S., Kangasniemi, M., & Winters, L. A. (2003). The brain drain: Curse or boon? *IZA Discussion Paper*, 809. Retrieved from http://repec.iza.org/dp809.pdf. DOA: 01.03.2017.

Connell, J. (2006). Medical tourism: Sea, sun, sand and … surgery. *Tourism Management*, 27(6), 1093–1100.

Coulter, A., & Jenkinson, C. (2005). European patients' views on the responsiveness of health systems and healthcare providers. *Health Services Research*, 15(4), 355–360.

Desjarlais-deKlerk, K., & Wallace, J. L. (2013). Instrumental and socioemotional communications in doctor – patient interactions in urban and rural clinics. *BMC Health Services Research*, 13(261). doi: 10.1186/1472-6963-13-261

Dias, S., Gama, A., Cargaleiro, H., & Martins, M. (2012). Health workers' attitudes towards immigrant patients: A cross-sectional survey in primary healthcare services. *Human Resources for Health*, 10, 14–20.

Durieux-Paillard, S. (2007). Differences in language, religious beliefs and culture: the need for culturally responsive health services. In B. Rechel, P. Mladovsky, W. Devillé, B. Rijks, R. Petrova-Benedict, & M. McKee (Eds.), *Migration and health in the EU*. Open University Press, 203–212. Retrieved from http://euro.who.int/__data/assets/pdf_file/0019/161560/e96458.pdf. DOA: 01.03.2017.

Emanuel, E. J., & Emanuel, L. L. (1992). Four models of the physician – patient relationship. *Journal of American Medical Association*, 267, 2221–2226.

Engel, G. L. (1988). How much longer must medicine's science be bound by a seventeenth century world view? In K. White (Ed.), *The task of medicine*. Menlo Park, CA: The Henry J. Kaiser Family Foundation, 113–136.

Espinel, A. G., Shah, R. K., McCormick, M. E., Krakovitz, P. R., & Boss, E. F. (2014). Patient satisfaction in pediatric surgical care: A systematic review. *Otolaryngology – Head and Neck Surgery*, 150(5), 739–749.

Farrell, E. J. (2008). *Negotiating identity: Discourses of migration and belonging* (Unpublished Ph.D. dissertation, Macquarie University).

Fletcher, R. H., O'Malley, M., Earp, J.-A., Littleton, T. A., Fletcher, S. W., Greganti, M. A., Davison, R. A., & Taylor, J. (1983). Patients' priorities for medical care. *Medical Care*, 21(2), 234–242.

Flick, U. (1998). *An introduction to qualitative research*. London: Sage.

Flick, U. (2000). Episodic interviewing. In M.W. Bauer & G. Gaskell (Eds.), *Qualitative researching with text, image and sound*. London: Sage, 75–92.

Forum 1. Retrieved from http://smartpolak.co.uk/forum/71909-co-sadzicie-o-lekarzach-angielskich

Forum 2. Retrieved from http://polacy.co.uk/forum/dyskusje/polski-pediatra-kontra-gp/103514

Fung, C. H., Elliott, M. N., Hays, R. D., Kahn, K. L., Kanouse, D. E., McGlynn, E. A., Spranca, M. D., & Shekelle, P. G. (2005). Patients' preferences for technical versus interpersonal quality when selecting a primary care physician. *Health Services Research*, 40, 957–977.

Glinos, I. A., Baeten, R., Helble, M., & Maarse, H. (2010). A typology of cross-border patient mobility. *Health & Place*, 16, 1145–1155.

Goodwin, R., Polek, E., Goodwin, K. (2012). Perceived changes in health and interactions with 'the Paracetamol force': A multimethod study. *Journal of Mixed Methods Research*, 7(2), 152–172.

Gromulska, L., Goryński, P., Supranowicz, P., & Wysocki, M. J. (2014). Responsiveness to the hospital patient needs in Poland. *Rocznik Państwowego Zakładu Higieny*, 65(2), 155–164.

Hall, J. A., Roter, D. L., & Katz, N. R. (1987). Task versus socioemotional behaviors in physicians. *Medical Care*, 25(5), 399–412.

Heszen-Klemens, I., & Łapińska, E. (1984). Doctor – patient interaction, patients health behavior and effects of treatment. *Social Science & Medicine*, 19, 9–18.

Hofstede, G., & Hofstede, G. J. (2005). *Cultures and organisations: Software of the mind* (Revised and expanded 2nd edition). New York: McGraw-Hill.

Jefferson, G. (2004). Glossary of transcript symbols with an introduction. In G. H. Learner (Ed.), *Conversation analysis: Studies from the first generation*. Amsterdam: John Benjamins, 12–31.

Jovchelovitch, S., & Bauer, M. W. 2000. *Narrative interviewing [online]*. London: LSE Research Online. Retrieved from http://eprints.lse.ac.uk/2633. DOA: 01.03.2017.

Kaczmarczyk, P. (Ed.). (2014). Recent trends in international migration in Poland. The 2012 SOPEMI Report. *CMR Working Paper*, 71(129). Retrieved from http://migracje.uw.edu.pl/publ/2373/. DOA: 01.03.2017.

La Barbera, M.C. (Ed.). (2015). *Identity and migration in Europe: Multidisciplinary perspectives*. Heidelberg: Springer.

Labov, W. (2013). *The language of life and death: The transformation of experience in oral narrative*. Cambridge: Cambridge University Press.

Lee, J.Y.-J., Kearns, R. A., & Friesen, W. (2010). Seeking affective healthcare: Korean immigrants' use of homeland medical services. *Health and Place*, 16, 108–115.

Leśniowska, J. (2007). Migration patterns of Polish doctors within the EU. *European Snapshots*, 13(4), 7–8.

Leśniowska, J. (2008). Poland's nursing brain drain to the west. *Health Affairs*, 27(2), 593.

Main, I. (2014). Medical travels of Polish female migrants in Europe. *Czech Sociological Review*, 50(6), 897–918.

Marcinowicz, L., Chlabicz, S., & Grebowski, R. (2009). Patient satisfaction with healthcare provided by family doctors: Primary dimensions and an attempt at typology. *BMC Health Services Research*, 9(63). doi:10.1186/1472-6963-9-63

Marcinowicz, L., Chlabicz, S., & Grebowski, R. (2010). Understanding patient satisfaction with family doctor care. *Journal of Evaluation in Clinical Practice*, 16, 712–715.

Meeuwesen, L., Brink-Muinen, A. van den, & Hofstede, G. (2009). Can dimensions of national culture predict cross-national differences in medical communication? *Patient Education and Counseling*, 75, 58–66.

Migge, B., & Gilmartin, M. (2011). Migrants and healthcare: Investigating patient mobility among migrants in Ireland. *Health & Place*, 17, 1144–1149.

Młynarski, J. (2007, November). Wyleczy cię doktor Paracetamol. *Polish Express Online*. Retrieved from http://polishexpress.co.uk/wyleczy-cie-doktor-paracetamol/. DOA: 01.03.2017.

Nielsen, S. Smith, Yazici, S., Petersen, S. Gronwald, Blaakilde, A. L., & Krasnik, A. (2010). Use of cross-border healthcare services among ethnic Danes, Turkish immigrants and Turkish descendants in Denmark: A combined survey and registry study. *Health Services Research,* 12(390). doi:10.1186/1472-6963-12-390

Ognyanova, D., Maierb, C. B., Wismarb, M., Girasekc, E., & Bussea, R. (2012). Mobility of health professionals pre and post 2004 and 2007 EU enlargements: Evidence from the EU project PROMeTHEUS. *Health Policy*, 108, 122–132.

Osipovič, D. (2013). 'If I get ill, it's onto the plane, and off to Poland.' Use of health care services by Polish migrants in London. *Central and Eastern European Migration Review*, 2(2), 98–114.

Parson, T. (1951). *The social system*. Glencoe, IL: The Free Press.

Pawelczyk, J. (2011). *Talk as therapy: Psychotherapy in a linguistic perspective*. Boston: Mouton.

PEO (2015, December). Moja rodzina nie otrzymała żadnej innej pomocy lekarskiej oprócz paracetamolu. *Polish Express Online*. Retrieved from http://polishexpress.co.uk/moja-rodzina-nie-otrzymala-zadnej-innej-pomocy-lekarskiej-oprocz-paracetamolu/

Petersoo, P. (2007). What does 'we' mean? National deixis in the media. *Journal of Language and Politics*, 6(3), 419–436.

President's Commission for the study of ethical problems in medicine and biomedical and behavioral research. (1982). Washington, DC: Government Printing Office.

Rees, C. E., Monrouxe, L., & Wilkinson, C. E. (2007). Doctors being up there and we being down here: A metaphorical analysis of talk about student/doctor – patient relationships. *Social Science & Medicine*, 65, 725–737.

Rienzo, C., & Vargas-Silva, C. (2014). *Migrants in the UK: An overview, Migration Observatory briefing*. COMPAS, Oxford University. Retrieved from http://migrationobservatory.ox.ac.uk. DOA: 01.03.2017.

Ronellenfitsch, U., & Razum, O. (2004). Deteriorating health satisfaction among immigrants from Eastern Europe to Germany. *International Journal for Equity in Health*, 3(4), 1–10.

Roter, D., & Stewart, M. (1989). Which facets of communication have strong effects on outcome – a meta-analysis. In M. Stewart & D. Roter (Eds.), *Communicating with medical patients, impact of the doctor – patient relationship on outcomes of chronic disease*. Thousand Oaks, CA: Sage, 228–245.

Roter, D. L., Stewart, M., Putnam, S. M., Lipkin, M. Jr, Stiles, W., & Inui, T. S. (1997). Communication patterns of primary care physicians. *Journal of American Medical Association*, 277(4), 350–356.

Różalski, J. (2015, April). Polska to medyczny raj. Dlaczego emigranci i cudzoziemcy z Zachodu masowo leczą się u nas? *Gazeta.pl*. Retrieved from http://wyborcza.pl/1,87648,17754857,Polska_to_medyczny_raj__Dlaczego_emigranci_i_cudzoziemcy.html. DOA: 01.03.2017.

Sarangi, S., & Roberts, C. (Eds.). (1999). *Talk, work and institutional order: Discourse in medical, mediation and management settings*. Berlin: Mouton de Gruyter.

Schegloff, E. A. (2007). *Sequence organization in interaction: A primer in conversation analysis*. Cambridge: Cambridge University Press.

Segall, A., & Burnett, M. (1980). Patient evaluation of physician role performance. *Social Science & Medicine*, 14A, 269–278.

Sime, D. (2014). 'I think that Polish doctors are better': Newly arrived migrant children and their parents' experiences and views of health services in Scotland. *Health and Place*, 30, 86–93.

Ślęzak, E. (2014). The post-2004 migration of the Polish medical personnel to the United Kingdom and its impact on societies and economies. Preliminary remarks. *International Business and Global Economy*, 33, 154–165.

Ślęzak, E. (2016). The intergenerational relations of Polish medical migrants in the UK. *Lidé města*, 2, 231–252.

Szasz, T. S., & Hollender, M. (1956). A contribution to the philosophy of medicine: The basic models of the doctor – patient relationship. *AMA Archives of Internal Medicine*, 97(5), 585–592.

Vick, S., & Scott, A. 1998. "Agency in health care. Examining patients' preferences for attributes of the doctor – patient relationship", *Journal of Health Economics*, 17(5), 587–605.

Watts, J. H. (2008). Emotion, empathy and exit: reflections on doing ethnographic qualitative research on sensitive topics. *Medical Sociology Online*, 3(2), 3–14.

Watts, J. H. (2010). Ethical and practical challenges of participant observation in sensitive health research. *International Journal of Social Research Methodology*, 14(4), 301–312.

Wodak, R., de Cillia, R., Reisigl, M., & Liebhart, K. (1999). *The discursive construction of national identity* (2nd edition). Edinburgh: Edinburgh University Press.

Wyrozębska, A., Wyrozębski, P., & Dmoch-Gajzlerska, E. (2013). Why do Polish healthworkers want to work abroad? *Electronic International Interdisciplinary Conference*, 2(6), 270–274.

Appendix

Transcription conventions (Jefferson, 2004; Schegloff, 2007):

:	prolongation of a sound
-	abrupt cut off of sound
(.)	pause of less than one second
[...]	omitted talk

Grażyna Anna Bednarek

Faculty of Medicine, Nicolaus Copernicus University
in Toruń, Poland

Cultural and linguistic heterogeneity in courtroom discourse: Diverse methods of witness examination in criminal trials

Abstract: Dedicated to courtroom discourse, the present paper concentrates on the linguistic representation of the inquisitorial and adversarial procedures of witness examination in criminal trials under two entirely disparate legal systems – Civil Law and Common Law, respectively – as an instantiation of cultural and linguistic heterogeneity in courtroom discourse, as well as two dissimilar ways of communicating among legal professionals in courts.[1] This article sheds new light on courtroom discourse by providing a systematic and comprehensive comparative analysis of the *modus operandi* of witness examination under Common Law and Civil Law. Most previous works on courtroom discourse focused on the use of language in courtroom interaction within one legal system only, namely that of the Common Law, either in the United States of America, or the United Kingdom. Often the resulting picture of courtroom discourse suggested that the use of language in court throughout the world would be similar. This, however, is not at all true, because legal systems are divided by profound dissimilarities. These, in turn, affect the use of language in courtroom interaction to a great extent, which makes each courtroom discourse a phenomenon *sui generis*, a distinctive example of a linguistic genre.

1. Introduction

The language that lawyers use to articulate, endorse and interpret law differs from that of ordinary speech. It is widely perceived and known as complex and very difficult to understand, which is why it has become a popular object of research conducted by linguists, translators and lawyers (e.g. Mellinkoff, 1963; Tiersma, 1999). In general, the study of the language of law can be carried out from two linguistic perspectives: (1) formal and (2) functional. As concerns the former, investigation of the language of law concentrates on its formal aspects such as

1 The paper recapitulates the key findings of the research on courtroom discourse published in my monograph *Polish vs. American Courtroom Discourse: Adversarial and Inquisitorial Procedures of Witness Examination in Criminal Trials* (Bednarek, 2014).

lexis, syntax or semantics (Mellinkoff, 1963; Goodrich, 1987; Tiersma, 1999). As regards the latter, the relevant studies focus on the functions of particular forms used in the language of law beyond the level of sentence, with emphasis on entire texts and conversations (Atkinson & Drew, 1979; Danet & Bogoch, 1980; Dunstan, 1980; Philips, 1984; Woodbury, 1984; Matoesian, 1993; Luchjenbroers, 1997; Ehrlich, 2001; Cotterill, 2003; Cotterell, 2004; Archer, 2005). In this approach particular attention is also given to how the language of law is used within the speech communities concerned for informational and interactional purposes, as well as how the relevant users perform certain, very important social roles related to the legal context by means of the language of law. In other words, under functional linguistics, and more specifically within discourse analysis, researchers examine how the language of law is used in certain spatio-temporal milieus related to the legal profession and/or how this language operates in society in general.

The present study is a comparative analysis of two dissimilar procedures of witness examination, adversarial and inquisitorial, as applied in the USA under Common Law and in Poland under Civil Law, respectively, with both contexts being culturally and linguistically different, and both involving different methods of communication among the members of legal speech communities.

The research, first presented in Bednarek (2014) and now recapitulated in this present paper, is founded on two hypotheses. The first assumes that each courtroom discourse is culturally varied; the second presupposes that courtroom discourse is socially conditioned. The former hypothesis is based on the idea that courtroom discourse is highly influenced by the social, cultural, institutional and historical setting in which it occurs, whereas the latter relies on the idea that in a particular society citizens formulate legal norms that govern their lives, which, in turn, regulate the social roles that the representatives of this society (e.g. judges, prosecutors or attorneys at law) play in different legal interactions. As such, the research carried out by Bednarek (2014) not only lays foundations for the current contribution, but also opens a general discussion dedicated to the heterogeneity of the language of the law above the level of the sentence.

The current contribution seeks to demonstrate the *diverse representation* of the language of law in court with reference to criminal cases conducted in two distinct legal systems, Civil Law and Common Law, in Poland and the United States of America, respectively. The author of the present paper hopes that a thorough research devoted to courtroom discourse under other legal systems, such as the Far Eastern law, the Islamic law, the Hindu law, or the Socialist law, to name but a few, will follow shortly, thus showing to the world to what extent and why courtroom discourse looks entirely different in those particular settings in comparison to Polish and American courtroom discourse investigated here and in Bednarek (2014). Such studies will certainly offer new and original contributions to the field of forensic linguistics in particular, and discourse analysis in general, as well as spread knowledge and raise awareness about cultural and linguistic diversity among the citizens of the world.

Although, as I have indicated in Bednarek (2014, p. 9), my study of courtroom discourse is entrenched in linguistics, and more specifically in discourse analysis, I also draw on selected contributions from numerous disciplines including (1) the theory and philosophy of law; (2) comparative law; (3) sociology of law; (4) anthropology of law; (5) anthropology; (6) sociology; and (7) linguistic anthropology. As a result, both Bednarek (2014) and this paper are not only interdisciplinary in approach, but also provide a holistic image of Polish and American courtroom discourse, with a particular accent on the *modus operandi* of witness examination, which constitutes the foremost part of a criminal trial.

2. Theoretical background

Thus far, courtroom discourse has been approached from a number of diversified perspectives such as (1) legal history, (2) legal anthropology and sociology, (3) courtroom interpreting, (4) sociology, (5) linguistics, and (6) forensic linguistics.

Most research into courtroom discourse has been conducted by legal historians, including, *inter alia*, Beattie (1986), Langbein (2003), Hostettler (2006, 2009) or Hostettler and Braby (2009). The major subject theme which dominates in their contributions revolves around the origins and history of the adversary criminal trial, with particular attention paid to the historic reasons for the denial of the counsel for defense at the dawn of criminal justice. The relevant contributions literally flourish with material related to the emergence of the adversary criminal justice, starting with the lawyer-free times towards the lawyer-dominated era. They feature breathtaking stories about the times when the accused had to speak in their own defense in response to the charges brought against them to court. Although these contributions do not offer much linguistic insight into courtroom discourse, they are not to be underestimated, as they are the foremost source of information about the evolving socio-political, historical and institutional backdrop in which courtroom discourse existed for hundreds of years, and which exerted such an overwhelming influence on the language used in courtroom interaction.

As far as legal anthropology and sociology are concerned, a notable work is Conley and O'Barr (1990), who discuss how the lay public interact with the legal system, that is how lay people identify and analyze legal problems. In their contribution, which they founded on materials from courts collected in three different regions of the USA in the so-called small claims courts, Conley and O'Barr (1990) analyze data which encompass 466 cases recorded during 36 days in court and focus on the language of the litigants as the major object of enquiry. The methodology employed in this study, which is that of the ethnography of discourse, enabled the authors to observe and conduct an analysis of the language focused on such phenomena as e.g. how the litigants manage to handle questions of responsibility. The major aim of their monograph is to examine court talk, including verbal interaction, participants' accounts and narratives. The contribution offers an anthropological point of view on the legal system, in which legal anthropologists seek to explicate the means by which people maintain order and resolve disputes. In particular, Conley and O'Barr (1990) examine how the lawyers decide which topics the witnesses may or may not discuss during a trial. In their research the authors have registered and analyzed the litigants' voices as they move through the legal proceedings starting from the very filing of a case, its litigation, to finally reflect on their experiences. As such, the book offers insights into courtroom discourse presented from the perspective of legal professionals on the one hand, and lay people on the other.

An entirely distinct theme that has dominated another monograph authored by Conley and O'Barr ([1998] 2005) is the intricate relationship between the language of law, language and power. Here Conley and O'Barr (2005) examine the mechanisms through which power is enacted in court in the USA, as well as how rape victims become revictimized by lawyers who control witnesses through linguistic practices during the penal process.

As for the field of courtroom interpreting, a representative work is Berk-Seligson (1990), who argues on numerous occasions that courtroom interpreters are required to be conversant with courtroom discourse in order to provide a high level of interpretation services to guarantee a fair trial to any suspected person against whom legal proceedings in the USA are instituted. Berk-Seligson (1990) studies cross-cultural aspects of courtroom discourse in the light of courtroom interpreting in penal cases based on a seven-month ethnographic observation and tape-recording of the judicial proceedings conducted by the author, revealing the social role of courtroom interpreters during the penal trial.

By contrast, a contribution written from the point of view of sociology, *Order in Court: The organization of verbal interaction in judicial settings*, authored by Atkinson and Drew (1979), offers invaluable facts on the organization of courtroom interaction, with particular attention to the system of turn-taking during the witness examination stage of a penal trial by jury. The use of conversation analysis as the fundamental method of enquiry allowed Atkinson and Drew (1979) to analyze the pre-allocated nature of the turn-taking system in trials, while the application of the ethnomethodological program enabled them to unveil the social order with a focus on how the participants of courtroom interaction produce, manage and recognize their appearances.

An entirely different insight into courtroom discourse, although within the same field, was offered by Matoesian (1993), who addresses rape trials, and who focuses on how a woman's testimony in court may be manipulated by defense lawyers to change a sexual assault incident into consensual sexual experience.

Finally, within the area of linguistics, early research into courtroom discourse concentrates predominantly on the use of open and closed questions during direct examination and cross-examination, for instance addressed by Danet and Bogoch (1980) or Dunstan (1980). This line of research was followed by studies of the lawyer-witness dyadic relationship, with meticulous attention paid to the formal and functional properties of questions, as represented in the contributions by Harris (1984), Philips (1984), Woodbury (1984) or Luchjenbroers (1997).

The theme of rape hearings and revictimization of rape victims has also been analyzed from a linguistic perspective, for example being recurrent topic in the monograph authored by Ehrlich (2001). The author focuses, *inter alia*, on a sexual assault adjudication process based on a real case of a male student accused of two instances of sexual assault in Toronto. Ehrlich's (2001) monograph is generally considered to be the pioneering feminist linguistic analysis of the language of sexual assaults in the light of courtroom interaction with an emphasis on gender and cultural theory.

The first attempt to address courtroom discourse comprehensively and beyond the lawyer-witness dyad, concentrating on the complexities of the lawyer-witness-jury triad, was undertaken by Cotterill (2003). The work revolves around such intricate issues associated with courtroom discourse as interactional dynamics, formal and functional properties of questions and answers from the examination of the witness stage of the criminal trial, styles of testimony and their influence on the jury, power and ideology, and narrative in American courtroom discourse. Cotterill's (2003) eclectic research into American courtroom discourse by means of conversation analysis, interactional sociolinguistics, and corpus linguistics as the principal methods of enquiry, represents a thorough analysis of American courtroom discourse with ample and rewarding findings. The study is synchronic in nature and investigates O. J. Simpson's trial of the century.

By contrast, the study conducted by Archer (2005) offers a diachronic analysis of English courtroom discourse written from the point of view of historical socio-pragmatics, with attention to questions and answers produced during Early

Modern English trials. Based on twelve transcripts taken from the Salem Witchcraft Papers, the monograph provides a classification system of questions and answers with their interactional intent, force and form, and their strategic use in the context of a courtroom. The analysis of questions and answers, focused on who posed the questions in particular time periods, enabled Archer (2005) to characterize the social roles of the major participants in the period 1640–1760. It must be noted that the court discourse of the Early Modern English period was earlier examined by Kryk-Kastovsky (2000), who studied the system of turn-taking in two 1685 trials, that is The Trial of Titus Oates and The Trial of Lady Alice Lisle.

3. Methods and materials

The present paper refers to the study of courtroom discourse performed by Bednarek (2014), which is basically synchronic and qualitative in nature, but also encompasses quantitative analyses. It employs three major approaches to discourse analysis: (1) ethnography of communication, (2) Conversation Analysis (CA), and (3) pragmatics. The relevance of the use of ethnography of communication for the study of courtroom discourse results from the fact that ethnography of communication understands language as a socially situated cultural form. It enables the researcher to examine the way of speaking of one's own community, and contrast it with the ways other communities speak (Saville-Troike, 1982, p. 4). In applying ethnography of communication as one of the methods of analyzing courtroom discourse, it is essential to mention that while describing the context in which Polish and American penal trials take place by employing the SPEAKING grid (Hymes, 1972; see below), it provides an exhaustive picture of the communicative situation, the speech event and speech acts. Thus, it refers to courtroom discourse in the light of cognitive, social and cultural components which all make up the *communicative competence* of the participants, who can use this knowledge to successfully participate in a penal trial by performing their distinctive social roles.

Thus, the analysis of courtroom discourse by means of ethnography of communication makes it possible to depict the use of language in relation to the wider culture. In this monograph, it is the legal culture of the Common Law legal system in the USA and the Civil Law legal system in Poland. The analysis of courtroom discourse by means of the SPEAKING grid introduced by Hymes (1972) allows to investigate courtroom discourse with attention to the following aspects of American and Polish courtroom discourse: (1) **S** *setting*: where the speech event is positioned in time and place; (2) **P** *participants*: who takes part in the speech event, and in what role; (3) **E** *ends*: what the purpose of the speech event is, and what its outcome is meant to be; (4) **A** *act sequence*: what speech acts make up the speech event and what order they are performed in; (5) **K** *key*: the tone or manner of performance (serious or joking, sincere or ironic); (6) **I** *instrumentalities*: what channel or medium of communication is used (speaking, singing, writing); (7) **N** *norms of interaction*: what are the rules for producing and interpreting speech acts; (8) **G** *genres*: what type does a speech event belong to, and what other pre-existing conventional forms of speech are drawn on or cited in producing appropriate contributions.

The investigation of American and Polish courtroom discourse by means of ethnography of communication appears to provide the most general perspective of the study, and as such depicts the characteristics of the wider cultural context in which American and Polish courtroom discourse take place. The units of analysis within the ethnography of communication approach in discourse analysis which allow the researcher to examine the rules of speaking in particular settings include (1) the speech situation, (2) the speech event, and (3) speech acts.

As for Conversation Analysis (CA), which has developed from ethnomethodological research in sociology, its application to study courtroom discourse narrows the perspective in that it draws the attention of the researcher to the very conversation between interlocutors during the penal trial. Ensuing from the idea that language is an instantiation of primal human interaction (Goodwin & Heritage, 1990, p. 283), and that talk is socially organized as a social encounter (Goffman, 1964, pp. 133–136), CA allows the researcher to: (1) examine the organization of taking turns in courtroom discourse, (2) investigate courtroom interaction during the penal trial, (3) identify the social roles that key partakers play, as well as (4) analyze the question and answer adjacency pairs to find out what kind of questions are employed during the examination of witnesses under the Common and/or Civil Law legal systems. Thus, while the employment of the ethnography of communication method makes it possible to focus on language usage in relation to the wider cultural setting in which courtroom discourse occurs, CA concentrates on the institutionalized talk itself, and as such restricts the perspective of the overall research. The emphasis is laid on the *system of turn-taking* during the examination of witnesses and on questions and answers as instances of *adjacency pairs*.

Finally, the study of courtroom discourse from the perspective of pragmatics focuses on the ways in which context contributes to meaning and on speech acts, and is founded on the idea that when people say things they also do things. The philosophical roots of pragmatics date back to the extremely influential research conducted by J. L. Austin (1962), who identified a class of utterances which he called performatives, whereby interlocutors perform particular actions.

The choice of pragmatics, through the analysis of assorted speech acts in American and Polish criminal trials, gives the researcher the opportunity to study what actions people perform when they speak in the respective legal contexts. It also facilitates the investigation of how the meaning of certain utterances relates to its force, i.e. how the linguistic form of an utterance relates to its communicative function. By means of Austin's (1962) model pragmatic analysis enables the researcher to study how participants use spoken language to do things in court proceedings. Also, it provides methods to look into various instances of speech acts in order to find out whether the key partakers of American and Polish courtroom discourse comply with the co-operative principle (Grice, 1975), making their speech such as required at the stage at which it occurred by the accepted purpose or direction of the talk exchange in which they engage. It also gives the chance to investigate the extent of any possible flouting of Grice's (1975) maxims of conversation. As such, in the research carried out by Bednarek (2014) and recapitulated here, pragmatics offers an analysis of language in use with special attention paid to the smallest unit of spoken discourse, namely the *speech act*.

The present study relies on naturally occurring data. As concerns American courtroom discourse, the data come from a double murder trial of an American football player, Orenthal James Simpson, which spanned from 1994 to 1995. As far as the Polish courtroom is concerned, the data come from a criminal trial that took place at one of the Regional Courts in Poland, in which the author participated as an observer.

4. Findings

Sections 4.1, 4.2, and 4.3 demonstrate similarities and disparities between the inquisitorial and adversarial procedures of witness examination in criminal trials from the perspective of (1) ethnography of communication, (2) Conversation Analysis, and (3) pragmatics, respectively.

As far as ethnography of communication is concerned (section 4.1), the findings of the study point to profound dissimilarities between the two legal systems in which courtroom discourse takes place, entirely disparate methods of witness examination in Common Law and Civil Law, different education and competences of major participants (e.g. judge, prosecutor, counsel for defense), different methods of appointment to the positions, dissimilar structural organization of the procedures of witness examination, and different norms of interaction.

As concerns Conversation Analysis (section 4.2), the findings indicate that the inquisitorial and adversarial procedures of witness examination in Civil Law and

Common Law systems, respectively, vary with respect to: (1) the system of turn taking, (2) structural organization of the speech event, (3) the social roles of the judge, counsel for the prosecution, and counsel for the defense, and (4) the types and numbers of questions asked in these two legal systems.

Finally, the findings of pragmatic analysis (section 4.3) indicate that the participants in court proceedings under both Common Law and Civil Law observe Grice's (1975) conversational maxims, although instances of their flouting do occur. The analysis of the selected speech acts has shown that the speech communities participating in the examination of witnesses under Common Law and Civil law share the knowledge of how to make use of spoken language to perform various acts, e.g. how to warn witnesses of their criminal responsibility for providing true testimony. This knowledge enables judges, counsels for the prosecution and counsels for the defense under Common Law and Civil Law to consciously perform their social roles as established in the respective laws and regulations.

4.1. Inquisitorial and adversarial procedures of witness examination in Poland and the USA in the light of the ethnography of communication approach to discourse analysis

One of the approaches to courtroom discourse employed in my study is ethnography of communication, which enabled me to demonstrate the broad sociocultural, historical, institutional and legal setting in which the inquisitorial and adversarial procedures of witness examination occurred in Polish and American courtrooms. In particular, I used the SPEAKING grid introduced by Hymes (1972), whereby I could confirm that Polish and American courtroom discourses are *two culturally different phenomena*. The results of the relevant research are summarized below.

The study of the **S**: Setting in which American and Polish penal trials take place has revealed significant differences in these two contexts as well as in methods of witness examination, which result from two entirely distinct legal systems – Common Law and Civil Law, respectively. These legal systems are divided by profound dissimilarities with reference to (1) their historical development and origins, (2) methods of logical thinking, (3) sources of law, (4) legal institutions, and (5) ideology.

As far as methods of witness examination are concerned, Civil Law, which was formulated, compiled and updated in academic settings, is characterized by the *inquisitorial* procedure of witness examination. By contrast, Common Law, which was developed in and by courts, thus being mostly judge-made law, is characterized by the *adversarial* procedure of witness examination.[2] Another difference lies in the fact that while Civil Law draws from general principles, Common Law is based on judgments issued by judges in previous legal cases. Also, Civil Law is founded on the posited statutes, whereas Common Law is founded on precedents, i.e. previous decisions of judges and the principle of *stare decisis*, in other words by case law.

There are also differences between the two court systems in general. In Poland, under Civil Law, the court system encompasses (1) common courts (such as district courts, regional or circuit courts, and appellate courts), (2) administrative courts, and (3) military courts. By contrast, the court system in the USA, under Common Law, is a dual court system and includes (1) state courts and (2) federal courts, which then include the Supreme Court, courts of appeal, district courts and magistrate courts.

As for the **P**: Participants taking part in penal trials in the two systems, the study has shown that the professions of judge, prosecutor and attorney for defense are also different in Poland and in the USA with respect to (1) education, (2) appointment for the position, and (3) duties and responsibilities during the penal trial arising from the differences between Common Law and Civil Law. The study has also revealed that there are other participants who take part in penal trials, namely lay assessors in Poland and the jury in the USA. Both lay assessors and the jury play very important social roles during Polish and American penal trials, respectively.

Another topic of analysis within the ethnography of communication approach was the purpose (**E**: Ends) of penal trials perceived as speech events performed in Polish and American courts. It has been proven that the overall role of the criminal justice system in Poland and in the USA, as well as the major objectives of penal trials (perceived as speech events) in these two contexts appear to be similar, in that both of them seek to discover whether the crime was committed, who committed the crime and in what circumstances. However, it has also been

2 The main difference lies in the fact that while the inquisitorial method allows the witness to disclose all the information they know in connection with the committed crime in response to a single question asked by the Chairman/Judge who conducts the examination of witnesses, the adversarial method requires that the witness provide an exact answer to the question posed and forbids them to disclose all that they know in connection with the committed crime in the form of a narrative. In other words, under Common Law in the USA the facts in connection with the crime are revealed in the course of a meticulous questioning, during which witnesses are required to provide answers strictly to the questions. Volunteering information is strictly forbidden and prompts objections raised by the opposing party.

found that the specific discursive means through which these goals are attained in the USA and in Poland vary significantly, and thus make the two speech events totally different phenomena. Again, these differences result to some extent from two distinctive methods of witness examination: adversarial under Common Law and inquisitorial under Civil Law.

The investigation of specific acts and their sequences (**A**: Act sequence), which make up the speech events of penal trial, has revealed that Polish and American courtroom discourses also differ in this respect, two major reasons being differences in the legal basis on which the examination of witnesses is founded and differences in the organizational structure of the process of witness examination under the two legal systems. In particular, examination of witnesses under Civil Law is founded on the *principle of substantive truth*, whereas examination of witnesses under Common Law is based on the *principle of formal truth* (see section 4.2 for details). What follows is that in Poland, which represents the former case, examination of witnesses includes free and unrestricted explanation and free and unrestricted testimony of the defendant and witnesses, respectively. This is followed by asking supplementary questions by the judge and – if need arises – by the prosecutor and attorney for defense. By contrast, in the latter context, of which the USA is an example, examination of witnesses encompasses direct examination by attorneys for the prosecution and attorneys for the defense of their own witnesses and cross-examination of the witnesses of the opposing party.

The study of the tone and manner (**K**: Key) of the examination of witnesses in Poland and the USA has shown that both speech events were conducted in a very serious atmosphere.

The investigation of the **I**: Instrumentalities, that is the medium of communication used during penal trials, has revealed that both Polish and American speech events are delivered verbally. However, the languages used during penal trials under Common and Civil Law are two totally different specialized languages, which have developed in and for the specific purposes of these two disparate legal systems.

Moreover, differences have been found in terms of **N**: Norms of interaction employed during Polish and American penal trials. Again, the observed differences can be related to different norms that determine the *modus operandi* of witness examination.

Finally, the examination of the **G**: Genre to which the Polish and American speech events belong has shown that both criminal trials and speech events are examples of spoken communicative events. Yet again their construction differs, which can be associated with the differences in the methods of witness examination in the two legal systems.

4.2. Inquisitorial and adversarial procedures of witness examination in Poland and the USA in the light of Conversation Analysis

Conversation Analysis (CA) allowed me to focus on verbal interaction of the participants during Polish and American criminal trials, considered to be specific speech events. I focused on the following aspects of witness examination in these two contexts: (1) the system of turn-taking, (2) the structural organization of criminal trials as speech events, (3) courtroom interaction, (4) social roles of the participants, (5) the way in which the participants discursively reconstruct the crime event on the basis of testimony, and (6) types of questions employed in the examination of witnesses in Poland and in the USA.

As concerns the first point, the system of turn-taking during Polish and American criminal trials approached as speech events, the results show that although in both cases the system of taking turns is fixed and pre-allocated, i.e. only particular persons may ask questions and others are required to answer them, the examination of witnesses in Poland is conducted in an entirely different manner than it is in the USA. This is due to the use of the *inquisitorial,* as opposed to the *adversarial* method (see also section 4.1).

As for the second point, the structural organization of criminal trials as speech events, the results of the study based on the ethnography of communication approach (see section 4.1) show that examinations of witnesses vary significantly in terms of their structure.

Under Civil Law, in the first part of the examination of witnesses, the witness discloses all the information related to the circumstances of the committed crime in response to a single question of the judge e.g. "What do you know in connection with this case?" Following art. 171 § 1 of the Polish Code of Penal Procedure, witnesses give free and unrestricted explanations in the case of the defendant, and free and unrestricted testimony in the case of other witnesses. In the second part of the examination of witnesses, the judge or the attorney for defense may ask supplementary questions. If, however, in the course of the free and unrestricted explanation or testimony all the information has been revealed, supplementary questions are not asked.

By contrast, the examination of witnesses under Common Law involves direct examination by the attorney for prosecution or attorneys for defense of their own witnesses and then cross-examination conducted by the opposing party, which may be followed by re-direct examination and re-cross-examination of witnesses.

In this case witnesses are forbidden to give testimony in the form of a narrative, i.e. they cannot produce lengthy stories. Instead, they develop their stories related to the circumstances of the committed crime in the form of answers to hundreds or even thousands of questions posed during the trial, whereas volunteering more information than is required in a single question is strictly prohibited.

As for the third point, courtroom interaction, in Poland the judge is the only person responsible for questioning the witness, although prosecutors and attorneys for defense may ask supplementary questions during the trial (only after the judge has completed the interrogation of the witness). By contrast, in the USA it is the prosecutor and attorney for defense who ask witnesses questions; the judge may not do so. The prosecutor and attorney for defense are thus engaged in a combat or battle before the judge and the jury to demonstrate the guilt of the defendant or to discredit the testimony given by the prosecution witnesses, respectively. Therefore, under Common Law the truth comes out as a result of a courtroom battle between the parties.

Related with courtroom interaction are the social roles performed by the major participants in penal trials in Poland and in the USA. The findings (see Bednarek, 2014 for details) prove that the social roles played by the judge, prosecutor and attorney for defense vary significantly depending on the system. In fact, there are no similarities in this respect at all between the examination of witnesses during Polish and American penal trials. Specifically, in Poland the person responsible for the examination of witnesses is the judge, whereas in the USA the persons responsible are the prosecutor and attorney for defense.

The analysis of the fifth point, how the participants responsible for questioning the witnesses discursively reconstruct the crime event on the basis of the testimony, has also shown differences between the inquisitorial and adversarial procedures of witness examination. In this respect what matters is the fact that penal trials in the USA and in Poland are founded on two completely distinct legal principles, i.e.: *the principle of formal truth* and *the principle of substantive truth*, respectively (see Bednarek, 2014 for a more detailed discussion). As far as the former is concerned, Summers (1999, pp. 285–286) asserts that the "formal truth is whatever legal counsels find as the fact-finders". This implies that what the "prosecution or defense present to the jury and the judge is only their own version of events", that is it is the story based on what they as fact-finders were able to find out in connection with the committed crime. The prosecution and the defense thus present two conflicting versions of the story during the trial, each of which comprises the story of the crime and the story of the investigation. Such narratives enable the two parties to engage in combat before the judge and the jury to prove the defendant's guilt beyond reasonable doubt or prove his/her innocence, respectively. Whichever party is capable of providing a more credible story according to the members of the jury issuing the verdict wins.

As a result, in the USA the process of examining witnesses and the search for the truth are comparable to the process of storytelling because the prosecution and defense are allowed to present two different versions (discursive reconstructions) of the events related to the committed crime, obtained through meticulous questioning of their witnesses.

By contrast, the *principle of substantive truth*, on which the Polish criminal trial is founded, assumes that the process of fact-finding involves establishing the objective truth. The examination of witnesses is conducted by an impartial person – the judge – a person who represents neither the injured party nor the defendant. Such a procedure is supposed to guarantee an impartial trial and quest for the objective truth. As a result, the process of examining witnesses and the search for the truth in Poland cannot be compared to the process of telling a story.

The sixth and last point analyzed with the CA approach concerns the distribution and classification of questions employed to examine witnesses under the two legal systems. In this respect a quantitative study has shown significant disparities between Polish and American courtroom discourses with reference to the following issues: (1) the number of questions asked during the examination of witnesses in American and Polish criminal trials, and (2) preference of certain types of questions asked during the examination of witnesses in these two contexts.

As for the first point, the number of questions asked, Polish and American courtroom discourses differ greatly with respect to the number of questions asked during the evidential phase. Bednarek (2014, p. 173) notes that the number of questions "asked in the American criminal trial substantially exceeds the number of questions posed during the Polish criminal trial", which may be explained by the fundamentally different legal principles on which the two penal trials are based, the principle of formal truth and the principle of substantive truth, respectively (see above).

As for the second point, the types of questions asked, Bednarek (2014, p. 70) observes that "American prosecutors and attorneys for defense have a penchant to employ different types of questions during different parts of the evidential phase"; by contrast, "Polish judges use any types of questions that may help them find the objective truth" (Bednarek, 2014, p. 173) in relation to the committed crime. Also,

American prosecutors and attorneys for defense use leading questions, which Polish judges may not ask while examining witnesses.[3]

4.3. Inquisitorial and adversarial procedures of witness examination in Poland and the USA in the light of the pragmatic approach

The third and final approach applied to the study of American and Polish courtroom discourses was the pragmatic approach. The topics addressed include (1) the participants' observance of Grice's (1975) Co-operative Principle (CP), and (2) the speech acts used. The results are presented below.

In terms of the observance of Grice's (1975) Co-operation Principle (CP) by the participants in courtroom proceedings, the comparative analysis of penal trials indicates that, although the observance of CP's four maxims is an essential requirement for communication to be effective, examples of flouting any or all of them can be found in both American and Polish courtroom discourses. This suggests that there are in fact certain similarities between these two otherwise different contexts in this particular respect.

Specifically, as for the maxim of Quantity ("Make your contribution as informative as is required for the current purposes of the exchange" and "Do not make your contribution more informative than is required", Grice, 1975, p. 45), the study of American courtroom discourse has revealed that during direct examination and cross-examination witnesses generally conform to this maxim, that is they usually give as much information as is asked of them. However, there are also frequent situations in which some witnesses find it difficult to restrict their contributions to what is wanted of them, as they have more to say. As mentioned above, such situations cause immediate objections of the opposing party.

By contrast, the research into Polish criminal trials indicates that the inquisitorial nature of witness examination, which is typical of this context and founded on the principle of substantive truth, implies that when providing explanations or testimony neither the defendant nor the witnesses are restricted as to the length of their response. The structure of the examination of witnesses in Polish court allows them to reveal all the information that they possess in connection with the committed crime. In consequence, the maxim of Quantity may be violated. Also, the maxim can be violated when the defendant or a witness answers supplementary questions posed by the Chairman if the defendant or a witness does

3 Leading questions evoke the desired answers or simply contain the information which the examining lawyer seeks to confirm (e.g. "Were you at the site of the crime on the day when the crime was committed at 9 p.m.?")

not say all that she/he knows during the first part of the examination. Again, their answers are not limited with respect to length.

As for the second maxim, that of Quality ("Do not say what you believe to be false" and "Do not say that for which you lack adequate evidence", Grice, 1975, p. 46), the research has confirmed that not all witnesses comply with it in the American court. Similarly, the analysis of Polish courtroom discourse indicates that examples of providing false testimony do take place, although under art. 233 § 1 of the Polish Penal Code anyone who, in providing testimony which is to serve as evidence in court proceedings or other proceedings conducted on the basis of law, gives false testimony or conceals the truth is subject to the penalty of deprivation of liberty for up to three years.

As for third maxim, that of Relation ("Be relevant", Grice, 1975, p. 46), the results of the study of American courtroom discourse indicate that most of testimonial evidence appears to be relevant to the case. However, sometimes the prosecution and defense lawyers object to the issues, which, in their opinion, depart from the expected answers, and accuse the witnesses of providing irrelevant information. In such cases the judge decides whether the issue in question is or is not relevant to the case. A qualitative analysis of the explanations of the defendant and testimony of the witnesses in the selected Polish criminal trials has shown certain similarities to American ones in that all the witnesses except one of the three victims made their contributions relevant to the case.

Finally, in the case of the last maxim, that of Manner ("Be perspicuous", "Avoid obscurity of expression", "Avoid ambiguity", "Be brief (avoid unnecessary prolixity)" and "Be orderly", Grice, 1975, p. 46), the findings of the research into American courtroom discourse indicate that the testimony of lay witnesses does not appear to be problematic in this respect, and hence does not flout this maxim. Lay witnesses generally abide by this maxim. However, the study of the testimony given by expert witnesses indicates their tendency towards marked incomprehensibility, complexity and ambiguity resulting from the fact that when they provide testimony, expert witnesses explain very complex, elaborate and complicated issues from various branches of science such as medicine, bio-chemistry or forensic science. Understanding them requires considerable familiarity with the topic, field competence and experience in the relevant profession. Considering that their domains of expertise often represent vast areas of research, the testimony of expert witnesses is frequently quite lengthy.

By contrast, the results of the study of Polish criminal trials have revealed that the testimony given by various witnesses, including experts in psychiatry or psychology, are comprehensible, intelligible and clear, which in turn indicates that witnesses generally abide by the fourth maxim. However, owing to the fact that the procedural law in force in Poland allows witnesses to provide answers in the form of a narrative, which can sometimes be lengthy, certain utterances may seem rather convoluted, and for this reason may be considered examples of flouting this maxim.

The comparative analysis of speech acts performed in Polish and American courtroom discourses has also shown that the speech communities participating in the examination of witnesses under Civil Law and Common Law share the knowledge of how to use spoken language to perform certain acts. For instance, court officials generally know how to request the defendant to provide an explanation, or how to warn witnesses of their penal responsibility for providing false testimony, or how to order police officers to remove the defendant from the courtroom, or how to make the witnesses promise to tell the truth, the whole truth and nothing but the truth when giving testimony. In other words, there is a certain similarity between the two speech communities involved, each of which may be characterized as being competent as to how to communicate effectively with each other, as well as how to communicate with the witnesses. This competence enables Polish and American participants to make proper use of diverse speech acts, be it Representatives, Directives, Commissives, Expressives or Declaratives (Austin, 1962; Searle, 1969), for different communicative purposes. However, what appears to be different between Polish and American courtroom discourses with respect to the speech acts used is that they are presented in different ways depending on the legal system (see Bednarek, 2014, for details).

5. Conclusions

The major objective of the present paper has been to demonstrate linguistic and cultural heterogeneity in courtroom discourses under Civil Law (Poland) and Common Law (the USA). Based on a comprehensive study of discursive elements typical of the two legal systems I have identified, illustrated and explained the similarities and differences between the adversarial and inquisitorial methods of witness examination in the USA and in Poland (see Bednarek, 2014 for details). The study has demonstrated and explained how, by what means and to what extent the social (institutional), cultural and historical contexts shape the use of language in criminal trials. The results obtained have also substantiated the hypotheses that (1) the inquisitorial and adversarial procedures of witness examination are culturally varied and socially conditioned, and (2) they represent two entirely different linguistic genres, or rather two phenomena *sui generis* that were shaped by two dissimilar cultures.

References

Archer, D. (2005). *Questions and answers in the English courtroom (1640–1760). A sociopragmatic analysis*. Amsterdam & Philadelphia: John Benjamins Publishing Company.

Atkinson, J. M., & Drew, P. (1979). *Order in court: the organization of verbal interaction in judicial settings*. London: McMillan.

Austin, J. L. (1962). *How to do things with words*. Oxford: Oxford University Press.

Beattie, J. M. (1986). *Crime and Courts in England 1660–1800*. Oxford: Clarendon Press.

Bednarek, G. A. (2014). *Polish vs. American Courtroom Discourse: Inquisitorial and Adversarial Procedures of Witness Examination in Criminal Trials*. Basingstoke & New York: Palgrave Macmillan.

Berk-Seligson, S. (1990). *The bilingual courtroom: court interpreters in the judicial process*. Chicago & London: The University of Chicago Press.

Conley, J. M., & O'Barr, W. M. (1990). *Rules versus relationships: The ethnography of legal discourse*. London: The University of Chicago Press.

Conley, J. M., & O'Barr, W. M. ([1998] 2005). *Just words: Law, language and power*. Chicago & London: The University of Chicago Press.

Cotterill, J. (2003). *Language and power in court: A linguistic analysis of the O. J. Simpson trial*. Basingstoke: Palgrave Macmillan.

Cotterell, R. (2004). Law in culture. *Ratio juris*, 1, 1–14.

Danet, B., & Bogoch, B. (1980). Fixed fight or free-for-all? An empirical study of combativeness in the adversary system of justice. *British Journal of Law and Society*, 7, 36–60.

Dunstan, R. (1980). Context for coercion: Analyzing properties of courtroom questions. *British Journal of Law and Society*, 7, 61–67.

Ehrlich, S. (2001). *Reproducing rape*. London: Routledge.

Goffman, E. (1964). The neglected situation. *American Anthropologist*, 6(2), 133–136.

Goodrich, P. (1987). *Legal discourse: Studies in linguistics, rhetoric and legal analysis*. Hong Kong: The Macmillan Press Ltd.

Goodwin, Ch., & Heritage, J. (1990). Conversation analysis. *Annual Review of Anthropology*, 19, 283–307.

Grice, H. P. (1975). Logic and conversation. In P. Cole & J. L. Morgan (Eds.), *Syntax and semantics 3: Speech Acts*. New York: Academic Press, 41–58.

Harris, S. (1984). Questions as a mode of control in magistrates' courts. *International Journal of the Sociology of Language*, 49, 5–27.

Hostettler, J. (2006). *Fighting for justice: The history and origins of adversary trial.* Winchester: Waterside Press.

Hostettler, J. (2009). *A history of criminal justice in England and Wales*. Sherfield: Waterside Press.

Hostettler, J., & Braby, R. (2009). *Sir William Garrow. His Life, Times and Fight for Justice*. Sherfield: Waterside Press.

Hymes, D. (1972). On communicative competence. In J. B. Pride & J. Holmes (Eds.), *Sociolinguistics*. Harmondsworth: Penguin, 269–293.

Kryk-Kastovsky, B. (2000). Representations of orality in early modern English trial records. *Journal of Historical Pragmatics*, 1/2, 201–230.

Langbein, J. H. (2003). *The origins of adversary criminal trial.* Oxford: Oxford University Press.

Luchjenbroers, J. (1997). In your own words: Questions and Answers in a Supreme Court Trial. *Journal of Pragmatics*, 27, 477–503.

Matoesian, G. M. (1993). *Reproducing rape: Domination through talk in the courtroom*. Cambridge: Polity Press.

Mellinkoff, D. (1963). *The language of the law*. Boston: Little, Brown and Company.

Philips, S. U. (1984). The social organization of questions and answers in courtroom discourse: A study of changes of plea in an Arizona court. *TEXT*, 4(1/3), 225–248.

Saville-Troike, M. (1982). *The ethnography of communication: An introduction.* Oxford & New York: Oxford University Press.

Searle, J. (1969). *Speech acts: An essay in the philosophy of language*. London: Cambridge University Press.

Summers, R. S. (1999). Formal legal truth and substantive truth in judicial fact-finding – Their justified divergence in some particular cases. *Cornell Law Faculty Publications*. Retrieved from http://scholarship.law.cornell.edu/cgi/viewcontent.cgi?article=2388&context=facpub. DOA: 02.03.2017.

Tiersma, P. M. (1999). *Legal language*. Chicago: University of Chicago Press.

Woodbury, H. (1984). The strategic use of questions in court. *Semiotica*, 48(3/4), 197–228.

Part 4.
Discourses of power and politics

Małgorzata Rzeszutko-Iwan

Maria Curie-Skłodowska University, Lublin, Poland

Knowledge, power and order as constituents of public discourse

Abstract: The aim of this article is to present how the categories of knowledge, power and order function in public discourse based on judicial and media discourses. The theoretical underpinnings of the study are the works of the philosopher Michel Foucault. Specifically, the category of order is manifested in three areas: symbolic, non-verbal and verbal. Knowledge is understood as searching for the truth and the interpretation of the truth, as well as revealing the truth. Finally, the category of power takes on institutional meaning, which is either literal or linguistic (symbolic). Following Foucault, the relationship between the three categories can be described as follows. The immanent order manifests itself through knowledge and power, and the latter categories, in turn, constitute and create a discourse which plays a significant role of an institutional tool used to maintain internal order in a given institution. This kind of discourse guarantees consistent relationships between subjects: situational, contextual and thematic relationships on the one hand, and ideological, axiological and social ones on the other.

1. Introduction

Since the dawn of humanity, the categories of knowledge and power have aroused, and still arouse, a lot of emotion and controversy.[1] They function in public discourse, with *public* understood here as related to the concept of *public space*[2], itself understood as any places commonly available free of charge where an individual

---

1 See e.g. the reflections of N. Machiavelli (15th/16th c.) contained in *Książę* 'The Prince' (1984a) and *Rozważania nad pierwszym dziesięcioksięgiem historii Rzymu Liwiusza* 'Discourses on the First Ten Books of Livy' (1984b).

2 The public space in the sociological sense includes the Internet (social networks, multiplayer games, instant messaging services including Skype, Gadu-Gadu, IRC, etc.) and the media (newspapers, radio, television). Religiousness is also sometimes included as a component of the public space. The following synonyms function in social sciences: public sphere, public space, and public domain (Makowski, 2011, p. 87). The distinction between the private and the public, both in terms of diachronic and contemporary approaches, is discussed in e.g. Pietrzak, Szczepanik & Zaorski (2001, pp. 109–121). Cf. also public vs. private (as defined by the law): Nowacki (1992, pp. 8–18); Jabłońska-Bonca (2002, pp. 316–335).

may find oneself in the physical and non-physical sense. The key terms of the present considerations are thus: *discourse*, *knowledge*, *power*, and, finally, *order*. This study takes the works of Michel Foucault (2002a, b, 2006) as a point of departure for the analysis of the above-mentioned concepts.

The primary concept in this context is *order*, which manifests itself in *discourse*; the latter can function because of the implementation of the *knowledge* and *power* categories. Thus, *discourse* is regulated directly by *knowledge* and *power*, and that discourse warrants *order*.[3]

The aim of this paper is to present the functioning of the *knowledge* and *power* categories, as well as *order*, in public discourse, illustrated with examples of judicial and media discourses.

The research is based on the materials recorded by the author in the years 2002–2012.[4] These are court hearing transcripts from the Regional Court and the District Court of Lublin, and radio interviews from the programme *Gość Radia Zet* 'The Guest of Radio ZET'. The choice of this programme was determined by its nationwide range in Poland, popularity, audience ratings, and also the nature of the interview itself, resembling court hearings (one-to-one relationship between the interviewee and the interviewer), and thus comparable to court interactions represented in the second group of texts.

On the basis of the juxtaposition between radio interviews and court hearings it is possible to clearly identify the characteristics common to a dialog situation (interaction of two participants) and to emphasize the differences resulting, among others, from institutional dissimilarities. One can also point out factors of a general nature (social and cultural) justifying the juxtaposition between court hearings and interviews:

---

3 We may say that these concepts form a philosophical circle, which refers to *transcendentals* – term created by M. Foucault – including work, life and speech. They allow for an objective cognition of living beings, laws of linguistic production and forms. They are unknowable *per se*, but constitute the conditions of knowledge; they are based on the existence, reality, establishing law and order of what is to become known (Foucault, 2006, pp. 221–273).

4 The recordings comprise court hearings with a total duration of 75 hours, and radio interviews – 70 hours. Out of the corpus the following samples were randomly selected to be transcribed: (1) 720 minutes of court hearings, (2) 600 minutes of radio interviews. On average, 45 minutes of a court hearing takes 15 typewritten pages, and a 15 minutes of an interview – 8 pages, which amounts to over 560 typewritten pages (more than 240 pages of court hearing transcription and 320 pages of radio interviews). The reference plane for the randomly selected sample of court hearing recordings was the total duration of these recordings, not the number of hearings (Rzeszutko-Iwan, 2015).

1. variability and multi-directional humanistic reflection, attempt to communicate across boundaries in the public sphere;
2. changes of the traditional judicial system in democratic countries (an increasing number of incoming cases, organizational insufficiency of courts), e.g. in performing jurisdictional activities, involving the diversion from an imperious way of resolving disputes to the idea of an alternative way of resolving them, in terms of criminal, civil, and administrative law (Kalisz & Zienkiewicz, 2014).

The paper is structured as follows. Section 2 discusses the theoretical approach to the concepts of discourse, order, knowledge, and power, referring primarily to the theory of M. Foucault and partly to the French School of Discourse Analysis. Section 3 is analytical, and presents the author's observations on the functioning of the relevant categories in the public, judicial and media discourse, e.g. the dimensions of order and knowledge. It contains several samples, taken from specific court hearings and radio interviews, which confirm the interpretations presented. Section 4 provides the general conclusions of the study.

2. Discourse – order – knowledge – power

The source of understanding of the concept of discourse adopted in this study is Michel Foucault's (2002a, b, 2006) work, according to which discourse has an important function of being an institutional tool used for maintaining internal order, as well as being the guarantor of consistent subjective, situational, contextual, thematic, ideological, axiological, and social relationships (Howarth, 2008, pp. 81–134; Grzmil-Tylutki, 2009, p. 89).[5]

The understanding of this concept also draws upon the theory of culture put forward by Fleischer (1994, 2002) and Labocha (1996, 2008), where discourse appears to be a cultural category which indicates how a given community (cultural formation) participates in the process of (interpersonal) communication. Discourse thus includes everything that is typical, repetitive, and common to a given culture.

5 References to Foucault's sociological thought are also found in Critical Discourse Analysis (CDA) in its Anglo-American version (e.g. Fairclough, 2008). Cf. the discussion of the differences in the approach to the understanding of the concept of discourse in Polish Text Linguistics, the French School of Discourse Analysis, and Critical Discourse Analysis (Duszak & Fairclough, eds. 2008; Grzmil-Tylutki, 2009; Witosz, 2009). Consider also the approach to discourse as a communication event: (1) as using language, (2) as conveying ideas, and (3) as an interaction in social situations (van Dijk, 2001, p. 10).

The understanding of the term *discourse* adopted here also makes reference to the French School of Discourse Analysis.[6] According to its assumptions, the subjective and temporal relationships, the broadly understood context, semantics, subject matter, and ideology remain integral parts of discourse and contribute to its formation. Linguistic and social dimensions appear as indivisible elements which complement one another and constitute a whole. The concept of discourse is thus identified with a specific area of life – the area of human socio-linguistic activity. This means that discourse is a space of human activity, an 'institutionalized socio-linguistic ritual' (Grzmil-Tylutki, 2009, p. 90; translation mine). The criterion specifying and allowing one to isolate or identify particular types of discourse, which constitute communication as a whole, is therefore a sphere of human activity. The following types of discourses may thus be specified, indicating the key human activities (the list is by no means complete):

1. political discourse: diplomatic, military, etc.;
2. economic discourse;
3. scientific discourse;
4. public discourse: judicial, media, etc.

Discourse refers both to attitudes, behaviors and their social effects, and to rules and standards to be observed in the process of communication within a group (discursive community). It is a way of "imposing order on what is empirical" (Foucault, 2006, p. 200; translation mine).

The simplest order, as defined by Foucault (2006), is an elementary system in which one can point out to differences and similarities. It "manifests itself as the inner law of things" (Foucault, 2006, p. 9), which makes it inscribed in the existence, in the order of being; order is simply the "silent order of things" (Foucault, 2006, p. 9). Only on its basis can general theories of organizing things (in Foucault's, 2006 sense) and their resulting interpretations be built. Order is created in space, i.e. in a particular discourse, by means of language. The orders resulting therefrom subsequently appear as codes involved in specific cultural realities.

Order itself is maintained and ensured by the categories of knowledge and power. Immanent order manifests itself through these categories, and they, in turn, confirm that order.

6 The main representatives (and pillars) of the French School of Discourse Analysis are Dominique Maingueneau and Patrick Charaudeau (Grzmil-Tylutki, 2007, p. 21).

Following Foucault (2006), knowledge is understood in a dual way:

1. knowledge as interpretation,
2. knowledge as cognition, or looking for similarities and differences.

In the latter case, the basic operation related to the category of knowledge consists in searching for similarities, which is followed by establishing the existing differences (full cognition). It should also be added that in the sphere of knowledge there are multiple configurations of various empirical cognition forms; in the light of their variation and accumulation it can thus be concluded that "knowledge generates knowledge" (Foucault, 2006, p. 11). This is because "to know – is to speak as it should be spoken and in the way that is dictated by the proper conduct of the mind; to speak – is to know what can be known and according to what is imposed on one by models existing in a given time" (Foucault, 2006, p. 89).

Consequently, "discourse is the knowledge inscribed into a uniform order" (Foucault, 2006, p. 87), and at the same time it is a way "to impose order on what is empirical" (Foucault, 2006, p. 200), i.e. power. Discourse is therefore a carrier of power, which appears as an element of the ordering of the world. Foucault also believes that words and language are burdened with authority in the sense of one's capability of imposing something on others. This is the so-called "language's power of presentation" (Foucault, 2006, p. 55).

Summing up, the categories of knowledge and power create discourse, and are constituted by discourse at the same time. It may therefore be concluded that knowledge and power on the one hand, and discourse on the other stimulate one another, and together form a system.

3. The categories of order, knowledge and power in public discourse (as exemplified by court hearings and radio interviews)

3.1. Order

Court hearings and radio interviews build the space of public discourse in which there is a certain order resulting from the operation of knowledge and power categories. Speaking of order, we should indicate the following dimensions in which it manifests itself:

1. *symbolic dimension* – occurring beyond the specific space of the courtroom / the (radio) broadcast studio,

2. *non-verbal dimension* – within the specific space of the courtroom / the (radio) broadcast studio,
3. *verbal dimension* – in specific linguistic realizations used by the participants.

As for the symbolic dimension of judicial order, it is understood as being embedded in the system of norms[7], primarily legal norms. This is because society operates in accordance with the hierarchical system of these norms, legitimized by the state and sanctioned by state institutions, norms which are socially acceptable and aimed at regulating the conduct of the members of a given community. This assumption applies to the belief that all actions of individuals are always in relation to the legal system in force, in a group to which they belong (social, political, national etc.). This may be a relation of either confirmation, similarity, abiding by the law, or denial, difference, i.e. breaking the law. Norms included in the legal system create institutional and organizational structures, which organize the activities of particular groups, assign social roles to their members, and provide strictly specified ways and means of controling their implementation. An individual breaking the law goes to court which is an institution that protects law and order. The purpose of the activities taken in court and other law-protecting institutions by means of judicial discourse is to repair the disturbed order.[8]

By contrast, the symbolic dimension of order in media discourse (in the case of radio interviews: beyond the space of the radio broadcasting studio) concerns embedding the statements on all the topics discussed in the whole spectrum of media contextualization of these statements, their rhetoric, and construction. In the stream of statements on a given subject it appears important that they refer to the current situation, the reality of a given moment, and that they highlight differences and similarities in relation to other statements concerning a given topic.

---

7 In this paper, the concept of norm is narrowed down to a rule which is generally accepted as binding, and which is laid down by the organization of the state (i.e. legislative power, which in the case of the Polish political system is exercised by the Parliament), that is legal norm. Consequently, it does not include such principles as morality, sociocultural values, religion, etc. It should be emphasized that the scopes of the abovementioned rules often overlap; cf. Wronkowska and Ziembiński (1997, pp. 81–95).

8 For more information on the role of activities typical of the sphere of jurisdiction, i.e. the function of law and of the main proceedings, see e.g. Rzeszutko (2003, pp. 36–37, 40–41).

As for the second dimension, the non-verbal one, in the case of the courtroom space it is associated with an institutional, very expressive and strict division of roles: judge – arbitrator, parties to the proceedings, and witnesses. Each participant of the proceedings is assigned a defined social role (involving prohibitions, orders, procedures, guidance on the order of speaking, etc.). This order is emphasized, among others, by the spatial arrangement of all persons appearing in the courtroom.[9] Apart from the spatial plane, non-verbal ritualization also manifests itself at the object level (e.g. the presence of some 'stage props' in the courtroom)[10] and the kinesic level (e.g. the necessity to adopt an appropriate body posture while speaking in the courtroom).[11]

By contrast, in the radio broadcasting studio the non-verbal dimension of order is based on the interviewer (journalist)-interviewee relationship. It should be noted, however, that, in contrast to the courtroom, swapping these roles is possible. The only element that remains unchanged is the role of mass audience.[12] Unlike in the courtroom context, there are no spatial-object rituals.[13]

Finally, there is the verbal dimension of order, which manifests itself at the level of language. In the courtroom, there are strict guidelines and limitations concerning the way of addressing various participants of the proceedings, for example *wysoki sądzie* 'Your Honor', *panie prokuratorze/pani prokurator* 'Prosecutor + *vocative male/female*', *panie mecenasie/pani mecenas* 'Counselor/Attorney + *vocative male/female*', *proszę oskarżonego* (addressing the accused), *proszę świadka* (addressing the witness), *the counsel may approach,* or *the witness may step down,* etc.:

9 The seriousness of the positions occupied by the participants in court proceedings is also confirmed by some prejudices functioning among lawyers. For example, sitting down in the dock/at the defense table instead of the accused is forbidden, even if one is extremely fatigued, so as not to find oneself there as the accused.

10 For more information on the ritual aspect of court proceedings, see Rzeszutko (2002, 2003, pp. 51–61, 155–181).

11 In the courtroom, there is a kind of "good practice of jurisdiction" which does not allow trainees before passing their final exams to even try on the appropriate court dress. Therefore, trainees appearing at the hearing, e.g. substituting for their patron, participate in the proceedings in plain clothes.

12 It should be added that there are radio programs where the audience actively participates in the communication, for example debates or discussions. Such a situation, however, does not occur in the radio interviews analyzed here.

13 Spatial and object rituals are important in the case of television programs, involving both aural and visual communication channels, in contrast to the radio, where only the former is used.

(1)
Obrońca: [...] dlatego też mamy wątpliwości co do faktu popełnienia przestępstwa przez ***podejrz..., przepraszam, już oskarżonego****, bo akt oskarżenia wpłynął, ponieważ oskarżony nie przyznał się [...]*

[Defense counsel: (...) therefore we have doubt as to the fact of committing a crime by the **susp..., I'm sorry, well, the accused** now that an indictment has been brought, because the accused pleaded not guilty (...)][14]

An important aspect of interactions is not only the way of formulating statements, but also the capability of initiating interactions by particular persons involved (or lack thereof). For instance, different participants apply different strategies of verbalizing specific language functions. This is the case of e.g. the impressive function, whereby the judge can formulate direct orders, which at the same time have performative power:

(2)
Sędzia: [...] ***zarządzimy poszukiwanie*** *oskarżonego listem gończym [...],* ***zarządzimy doprowadzenie*** *[...]* ***przymusowe*** *przez policję obu świadków [...] Jeśli się świadkowie nie będą stawiać [...]* ***podejmiemy decyzję o ich aresztowaniu*** *[...]*

[Judge: (...) **we will issue an arrest warrant** (...), **we will issue a warrant for compulsory appearance (...)** of both witnesses (...) If the witnesses fail to appear (...) **we will decide to detain them** (...)]

By contrast, the accused, the defense counsel or the prosecutor would rather use e.g. requestive constructions to perform the impressive function:

(3)
Obrońca: [...] ***jeżeli Wysoki Sąd pozwoli,*** *to ...* ***argumentowałbym to*** *w sposób następujący [...]* ***Wnosiłbym*** *o nieprzedłużanie stosowania tego środka,* ***bądź jeżeli Wysoki Sąd dojdzie do wniosku,*** *że oskarżony musi podlegać jakimś specjalnym rygorom,* ***zastosowanie wobec niego innego środka*** *zapobiegawczego o charakterze wolnościowym [...]*

[Defense counsel: (...) **if you allow it, Your Honor** ... I **would argue** in the following way (...) **I would like to request** Your Honor not to extend the application of this measure, **or, if Your Honor concludes** that the accused must be subject to special rigors, **to take preventive measures** other than detention (...)]

Witnesses, on the other hand, have no possibility of performing the impressive function at all.

---

14 All examples provided in this paper are taken from the corpus gathered in 2002–2012 unless stated otherwise. The corpus contains texts transcribed in the original language (Polish) and then translated into English for the purposes of the present analysis.

As for the radio broadcasting studio, the verbal dimension of order does not entail any formal or institutional requirements.[15] Instead, there are applied norms of linguistic politeness appropriate to official communication and general rules of good manners. A whole range of expressions may thus be observed, including colloquialisms:

(4)
Osoba udzielająca wywiadu: ***No myślę,*** *że jeżeli porezerwuje zanadto, czyli to się nazywa w bankowości* ***zrobi zbyt duże sadełko*** *i to robią niektóre firmy, niektóre banki. Ja też patrzyłam, czy banki słusznie rezerwy celowe składają, czy nie, tak wysokie,* ***no to może być to za duże sadełko,*** *tak jak dla każdej innej firmy.*

Dziennikarz: ***No dobrze, ale czy słusznie Donald Tusk chce zjeść trochę tego sadełka.***

[Interviewee: **Well, I think** if one reserves too much, or in banking we say it **accumulates too much 'fat'**[16], and that's what some companies, some banks do. I also watched if the banks are right to accumulate such high appropriated reserves, or not, **well, there might be that excess "fat",** as for any other company.

Journalist: OK, but is **Donald Tusk** [then former Polish PM – MRI] **right in that he wants to eat some of this fat**?]

Grammatical errors also occur:

(5)
Osoba udzielająca wywiadu: W jakiś sposób PO dla mnie osobiście się kojarzy z partią, która chyba nie lubi niektórych słów, tak jak na przykład: naród, patriotyzm. ***Oni zamieniają to słowami osobowość,*** *nie lubią systemowego* ***rozwiązania*** *problemów* [...] *Zobaczymy,* ***jak będzie składały się losy tych Polaków,*** *którzy pojadą pracować do Niemiec,* ***kiedy stracimy jedną z naszych najlepszych kadr*** [...] *No właśnie zobaczymy, czy ludzie, którzy żyją w Polsce, czy im się żyje lepiej, czy gorzej, bo Donald Tusk kojarzy się z dobrobytem,* ***a patriotyzm to jest jakby na dłuższym miejscu, na dalszym miejscu.***

[Interviewee: For me, personally, the Civic Platform [Polish political party - MRI] is somehow associated with a political party which probably does not like certain words, such as, for example, 'nation', 'patriotism'. **They change these words with personality**[17],

---

15 For more information on the styles of conducting interviews (e.g. cooperation, negotiations, passive participation) with examples, see Rzeszutko-Iwan (2015, pp. 194–199, 220–233).

16 In this context *fat, to have the fat, to eat the fat* mean 'financial reserves', 'to accumulate financial reserves' and 'to consume financial reserves', respectively. These colloquialisms relate to financial reserves that banks want to keep for themselves, and the government aims to shift the assets and dispose of them for any purpose.

17 The phrase *zamieniają to słowami osobowość* [they change these words with personality] contains an incorrect number. There is also an incorrect verb, it should be *zastępują je* 'they substitute them with' – both lexical and grammatical mistakes.

don't like systematic problem **solution** (…) We'll see **how it will look like** the fate of the Poles who will travel to work to Germany, **when we lose one of our best human resources** (…) Well, we'll just see if the people who live in Poland, whether their lives are better or worse, because Donald Tusk is associated with prosperity, **and patriotism is as if sort of at the long position, to him it comes second.**]

Yet one can also find conversations meeting the criteria of careful speech:

(6)
Osoba udzielająca wywiadu: Muszę powiedzieć, że jako długoletni, chyba najdłużej funkcjonujący prezes Narodowego Banku Polskiego, przez 9 lat prawie, z różnymi rządami, mogę powiedzieć, że dwie rzeczy, a w szczególności zysk oraz stopy procentowe były taką kością niezgody. Pewnie niektórzy jeszcze pamiętają moje, że tak powiem, potyczki z wicepremierem Kołodką, tak że zysk rzeczywiście jest kwestią bardzo istotną dla budżetu. I w związku z tym można powiedzieć tak, pewne rzeczy w tym zysku są uznaniowe. To znaczy, pamiętam do dziś dnia z mojej historii taką rzecz, że komisja, wtedy bilansu, teraz jest to niezależny audytor, przekonywała mnie, że powinnam rozwiązać rezerwy na nasz dług wobec Bułgarii […]

[Interviewee: I must say that as a long-term, perhaps the longest serving President of the National Bank of Poland, for almost nine years, with different governments, I can say that two things, and in particular, profit, and interest rates, were the apple of discord. Some people may still remember my, so to speak, skirmishes with Deputy Prime Minister Kołodko [former Polish Deputy Prime Minister and Finance Minister – MRI], so the profit is really important for the budget. And, therefore, it can be said that some things in that profit are arbitrary. I mean, I do remember to this very day such a thing from my story as the President, that what was then Balance Sheet Committee, it is now an independent auditor, kept convincing me that I should release the reserve for our debt to Bulgaria (…)]

To sum up, the category of order functions in both types of public discourse. However, in the space of the court discourse it has a very distinctive anchoring in

---

Rozwiązania 'solutions' – should be *rozwiązywania* 'solving', as it refers to an ongoing process – a grammatical mistake.
Jak będzie składały się losy tych Polaków [how it will look like the fate of the Poles] – should be *Jak ułożą się losy* [what the fate of those Poles would be like] – lexical and grammar mistakes (in Polish singular verb, *będzie składały*, instead of the plural *ułożą się*) – a grammatical mistake (wrong verb aspect).
Kiedy stracimy jedną z najlepszych kadr [when we lose one of our best human resources] – should be *stracimy część najlepiej wykształconych ludzi* [when we lose some best educated people] – a lexical mistake.
Patriotyzm to jest jakby na dłuższym miejscu [patriotism is as if sort of at the long position] should be *na dalszym planie* [is further in the background] – a lexical mistake.

the legal system, as well as specific formal determinants, e.g. obligatory language realizations. In the media, on the other hand, it remains in relation to cultural conventions, politeness, and the accepted standards of behavior.

3.2. Knowledge

The research of the discursive elements of court hearings and radio interviews has revealed that in public discourse, the category of knowledge manifests itself in two dimensions:

1. knowledge as searching, learning (and cognition), approaching the truth,
2. knowledge as interpreting, revealing the truth.

The former, cognitive dimension, includes noticing similarities of specific behaviors, views, and then pointing out the differences within the previously distinguished groups. Various forms of cognition appear in the space of knowledge. Both the above-listed dimensions involve noting the similarity of certain behaviors and views, and the subsequent indication of differences between them.

In the judicial sphere, the approaching-the-truth dimension manifests itself in a variety of ways (e.g. witness statements, explanations of the accused, reconstruction of the crime scene, material evidence, etc.). There are also different initial points for each of the participants. For instance, the accused, from the beginning of the proceedings, has full knowledge of the events and behaviors that are associated with the breach of a particular legal norm.[18] (S)he knows for sure whether, to what extent, and in which way, (s)he breached the established norms. Simply speaking, (s)he knows what (s)he did. However, (s)he does not know with indisputable certainty to what extent other participants in the proceedings are familiar with the picture of the events. (S)he has access to the case files, i.e. to the documented knowledge of the judge and the prosecutor. (S)he is not certain, however, as to the contents of the witnesses' statements. Sometimes (s)he knows only some witnesses, and is unaware of others.

Similarly, the defense counsel has extensive knowledge. The knowledge of both the prosecutor and the judge is similar, profiled at a certain angle. The state of knowledge of the judge, like the knowledge of all the other participants in the

18 I do not take into consideration cases of unconscious actions, i.e. law-breaking actions resulting from ignorance or the lack of control over one's behavior.

proceeding, changes, however, in the course of its duration. A significant part of the judge's activities consists in searching, exploring and investigating the truth:

(7)
Sędzia: […] ***Trudno mi wypowiadać się w sposób jednoznaczny co do postawionego zarzutu*** *[…] bo czynić tego nie mogę w tej chwili, gdyż jestem referentem tej sprawy, a więc […] będę orzekał w tej sprawie […]*

[Judge: (…) **It is hard for me to speak unequivocally about the objection made** (…) because I can't do it right now as I'm the reporting judge, that's why (…) I'll be adjudicating in this case (…)]

Then, in the final phase of judicial actions, the judge moves on to the dimension of knowledge as interpretation, for example:

(8)
Sędzia: […] ***sąd nie dał wiary*** *wyjaśnieniom oskarżonego,* ***w ocenie sądu*** *bezsprzeczne jest, że oskarżony dokonał zarzucanego mu czynu. […]*

[Judge: (…) **the court did not acknowledge** the explanations provided by the accused to be fact. **In the opinion of the court** it is undeniable that the defendant committed the alleged act (…).]

On the basis of the conducted proceedings, the judge must decide on the legitimacy, or lack thereof, of the indictment. (S)he is, therefore, obliged to continuously assess the information provided by the participants during the proceedings. The fact of interpreting information is repeatedly reflected in the statements of the presiding judge:

(9)
[…] zarzut […] z punktu drugiego zagrożony jest karą do dziesięciu lat pozbawienia wolności. ***W związku z tym, chociażby przez sam fakt zagrożenia, zachodzi domniemanie możliwości uchylania się od wymierzenia kary i tym samym nieodbycia kary ... przez oskarżonego, co już byłoby*** *[…]* ***podstawą do stosowania tego tymczasowego aresztowania*** *[…],*

[…] ***biorąc pod uwagę wyrok łączny – jedenastokrotnie karany, w tym z recydywą*** *z art. 60§2, ostatnio już nawet w takiej postaci.* ***Sąd jak na dzień dzisiejszy nie widzi podstaw do uchylenia tymczasowego aresztowania*** *[…]* ***areszt, będzie w dalszym ciągu stosowany,***

[…] ***może to być podstawą do rozważenia o uchyleniu tymczasowego aresztowania, jeśli stan zdrowia jego rzeczywiście się pogorszył***

[(…) the charge (…) from point 2 carries the penalty of up to ten years' imprisonment. **Therefore, even because of that very fact, there is a presumed possibility of evasion of punishment by the defendant and thus non-execution of the penalty …, which would be** (…) **the basis to justify the use of pre-trial detention** (…)

(...) **taking into account the cumulative judgment - eleven prior criminal convictions, including recidivism pursuant to art. 60§2**, and recently even as such. **As of today, this court sees no basis for revoking the pre-trial detention order** (...) **which will continue to be in effect**, (...)

if his health has really deteriorated, that fact may provide the basis for considering the detention repeal.]

Knowledge understood as interpretation is always equivalent to the presentation of a particular point of view.

As far as radio interviews are concerned, the situation is completely different. Both the journalist and the interviewee in the studio have a relatively broad knowledge concerning the subject matter of the interview. Various sources of information are equally available to both parties, such as other interviews, statements made by others, etc.:

(10)
*Dziennikarz: Jak będzie wyglądał w tym roku 1 sierpnia? **„Gazeta Wyborcza" pisze, że** znowu jest awantura wokół uroczystości, wokół 1 sierpnia* [...]

*Dziennikarz: Proszę posłuchać, **to z „Gazety Wyborczej":** „Nie będzie polityków, nie będzie okrzyków, ani barier, które zakłócają spokój tego miejsca" – napisali w liście do organizatorów. Taki list trafił do Komitetu Organizacyjnego obchodów 65. rocznicy wybuchu Powstania Warszawskiego* [...]

Dziennikarz: [...] ***cytuję z tego raportu:** „Ostentacyjne akcentowanie przez Donalda Tuska swojej kaszubskości".*

[Journalist: What will August 1st be like this year? **"Gazeta Wyborcza"** [Polish daily newspaper - MRI] **reports that** again there is a row about the festivities around August 1st (...)

Journalist: Please listen to what **"Gazeta Wyborcza" says:** "There will be no politicians, not shouting or barriers that disturb the peace of this place," – they wrote in a letter to the organizers. Such a letter was sent to the Organizing Committee of the 65th Anniversary of the Warsaw Uprising (...)

Journalist: (...) **I quote from this report:** "Ostentatious accenting his Kashubian origin by Donald Tusk".]

Also, in certain situations, the knowledge of the journalist and the interviewee seem to be complementary:

(11)
*Dziennikarz: Ale **chęć brania pieniędzy z rezerw przypomina to, co chciał Andrzej Lepper i to co chciał Grzegorz Kołodko.***

*Osoba udzielająca wywiadu: Nie, nie, to już **nie można równać Kołodki z Lepperem, a tym bardziej teraz premiera.** Dlaczego? Dlatego że **Andrzej Lepper** z tego, co pamiętam **chciał rezerwy dewizowe brać.** I to **jest różnica między rezerwą dewizową a rezerwą***

na kursy, *to jest taka mniej więcej jak między zamkiem w drzwiach, a zamkiem, który stoi jako budynek.*

Dziennikarz: No, ale ktoś ten zamek chce zabrać.

Osoba udzielająca wywiadu: Więc nie można porównać tego do Leppera, trochę mnie to zdziwiło, że nie pamiętano, że on chciał te 30 miliardów wówczas, a teraz pewnie dużo więcej miliardów dolarów rezerw, znaczy dolarów i euro.

Dziennikarz: Ale jak pisze Witold Gadomski ***można nazwać Donalda Tuska uczniem Leppera,*** *no bo jednak…*

Osoba udzielająca wywiadu: ***Nie, ja bym powiedziała, że prędzej Kołodko,*** *w sposób powiedziałam, taki bardziej profesjonalny* ***próbował ten zysk ode mnie wydobyć*** *i ewentualnie…*

Dziennikarz: ***I od Leszka Balcerowicza,*** *potem od Leszka Balcerowicza, który powiedział. Od Leszka Balcerowicza chciał wydobyć pieniądze z NBP i Leszek Balcerowicz postawił tamę temu* ***i teraz znowu próbuje pan premier.***

Osoba udzielająca wywiadu: ***To znaczy,*** *powiem szczerze,* ***takie rozmowy odbywały się zawsze.*** *Ja rozmawiałam i z ministrami finansów jako prezes NBP i rozmawiałam czasami z prezydentem, to był najdłużej funkcjonujący prezydent, kiedy ja byłam prezesem, z prezydentem Kwaśniewskim.* ***Nigdy to nie było zmuszanie,*** *może szkoda, że to wyszło na zewnątrz, bo takie rozmowy powinny być wewnątrz.*

[Journalist: But **the willingness to take money from the reserves looks similar to what Andrzej Lepper** [former Polish Deputy Prime Minister – MRI] **and Grzegorz Kołodko wanted to do.**

Interviewee: No, no, **you can't compare Kołodko with Lepper, and even less so the present Prime Minister**. Why not? Because, as far as I remember, **Andrzej Lepper wanted to take foreign currency reserves.** And **there is a difference between foreign currency reserves and reserves on rate moves**, they are, more or less, as different as a bar of gold and a bar to have a drink at.

Journalist: Yes, but somebody wants to take that bar of gold.

Interviewee: So you can't compare him to Lepper, and that surprised me a bit, that nobody remembered that Lepper had wanted that 30 billion then, and now that would be a good many more billion dollars of the reserves, dollars and euro that is.

Journalist: But, as Witold Gadomski [Polish journalist – MRI] writes, **Donald Tusk may be called Lepper's disciple,** because, one way or another….

Interviewee: **No, I'd sooner say that it was Kołodko that**, as I would say, in a more professional way, **to get that the profit from me** and possibly …

Journalist: **And from Leszek Balcerowicz** [former Polish Finance Minister – MRI]. Who said he wanted to get that money from Leszek Balcerowicz from the National Bank of Poland and Leszek Balcerowicz put an end to that, and **now Mr Prime Minister is trying to do that again.**

Interviewee: **I mean**, to be perfectly honest, **such talks always took place**. I talked with finance ministers as the President of the National Bank of Poland and sometimes with the President [of Poland], he was the longest serving President [of Poland], when I was the Bank President, with President Kwaśniewski [former President of Poland – MRI]. **It was never a matter of forcing**, it's a pity, perhaps, that it has leaked out, because such talks should be kept private.]

Furthermore, the interview situation can emphasize the subjectivity of the interviewee's knowledge:

(12)
Osoba udzielająca wywiadu: Dobrze by było, tak, ***uważam, że*** *najpierw powinny być takie rozmowy wewnętrzne, tylko tak jak mówię,* ***no nie wiem, na ile jest komunikatywny pan prezes*** [...] ***jak go oglądam na konferencjach prasowych, to jest wyjątkowo mało komunikatywny*** [...] ***jest traktowany jako trochę były pracownik NIK i wiceprezydent za Lecha Kaczyńskiego*** *i to powoduje, powiedziałam, jak gdyby takie skierowanie na prezydenta.*

Dziennikarz: ***No szkoda, że pan się tak wstrząsnął koncertem Madonny, a ta sprawa panem nie wstrząsa,*** *żeby przed 1 sierpnia...*

[Interviewee: It would be good, yes, **I believe** there should be some internal talks like these first, but like I'm saying, well, **I don't know how communicative Mr President** [of the National Bank of Poland, Sławomir Skrzypek – MRI] **is (...) when I watch him at press conferences, he is extremely uncommunicative (...) he is treated a bit like an ex-employee of the Supreme Audit Office and Deputy Mayor when Lech Kaczyński was the Mayor** [of Warsaw] and that brings about, I said, something like an association with the Mayor.

Journalist: **Well, it's a shame that you were so shocked by the Madonna concert and that this issue does not shock you**, so as to before August 1st ...]

By contrast, mass audience (listeners) may have no knowledge of the subject matter discussed at all.

To sum up, a significant difference between the judicial and the media discourses is the domination of knowledge as interpretation and revealing the truth, and not seeking it in the latter case. There is also a clear difference in the position of the center of gravity: in the courtroom, it lies in seeking the truth, objectivity, versatility of overview, i.e. taking into consideration different points of view, etc., whereas in interviews it is about showing, disclosure of the truth, subjectivity and presentation of the interviewee's own point of view.

3.3. Power

The category of order implies a situation in which both the social roles of the participants and the institutional functions are precisely defined. The degree of power held by any of the participants involved is also common knowledge to all of them. Therefore, two dimensions of power can be distinguished:

1. *institutional dimension* (official), i.e. power resulting from performing a certain official function; it is the actual (real) power;
2. *linguistic dimension*, i.e. power resulting from the very possibility of speaking; anyone allowed to speak in a given context has an advantage over the silent participants of the discourse; the former participant(s) have power – symbolic power, in this case.

The institutional dimension of power functions basically only in the judicial space, where it is realized primarily through the speech of the presiding judge.[19] The judge has a very wide range of *exclusion systems*, i.e. procedures of controlling the discourse, at his/her disposal. The ways of manifesting the category of power available to the judge are thus:

1. procedures of entering into discourse,
2. prohibition or injunction,
3. division and rejection (what is acceptable or unacceptable),
4. the opposition of truth and falsehood (what is considered true or false).[20]

---

19 Institutional participants in courtroom proceedings (judge, prosecutor, defense counsel) are vested with the institutional dimension of power, i.e. actual power. The participants from beyond the institution (the accused, witnesses) are vested with the linguistic dimension of power, i.e. symbolic power. The consequence of this division is, e.g. the privileges resulting from that fact, due to which the judge, the prosecutor, and the defense counsel may never be asked questions about the events occurring in the course of the case. The aforementioned participants, however, are entitled to exercise such power in relation to other persons (Rzeszutko, 2001, p. 3).

20 According to the line of defense adopted, the accused may, for example, deny having committed the alleged act. The defense counsel supports the actions of his/her client; cf. the contemporary formulation of the defense counsel's duties presented in legal literature (Śliwiński, 1984, p. 401):

> *Obrońca nie musi [...] działać zgodnie ze swym przekonaniem o winie lub niewinności oskarżonego. Chociaż jest przekonany o winie oskarżonego lub o słuszności niekorzystnej dla oskarżonego wykładni jakiegoś przepisu ustawy, ma wytoczyć wszystko przed oblicze sądu, tak pod względem faktycznym jak i prawnym, co mogłoby przemawiać na korzyść oskarżonego, działa bowiem na procesie nie tyle w tym celu, aby wyrobić sobie sąd o czynie swego klienta, lecz w tym celu by przeciw oskarżycielowi stanął ktoś, kto zapomniawszy o swym subiektywnym przekonaniu, szuka okoliczności obiektywnie na korzyść oskarżonego przemawiających. Obrońca ma prawo i obowiązek powstrzymać swego klienta od tych czynności procesowych, które są szkodliwe dla oskarżonego.*

All events that take place in the courtroom space must have the judge's permission. Starting from organizational activities, ordering (e.g. signaling the order in which other participants appear), indicating the sequence of the statements made by them, up to the admissibility of the appearance of specific persons or evidence, or lack thereof. At any moment the judge may take back the floor or give the floor to another participant of the proceedings. In effect, prohibitions very clearly show the relationship between the categories of discourse and power.

Among the dyadic communication systems, the interactions: judge – prosecutor, judge – the accused, judge – defense counsel, judge – witness, and judge – expert witness are always asymmetrical. This is related precisely to the category of power and action on behalf of the state. The institutional dimension of power is thus connected with the hierarchy of participants in the proceedings.[21] Moreover, it is emphasized by various forms of ritual behavior.[22]

As for radio interviews, one can note only the existence of symbolic power. Anyone who is speaking has an advantage over the silent participants of the discourse, has power. The listeners, then, may not have any power at all. It should also be noted that the full extent of power is granted to those participants in the media discourse who, in addition to presenting their views, also have the greatest knowledge:

(13)

Dziennikarz: Pani poseł, proszę powiedzieć, ***czy czytała pani raport*** *napisany przez Jarosława Kaczyńskiego?*

Osoba udzielająca wywiadu: ***Nie, nie czytałam, ale słyszałam o nim****.*

Dziennikarz: [...] *w tym raporcie jest mowa o tym, że PO to jest partia antyzasad i antywartości. Tak?* ***Zgadza się pani z tym, że*** *jest partią antyzasad* [...]*? W raporcie*

[The defense counsel has no obligation (...) to act in accordance with his/her belief in the guilt or innocence of the accused. Although (s)he is convinced of the guilt of the accused or the rightness of the interpretation of some provision of a legal act which is unfavorable for the accused, his/her role is to bring everything to court, both in terms of facts and law, that may speak in favor of the accused. Actually, during the proceedings, the defense counsel's role is not so much to form his/her own judgment about the action of his/her client but to stand against the prosecutor, to be someone who has forgotten his/her subjective belief and who is seeking circumstances being objectively in favor of the accused. The defense counsel has the right and duty to protect his client from those procedural actions that are detrimental to the accused.]

21 See also the types of strategies used by particular participants in court proceedings (Rzeszutko-Iwan, 2015, pp. 127–189).

22 For more information on the ritual aspect of court proceedings, see Rzeszutko (2002, 2003, pp. 51–61, 155–181).

Jarosław Kaczyński zarzuca Tuskowi, że ostentacyjnie podkreśla kaszubskość. Nie można mówić, że jest się Kaszubem?

Osoba udzielająca wywiadu: [...] ***trudno mi mówić o raporcie, którego nie czytałam.***

Dziennikarz: Ale ja pani cytuję z tego raportu: „Ostentacyjne akcentowanie przez Donalda Tuska swojej kaszubskości".

Osoba udzielająca wywiadu: Coś ***nie chce mi się wierzyć w to, żeby tak było napisane.*** *[...] ja szczerze mówiąc nie chciałabym rozmawiać o Donaldzie Tusku, bo nie ma o czym rozmawiać.*

Dziennikarz: No, ale cały ten raport jest poświęcony Platformie Obywatelskiej i Donaldowi Tuskowi. ***No to jak możemy o tym nie rozmawiać?*** *To prezes stracił czas, napisał 116 stron na marne?*

Osoba udzielająca wywiadu: Bo ja chciałabym rozmawiać o sprawach, których nie załatwia Donald Tusk [...]

Dziennikarz: No dobrze, pani poseł, ale pani jest posłanką Prawa i Sprawiedliwości i ***dzisiaj najważniejszym wydarzeniem to jest właśnie tenże raport,*** *to co mówi Jarosław Kaczyński. Na przykład mówi o tym, że jest „bezrozumna polityka zagraniczna", co to znaczy [...]?*

Osoba udzielająca wywiadu: [...]

Dziennikarz: ***Dobrze, ale jeszcze wracając do raportu,*** *tu jest taka mowa o tym, że „trzeba się zastanowić" – na temat Jacka Rostowskiego, ministra finansów: „osoba, której droga do rządu wymagałaby precyzyjnego wyjaśnienia", znaczy rozumiem, że Jarosław Kaczyński zastanawia się, w jaki sposób Jacek Rostowski został ministrem finansów, i że to jest takie podejrzane, że on właśnie został ministrem finansów. Czy pani się wydaje to podejrzane, że właśnie Jacek Rostowski został ministrem finansów, i że trzeba to zbadać dlaczego on został?*

Osoba udzielająca wywiadu: [...] ***Ja nie znam szczegółów.***

[Journalist: Madam the Honorable Member of Parliament, **have you read the report** written by Jarosław Kaczyński [Polish Law and Justice party leader – MRI]?

Interviewee: **No, I haven't read it but I've heard of it.**

Journalist: (...) in that report, the Civic Platform is referred to as a party of anti-principles and anti-values. Is it? **Do you agree with** the opinion that it is a party of anti-principles (...)? In the report, Jarosław Kaczyński criticizes [Donald] Tusk for Tusk's ostentatious stressing Kashubian origin. Is it forbidden for one to say one is a Kashubian?

Interviewee: (...) **it's hard for me to talk about a report I haven't read**.

Journalist: But I'm quoting from that report: "Ostentatious accenting his Kashubian origin by Donald Tusk"

Interviewee: **I somehow can't believe it is said this way** (...) to be honest, I wouldn't like to talk about Donald Tusk, because there's nothing to talk about.

Journalist: But that whole report concerns the Civic Platform and Donald Tusk. **So how can't we talk about it?** Does that mean the Chairman [Kaczyński] has wasted his time, has he written 116 pages to go down the drain?

Interviewee: Because I would like to talk about things Donald Tusk doesn't take care of (…)

Journalist: OK, Madam the Honorable Member of Parliament, but you represent the Law and Justice and **the most important news today is that report**, or what Jarosław Kaczyński says. For example he says that there is "thoughtless foreign policy", what does it mean (…)?

Interviewee: (…)

Journalist: **OK, but still going back to the report**, there is a fragment about the fact that "one has to think about" – about Jacek Rostowski, the Finance Minister: "a person whose way to the government would require a precise explanation", I mean, I understand that Jarosław Kaczyński wonders how Jacek Rostowski has become the Finance Minister, and that it is the fact that he has become Finance Minister is so suspicious. Does it look suspicious to you that it was Jacek Rostowski who has become the Finance Minister and do you believe that the fact that he has become the Finance Minister should be investigated?

Interviewee: (…) **I don't know any details.**]

As can be seen in excerpt (13), a well-prepared journalist has an advantage over the interviewee. She knows exactly what she wants to ask the interviewee about; she also has the power to comment and interpret the statements of the interviewee. The scope of the journalist's knowledge thus makes it possible for her to control the course of the interview.[23]

To sum up, it may be stated that in judicial discourse full power, in both dimensions, is revealed when it coincides with the category of knowledge, and such is the situation of the judge in the final phase of the proceedings. The judge has institutional power by default and holds it continually from the very beginning of the hearing. The state of his/her knowledge expands during the subsequent judicial proceedings. Therefore, in the final phase, with full knowledge and power, the judge makes the ruling in the case. The remaining participants broaden their knowledge but their power in the institutional dimension does not change. This happens only with the accused, whose scope of rights increases in the case of acquittal or is dramatically reduced at the moment of his/her guilt being declared.[24]

In media discourse, by contrast, one may hypothesize that the category of power comes down to the category of knowledge. That knowledge, however, is

---

23 See also the means of creating individual strategies of the journalist and the interviewee in the studio, exemplified by radio interviews (Rzeszutko-Iwan, 2015, pp. 189–233). See also Pałuszyńska's (2012) extensive monograph on the strategies used by both journalists and their interlocutors in public media discourse.

24 For more information on the performative function of the final decision see Rzeszutko (2003, pp. 105–124).

always symbolic. In the case of media discourse then, there is no category of power in the institutional dimension. The dominant position is held by the interlocutor who has a broader view of reality, has discussed certain issues, and, in the case of sensitive subjects, the one who wants to make a final point.

4. Conclusion

Public discourse, understood as an "institutionalized socio-linguistic ritual" (Grzmil-Tylutki, 2009, p. 90), functions on the basis of appropriate discursive regularities, namely the categories of knowledge and power. A question can be asked which of these categories – if either – is superior. In the context of the present analysis it can be concluded that in the judicial discourse the dominant category is by far that of power, and in the media discourse it is knowledge. Thus, the results of the research indicate a close relationship between the three concepts: discourse, power and knowledge. It has also been confirmed that in the contexts analyzed the function of both power and knowledge is to maintain immanent order, which proves the thesis stated in Foucault's theory.

All in all, in the light of the present study, the hypothesis formulated by Foucault (2002b, p. 7) that "in every society the production of discourse is at once controlled, selected, organized and redistributed by a certain number of procedures whose role is to ward off its powers and dangers, to gain mastery over its chance events" appears to be correct. The immanent order manifests itself through the categories of knowledge and power, and these categories, in turn, shape discourse.

References

van Dijk, T. A. (Ed.) (2001). *Dyskurs jako struktura i proces*. Warszawa: Wydawnictwo Naukowe PWN.

Duszak, A., & Fairclough, N. (Eds.) (2008). *Krytyczna analiza dyskursu. Interdyscyplinarne podejście do komunikacji społecznej*. Kraków: Universitas.

Fleischer, M. (1994). *Problemy i hipotezy systemowej teorii kultury*. Wrocław: "Leopoldinum" – Wydawnictwo Fundacji dla Uniwersytetu Wrocławskiego.

Fleischer, M. (2002). *Teoria kultury i komunikacji. Systemowe i ewolucyjne podstawy*. Wrocław: Wydawnictwo Dolnośląskiej Szkoły Wyższej.

Foucault, M. (2002a). *Archeologia wiedzy*. Warszawa: De Agostini.

Foucault, M. (2002b). *Porządek dyskursu*. Gdańsk: Słowo/Obraz Terytoria.

Foucault, M. (2006). *Słowa i rzeczy. Archeologia nauk humanistycznych*. Gdańsk: Słowo/Obraz Terytoria.

Grzmil-Tylutki, H. (2007). *Gatunek w świetle francuskiej teorii dyskursu*. Kraków: Uniwersitas.

Grzmil-Tylutki, H. (2009). Gatunek – kategoria analizy dyskursu. *Biuletyn Polskiego Towarzystwa Językoznawczego*, LXV, 89–99.

Howarth, D. (2008). *Dyskurs*. Warszawa: Oficyna Naukowa.

Jabłońska-Bonca, J. (2002). *Podstawy prawa dla ekonomistów*. Warszawa: Wydawnictwo Prawnicze LexisNexis.

Kalisz, A., & Zienkiewicz, A. (2014). *Mediacja sądowa i pozasądowa*. Warszawa: Wydawnictwo Wolters-Kluwers.

Labocha, J. (1996). Tekst, wypowiedź, dyskurs. In S. Gajda & M. Balowski (Eds.), *Styl a tekst*. Opole: Uniwersytet Opolski, 49–55.

Labocha, J. (2008). *Tekst, wypowiedź, dyskurs w procesie komunikacji językowej*. Kraków: Wydawnictwo Uniwersytetu Jagiellońskiego.

Machiavelli, N. (1984a). *Książę*. Warszawa: PWN.

Machiavelli, N. (1984b). *Rozważania nad pierwszym dziesięcioksięgiem historii Rzymu Liwiusza*, Warszawa: PWN.

Makowski, P. (2011). *Sfera publiczna* i detranscendentalizacja intersubiektywności. Uwagi na temat normatywności teorii społecznych. In P. Pluciński & M. Nowak (Eds.), *O miejskiej sferze publicznej, Obywatelskość i konflikty o przestrzeń*. Kraków: Wydawnictwo Ha!art, 87–102.

Nowacki, J. (1992). *Prawo publiczne – prawo prywatne*, Katowice: Wydawnictwo UŚ.

Pałuszyńska, E. (2012). *Strategie dziennikarzy i ich rozmówców w medialnym dyskursie publicznym*, Łódź: Wydawnictwo Uniwersytetu Łódzkiego.

Pietrzak, E., Szczepanik, R., & Zaorski-Sikora, Ł. (2011). *Aksjologia życia publicznego*, Łódź: Wydawnictwo AHE.

Rzeszutko, M. (2001). Kategorialne wyznaczniki gry w tekście rozprawy sądowej. *Poradnik Językowy*, 10, 1–9.

Rzeszutko, M. (2002). Rytualny charakter interakcji w rozprawie sądowej. In G. Szpila (Ed.), *Język trzeciego tysiąclecia II, t. 1: Nowe oblicza komunikacji we współczesnej polszczyźnie*. Kraków: Uniwersitas, 193–203.

Rzeszutko, M. (2003). *Rozprawa sądowa w świetle lingwistyki tekstu*, Lublin: Wydawnictwo Uniwersytetu Marii Curie-Skłodowskiej.

Rzeszutko-Iwan, M. (2015). *Zarys paradygmatu strategii w przestrzeni dyskursu publicznego (przesłuchania sądowe a/i wywiady radiowe)*, Lublin: Wydawnictwo Uniwersytetu Marii Curie-Skłodowskiej.

Śliwiński, S. (1984). *Proces*, Warszawa: PWN.

Witosz, B. (2009). Gatunek tekstu wobec porządku dyskursu. *Biuletyn Polskiego Towarzystwa Językoznawczego*, LXV, 99–111.

Wronkowska, S., & Ziembiński, Z. (1997). *Zarys teorii prawa*, Warszawa: PWN.

Adam Warzecha

University of Silesia, Katowice, Poland

Shockvertising, scandalization and viral communication in discursive struggle: Nergal in *The Voice of Poland*

Abstract: Participation of Adam "Nergal" Darski, the leader of the death metal band *Behemoth*, in the television talent–show *The Voice of Poland* in autumn 2011 caused a media storm and fierce public debate in Poland.[1] This story has focused as in a lens Polish social, political and religious life. Here heavy metal intersects with the popular media and culture, controversial stage image with court trials, Nergal's fight against leukemia with advertising, Satanism and its symbols with Christianity, political struggle during the parliamentary election campaign with religious life, freedom of speech and artistic expression with religious freedom.

This paper aims to answer two fundamental questions about those events: (1) How various discourses involved influenced each other?; (2) Which communication mechanisms have been used? Methodologically I use the Critical Discourse Analysis approach of Norman Fairclough (2003, 2005) and the case study method (Gerring, 2007; also Stacks, 2005, 2011) to identify three intertwining and interacting processes of communication: (1) Nergal's *shockvertising/publicity* in the death metal niche; (2) Nergal's *shockvertising/publicity* in TVP when promoting *The Voice of Poland* to mass audience; (3) *political and religious scandalization* performed by specific activists (various political, church and religious organizations, bishops etc.)

1. Background

Nergal is the stage name of Adam Michał Darski (b. 1977), the leader of the death metal band *Behemoth* (est. 1991)[2]; the pseudonym refers to the Mesopotamian chthonic god-ruler of the underworld (Jordan, 2004, p. 218). Nergal's songs touch directly on satanic topics and symbolism, especially the anti-Christian and

---

1 I adapted here one of the three case studies from my doctoral dissertation: A. Warzecha (2013), *Działania public relations Kościoła katolickiego w Polsce z perspektywy Krytycznej Analizy Dyskursu*. Rozprawa doktorska napisana pod kierunkiem prof. dr. hab. UŚ Jacka Warchali, Katowice, 2013, pp. 234–348.

2 http://www.behemoth.pl; DOA: 17.11.2016; http://www.metalstorm.net/bands/band.php?band_id=50&bandname=Behemoth; DOA: 17.11.2016.

neo-pagan.[3] For several years, the band existed mainly in the heavy metal niche, but then in 2007–2008 *Behemoth* consolidated its position on the music market. The band became the most famous Polish group abroad, which performs on all continents, has sold several million records, and was the first Polish artist on the Billboard 200 list.[4] It is considered a precursor of black/death metal and one of the best bands of the genre. *Behemoth* supported concert tours of such rock and metal legends as *Anthrax*, *Marilyn Manson*, *Metallica* or *Slayer*.[5] They were also awarded by such music magazines as *Metal Hammer*, *Mystic Art*, *Decibel Magazine*, *Terrorizer* or *metalstorm.net*.[6]

Crucial for Nergal and *Behemoth* popularity was the year 2009.[7] In May, Nergal met the pop-singer Doda (Dorota Rabczewska) and became the target of the paparazzi and various celebrity gossip websites. They followed them, their engagement on the New Year's Day 2010, Nergal's winning battle against leukemia and his appearance in the promotion campaign for bone marrow donation (August 2010–January 2011), until the couple's break-up in March 2011.[8]

By further provocations, Nergal drew public attention to himself and built his controversial image. As is discussed in section 4, his actions in this respect involved *publicity* (Grunig & Hunt, 1984), realized mainly by *shockvertising* (Dahl, Frankenberger & Manchanda, 2003) and – quite unusually – some aspects of the *public information* model (e.g. Grunig & Hunt, 1984), especially during his leukemia treatment, when he took part in the campaign for promoting stem cell registration. Consequently, Darski began to appear not only in the music or gossip media, but also in the mainstream and opinion-forming ones, transforming gradually himself from an underground rocker to a pop icon. This tactic, consisting in sending contradictory signals – a shocking artist and a socially responsible citizen – proved effective. In November 2011, the weekly magazine *Wprost* listed Darski among the hundred most influential Poles.[9]

3 http://www.behemoth.pl/site/interviews/metalmaniacs.html; DOA: 17.11.2016.

4 http://www.billboard.com/artist/281109/behemoth/chart; DOA: 17.11.2016.

5 http://www.behemoth.pl/site/index.php/pol#archiwum_news2009; DOA: 17.11.2016.

6 http://www.completemusicupdate.com/article/metal-hammer-golden-gods-nominations-announced/; DOA: 17.11.2016; http://www.metalstorm.net/awards/archive.php?year=2004; DOA: 17.11.2016.

7 http://muzyka.interia.pl/metal/news-to-nie-fenomen-to-cud,nId,1640974; DOA: 17.11.2016.

8 http://www.fakt.pl/kobieta/plotki/nergal-nie-jest-juz-z-doda-to-koniec/pd50vpn; DOA: 17.11.2016.

9 "100 najbardziej wpływowych Polaków", *Wprost* 45/2011 (1500), 07.11.2011, p. 44.

2. Bible tearing

On 13th September 2007, during a concert in Gdynia club *Ucho*, announcing the song "Christgrinding Avenue", Nergal tore the Bible (00'45" – 01'00"):

> *To piosenka z nowego albumu… z albumu „The Apostasy", która opowiada o naszej wizycie w tak zwanym Świętym Mieście, Jerozolimie. Pojechaliśmy tam, żeby osobiście rozprawić się z mitem, który pokutuje już od dwóch tysięcy pieprzonych lat. Mitem, którego głównym bohaterem jest człowiek ukrzyżowany między dwoma zbrodniarzami. Mitem, którego bohaterem jest największa, najbardziej zbrodnicza sekta, jaka istniała na Ziemi. To jest Pismo Święte, jak mówią… Ja mówię, to jest księga kłamstw. Pieprzyć to gówno. Pieprzyć tą hipokryzję. Żryjcie z tego gówna. Ten kawałek jest naszym komentarzem na temat tego właśnie gówna.*
>
> (http://www.youtube.com/watch?v=Nrvv0HRKgqg; DOA: 17.11.2016)[10]

> [This is a song from the new album… from the album *The Apostasy*, which tells about our visit to the so-called Holy City, Jerusalem. We went there to personally deal with the myth that lingers from two thousand fucking years. With the myth, whose protagonist is a man crucified between two criminals. With the myth whose protagonist is the largest, the most criminal sect that existed on Earth. This is the Holy Scripture, as they say… I say this is the book of lies. Fuck this shit. Fuck this hypocrisy. Gobble from this shit. This piece is our commentary on this particular shit.]

On the recording, it can be seen that the audience burn the Bible and trample on it (02'41"). The act was deliberately planned and staged. One of the pieces of evidence is handwritten annotations on the setlist found by journalists just after the concert.[11] Moreover, Nergal repeated that announcement on other concerts, saying e.g. "Fuck it! Burn it! Piss on it!" (e.g. in Paris on 17th February 2008) and "Fuck Jesus Christ!" (e.g. in New York City on 18th November 2007).[12]

Apart from a few press texts, the event did not cause any public reaction then. Neither was there any public reaction five months later, when on 4th February 2008, Ryszard Nowak, the chairman of the National Committee for Protection against Sects, reported to the Polish Prosecutor General that by tearing the Bible

---

10 See also: http://www.gazetaswietojanska.org/index.php?id=2&t=1&page=913; DOA: 17.11.2016.

11 http://www.gazetaswietojanska.org/index.php?id=2&t=1&page=919; DOA: 17.11.2016.

12 http://www.dziennikbaltycki.pl/artykul/798069,nowak-ponownie-oskarza-nergala-muzyk-zniszczyl-biblie-kilkanascie-razy,id,t.html; DOA: 17.11.2016. http://www.youtube.com/watch?v=y11y0WK-qqs (rec. 17.02.2008); DOA: 17.11.2016; http://kinoplay.pl/behemoth_evangelia_heretika,72,390.html; DOA: 17.11.2016; http://www.youtube.com/watch?v=S21-0F_KpqQ (rec. 26.06.2008); DOA: 17.11.2016; https://www.youtube.com/watch?v=WCDtrGL76jo (rec. 18.11.2007); DOA: 17.11.2016.

Darski insulted his religious feelings, following Article 196 of the Polish penal code, which bans actions that can offend religious feelings or sentiment.[13] On 21st August 2011, the Regional Court in Gdynia acquitted Darski of the accusation.[14] The verdict was appealed and the case was brought before the Polish Supreme Court, which, on 5th March 2015, finally stated that in the case "the constitutive elements of offence" (*znamiona przestępstwa*) were not fulfilled "for the artist's message was addressed to a specific group of people, who shared his beliefs" (*przekaz artysty był skierowany do określonej grupy osób, które podzielały jego przekonania*). Yet "this does not mean that the behavior of Adam D. is accepted" (*nie oznacza to, że zachowanie Adama D. jest akceptowane*).[15]

The case received wide coverage only in the autumn of 2011, when Darski became the juror-coach in the talent-show *The Voice of Poland* aired by TVP2, the second channel of Polish public television (*Telewizja Polska*, TVP).[16] However, reactions did not appear at once. The first press releases on Nergal's participation in the show were published on 16th May 2011, and the first protests took place only in early July, i.e. after the first hearing on Nowak vs. Darski, which was previously postponed due to the latter's health condition.[17] Still at the time the case did not cause much interest of any church institution nor organization, either religious or political. *Scandalization* (Kepplinger, 2008; see section 4.3) only began in mid–August 2011, at the beginning of the election campaign for parliament, after Darski's acquittal by the Regional Court in Gdynia, just before the first episode of the show was broadcast.[18] Only then did the representatives

---

13 Art. 196 Ustawa z dnia 6 czerwca 1997 r. – Kodeks karny (Dz. U. z 1997 r. Nr 88, poz. 553 z późn. zm.). See also: http://www.trojmiasto.pl/wiadomosci/Czy-Behemoth-obrazil-uczucia-religijne-n26713.html; DOA: 17.11.2016.

14 http://www.tvn24.pl/wiadomosci-z-kraju,3/nergal-niewinny-darcie-biblii-forma-sztuki,181508.html; DOA: 17.11.2016.

15 http://www.sn.pl/aktualnosci/SitePages/Komunikaty_o_sprawach.aspx?ItemID=46&ListName=Komunikaty_o_sprawach&rok=2015; DOA: 17.11.2016.

16 *The Voice of...* is the television format created in the Netherlands by the Talpa Media Group in 2010. In April 2011 the American version of the show appeared on NBC; that version became the model for the Polish one: http://muzyka.interia.pl/pop/news-w-nowym-show-oceniaja-uczestnikow-nie-widzac-ich,nId,1652080; DOA: 17.11.2016.

17 http://www.radaetykimediow.pl/index.php?option=com_content&view=article&id=207:w-sprawie-adama-darskiego-&catid=33:nasze-stanowisko&Itemid=40; DOA: 17.11.2016.

18 http://www.wirtualnemedia.pl/artykul/show-the-voice-jesienia-w-tvp-2-trwaja-prace-wideo; DOA: 17.11.2016; http://dziennikustaw.gov.pl/du/2011/s/162/978/1; DOA: 17.11.2016.

of political parties and various religious organizations, also some bishops, begin to voice their opinions. The person most involved in this case was Wiesław Mering, Bishop of Włoclawek. In late August, the Catholic Association of Journalists published a petition against the promotion of satanism in TVP, which in a few weeks was signed by more than 42 thousand people.[19] Interestingly, the protests subsided after the election Sunday, 9th October 2011.

3. Methodology

In this study I have used the Critical Discourse Analysis approach of Norman Fairclough (2003, 2005) as described in Warzecha (2012, 2013, 2014). I have also used the *case study* method, which, according to Gerring (2007, p. 20), "may be understood as the intensive study of a single case where the purpose of that study is – at least in part – to shed light on a larger class of cases (a population)". I also adopted Don Stacks' (2005, 2011) *process-oriented case study* approach. In relevant places I also refer to Hans M. Kepplinger's (2008) *scandalization* mechanisms, Stanisław Barańczak's (1975) *persuasion* mechanisms, and the concept of *the political* discussed by Carl Schmitt (2007).

The model applied allowed for the identification of three intertwining and interacting processes of communication: (1) Nergal's *shockvertising/publicity* in the death metal niche; (2) Nergal's *shockvertising/publicity* used and enhanced by TVP in promoting *The Voice of Poland* to mass audience, and (3) *political–religious scandalization* conducted by the activists (various political, church and religious organizations, bishops etc.).

4. Case study

A query based on the corpus of texts published between 2008 and 2011 in 1100 various Polish newspapers and periodicals has shown a sharp increase in the media interest in Adam Darski in 2011.[20] Specifically, in 2008 he was mentioned only in 61 press texts, in 2009–543, in 2010–1259, and in 2011–2755. More than two-thirds of the texts in the corpus appeared in the last four months of

19 http://ksd.media.pl/component/content/article/1-news/393-ksd-protestuje-wobec-promocji-satanizmu-w-tvp; DOA: 17.11.2016; http://ksd.media.pl/aktualnosci/403-prezes-ksd-odpowiada-prezesowi-tvp; DOA: 17.11.2016.

20 The query concerning the phrase "Adam Darski OR Nergal" (in all declensional cases) according to PRESS-SERVICE data by courtesy of Ms. Marlena Sosnowska, Spokesperson and Public Relation Manager, PRESS-SERVICE Monitoring Mediów Sp. z o.o., ul. Grunwaldzka 19, 60–782 Poznań, Poland.

2011, when *The Voice of Poland* was on the air (September – 776, October – 557, November – 305, December – 230).

As far as collocations with Adam Darski/Nergal are concerned, in 2011 it co-occurred mostly with *Kościół* 'Church' (725 occurrences), *Voice of Poland* (680), *Doda* / Dorota Rabczewska (608) and *białaczka* 'leukemia' (213).[21] In 2010, the most common collocations included references to *Doda* / Dorota Rabczewska (693), *białaczka* 'leukemia' (322) and *Kościół* 'Church' (111), whilst in 2009 – *Doda* / Dorota Rabczewska (338).[22]

Figure 1. Quantity of press texts about Nergal in 2011 (courtesy of PRESS-SERVICE)

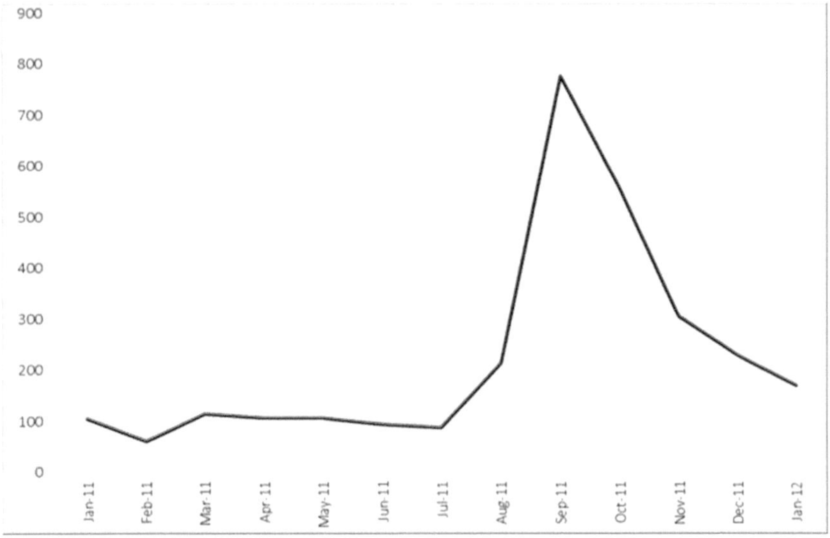

The peak in the interest in August–October 2011, as shown in Figure 1, is concurrent with the then ongoing election campaign for parliament (5th August 2011 – 7th October 2011), but also with the second phase of *The Voice of Poland* advertising campaign (15th August 2011 – 30th September 2011), and the broadcasting of the

21 Number of press articles in which the phrase "Adam Darski OR Nergal" co-occured with "Kościół", "The Voice of Poland", "Doda OR Dorota Rabczewska" and "białaczka" (in all declensional cases) according to PRESS-SERVICE.

22 The results for "Kościół", "The Voice of Poland", "Doda / Dorota Rabczewska" and "białaczka" in the subsequent years were respectively: in 2008 – 25, 0, 0, 0; in 2009 – 69, 0, 338, 0, and in 2010 – 111, 0, 693, 322.

first episodes of the program, the first being aired on Saturday, 3rd September 2011, at 8 PM, i.e. in the prime time.[23]

4.1. Shockvertising

The first process involved in the media communication on Nergal in the period analyzed is *self-scandalization*, which is addressed to fans of the artist in the death metal niche. It can be seen in terms of shockvertising, or "shocking advertising content" (Dahl et al., 2003), which

> attempts to surprise an audience by deliberately violating norms for societal values and personal ideals. It is the norm violation aspect of the shock appeal that is assumed to underlie its ability to break through advertising clutter and capture the attention of a target audience who then listens and acts on the related message
>
> (Dahl et al., 2003, p. 269).

As Parry, Jones, Stern & Robinson (2013, pp. 212–213) add, "examples of shock advertising can include the visual display of obscene sexual references, profanity or gratuitous violence".

Shockvertising allowed Nergal to draw attention of his target group, i.e. current and potential customers: fans, concert audience, and buyers of CD, DVD, other publications and merchandise. In terms proposed by Dahl et al. (2003, p. 269), Nergal has surprised a (general) *audience* "to capture the attention of a *target audience*", at the same time setting a high threshold (shock), which allows him to separate the target audience from the unprepared one (see also Parry et. al., 2013, pp. 112–113).

According to Darski, none of the hundreds of people present at the concert in 2007 felt offended by him tearing the Bible. In fact, participants of the concert, declaring the Christian faith and testifying in the process as witnesses, admitted that his behavior did not offend their feelings: *Obrażone zostały natomiast osoby, które nie były na koncercie, które nie rozumieją kontekstu i przekazu* [Instead, offended were the persons absent on the concert, who do not understand the context and the message].[24] That was primarily Ryszard Nowak, who acknowledged Darski to be 'a dangerous person': *Na jego koncerty w większości chodzi niepełnoletnia młodzież, a on w czasie koncertów propaguje satanizm – ideologię śmierci* [It is

23 http://www.wirtualnemedia.pl/artykul/the-voice-of-poland-jesienia-w-tvp-2-emisja-w-soboty-wideo; DOA: 17.11.2016.

24 http://www.tvp.info/4791511/nergal-stanal-przed-sadem; DOA: 17.11.2016; http://www.tvn24.pl/wiadomosci-z-kraju,3/nergal-niewinny-darcie-biblii-forma-sztuki,181508.html; DOA: 17.11.2016.

mostly underage youth that are going to his concerts, during which he propagates satanism – ideology of death].[25] However, due to the limited communication potential of Nowak and his followers, his opinion did not set up a considerable resonance.

4.2. Amplification

Subsequent to self-scandalization/shockvertising was *amplification*, whose function was to publicize the first process and amplify it during the advertising campaign of *The Voice of Poland* talent show. The following shock resulted mainly from 'pulling out' Nergal from his extreme, death metal, iconoclastic niche and 'inserting' him into a popular TV production intended for mass audience. In fact, shock and its amplification were pivotal to *The Voice of Poland*'s advertising campaign, which otherwise was rather modest, consisting mainly of self-promotion on TVP's own channels, radio and Internet ads, and video spots in sea resorts. Darski was later upset with TVP for not organizing an outdoor campaign and for putting the main emphasis on creating publicity and using controversies surrounding him, as he observes in an interview:

> **Piotr Najsztub**: Z tego, co wiem, nie było pieniędzy na promocję tego programu, ty swoją osobą załatwiłeś promocję.
>
> **Adam Darski (Nergal)**: *Jesteś dobrze zorientowany. Mam żal do Dwójki, że nie zdecydowała się na porządną kampanię billboardową. My daliśmy z siebie wszystko, ale skrzydła podcinała nam telewizja, nie robiąc nic, żeby „Voice" wypromować z klasą i rozmachem. Sam biskup Mering promocyjnie nie pociągnie programu. „Voice" potrzebował dużo więcej wsparcia niż tabloidowe kłamstwa i ujadanie moich nawiedzonych adwersarzy.*
>
> (Darski, 2011, p. 41)
>
> [**Piotr Najsztub**: As far as I know, there was no money to promote this program, and you made publicity with your own person.
>
> **Adam Darski (Nergal)**: You are well versed. I regret that the Two [TVP2] did not decided to perform a decent billboard campaign. We did our best, but television clipped our wings, not doing anything to promote „The Voice" with flair and verve. Bp. Mering himself does not pull the program promotionally. „The Voice" needed a lot more support than tabloid lies and baying of my cranky adversaries.]

Despite vivid social reaction, the program did not have a good audience. *The Voice of Poland* was watched by an average 2.27 million viewers, which gave TVP2 15.69% share in the group of TV viewers over the age of 4 and 14.85% in the group

25 http://www.tvp.info/4791511/nergal-stanal-przed-sadem; DOA: 17.11.2016.

aged 16–49 years.[26] Consequently, *The Voice of Poland* took only the third place in the sweeps, after TVN *I've got talent!* and TVP1 feature films aired at the same time. The TVP2 talent-show was viewed mostly by the middle aged and older female residents of rural areas.

4.3. Scandalization

Following self-scandalization/shockvertising and their amplification, the second process of communication involved in the case discussed is *scandalization*, which involved various publics protesting against Nergal's participation in the public television program. In this case scandalization can be seen as (1) a reaction to the shock provoked by earlier promotional campaigns; however, it also reveals (2) complex relationships between various religious, political, media and show–business discourses. Changing the context of communication, from the heavy metal niche into the public sphere on the one hand, and its amplification on the other caused resonance among the social groups and individuals so far unfamiliar with Nergal. In general, the protesters and activists exerted pressure on TVP rather by social media Internet activism than by legacy media activism (Coombs & Holladay, 2014, pp. 74, 85–86). Of course, they also used such resources as petitions, sermons, letters, parish bulletins, catechesis, radio and television or letters of support, but first of all they employed websites, forums, comments, Facebook, Twitter etc. for their purposes.[27] Following Vilpponen, Winter & Sundqvis (2006, p. 66), such forms of protest can be seen as a multilevel word–of–mouth/viral communication with active opinion leader/leaders and positive resonance of their "networks".

In the process of scandalization communication had three functions: (1) religious protest against Bible tearing, which aimed at removing the blasphemer from the public sphere; founded on the religious protest is the (2) political protest, which aimed at changing the TVP's managerial board and later achieving good parliamentary election results by the conservative (see below); (3) publicity and positioning of social actors participating in this discursive struggle – primarily Darski and Bp. Mering – performed in viral communication. In the following sections I discuss these three aspects of scandalization in detail.

26 http://www.wirtualnemedia.pl/artykul/the-voice-of-poland-przegral-z-tvn-i-tvp-1-27-mln-zl-z-reklam; DOA: 17.11.2016.

27 http://ksd.media.pl/component/content/article/1-news/397-bp-mering-popar-petycj-ksd; DOA: 17.11.2016.

4.3.1. Religious protests

Initially the protests had a religious character; the protesters argued that Darski's tearing of the Bible "offended their religious feelings". The act was called "the lack of culture" (*brak kultury*) e.g. by Fr. Boniecki, Bp. Tomasik and Bp. Mering, and "the manifestation of unprecedented intellectual barbarity" (*przejaw niesłychanego intelektualnego barbarzyństwa*) by Marcin Przeciszewski, editor-in-chief of KAI, Polish Catholic Press Agency.[28] According to Bp. Mering, "[e]mployment of a follower of satanism, a blasphemer, a man without a basic culture in the public TV transgresses all bounds of decency" (*Zatrudnienie wyznawcy satanizmu, bluźniercy, człowieka bez podstawowej kultury w TV publicznej bije wszelkie granice przyzwoitości*), and "there are boundaries of what is proper and what is not proper in the public sphere" (*są granice tego, co wypada i co nie wypada w sferze publicznej*).[29]

A violent eruption of protests almost four years after the concert in *Ucho* club may indicate that Darski is somehow tolerated as long as he remains in his subcultural niche: "We missed that moment, the evil felt strong, so today they give that follower of Satan with his beliefs a television airtime" (*Przespaliśmy tamten moment, zło poczuło się mocne, więc dzisiaj dają temu wyznawcy Szatana z jego poglądami czas na antenie telewizyjnej*) (Bp. Kaszak).[30] Reference to Darski's performance is also made by Cardinal Dziwisz: "We cannot remain silent when the Bible is torn up on stage. We cannot remain silent when in the public media are promoted people, who combined the sign of the cross into satanic shows" (*Nie możemy milczeć, gdy na scenie rwie się na strzępy Pismo Święte. Nie możemy milczeć, gdy promuje się w publicznych mediach osoby, które znak krzyża włączyły w satanistyczne widowiska*).[31] In response TVP argued that Darski "in this program is to speak out – and this is clearly established – in matters of music, and not in

---

28 http://wideo.onet.pl/religia-czy-protest-to-najlepsza-forma-wyrazania-pogladow,26468, w.html; DOA: 17.11.2016; https://ekai.pl/diecezje/radomska/x45404/bp-tomasik-mocniej-reagujmy-na-profanacje-symboli-chrzescijanstwa/; DOA: 17.11.2016; http://ekai.pl/wydarzenia/polska/x45953/apeluje-o-rezygnacje-z-uslug-nergala/; DOA: 17.11.2016.

29 http://www.diecezja.wloclawek.pl/pl/news/20,aktualnosci/367,najwazniejsze-wydarzenia-mijajacego-roku-sprzeciw-wobec-promocji-satanizmu-w-publicznych-mediach; DOA: 17.11.2016; http://prasa.wiara.pl/doc/1020920.Nergal-dziekowal-mi-za-reklame; DOA: 17.11.2016.

30 https://ekai.pl/diecezje/x45967/bp-kaszak-do-ksiezy-nie-wolno-nam-milczec-gdy-atakuje-zlo/; DOA: 17.11.2016.

31 https://ekai.pl/wydarzenia/polska/x45862/nie-mozemy-milczec-gdy-rwie-sie-pismo-swiete/; DOA: 17.11.2016.

others. If he spoke in other matters, it would be a breach of contract, which was concluded with him" (*W tym programie ma wypowiadać się – i jest to wyraźnie ustalone – w sprawach muzyki, a nie w innych. Gdyby wypowiadał się w innych sprawach, byłoby to naruszeniem umowy, jaka z nim została zawarta*) (Juliusz Braun, TVP's CEO in 2011–2015).[32] As it has later turned out, the musician in the program behaved culturally, which Fr. Boniecki commented on "if there was something shocking that was that he is not shocking at all" (*Zachowuje się kulturalnie i delikatnie. Jeśli czymś zaszokował, to właśnie tym, że nie szokuje*).[33]

The protesters adopted quite a different point of view. For example, Bp. Mering wrote to Fr. Boniecki: "Can't you see Father the relationship between Nergal as a Satanist and as a juror? Thus, please treat yourself to eye examinations" (*Nie widzi Ksiądz związku między Nergalem jako satanistą i jako jurorem? Proszę zatem zafundować sobie badania okulistyczne*).[34] The protesters saw Darski's appearance in the show as a satanic manifestation, as if it were a hypertext link referring "Darski-juror" to "Darski-Nergal" and his controversial stage image. This very image provides for them an important "anti-Christian" context in which Darski's 'neutral' participation in the television entertainment show gains another i.e. somehow "religious" meaning. Even if "Darski–juror" is only to assess the voice quality and singing skills of the participants, and would not talk about religion or worldview issues at all, he will still remain "Darski-Nergal" to the protesters.

This is also an example of how the mass media have become the *hypertext system* for the public opinion, or – in Henry Jenkins' terms – an example of *media convergence*, i.e.

> [...] the flow of content across multiple media platforms, the cooperation between multiple media industries, and the migratory behavior of media audiences who will go almost anywhere in search of the kinds of entertainment experiences they want.
>
> [...] Convergence does not occur through media appliances, however sophisticated they may become. Convergence occurs within the brains of individual consumers and through their social interactions with others. Each of us constructs our own personal mythology from bits and fragments of information extracted from the media flow and transformed into resources through which we make sense of our everyday lives.
>
> (Jenkins, 2006, pp. 2–4)

32 http://orka.sejm.gov.pl/Biuletyn.nsf/wgskrnr6/KSP-180; DOA: 17.11.2016.

33 http://fakty.tvn24.pl/ogladaj-online,60/fakty-po-faktach,184613.html (especially 33' 20"-34'09" of the video); DOA: 17.11.2016.

34 http://www.diecezja.wloclawek.pl/pl/news/20,aktualnosci/265,list-otwarty-bp-wieslawa-meringa-do-ks-adama-span-style-background-fff000-boniecki-span-ego-redaktora-seniora-tygodnika-powszechnego; DOA: 17.11.2016.

One could see this "circulation of media content – across different media systems" (Jenkins, 2006, p. 3) or "an information medium that links verbal and nonverbal information" (Landow, 2006, p. 3), when television news and studio discussion programs broadcast in 2011 were illustrated with the footage from *Ucho* club shot in 2007. Consequently, the Bible tearing has suddenly become a present event, and Darski starring in the show has been equated with blasphemy.

4.3.2. Political protests

Religious protests also had a political dimension, which was highlighted by scandalization and the mechanisms of persuasion and elements of political language used in this framework.

According to Kepplinger (2008, pp. 59–60), one of the features of scandals is the occurrence of "culprits, who can be held liable", people whose guilts require penance, and "painful personal consequences", i.e. their dismissal, discharge or resignation. A scandal is thus the result of "behavior of persons acting from ulterior motives who are aware of the negative effects of their conduct" (Kepplinger, 2008, p. 59).

In the case discussed the protesters demanded that Darski is removed from the program, which action, if successful, would prove the incompetence of the TVP's CEO, and in turn entail his eventual resignation or dismissal. The protesters emphasized not only CEO's Braun's failures in management, but also negative traits of his character. For example, further allegations which circulated at the time pointed out that he treated the public media company like a "private playground" (*traktujecie państwo media publiczne jak prywatny folwark*), "does not control it" (*pan nad tym nie panuje*), and pays the satanist a fee from the monthly subscription paid by Poles, i.e. Catholics (Anna Sobecka MP).[35] It was also argued that by employing Darski Braun "violates the law" (*prawo narusza* [...] *kierownictwo*) (Marek Jurek, former conservative MP).[36] Juliusz Braun was also accused of acting in bad faith – according to Bp. Mering, Braun "does not have the will to listen to thousands of people" (*nie ma woli wysłuchania tysięcy ludzi*).[37] All these allegations were to discredit Braun and to convince the public of his guilt. Although Braun repeatedly assured that employing Darski was wrong and cooperation with him would not be

35 http://orka.sejm.gov.pl/Biuletyn.nsf/wgskrnr6/KSP-180; DOA: 17.11.2016.

36 https://ekai.pl/wydarzenia/x45806/prawica-rp-dziekuje-biskupom/; DOA: 17.11.2016.

37 http://www.diecezja.wloclawek.pl/pl/news/20,aktualnosci/263,list-bp-ordynariusza-wieslawa-meringa-do-kaplanow-i-wiernych-swieckich-kosciola-wloclawskiego-w-sprawie-wycofania-nergala-z-2-programu-tvp; DOA: 17.11.2016.

continued, some protesters actually acknowledged their defeat in the protest: "The battle against Nergal we lost..." (*Tę bitwę z Nergalem przegraliśmy...*), indicating their original intention and target of protest.[38]

4.3.3. Persuasion strategies in religious and political protests

Discourses of both religious and political protests have employed diverse mechanisms of persuasion[39], including (1) *emotionalization of reception*, (2) *non-alternative reception*, (3) *simplification of the decomposing of values*, and finally (4) *the mutual world and language*. They are discussed one by one below.

Firstly, emotionalization of reception was realized in the protesters' discourse mainly by using affect-marked lexemes (Moore, 2014), which, among others, clearly demonized Darski. For example, he was called "a practising satanist" (*praktykujący satanista*) by *Katolickie Stowarzyszenie Dziennikarzy* 'Journalists' Catholic Association' or Abp. Głódź, "a declared satanist" (*zdeklarowany satanista*) by *Akcja Katolicka archidiecezji częstochowskiej* 'Catholic Action of the Częstochowa archdiocese', "the enemy of Christian values" (*wróg chrześcijańskich wartości*) by *Katolickie Stowarzyszenie Dziennikarzy* 'Journalists' Catholic Association', or "known for spreading hatred towards the Catholic Church" (*znany* [...] *z* [...] *krzewienia nienawiści wobec Kościoła katolickiego*) by *Polska Federacja Ruchów Obrony Życia* 'Polish Federation of Pro-Life Movement'.[40]

Secondly, the mechanism of non-alternative reception has been used. In the mechanism

> [...] on every of specific states of the process of receive and on every 'level' of this receive – from the language to the world outlook generalizations – the persuasive measures are directing the listener in such a way that in every moment he had only one choice: without any alternative and without any choice.
>
> (Barańczak, 1975, p. 53, cited in Olczyk, 2011)

38 http://ksd.media.pl/aktualnosci/481-wasiukiewicz-t-bitwe-z-nergalem-przegralimy; DOA: 17.11.2016.

39 On persuasive mechanisms in political communication, see Barańczak (1975) and Olczyk (2011).

40 http://ksd.media.pl/component/content/article/1-news/393-ksd-protestuje-wobec-promocji-satanizmu-w-tvp; DOA: 17.11.2016; https://ekai.pl/wydarzenia/polska/x45689/abp-glodz-oburzony-promowaniem-nergala-w-tvp/; DOA: 17.11.2016; https://ekai.pl/diecezje/czestochowska/x46100/akcja-katolicka-archidiecezji-czestochowskiej-protestuje-przeciw-obecnosci-nergala-w-tvp/; DOA: 17.11.2016; http://federacjazycia.pl/pg/pl/wiadomosci/sprzeciw_wobec_promocji_nergala.html; DOA: 17.11.2016.

Such a non-alternative reception was achieved by protesters' using various binary pairs and substitutions in the context. For example, Nergal is Satan and the protagonist is [with] God: "we'll see, if Satan wins in the second instance" (*zobaczymy, czy szatan zwycięży w drugiej instancji* – Ryszard Nowak), Nergal is "the follower of Satan" and we are "the followers of Christ" (*wyznawca Szatana* – Bp. Kaszak), "it is not Nergal who is in danger today, it is Christ in our hearts who is in danger" (*to nie Nergal jest dzisiaj zagrożony, to Chrystus w naszych sercach jest zagrożony* – Bp. Mering), "God is God and Satan is Satan" (*Bóg to jest Bóg, a Szatan to jest Szatan* – Bp. Mering), "we can't elect those who will mock Christ" (*My nie możemy wybierać tych, którzy będą szydzili z Chrystusa* – Bp. Mering).[41] Even if it looks as a choice logically, the receiver has no real choice at all, and so is exempted from decision making.

Thirdly, simplification of the decomposing of values can be seen as convergent with tabloidization. The latter term I understand here as a trend in journalism "towards values characteristic of tabloid newspapers, [which] can be identified as personalization and sensationalism, and the linguistic features through which these values are represented" (Lefkowitz, 2016, p. 2), "dumbing-down" and "entertainization" of newspaper discourse (Ornebring & Jonsson, 2004, p. 284; Rantanen, 2012, pp. 146–147; Van den Bulck, Paulussen & Bels, 2016, p. 4).

What these mechanisms have in common is that they are employed to reject any information inconsistent with the desired image. In the case discussed this can be observed in messages such as *Nergal* [...] *nie jest satanistą*, [...] *odgrywa szatana* [...] *moim zdaniem to jest jasełkowy szatan* [Nergal ... is not a satanist, ... he plays Satan ... in my opinion it is Satan from nativity plays] (Fr. Boniecki), or *nawet jeśli w dużej mierze jest to plastikowy pseudo-satanizm, sceniczna poza* [even if it is largely a plastic pseudo-Satanism, a stage pose] (Fronda.pl).[42] Other examples

41 http://trojmiasto.wyborcza.pl/trojmiasto/1,35612,10375418,Sprawa_Nergala__czyli_czy_szatan_zwyciezy_w_II_instancji.html; DOA: 17.11.2016; https://ekai.pl/diecezje/x45967/bp-kaszak-do-ksiezy-nie-wolno-nam-milczec-gdy-atakuje-zlo/; DOA: 17.11.2016; http://www.diecezja.wloclawek.pl/pl/news/20,aktualnosci/270,bp-mering-do-gimnazjalistow-nie-bronmy-nergala-bo-to-nie-on-jest-dzisiaj-zagrozony-to-chrystus-w-naszych-sercach-jest-zagrozony; DOA: 17.11.2016; http://www.diecezja.wloclawek.pl/site/pliki/pliki/2838023a778dfaecdc212708f721b788.mp3 (especially 14'09" and 9'41" of the audio); DOA: 17.11.2016.

42 http://video.gazeta.pl/9/10834/187667_gazeta_boniecki_nergal_17_12_11.mp4 (especially 0'44"–1'16" of the video); DOA: 17.11.2016; http://wiadomosci.gazeta.pl/wiadomosci/1,114873,10835258,_Zeby_wystapic_w_Radiu_Maryja_musialbym_sie_wyrzec.html; DOA: 17.11.2016; http://fakty.tvn24.pl/ogladaj-online,60/fakty-po-faktach,184613.html; DOA: 17.11.2016; http://www.fronda.pl/a/fronda-modli-sie-za-nergala-i-jego-fanow,14491.html; DOA: 17.11.2016; http://www.tvn24.pl/

of simplification of the decomposing values are e.g. lack of acceptance of certain facts, for instance that Darski as a baptized person is a member of the Church[43], or that he was admitted as godfather of his nephew, or, finally, that the verdict of the Regional District Court in Gdynia of 18th August 2011 acquitted Darski of the charge of offending religious feelings etc.[44]

Other rhetorical resources used for simplification of the decomposing values include metonymies, shifts in meaning and context changing. For example, in one interview politician Sławomir Nowak (*Platforma Obywatelska*, Civic Platform) called Darski using the slang word *ziomal*, which depending on the context may be positive or pejorative (meaning more or less 'homie', 'compatriot', 'countryman', 'companion', 'fellow', but also 'dude', 'mate', 'buddy', or 'bro'), in the sense of a person originating from the same area or someone we know or like.[45] Later, referring to this statement, another politician, Tomasz Nałęcz (*Socjaldemokracja Polska*, Polish Socialdemocracy), used a similar word *krajan* ('compatriot', 'fellow–citizen').[46] Their words were, however, interpreted to mean 'friend', and raised an objection against both of them; the opponents described them in terms of "flirting with satanists" (*flirtować z satanistami*).[47] The right-wing media then published texts about the alliance of liberals, the Left, and satanism[48], which accentuated the crucial political opposition *we* vs. *they*. Other examples of related oppositions are Christianity vs. satanism, the Right vs. the Left, *Prawo i Sprawiedliwość* (PiS, Law and Justice, right wing, radical-conservative party) vs. *Platforma Obywatelska* (PO, Civic Platform, centrists, liberal-democratic party), *Telewizja Polska* (TVP, Polish national television

---

wiadomosci-z-kraju,3/nergal-niewinny-darcie-biblii-forma-sztuki,181508.html; DOA: 17.11.2016; http://polska.newsweek.pl/nergal--polacy-to-waleczni-glupcy,81912,1,1.html; DOA: 17.11.2016.

43 Darski made an act of apostasy, but it took place only a few months after the events discussed, 18th June 2012 – see Darski, Weltrowski and Azarewicz (2012).

44 http://www.newsweek.pl/polska/nergal--polacy-to-waleczni-glupcy,81912,1,1.html; DOA: 17.11.2016; http://www.tvn24.pl/wiadomosci-z-kraju,3/nergal-niewinny-darcie-biblii-forma-sztuki,181508.html; DOA: 17.11.2016.

45 http://wiadomosci.onet.pl/tylko-w-onecie/nowak-nergal-mi-nie-przeszkadza-to-moj-ziomal/mpsm6; DOA: 17.11.2016.

46 http://wiadomosci.wp.pl/kat,1342,title,Nergal-to-moj-krajan-Nie-mozemy-go-eliminowac-z-TVP,wid,13794130,wiadomosc.html?ticaid=116bbe&_ticrsn=3; DOA: 17.11.2016.

47 http://www.fronda.pl/a/terlikowski-czy-prezydent-komorowski-chce-miec-takich-ziomali,14465.html; DOA: 17.11.2016.

48 http://www.fronda.pl/blogi/na-szancach-sw-trojcy/sojusz-liberalizmu-lewicy-ks-bonieckiego-i-satanizmu,22714.html; DOA: 17.11.2016.

broadcaster) vs. *Telewizja Trwam* (private-owned, religious, right-wing television broadcaster), "mohair Christians" (traditional, conservative religiosity) vs. "asphyxiated Christians" (modern, liberal religiosity), or majority vs. minority.

Also, the material analyzed contains instances of the mechanism of exclusion from the discourse, whereby Darski, Fr. Boniecki and political opponents were excluded from public – and religious – discourse. One of the examples of the exclusion mechanisms employed in this discursive struggle between the parties involved is the use of the quite widespread, although colloquial interpretation of the words of Jesus from the Sermon on the Mount: "All you need say is «Yes» if you mean yes, «No» if you mean no; anything more than this comes from the Evil One" (Matthew 5:37; Wansbrough, 1985). The verse from the Gospel of Matthew usually appears in bombastic, strongly affect-marked religious texts. The words "say yes–yes or no–no" are often interpreted as the call for simplification of the Christian discourse, the confirmation of the materialization of the absolutized opposition of Good vs. Evil, the call for clarity, unambiguousness, and radicalism (e.g. Rydzyk, 2002). As a result, more balanced and complex approaches are identified with unacceptable moral relativism. In this very sense these words were used by Bp. Mering, who criticized Fr. Boniecki's view on Darski's participation in *The Voice of Poland*: *Trzeba nam zatem trzymać się pouczenia Jezusa: wasza mowa niech będzie «tak – tak, nie – nie», a co nadto jest, od złego pochodzi. Nie możemy rozmywać prawdy.* [Therefore we have to stick to Jesus' teaching: let your speech be «yes – yes, no – no», and anything more than this comes from evil. We should not blur the truth], or in another text *'Ani jedna Jota' nie może być zmieniona w Ewangelii, a nasze wypowiedzi powinny być: 'Tak, tak – nie, nie!'* ["Not one iota" can be changed in the Gospel and our speeches should be "Yes, yes – no, no"].[49]

Such an interpretation, however, ignores the proper context of the verse, i.e. Matthew 5:33–5:37, and in this way changes its actual meaning. In fact, the passage refers to the second commandment, which forbids the abuse of God's name, and also to the eighth, which forbids false testimony.[50] According to Abp. Życiński,

49 http://www.diecezja.wloclawek.pl/pl/news/20,aktualnosci/253,milczenie-oznac zaloby-zgode-wywiad-zks-bp-wieslawem-meringiem-dla-naszego-dziennika-; DOA: 17.11.2016; http://www.diecezja.wloclawek.pl/pl/news/20,aktualnosci/265,list-otwarty-bpwieslawa-meringa-do-ks-adama-bonieckiego-redaktora-seniora-tygod nika-powszechnego; DOA: 17.11.2016.

50 Cf. Matthew 5:33–37 and Jacob 5:12, both referring to Exodus 20:7; Leviticus 19:12; Number 30:3 and Deuteronomy 5:11.
The Greek New Testament critical apparatus also lists Deuteronomy 23:22; Isaiah 66:11; Matthew 23:22; Acts of Apostles 7:40; Psalms 48:2, regarding oath (vow), and referring

the popularity of the 'radical' and 'black and white' interpretation of the passage stems, on the one hand, from Manichaean dualism rejected by Christianity, and on the other, from radical antitheses of Marxism:

Można obawiać się, że nauczanie Chalcedonu zostało dziś zarzucone przez środowiska, które widzą we współczesnej kulturze przede wszystkim walkę absolutnego dobra z absolutnym złem. Po co wysilać się, by poszukiwać ukrytej jedności, gdy wystarczy przyjąć, że istnieje tylko jeden rodzaj dobra, rozdzielanego w dodatku z klucza partyjnego.
(http://www.jozefzycinski.pl/index.php/tesci-kokruchy/4-okruchy/247-chalcedon-zapomniany; DOA: 17.11.2016)

[One can fear that the teaching of Chalcedon is today abandoned by the communities who most of all see in the contemporary culture the fight between absolute good and absolute evil. Why make the efforts to look for the hidden unity if it is enough to assume there is only one kind of the good, additionally divided on a party basis.]

In the course of time the simple interpretation of the verse was adopted as a criterion for evaluation of religious discourse, and is still used to eliminate from the discourse community people who present a different view, and thus are treated as discursive opponents.[51] This practice stands in clear contradiction to both rules of social communication adopted by the Church, "which is seen first of all as dialogue, exchange, solidarity and the creation of positive relations", and the Christian way of communicating, which takes "the form of a communication which is honest and open, responsible and respectful of others", and manifests itself "in the way one communicates choices, preferences and judgements that are fully consistent with the Gospel, even when it is not spoken of specifically" (Benedict XVI, 2011).

In terms of Grunig's (1997, 2005) *situational theory of publics*, the above-discussed process can activate what he calls *aware* vs. *latent publics*; or *activating* vs. *arousal* publics in Hallahan's (2000) terms, or *activating latent* vs. *apathetic* vs. *aware* publics in Smith's (2013) terms. In general, these concepts correspond with

---

to verse 37 also: 2 Corinthians 1:17 and Jacob 5:12, paralleling with „ναὶ ναί, οὒ οὔ" („yes yes, no no"): cf. Aland, Black, Martini, Metzger and Wikgren (1988, pp. 15, 789). The second and eighth commandments are also referred to in the *Catechism of the Catholic Church* (1997, pp. 518–522, 591–601) in CCC 2142–2167 and 2464–2513, which recommends "discretion in calling upon God" (CCC 2153); http://ccc.usccb.org/flipbooks/catechism/index.html; DOA: 17.11.2016.

51 Cf.: http://barykada.salon24.pl/278520,niech-wasza-mowa-bedzie-tak-tak-nie-nie-zdrada, DOA: 17.11.2016; http://info.wiara.pl/doc/555920.tak-tak-nie-nie, DOA: 17.11.2016.

the basic friend vs. enemy antithesis, or a more complex one distinguishing the other, the stranger, the different, and the alien as presented in Schmitt's (2007, pp. 26–27) concept of the *political*. According to Schmitt's (2007) model,

> [e]motionally the enemy is easily treated as being evil and ugly, because every distinction, most of all the political, as the strongest and most intense of the distinctions and categorizations, draws upon other distinctions for support. This does not alter the autonomy of such distinctions. […] The morally good, aesthetically beautiful, and economically profitable need not necessarily become the friend in the specifically political sense of the word.
> (Schmitt, 2007, p. 27)

The first element of the model (treating enemy as being evil) is present in the protesters' discourse in demonization of Darski and other political opponents, whilst the second element (who is a friend?) in their using the political category as the overriding criterion of inclusion or exclusion of the other's being friend. In this case 'the friend' does need to be another believer (e.g. Fr. Boniecki, "asphyxiated Christians" etc.).

The analyzed case also reveals a struggle between political and religious discourses in general. Religious discourse becomes a function of the political one: the former substantiates and strengthens the latter, and, as a result, persuades the public to vote for the suggested party. A relevant example in the case examined is Fronda.pl, a Polish right-wing portal, which defines their initiative to pray for Nergal as 'alternative', in contrast to 'mainstream' political actions taken by the activists.[52] Likewise, some statements made by certain bishops (e.g. Bp. Mering, Abp. Głódz, Abp. Michalik etc.) due to their ecclesiastical jurisdiction cannot be regarded as official statements of the Roman Catholic Church in Poland. Exceptions to this line are the moderate statement of the Polish Episcopal Conference and cautious remarks of its spokesman, Fr. Dr. Józef Kloch.[53] While some of these statements can be considered to be messages used in religious communication with the officials' respective diocesans, most of them were political in their character.

The described tensions and struggles between politics and religion can also be considered to form a new *nodal discourse* (Fairclough, 2005, p. 81), which term refers to a particular kind of discourse which imagines, operationalizes and

52 http://www.fronda.pl/a/fronda-modli-sie-za-nergala-i-jego-fanow,14491.html; DOA: 17.11.2016.

53 http://ekai.pl/wydarzenia/polska/x45819/reakcja-biskupow-nie-jest-przesadzona; DOA: 17.11.2016; http://old.episkopat.pl/dokumenty/komunikaty_zp_kep/4575.0,Komunikat_z_356_Zebrania_Plenarnego_Konferencji_Episkopatu_Polski.prn, DOA: 17.11.2016;

actualizes a new political-social-religious fix/order. In other words, it is a process of subsuming, articulating, simplifying, and condensing other discourses. As a result of this process some discourses are dominated, or hegemonized by others.

4.4. Publicity and viral communication

The third process of communication involved in the events discussed is of viral nature, and in the case discussed it served to position social agents (in particular Darski and Bp. Mering) in their publics. In the case of Nergal, as in the self-scandalization/shockvertising and their amplification performed in *The Voice of Poland* campaign, publicity contributed to attracting his target audience from the general audience, and strengthened his position among the fans. In the case of Bp. Mering, publicity positioned him among one group in the Polish Episcopate. This positioning is evidenced in a number of statements made by other hierarchs (e.g. Abp. Głódź); the intended response of their social networks was viral replication (i.e. citing the protagonists' names), which tactic proved effective given the sheer number of related media publications. The social actors involved appear to have realized this fact; for instance, Bp. Mering later commented:

> *Doniesiono mi, że sam Nergal dziękował za reklamę, jaką mu zrobiłem. Uważam jednak, że ta „reklama" zawsze działa w obie strony. Być może dzięki mojej reakcji bardzo wielu ludzi dowiedziało się o Nergalu, ale też wielu zorientowało się, kim on jest. Wszyscy już wiedzą, że ogromna część społeczeństwa katolickiego nie życzy sobie w sferze publicznej takich zachowań jak zachowania Nergala. Można zatem powiedzieć, że i Nergal zrobił katolikom reklamę.*
>
> (http://prasa.wiara.pl/doc/1020920.Nergal-dziekowal-mi-za-reklame/4; DOA: 17.11.2016)
>
> [It was reported to me that Nergal himself thanked for advertising which I did to him. However, I believe that this "advertisement" always works both ways. Maybe thanks to my reaction many people have found out Nergal, but also many of them have figured out who he is. Everyone already knows that the huge part of the Catholic society does not wish such behaviors as Nergal's in the public sphere. It can be said that also Nergal has done advertising to Catholics.]

Nergal has also considered "tabloid lies and baying of [his] cranky adversaries" (*tabloidowe kłamstwa i ujadanie moich nawiedzonych adwersarzy*) to contribute to his promotion: *Kościół znuff mnie wspiera, za co dziękuję bardzo* [the Church supports me again, for which I thank you very much] (Darski, 2011, p. 41; the quote is a comment on the book by Posacki, 2011). Interestingly, this point has also been stated by Fronda.pl: *Jesteśmy również świadomi, że kolejne bojkoty to darmowa reklama dla Nergala i jego poglądów* [we are ... aware that further boycotts are free advertising for Nergal and his views].[54] In addition, Fr. Boniecki is of the opinion that Darski is the one who benefits from the situation: *Rozdmuchiwanie tej sprawy może przynieść protestującym skutek odwrotny od zamierzonego* [Hyping the case may be counterproductive for the protesters].[55]

5. Conclusions

The study of the scandal caused by Nergal's participation in the talent show *The Voice of Poland* has shown how political discourse hegemonizes religious discourse. The observed tensions and struggles between various social agents involved exhibit the process of formation of a new nodal discourse, which articulates, condenses, subsumes and simplifies various political, social and religious threads into a new order. Scandalization and diverse persuasive mechanisms as well as the political category of the enemy were widely used in the process. It has been revealed that application of publicity, activism, and propaganda at the interface between politics, religion, and mass culture can cause big social repercussions in Poland. Metonymies, shifts in meaning, context changing, hyperbolization and generalization were also used to supersede the religious category of the *neighbor* by the political category of the *enemy*. The identified shifts in the religious language in favor of the political could affect the Church's message and mission, leading to their both disruptions and simplifications (tabloidization).

References

Anonymous. (2011). 100 najbardziej wpływowych Polaków. *Wprost*, 45/2011 (1500). 7th November 2011, 16–75.

Aland, K., Black, M., Martini, C. M., Metzger, B. M., & Wikgren, A. (Eds.) (1988). *The Greek New Testament*, Stuttgart: United Bible Societies.

Barańczak, S. (1975). Słowo–perswazja–kultura masowa. *Twórczość*, 7, 44–59.

Benedict XVI (2001). *Truth, Proclamation and Authenticity of Life in the Digital Age*. Message of His Holiness Pope Benedict XVI for the 45th World Communications Day, Vatican.

Catechism of the Catholic Church. (1997). Vatican: United States Catholic Conference, Inc. & Libreria Editrice Vaticana.

---

54 http://www.fronda.pl/a/fronda-modli-sie-za-nergala-i-jego-fanow,14491.html; DOA: 17.11.2016.

55 http://www.gazetakrakowska.pl/artykul/451199,krakow-kardynal-dziwisz-pietnuje-nergala,id,t.html; DOA: 17.11.2016.

Coombs, W. T., & Holladay, S. J. (2014). *It's Not Just PR: Public Relations in Society.* Chichester: Wiley Blackwell.

Dahl, D. W., Frankenberger, K. D., & Manchanda, R. V. (2003). Does it pay to shock? Reactions to shocking and nonshocking advertising content among university students. *Journal of Advertising Research*, 43(3), 268–280.

Darski, A. (2011). Nergal dziękuje Kościołowi. Rozmowę przeprowadził P. Najsztub. *Wprost*, 50/2011(1505), 38–42.

Darski, A., Weltrowski, P., & Azarewicz, K. (2012) *Spowiedź heretyka. Sacrum profanum.* Warszawa: G+J.

Fairclough, N. (2003). *Analysing Discourse: Textual analysis for social research.* London: Routledge.

Fairclough, N. (2005). Critical discourse analysis. *Marges Linguistiques*, 9, 76–94.

Gerring, J. (2007). *Case Study Research: Principles and Practices.* Cambridge: Cambridge University Press.

Grunig, J. E. (1997). A situational theory of publics: Conceptual history, recent challenges, and new research. In D. Moss, T. McManus & D. Verčič (Eds.), *Public relations research: An international perspective.* Boston: International Thomson Business Press, 3–46.

Grunig, J. E. (2005). Situational theory of publics. In R. L. Heath (Ed.), *Encyclopedia of public relations*, Vol. 2. Thousand Oaks, London & New Delhi: Sage Publications Inc., 778–780.

Grunig, J. E., & Hunt, T. (1984). *Managing Public Relations.* New York: Holt, Rinehart and Winston.

Hallahan, K. (2000). Inactive Publics: The Forgotten Publics in Public Relations. *Public Relations Review*, 26(4), 499–515.

Jenkins, H. (2006) *Convergence culture: where old and new media collide.* New York & London: New York University Press.

Jordan, M. (2004). *Dictionary of Gods and Goddesses*, New York: Facts On File, 218.

Kepplinger, H. M. (2008). *Mechanizmy skandalizacji w mediach.* Translated by A. Kożuch, Kraków: Wydawnictwo Uniwersytetu Jagiellońskiego.

Landow, G. P. (2006) *Hypertext 3.0: Critical Theory and New Media in an Era of Globalization.* Baltimore: The Johns Hopkins University Press.

Lefkowitz, J. (2016). 'Tabloidization' or Dual-Convergence. Quoted speech in tabloid and 'quality' British newspapers 1970–2010. *Journalism Studies.* doi: 10.1080/1461670X.2016.1190662.

Moore, R. L. (2014). Affect-marked Lexemes and Their Relational Model Correlates. *Faculty Publications. Paper 107.* Retrieved from: http://scholarship.rollins.edu/as_facpub/107; DOA: 17.11.2016.

Olczyk, T. (2011) We, them and the virtual universes of the tv political advertisement. *Forum Artis Rhetoricae*, 26(3) 2011. Retrieved from: http://www.retoryka.edu.pl/index.php?option=com_content&view=article&id=55. DOA: 17.11.2016.

Ornebring, H., & Jonsson, A. M. (2004). Tabloid Journalism and the Public Sphere: A Historical Perspective on Tabloid Journalism. *Journalism Studies*, 5(3), 283–295.

Parry, S., Jones, R., Stern, P., & Robinson, M. (2013). 'Shockvertising': An exploratory investigation into attitudinal variations and emotional reactions to shock advertising. *Journal of Consumer Behaviour*, 12(2), 112–121.

Posacki, A. (2011). *Jak przeciwstawiać się złu? Demonologia na dzisiejsze czasy*. Kraków: Wydawnictwo M.

Rantanen, T. (2012) In Nationalism We Trust? In M. Castells, J. Caraca & G. Carduso (Eds.), *Aftermath: The Cultures of the Economic Crisis*, Oxford: Oxford University Press, 132–153.

Rydzyk, T. (2002). *Tak – tak, nie – nie*. Warszawa: Wydawnictwo Sióstr Loretanek.

Schmitt, C. (2007). *The Concept of the Political*. Translated by G. Schwab. Chicago & London: The University of Chicago Press.

Smith, R. D. (2013). *Strategic Planning for Public Relations*. New York & London: Routledge.

Stacks, D. W. (2005). Case Study. In R. L. Heath (ed.), *Encyclopedia of public relations*, Vol. 1. Thousand Oaks, London & New Delhi: Sage Publications Inc., 117–118.

Stacks, D. W. (2011). *Primer of public relations research*. New York & London: The Guilford Press.

Anonymous. (1997). *Ustawa z dnia 6 czerwca 1997 r. – Kodeks karny* (Dz. U. z 1997 r. Nr 88, poz. 553 z późn. zm.)

Van den Bulck, H., Paulussen, S., & Bels, A. (2016). Celebrity news as hybrid journalism: An assessment of celebrity coverage in Flemish newspapers and magazines. *Journalism* 1464884916657523, first published on 8th July 2016 as doi:10.1177/1464884916657523.

Vilpponen, A., Winter, S., & Sundqvis, S. (2006). Electronic Word-of-Mouth in Online Environments: Exploring Referral Network Structure and Adoption Behavior. *Journal of Interactive Advertising*, 6(2), 63–77.

Wansbrough, H. (Ed.) (1985) *The New Jerusalem Bible*. New York & London: Doubleday & Darton, Longman & Todd.

Warzecha, A. (2012). Krytyczna Analiza Dyskursu w public relations (koncepcja badania). *Konteksty Kultury*, 9, 189–205.

Warzecha, A. (2013). *Działania public relations Kościoła katolickiego w Polsce z perspektywy Krytycznej Analizy Dyskursu*. Rozprawa doktorska napisana pod kierunkiem prof. dr. hab. UŚ Jacka Warcholi. Katowice.

Warzecha, A. (2014). Krytyczna Analiza Dyskursu (KAD) w ujęciu Normana Fairclougha. Zarys problematyki. *Konteksty Kultury*, 11(2), 164–189.

Julita Śmigielska

University of Warsaw, Poland

Legitimation strategies in Russian political discourse on the annexation of Crimea

Abstract: The paper analyzes legitimation strategies in Russian political discourse concerning the annexation of Crimea on the example of Vladimir Putin's speech of 18th March 2014. Carried out with methods of (Critical) Discourse Analysis the study investigates relevant linguistic phenomena in their social context and reveals ideological properties inherent to political discourse. The analytical categories applied in the paper include mainly classification of legitimation strategies proposed by van Leeuwen (2008): *authorization*, *moral evaluation* and *rationalization* as well as the *Us vs. Them* polarization typical of political discourse. The results of the study show that the main conceptualization frame of the analyzed discourse is based on the thesis-antithesis construction: the attribution of lexical items with positive axiological value to the in-group and negative evaluation of the out-group, whereas argumentation strategies used for legitimation predominantly refer to history and law.

1. Introduction

Symbolic power relations in society, *ideology* and *manipulation* in language are notions of central importance for Critical Discourse Analysis (Fairclough, 1999; Wodak, 2007; Duszak & Fairclough, 2008). Focusing on these aspects, critical discourse studies investigate, among others, discursive practices immersed in the broader social, cultural and historical contexts. One domain in which relations between symbolic power and language are probably most evident and hence have frequently been subject to CDA studies (e.g. Chilton, 2004; Okulska & Cap, 2010a, b; Wodak, 2012) is politics, in which area a particularly interesting aspect involving such relations is *legitimation* (Cap, 2008; van Leeuwen, 2008; Verschueren, 2012). Specifically, legitimation as a discursive phenomenon aims at the implementation of ideology by providing justification against the (possible) accusations of illegal actions allegedly performed by the political body concerned, gaining in turn social acceptance for controversial political issues and presenting the agent's concerned positive self-image (Cap, 2013).

The article presents a short overview of linguistic legitimation strategies in Russian political discourse on the example of the speech by Vladimir Putin of

18th March 2014, which is arguably the most representative example of Russian political rhetoric concerning the annexation of Crimea. The paper is structured as follows: in section 2 I discuss theoretical underpinnings of the research, while section 3 presents the results of qualitative-methods based critical discourse analysis of Vladimir Putin's speech. Following Fairclough's ([1989] 2001) model, the analysis includes three main steps: *description*, *interpretation* and *explanation*.

2. Theoretical underpinnings of the study

In this section I present the main theoretical concepts discussed in the paper: *discourse* and *genre* (section 2.1), *political discourse* (section 2.2), *political speech* as a genre of political discourse (section 2.3), and *legitimation* (section 2.4).

2.1. Discourse and genre

The notion of *discourse* is a vague concept which has been defined in different ways. Firstly, it reflects the relationship between language and social practices. Accordingly, discourse may be understood as an abstract notion, while a text is its particular realization (Wodak, 2008, p. 6). In a broader sense, discourse is conceptualized as a *text in context.* It may be also viewed as a kind of social activity involving verbal communication (language) and nonverbal elements. In this approach discourse is seen as "*linguistic action*, be it written, visual or oral communication, verbal or nonverbal, undertaken by social actors in specific setting determined by social rules, norms and conventions" (Wodak, 2008, p. 5).

By contrast, a socially constructed relationship between communicative acts and their aims is represented in the notion of *genre* (Duszak & Fairclough, 2008, p. 9). Like *discourse*, the term is defined in different ways. In an early definition of the concept Bakhtin ([1986] 2000) defines s*peech genres* as "relatively stable types of utterances" in a particular field of language use. By contrast, Swales (1990, p. 58) defines *genre* as "a class of communicative events, the members of which share some set of communicative purposes". The central notion in his theory is the concept of *discourse community* that determines common goals of communication and, as a result, stimulates the emergence of new genres.

In general, it can be argued that genres reflect particular patterns in language use and social effects of texts. They are described as sets of texts typical of a particular communication event and performing the same function in a given social, cultural, historical and socio-pragmatic context (Duszak, 1998, p. 214).

2.2. Political discourse

The topic of the present study is the role of language in political communication. As has been already said, political discourse is the type of discourse in which the relationship between language use and symbolic power relations in society is arguably best reflected. According to Wilson (2001, p. 398), political discourse includes "formal/informal political contexts and political actors [...], that is, *inter alia,* politicians, political institutions, governments, political media, and political supporters operating in political environments to achieve political goals". *Political discourse* can thus be defined as the discourse of political actors used in the institutional context. By contrast, a definition based on some of the main characteristics of political discourse (e.g. *power, conflict, control* or *determination*) is problematic, since these qualities may also be found in other domains of social life and, consequently, in other discourses (Wilson, 2001, p. 398).

Discussing the relation between political discourse and its social impact, Chilton (2004, p. 14) observes that "political actors recognize the role of language because its use has effects". A text produced becomes a social event which has real effects – it can influence the audience's knowledge, beliefs and/or attitudes, and can also shape people's behaviour. Political texts, likewise, can affect social cognition, in particular by (re)producing specific ideologies and implementing them in the given social context (Fairclough, 2001).

A distinctive property of political discourse is its persuasive and goal-oriented character, in that each linguistic means may fulfill some political function, for instance legitimating political decisions or creating a politician's positive self-image.

Considering the above-discussed features political discourse is a frequent topic of discourse studies (Chilton, 2004; Okulska & Cap, 2010b; Wodak 2012), generally characterized by the *reflective-interpretative* nature (Okulska & Cap, 2010b, p. 402). Such an approach not only offers a description of political processes (*reflection*), but also offers insights into social processes (*interpretation*).

As far as contemporary Russian political discourse is concerned, the research in this field includes such topics as e.g. the use of the personal pronoun 'us' in Russian political discourse (Pyykkö, 2002), the discursive construction of Russia in the international news coverage (Macgilchrist, 2011), pragmatic aspects of political questions and answers (Sivenkova, 2013), the semantic field of power (Dobrovolskij & Pöppel, 2013), analysis of grammatical markers of ideology on the example of political parties programmes (Karamova, 2014), or Russian politicians' rhetoric concerning Russia-EU relations (Schiffers, 2015).

2.3. Political speech as a genre

Critical Discourse Analysis views *political speech* in terms of the relation between linguistic entities and political, social and cultural background of the utterance. Charteris-Black (2014, p. xiii) defines *political speech* as a "coherent stream of spoken language that is usually prepared for delivery by a speaker to an audience for a purpose on a political occasion". Its most important definitional aspects are related to the question of how its language is adjusted to the given social and cultural context, who the audience is, and what the goal of the speaker is (Charteris-Black, 2014).

There are several contextual components of a political speech that should be considered in the process of its preparation and delivery. The most important are: the audience (which may be further divided into *direct audience* present at the place of the communication event and *second-frame audience*, which is reached by the political actor through the media), the aim of the speech, shared knowledge between the speaker and the audience, and the speaker's assumptions about the addressee's knowledge (Charteris-Black, 2014, p. xvi). Furthermore, the process of communication is affected by the level of shared knowledge between the speaker and the audience, as the amount of information expressed implicitly and explicitly in the speech is adjusted to the estimated scope of knowledge of the audience.

As far as the internal structure of the political speech is concerned, speeches have their distinctive rhetorical tropes and figures, strategies of argumentation and legitimation (Wodak, 2008, p. 18), the latter being of particular interest in this study. What is more, the character of political activity is reflected in the goal-oriented strategies in political discourse. Thus not only the choice of particular lexical items, but, most importantly, the choice of information presented in the speech are dictated by the goal of the speaker. The latter is much centered on the legitimation of political activity, presentation of axiological opposition between political supporters and opponents and/or presenting the politician's positive self-image.

2.4. Legitimation in political discourse

Legitimation is a complex phenomenon that can be analyzed from different perspectives: linguistic, political, psychological and sociological. It can be defined as "establishing one's interests as broadly acceptable" (Eagleton, [1991] 2007, p. 34). In linguistics, the concept of legitimation was described e.g. by van Dijk (1998), Chilton (2004) and Cap (2008, 2013). According to Cap (2008, p. 22), legitimation can be defined as "a linguistic enactment of the speaker's right to be obeyed".

One of the key concepts for legitimation is the *symbolic power*, which is a form of domination in society defined "in terms of the *preferential access to, or control over, public discourse*" (van Dijk, 2008, p. 14; original emphasis). In contemporary society symbolic power differentials can be found in certain social domains, e.g. politics, economy or education. Each of these fields has its own range of genres, styles, aims and internal structure of institution, which, among others, indicate the preferred modes of communication (van Dijk, 2008, p. 40). As for social power, it can be viewed as a form of control over public discourse: "[p]ower does not derive from language, but language can be used to challenge power, to subvert it, to alter distributions of power in the short and long term" (Wodak, 2007, p. 11). In this model, political institutions with their privileged position in public discourse are referred to as *symbolic elites* (van Dijk, 2008).

From a pragmatic point of view, legitimation is a speech act used for providing justification for past or present actions that may be criticized (van Dijk, 1998, p. 255). Justification of a political actor's actions and reasons why his/her policy should be obeyed is communicated explicitly or implicitly by means of ideological meanings or reference to moral values (van Dijk, 1998).

Accordingly, the process of legitimation is strictly connected with the naturalization of ideology and common sense (van Dijk, 1998), which means that the speaker's views are presented as a natural organization of discourse. Additionally, a value system broadly recognized in a given society, authority of tradition and custom, and expert knowledge are of crucial significance in the process of legitimation, whose overall effect is enhanced through the choice of specific lexicogrammatical resources (Cap, 2013).

It should be also noted that legitimation has the opposite concept *delegitimation*, which stands for the negative construction of the political opponent's image, questioning his/her morality and rationality of actions undertaken by him/her (van Dijk, 1998).

The classification of legitimation strategies applied in the present analysis was proposed by van Leeuwen (2008, p. 105) and includes the following categories:

1. *Authorization*, that is, legitimation by reference to the authority of tradition, custom, law, and/or person in whom institutional authority of some kind is vested.
2. *Moral evaluation*, that is, legitimation by (often very oblique) reference to value systems.
3. *Rationalization*, that is, legitimation by reference to the goals and uses of institutionalized social action and to the knowledge that society has constructed to endow them with cognitive validity.
4. *Mythopoesis*, that is, legitimation conveyed through narratives whose outcomes reward legitimate actions and punish nonlegitimate actions.

(van Leeuwen, 2008, p. 105)

The above-mentioned classification (and similar ones) helps to grasp all the important constituents of political discourse, as it relates to as diverse issues as moral values, political context or institutional authority. Despite the differences in the premises used for justification, one element which is present in all kinds of legitimation is *inclusion* and *exclusion* (van Dijk, 1998), i.e. strategies of positive self-presentation (*Us*) and negative other-presentation (*Them*). In texts this division is connected, *inter alia,* with the inclusive and exclusive use of the personal pronoun *we*. In particular, the inclusive *we* has an important persuasive function in a political speech. It is often used by the speaker to emphasize the unity with the audience, which is represented as a part of the speaker's in-group (Gruszczyńska, 2012, p. 157). The persuasive use of the inclusive *we* also implies the unity of actions and/or interests between the speaker and the audience (Kłosińska, 2004, p. 28).

3. Legitimation strategies in the discourse on the annexation of Crimea

This section presents the results of an analysis of legitimation strategies in Russian political discourse on the annexation of Crimea. The material selected for this purpose is arguably one of the most representative examples of the Russian legitimation rhetoric concerning the annexation of Crimea, that is Vladimir Putin's address delivered in Kremlin on 18th March 2014. The event took place two days after the referendum on the status of Crimea, which was recognized invalid by the international community.

Putin's speech may be divided into several moves: (1a) announcing the results of the referendum in Crimea and (1b) describing it as a manifestation of the free will of its inhabitants, (2) persuading the audience about the referendum's compliance with international regulations, (3a) providing a historical justification of the described events, (3b) presenting the mutual history of Crimea and Russia as the main uniting factor, (4) informing the audience about the moral obligation of Russia to protect the Russian-speaking population outside the country and, finally, (5) polemics with Western countries opposing the annexation of Crimea (their stances being constructed on delegitimation strategies). As is shown below, legitimation in the analyzed speech is based on what van Leeuwen (2008) refers to as *authorization, moral evaluation* and *rationalization* (see also section 2.4).

Following Charteris-Black's (2014) model (see section 2.3), the audience of the speech may be divided into direct audience (people present in the Kremlin) and second-frame audience (media audience in Russia and abroad). Therefore, taking the context into consideration, it may be stated that Putin's legitimation strategies were aimed both at the Russian audience and the international community.

The first legitimation strategy used in the text is *authorization* by the reference to history; in fact, historical motives are present in Putin's speech from the very beginning. The Russian president begins his address with an introduction in which he claims that the background of the referendum's results is connected directly to historical motives.

(1)
Чтобы понять, почему был сделан именно такой выбор, достаточно знать историю Крыма, знать, что ***значила и значит*** *Россия для Крыма и Крым для России.*[1]

[To understand the reason behind such a choice it is enough to know the history of Crimea and what Russia and Crimea **have always meant** for each other.][2]

As example (1) shows, it is implied that there exists a special bond between Crimea and Russia. The importance of this relationship is emphasized by the reference both to the past and present times; the sense of continuity of this relation is reflected by the use of verb *значить* 'to mean' used twice, in the past and present tenses (*значила и значит* '*lit.* meant and means'). References to the past serve as a ground for granting the same importance of the territory of Crimea for Russia nowadays. Putin also stresses the mutual character of the relationship between Crimea and Russia as reflected in the results of the referendum by repeating the geographical names *Россия* 'Russia' and *Крым* 'Crimea' in two different orders saying that not only is Crimea important for Russia, but also Russia for Crimea.

Another instance of *authorization* by the reference to history is providing the historical background from the beginnings of Rus, through the Communism and the collapse of the USSR up to present times. Putin builds his argumentation on the premises of historical continuity, having its origins in ancient times and the origin of Russian nationality.

1 Transcription of the original version of the speech available at the Official website of the President of Russia, URL: http://news.kremlin.ru/news/20603. DOA: 06.06.2015.

2 Transcription of the English translation of the speech available at the Official website of the President of Russia, URL: http://eng.kremlin.ru/transcripts/6889. DOA: 06.06.2015.

(2)

В Крыму буквально всё пронизано нашей общей историей и гордостью. Здесь древний Херсонес, где принял крещение святой князь Владимир. Его духовный подвиг – обращение к православию – предопределил общую культурную, ценностную, цивилизационную основу, которая объединяет народы России, Украины и Белоруссии. В Крыму – могилы русских солдат, мужеством которых Крым в 1783 году был взят под Российскую державу. Крым – это Севастополь, город -легенда, город великой судьбы, город-крепость и Родина русского черноморского военного флота. Крым – это Балаклава и Керчь, Малахов курган и Сапун-гора. Каждое из этих мест свято для нас, это символы русской воинской славы и невиданной доблести.

[Everything in Crimea speaks of our shared history and pride. This is the location of ancient Khersones, where Prince Vladimir was baptised. His spiritual feat of adopting Orthodoxy predetermined the overall basis of the culture, civilisation and human values that unite the peoples of Russia, Ukraine and Belarus. The graves of Russian soldiers whose bravery brought Crimea into the Russian empire are also in Crimea. This is also Sevastopol – a legendary city with an outstanding history, a fortress that serves as the birthplace of Russia's Black Sea Fleet. Crimea is Balaklava and Kerch, Malakhov Kurgan and Sapun Ridge. Each one of these places is dear to our hearts, symbolising Russian military glory and outstanding valour.]

Example (2) shows that in Putin's rhetoric historical events occurring in Crimea are given the status of triggers of the momentous change in the nation's life, a source of Crimeans' and Russians' mutual culture, heritage and spiritual life. The axiological construction of arguments relies on some universal values uniting the Eastern world and religion as a source of tradition and culture (hence *authorization by the reference to tradition*). Putin mentions historical events in order to connect associations about Crimea with the feeling of national pride among Russian people: *Каждое из этих мест свято для нас* [Each one of these places is dear to our hearts]. The message is further intensified by the opening assertion: *В Крыму буквально всё пронизано нашей общей историей и гордостью* [Everything in Crimea speaks of our shared history and pride].

Putin's rhetoric is constructed on the opposition between the "glorious" Russian chapter in Crimean history and the "tragic" Ukrainian times; this contrast is expressed in the form of a classic thesis-antithesis construction. At the lexical level, for instance, this opposition is expressed with antonymous evaluative vocabulary. Thus, the description of the shared Russian-Crimean history makes use of words and expressions with positive connotations: *гордость* 'pride'; *культурная, ценностная, цивилизационная основа* 'basis of the culture, civilization, human values'; *город-легенда* 'legendary city'; *воинская слава и невиданная доблесть* 'military glory, outstanding valour'. By contrast, the description of the later period in the history of Crimea, and Ukraine itself, includes negatively connoted items: *вопиющая историческая несправедливость* 'outrageous historical injustice'; *политический и государственный кризис* 'political and state crisis'; *принудительная ассимиляции* 'forced assimilation'.

Negative evaluation is also present in the descriptions of the actions of Russia's alleged adversaries, which feature lexical items connected with crime. Thus, for instance, when referring to Crimea as a part of Ukraine, the speaker presents this event as the "historical injustice", using the verbs *обокрали* 'robbed' and *ограбили* 'plundered', whose sequence is based on the gradual increase in the semantics of crime weight. On the other hand, such conceptualization depicts the resulting situation as a tragedy of the Russian nation.

In his speech Putin also comments on the internal situation of Russia in the past, justifying its "passiveness" towards Crimea so far. Following the collapse of the Soviet Union, Russia is presented metaphorically as a person, humbly accepting the will imposed by external circumstances (cf. *Опустила голову и смирилась, проглотила эту обиду* [It humbly accepted the situation]). Such illustration of events from the history serves as another legitimation strategy for the annexation of Crimea in the speech.

In sum, the thesis-antithesis construction is one of the main conceptualization frames aimed at persuading the audience to accept the speaker's arguments. By using this rhetorical technique Putin presents two contrastive interpretations of past and present events. The moment when Crimea became a part of Ukraine in the 1950s is constructed in his discourse as the unlawful decision made with neither the consent of the people nor consideration of their ethnical background. By contrast, the annexation of Crimea by Russia is conceptualized as acting in the name of the people's free will.

Putin's rhetoric on the annexation of Crimea is framed as a discourse of historic change. The president presents the decision about the annexation of Crimea as a momentous event in the life of the Russian nation. The feeling of success and pride at the time of the event affects the interpretation of the further content of his speech. To achieve this goal Putin increasingly uses lexical items emphasizing the great importance of the said event for Russia, e.g. *жизненно важное значение, историческое значение* 'vital, historic significance'; *переломные исторические моменты* 'historic turning points' in examples (3) and (4):

(3)
[…] *сегодня мы собрались по вопросу, который имеет* ***жизненно важное значение, историческое значение*** *для всех нас*

[(…) we have gathered here today in connection with an issue that is of **vital, historic significance** to all of us]

(4)
Именно в такие ***переломные исторические моменты*** *проверяется зрелось и сила духа нации.*

[It is at **historic turning points** such as these that a nation demonstrates its maturity and strength of spirit.]

Another legitimation strategy used in Putin's speech is *authorization* by the reference to law. It involves two main arguments presented from the speaker's point of view: the request of Crimean authorities for protection of the rights of Crimea residents and the referendum held in Crimea on 16th March 2014. The outcome of the referendum is presented in Putin's rhetoric as a manifestation of the people's will and the main legal basis for the annexation of Crimea by the Russian Federation.

The following excerpt from Putin's speech exemplifies one of the core argumentation schemes of his rhetoric, *authorization*:

(5)
Дело – за политическим решением самой России. А оно может быть ***основано только на воле народа****, потому что только народ является* ***источником любой власти****.*

[Now this is a matter for Russia's own political decision, and any decision here can be **based only on the people's will**, because the people is the ultimate **source of all authority**.]

Here Putin directly refers to the 'people's will' as the "source of all authority" and the only premise for legitimation of his political decisions.

An additional argument used in the speech for legitimation of Russian actions undertaken in Crimea is the need for protection of the Russian-speaking population in Crimea (see example 6). The role of Russia in the 'separation' of Crimea from Ukraine is conceptualized as purely supportive, not decisive. In this respect Putin speaks about the help to "create" conditions for voting, but at the same time denies the presence of Russian armed forces in Crimea. The temporal aspect of the referendum is stressed here by the use of the expression *первый раз в истории* [for the first time in history].

(6)
Прежде всего нужно было помочь создать условия для мирного, свободного волеизъявления, чтобы крымчане могли сами определить свою судьбу ***первый раз в истории****.*

[First, we had to help create conditions so that the residents of Crimea **for the first time in history** were able to peacefully express their free will regarding their own future.]

In his speech Putin employs analogies in an attempt to present the decision about the annexation as consistent with democratic values. Specifically, he tries to draw an analogy between the annexation of Crimea, conceptualized by him as an expression of the people's free will, and specific momentous events in the world history, which are perceived as a manifestation of the struggle for freedom. As for the latter, he refers to the issuing of the Declaration of Independence in the USA and the unification of West and East Germany. Putin recalls these specific symbolic events to further refer to common ideals of freedom, liberty and national unity (*legitimation by moral evaluation;* see also below).

(7)

Сегодня я хочу обратиться и к народу Соединённых Штатов Америки, к людям, которые со времён основания этого государства, принятия Декларации независимости гордятся тем, что свобода для них превыше всего. Разве стремление жителей Крыма к свободному выбору своей судьбы не является такой же ценностью? Поймите нас.

Верю, что меня поймут и европейцы, и прежде всего немцы. Напомню, что в ходе политических консультаций по объединению ФРГ и ГДР на, мягко говоря, экспертном, но очень высоком уровне представители далеко не всех стран, которые являются и являлись тогда союзниками Германии, поддержали саму идею объединения. А наша страна, напротив, однозначно поддержала искреннее, неудержимое стремление немцев к национальному единству. Уверен, что вы этого не забыли, и рассчитываю, что граждане Германии также поддержат стремление русского мира, исторической России к восстановлению единства.

[Today, I would like to address the people of the United States of America, the people who, since the foundation of their nation and adoption of the Declaration of Independence, have been of Independence, have been proud to hold freedom above all else. Isn't the desire of Crimea's residents to freely choose their fate such a value? Please understand us.

I believe that the Europeans, first and foremost, the Germans, will also understand me. Let me remind you that in the course of political consultations on the unification of East and West Germany, at the expert, though very high level, some nations that were then and are now Germany's allies did not support the idea of unification. Our nation, however, unequivocally supported the sincere, unstoppable desire of the Germans for national unity. I am confident that you have not forgotten this, and I expect that the citizens of Germany will also support the aspiration of the Russians, of historical Russia, to restore unity.]

Apart from authorization (especially by reference to history and law), Putin also applies another legitimation strategy – *moral evaluation*. For instance, in example (8) such universal values as truth and justice are mentioned to explain the strong relationship between Crimea and Russia in the past and in the present times. A reference to the fundamental values of humanity plays the role of the 'universalizing' aspect of Putin's ideology. Again, the assertion of continuity is enhanced by the use of the verbs in the past and present tenses in one sentence:

(8)
В сердце, в сознании людей Крым всегда ***был*** *и* ***остаётся*** *неотъемлемой частью России.* ***Эта убеждённость, основанная на правде и справедливости****, была непоколебимой, передавалась из поколения в поколение, перед ней были бессильны и время, и обстоятельства, бессильны все драматические перемены, которые мы переживали, переживала наша страна в течение всего XX века.*

[In people's hearts and minds, Crimea **has always been** an inseparable part of Russia. **This firm conviction is based on truth and justice** and was passed from generation to generation, over time, under any circumstances, despite all the dramatic changes our country went through during the entire 20th century.]

In addition to legitimation strategies Putin's speech contains elements of delegitimation, used to attack the speaker's adversary. An important part of delegitimation is the organization of the deictic center, on which basis in- and out-group categorization is developed. The group identity of both insiders and outsiders is reflected in social indexicals and the use of personal pronouns *we* and *they*, respectively. In Putin's speech these resources are used for delegitimation directed at the Ukrainian authorities and Western countries.

In his speech the Russian president uses the in- and out-group personal pronouns *мы* 'we' and *они* 'they', by which means he indicates the social proximity and distance between the groups concerned. With the first-person plural pronouns Putin refers to Russian authorities, Russian citizens and Russian-speaking people. Yet the in-group consists not only of Russians, but also of residents of Crimea, Belarusians and Ukrainians in the historical perspective. Broadly speaking, the speech is an attempt to construct the in-group solidarity among all the people who share the same worldview as Russian politicians and support the same ideology.

At the lexical level the in-group members are characterized with the items denoting positive values. The following fragment exemplifies the attribution of positive values and high morals to the in-group:

(9)
Разумеется, мы не могли не откликнуться на эту просьбу, не могли оставить Крым и его жителей в беде, иначе это было бы просто предательством.

[Naturally, we could not leave this plea unheeded; we could not abandon Crimea and its residents in distress. This would have been betrayal on our part.]

Also, the frequent use of the personal pronoun *мы* 'we' builds the group identity among the participants of the communicative event (the speaker with the audience) as well as between Russian people and Crimeans. Putin emphasizes the importance of Crimea for Russia at the symbolic and historical level, referring to the notion of national pride. What is more, references to the past are strategically employed to influence the audience's emotions and to evoke sentiments of the Russian people for the Russian Empire as a symbol of strength and military glory (see also example 2).

On the other hand, the out-group is represented by Ukrainian authorities and Western countries, who are conceptualized in the analyzed discourse as led by negative premises and not recognizing the basic democratic and human values.

(10)
[…] *Однако что же мы слышим сегодня от наших коллег из Западной Европы, из Северной Америки? Нам говорят, что мы нарушаем нормы международного права. Во-первых, хорошо, что они хоть вспомнили о том, что существует международное право, и на том спасибо, лучше поздно, чем никогда.*

[(…) However, what do we hear from our colleagues in Western Europe and North America? They say we are violating norms of international law. Firstly, it's a good thing that they at least remember that there exists such a thing as international law – better late than never.]

(11)
От тех же Соединённых Штатов и Европы мы слышим, что Косово – это, мол, опять какой то особый случай. […] *И потом, знаете, это даже уже не двойные стандарты. Это какой то удивительный примитивный и прямолинейный цинизм. Нельзя же всё так грубо подвёрстывать под свои интересы, один и тот же предмет сегодня называть белым, а завтра – чёрным.*

[We keep hearing from the United States and Western Europe that Kosovo is some special case. (…) This is not even double standards; this is amazing, primitive, blunt cynicism. One should not try so crudely to make everything suit their interests, calling the same thing white today and black tomorrow.]

(12)
Наши западные партнёры во главе с Соединёнными Штатами Америки предпочитают в своей практической политике руководствоваться не международным правом, а правом сильного.

[Our western partners, led by the United States of America, prefer not to be guided by international law in their practical policies, but by the rule of the gun.]

Additionally, the Russian president questions the legitimacy of Ukrainian authorities after the Maidan.

(13)
Первым делом новые так называемые «власти» внесли скандальный законопроект о пересмотре языковой политики, который прямо ущемлял права национальных

> *меньшинств. Правда, зарубежные спонсоры этих сегодняшних «политиков», кураторы сегодняшних «властей» сразу одёрнули инициаторов этой затеи.* [...]
>
> [The new so-called authorities began by introducing a draft law to revise the language policy, which was a direct infringement on the rights of ethnic minorities. However, they were immediately 'disciplined' by the foreign sponsors of these so-called politicians. (...)]

The expression *так называемые «власти»* 'so-called politicians' emphasizes that Putin does not consider them a legitimate authority. What is more, Putin accuses them of being not sovereign, supported by 'foreign sponsors' (*зарубежные спонсоры*), who are not explicitly named in the text. The conceptualization of Ukraine immersed in a state of total chaos is aimed at presenting Russia as a strong country, which offers the only alternative for Crimea. In short, the values represented in the discourse by the in-group and out-group may be placed at the opposing ends of the axiological axis in terms of moral behaviour.

> (14)
> ***Ясно*** *и то, что легитимной исполнительной власти на Украине до сих пор нет, разговаривать не с кем.*
>
> [**It is also obvious** that there is no legitimate executive authority in Ukraine now, nobody to talk to.]

Finally, in example (14), Putin further strengthens his message with the legitimation strategy of *rationalization*, i.e. use of lexical items referring to obviousness and public knowledge (*Ясно* 'It is obvious'). This strategy is aimed at achieving the effect of the audience's approving the speaker's controversial ideas.

4. Conclusions

Recognizing that political speech is a powerful discursive tool of (re)construction of social attitudes, knowledge and identities, this paper highlighted some of the linguistic devices used for legitimation in Russian political discourse, in particular those concerning the annexation of Crimea on the example of Vladimir Putin's speech of 18th March 2014.

The qualitative analysis of empirical material was preceded by the introduction of several theoretical concepts in sections 1 and 2: *discourse*, *political discourse*, *political speech* and *legitimation*.

The methodological model adopted in the analysis helped to investigate typical rhetorical devices used in Putin's speech in terms of its strategic function: legitimation of the annexation of Crimea (gaining social approval and preventing possible accusations of illegal actions) and delegitimation of his opponent's stance.

The analysis revealed some typical elements of Russian political discourse concerning international politics: promoting the speaker's/in-group's positive self-image by ascribing positive values to his/her own actions (concepts such as respect for tradition and history, or the topos of the 'free will of people') and enhancing the negative image of Western states on the basis of thesis-antithesis construction. Building a strong in-group solidarity by the reference to common goals and universal values is used as the basis for the construction of social identity.

As has been shown in the analysis, apart from the strategy of *moral evaluation,* legitimation in Putin's speech is also based on *authorization* by the reference to historical motives and law, which involves re-construction of social reality from the speaker's perspective. The speech includes explicit and implicit messages aimed at shaping social attitudes and promoting the speaker's ideology. Here, the strategy of *rationalization* functions on the principle of granting controversial ideas the status of obvious facts.

References

Bakhtin, M. ([1986] 2000). *The problem of speech genres.* In A. Jaworski & N. Coupland (Eds.), *The discourse reader.* London: Routledge, 121–132.

Cap, P. (2008). Towards the Proximization Model of the Analysis of Legitimization in Political Discourse. *Journal of Pragmatics*, 40, 17–41.

Cap, P. (2013). *Proximization. The Pragmatics of Symbolic Distance Crossing.* Amsterdam: John Benjamins.

Charteris-Black, J. (2014). *Analysing Political Speeches. Rhetoric, Discourse and Metaphor.* Basingstoke: Palgrave Macmillan.

Chilton, P. (2004). *Analysing political discourse: theory and practice.* London: Routledge.

van Dijk, T. (1998). *Ideology. A Multidisciplinary Approach.* London: Sage Publications.

van Dijk, T. (2008). *Discourse and power.* Basingstoke & New York: Palgrave Macmillan.

Dobrovolskij, D., & Pöppel, L. (2013). The semantic field of POWER and political propaganda: революция (revolution) vs. переворот (coup) andвосстание (uprising) vs. мятеж (revolt). In K. Senkbeil & B. Kress (Eds.), *Totalitarian Political Discourse?: Tolerance and Intolerance in Eastern and East Central European Countries: Diachronic and Synchronic Aspects.* Frankfurt am Main: Peter Lang AG, 73–90.

Duszak, A. (1998). *Tekst, dyskurs, komunikacja międzykulturowa.* Warszawa: Wydawnictwo Naukowe PWN.

Duszak, A., & Fairclough, N. (2008). Wstęp. Krytyczna analiza dyskursu – nowy obszar badawczy dla lingwistyki i nauk społecznych. In A. Duszak & N. Fairclough (Eds.), *Krytyczna analiza dyskursu.* Kraków: Universitas, 7–32.

Eagleton, T. ([1991] 2007). *Ideology: An Introduction.* London & New York: Verso.

Fairclough, N. ([1989] 2001). *Language and power.* Harlow: Longman.

Fairclough, N. (1999). *Critical discourse analysis. The critical study of language.* London: Longman.

Gruszczyńska, E. (2012). *Dawne polskie przekłady prasowe. Informacja-perswazja-manipulacja.* Warszawa: ASPRA-JR.

Karamova, A. (2014). Grammaticheskije sredstva ideologichnosti politicheskogo diskursa. *Politicheskaja lingvistika,* 2(48), 143–148.

Kłosińska, K. (2004). Retoryka form osobowych w dyskursie politycznym. *Poradnik językowy,* 1, 19–39.

van Leeuwen, T. (2008). *Discourse in practice: a new tool for critical discourse analysis.* Oxford: Oxford University Press.

Macgilchrist, F. (2011). *Journalism and the Political: Discursive Tensions in News Coverage of Russia.* Amsterdam: John Benjamins Publishing Company.

Okulska, U., & Cap, P. (2010a). Analysis of Political Discourse: Landmarks, challenges and prospects. In U. Okulska & P. Cap (Eds.), *Perspectives in Politics and Discourse.* Amsterdam: John Benjamins Publishing Company, 3–20.

Okulska, U., & Cap, P. (2010b). Exploring 'political communication(s)': Contexts, procedures and outlook. In P. Cap & U. Okulska (Eds.), *Perspectives in Politics and Discourse.* Amsterdam: John Benjamins Publishing Company, 399–406.

Pyykkö, R. (2002). Who Is 'Us' in Russian Political Discourse. In A. Duszak (Ed.), *Us and Others: Social Identities across Languages, Discourses and Cultures".* Amsterdam: John Benjamins Publishing Company, 233–248.

Schiffers, S. (2015). A Decade of Othering: Russian Political Leaders' Discourse on Russia-EU Relations 2004–2014. *East European Quarterly,* 43(1), 1–27.

Sivenkova, M. (2013). On the metapragmatics of British, German and Russian political questions and answers. In A. Fetzer (Ed.), *The Pragmatics of Political Discourse: Explorations Across Cultures.* Amsterdam: John Benjamins, 21–46.

Swales, J. (1990). *Genre analysis: English in academic and research settings.* Cambrige: Cambridge University Press.

Verschueren, J. (2012). *Ideology in Language Use.* Cambridge & New York: Cambridge University Press.

Wilson, J. (2001). Political Discourse. In D. Schiffrin, D. Tannen & H. Hamilton (Eds.), *The Handbook of Discourse Analysis.* Malden, Oxford: Blackwell, 398–411.

Wodak, R (2007). What Critical Discourse Analysis is about – a summary of its history, important concepts and its developments. In R. Wodak & M. Meyer (Eds.), *Methods of critical discourse analysis*. Los Angeles: Sage, 1–14.

Wodak, R. (2008). Introduction: Discourse Studies – Important Concepts and Terms. In R. Wodak & M. Krzyżanowski (Eds.), *Qualitative Discourse Analysis in the Social Sciences*. Basingstoke: Palgrave Macmillan, 1–29.

Wodak, R. (2012). Politics as usual. In J. Gee & M. Hanford (Eds.), *The Routledge Handbook of Discourse Analysis*. London: Routledge, 525–540.

Sources

Vladimir Putin's address, 18th March, 2014.

Source: Official website of the President of Russia, URL: http://news.kremlin.ru/news/20603, DOA: 06.06.2015.

Source of the English translation: Official website of the President of Russia, URL: http://eng.kremlin.ru/transcripts/6889, DOA: 06.06.2015.

Ludmilla A'Beckett

Monash University, Australia / University of the Free State, South Africa

Fragmentation of the discourse community through the lens of metaphor analysis: A case study of RUSSIANS AND UKRAINIANS ARE BROTHERS

Abstract: This paper reconstructs virtual communication between Russians and Ukrainians centered around the metaphor BROTHERS. The research demonstrates that ubiquitous use of the metaphoric concept does not ensure coherent views of discourse participants. The frequently used metaphor often points to a clash of ideological positions rather than to a unanimous acceptance of the interpretative frame imposed by a power group. The focus on different attitudes expressed toward the dominant metaphoric proposition allows for profiling diverse perspectives of the discourse community members in relation to the same ideological issue.

1. Introduction

The power of metaphor in constructing and reflecting discourse ideology has been widely acknowledged and explored (Lakoff, 1996; Semino & Masci, 1996; Santa Anna, 1999; Koller, 2004, 2005; Musolff, 2004; Chiang & Duann, 2007, and many others). Scholars who attempt to unveil ideological aspects in texts have frequently been tempted to draw on several aspects of the conceptual metaphor theory (Lakoff & Johnson, 1980). Popular aspects of metaphor-based discourse analysis include the extraction of conventional mappings or patterns of thought represented by ubiquitous metaphors (Nerlich & Jaspal, 2012; Ly, 2013), speculations on metaphor framing effects in the text (Schȍn, 1993; Ritchie & Cameron, 2014), and the emotive stance provoked in the putative audience (Cisneros, 2008; Lakoff, 2013). In sum, the lexical choices of discourse participants are usually interpreted as pointers to cognitive models which gain salience in public discourse. The authorial intentions and the impact of these cognitive models on a putative reader were discussed in terms of 'ideological' or 'evaluative biases' (cf. Musolff, 2006; Cameron, 2010). For instance, Santa Anna (1999) analyzed metaphoric representations of migrants in US public discourse and concluded that migrants were frequently portrayed as animals. This salient conceptual model encouraged the dehumanization and stigmatization of immigrants among other members of the discourse community. It should be noted, though, that some of Santa Anna's interpretations of metaphors were later questioned by Deignan (2010, p. 54).

Similarly, in her study of business media, Koller (2004, 2005) found that the topic of mergers and acquisitions was frequently presented through STRUGGLE FOR SURVIVING metaphors, i.e. FIGHTING, FEEDING and MATING. These metaphors lead to the emergence of a global hegemonic masculinity (Koller, 2004, pp. 34–35, 40–41, 172–175). Koller suggests that the cognitive models underlying the STRUGGLE FOR SURVIVING metaphors position women as out-group members. It was argued that the widespread use of aggressive and competitive models in business media sustains masculine culture and values (Koller, 2005, p. 219; see also Koller, 2004, p. 173).

It has also been discussed how people in power impose their metaphors on others (Lakoff & Johnson, 1980, p. 157). The adoption of a certain set of metaphors by either group has been viewed as an attempt to solicit a particular viewpoint. Lakoff and Johnson (1980, p. 156) provided general guidance to scholars investigating discourse into how the choice of metaphors can reflect and construct social experience:

> Metaphors […] highlight and make coherent certain aspects of our experience […] metaphors may create realities for us, especially social realities. A metaphor may thus be a guide for a future action […] this will, in turn, reinforce the power of the metaphor to make experience coherent. In this sense metaphors can be self-fulfilling prophecies.

This claim has stimulated linguists to address metaphoric models in texts. It was assumed that the position of power often dwells on the metaphors that are widely shared among discourse community members. It has been argued that frequently used metaphors shape people's judgements and motivate their real-life choices (Howe, 1988; Semino & Masci, 1996; Santa Anna, 1999). It has also been assumed that speakers can manipulate their audiences through the choice of metaphoric expressions that exemplify particular cognitive models. Lakoff's (1996) view was that change in the selection of metaphors can drive changes in political and social developments.

However, despite the recognized popularity of these statements, their authors and followers seem to have neglected some aspects of metaphor use in discourse. In this paper I show that ubiquitous use of a metaphor does not necessarily mean that the discourse community as a whole accepts it as a unified *gestalt*. Neither does it mean that all members of that discourse community make their choices and create allegiances under the cognitive impact of a popular metaphor. Furthermore,

I will show in this paper that the frequent use of the metaphor NATIONS ARE BROTHERS in Russophone discourse is a result of (1) uncritical acceptance of the metaphor by some speakers, (2) negotiation of relevant parameters of correlations between its source and target by discourse participants, and (3) various techniques of rejecting and questioning the analogy between the ideal family and neighboring nations. The paper purports to recreate the diversity of the discourse community as observed in different attitudes toward a metaphor promulgated by people in power.

The paper is structured as follows. In section 2 several case studies are revisited to show correlations between dominant metaphors and discourse ideologies. This section also focuses on instances of incoherent viewpoints introduced by the same or similar metaphoric vehicles. Section 3 further discusses the play of voices around a metaphoric proposition in discourse and the means of locating different interest groups among discourse participants. The main case study on the multiplicity of stances expressed toward the metaphoric analogies UKRAINIANS AND RUSSIANS ARE BROTHERS in Russian public discourse can be found in Section 4. The paper concludes with the observation on the metaphor's semantic variation and pragmatic adaptability in Russo-Ukrainian debates.

2. Reflections on previous case studies

The investigation of the links between metaphoric models and discourse ideologies can be approached from two different directions. The first way is to compile a totality of texts representing the same topic (Koller, 2004, p. 18), locate ubiquitous metaphors in this collection of texts, and then analyze the dominant views anchored to these metaphors. The second way is to collect a "metaphor discourse", i.e. patterns of metaphor use by different speakers. The first model can be exemplified by Koller's (2004, 2005) research on metaphors used in the business media discourse and by Chiang and Duann's (2007) investigation on newspaper reports about the epidemics of SARS in Taiwan and China. The second one is represented by Musolff's (2013) research of the discursive carrier of 'the heart of Europe' in Great Britain.

The present study on the functions of the metaphor RUSSIANS AND UKRAINIANS ARE BROTHERS follows the pattern of Musolff's research. Nevertheless, the results of the investigations dealing with the distribution of prominent metaphors in thematic collections of texts, as exemplified by Koller's (2004, 2005) research on mergers and acquisitions in business media discourse and by Chiang and Duann's (2007) study of the SARS discourse in Taiwan and China, need to be discussed as well, as they illustrate different types of correlations between ubiquitous metaphors and discursive ideology/ies.

Koller's analysis resulted in locating the prominence of the metaphoric model of evolutionary struggle (Koller, 2005, p. 199; see also Koller, 2004, p. 164) in the world of business and finance. Koller (2005, p. 204) suggested that the prominence of this conceptualization supports existing power relations, which are asymmetrical in nature. The pool of cognitive resources in texts dedicated to business mergers and acquisitions is filled with FIGHTING, MATING and FEEDING metaphors. Koller argues that all evolutionary struggle metaphors construct very similar perspectives: "[f]ighting, mating and feeding alike serve the ulterior survival motive that is conceptualized in antagonistic terms, as competition and struggle rather than cooperation and mutual benefit" (Koller, 2005, p. 216; see also Koller, 2004, p. 132). Koller's influential and thorough investigation also revealed that in the whole corpus dedicated to mergers and acquisitions there was little questioning or negating of the dominant metaphors.

Nevertheless, if other metaphor researchers were keen on extrapolating Koller's conclusions for a set of data from different texts, these authors might mislead their audiences about the coherence of beliefs associated with EATING and MATING metaphors. For instance, in a fiction book about business and academic culture, *Scandalous* by Tilly Bagshave (2010), we can find that MATING and FEEDING metaphors correspond to different prospects for the main character and that they are in complementary distribution:

> Give it a year and Ceris'll be completely subsumed. Two years and no one will even remember the name. We did not **get married**. We **got eaten**.
>
> (Bagshave, 2010, pp. 373–374, emphasis mine)

Even if we agree that marriage, as an instantiation of MATING metaphors, is a defense mechanism and a response to threat in the business world (Koller, 2005, p. 216), the future of companies that have been swallowed and of the ones that found a caring spouse are perceived as different. Koller's examples about 'marriages' from the business media, e.g. MERGERS AND ACQUISITIONS ACTIVITIES ARE COERCING A WOMAN (COMPANY) INTO MARRIAGE, emphasize the dominance of aggressive strategies in the world of business (Koller, 2004, p. 164).

If we look at the example from Bagshave's novel *Scandalous* the opposition between EATING and MATING highlights a voluntary action in 'marriage' and a passive victim in the case of 'being eaten'. Hence, in Lakoff and Johnson's (1980, p. 156) terms, the 'marriage' and 'eating' metaphors in the example above are associated with 'different guides for future actions', and hence activate different evaluative biases. In addition to this, the hypothetical 'marriage' from *Scandalous* does not accentuate aggression, which is "particularly salient in so-called romantic contexts when we focus on the sexual aspect of the MATING metaphor"

(Koller, 2004, p. 167). Thus, a ubiquitous metaphor does not always represent a uniform conceptualization of power relations which was assessed as a domination of masculine power and behavior represented by "attributes such as aggressive, unemotional, competitive, logical, adventurous, self-confident, and ambitious" in business media discourse on mergers and acquisitions (Koller, 2004, p. 173).

Recontextualization of the same metaphor vehicle can change an attitude commonly associated with this vehicle. In the analyzed example from Tilly Bagshave the vehicles 'being married' and 'being eaten', which allegedly represent the same conceptual bias, e.g. a culture of aggression, were opposed to each other and, as a result, aggression and coercion was carried by only one vehicle, i.e. 'being eaten'.

The same metaphor vehicle can carry incoherent viewpoints also due to abilities of discourse participants to allocate dissimilar roles within the same conceptual frame to characters featuring in discourse. In other words, the selection of positions for social agents in a scheme of experience such as FIGHT or WAR can vary in different texts. For instance, Chiang and Duann (2007) analyzed the coverage of the spread of SARS infection in two Taiwanese and one Chinese newspapers. All newspapers used FIGHTING (WAR) metaphors. However, the FIGHTING or WAR could be carried out by different agents within this conceptual frame. The pro-government Taiwanese newspaper attributed the role of 'aggressors' and 'invaders' to China, where the virus supposedly originated. The Taiwanese opposition was depicted as 'saboteurs' and 'assistants of the invasion' since the opposition compromised the defense lines. By contrast, the Taiwanese government was the 'chief combatant' with 'aggressors' and was the 'people's protector'. As for the Chinese newspaper, it assigned the role of 'guardian' to the Chinese government, the 'main protector' of the people defying and resisting the SARS invasion. The Taiwanese opposition newspaper, however, attributed the role of the 'guardians' and 'fighters' to the medical workers who were at the frontier of the war while the government revealed its incompetence and inability to lead the 'battle'.

Chiang and Duann (2007, pp. 191–194) argue that the attribution of roles to social actors as constructed in the newspapers analyzed is consistent, and hence can be taken as evidence of discourse cohesion in the totality of articles about SARS in each newspaper. However, if we define discourse as 'the virtual conversation within and between communities' (Musolff, 2004, p. 5), then the texts of the government and opposition newspapers in Taiwan can be treated as voices from the same discourse. In this instance, metaphor vehicles (e.g. 'war' or 'to fight') in isolation from their contexts are not indicative of an attitudinal bias. The FIGHTING metaphors do not necessarily carry the perception of hegemonic masculinity (as suggested by Koller, 2004, 2005; see also Howe, 1988) if we consider contexts provided by Chiang and Duann (2007).

The allotment of FIGHTING metaphors in the SARS discourse is more indicative of the contribution of different parties to the noble cause of curing the society and resisting 'hostile intrusions'. The more a social agent carries 'fighting', the bigger his/her share in the problem solving. It can be concluded that identical or similar metaphor vehicles (e.g. 'a fight' and 'to fight') carry dissimilar attitudinal biases in different contexts and discourses, especially if we compare their fields of references (e.g. 'to fight against SARS' and 'to fight for the company's independence and solvency'). The 'fight' and 'struggle' is usually positively charged if it is directed against an 'aggressor' and 'invader'. 'Protectors', 'guardians' and 'custodians' usually 'fight' for a noble cause when trying to defend those who are entrusted in their care. 'Predators' cause trouble, and therefore evoke negative perceptions but, nevertheless, represent the rewarding model of *macho* conduct in the business discourse.

The above overview of works in the field shows that there are several discourse factors which can undermine the assumption that the common interpretative repertoire of discourse participants always supports the existing power relations and carries similar viewpoints. It can be suggested that a mere change in the argumentative patterns of a ubiquitous metaphor such as positioning it in a context highlighting contrasts between two options or ironical proposition induces a different perspective in their understanding.

Koller (2004, 2005) also argues that the aggressiveness of the hegemonic STRUGGLE FOR SURVIVING metaphor could be mitigated if the metaphor was negated, questioned or countered in the discourse. However, such instances did not surface much in her data on mergers and acquisitions. Still, the example from Bagshave's novel can fill this gap in the available evidence and demonstrate that not all metaphors qualified by Koller as the EVOLUTIONARY STRUGGLE model are charged with aggression or perceived to carry wide-spread *machismo*.

Furthermore, role attribution within a given cognitive frame can vary between different ideological players. The study by Chiang and Duann (2007) showed that conflicting parties often rely on the same conceptual frame but assign different points of reference to social agents within the overarching scheme. Metaphor researchers can misrepresent the attitudinal trajectories of discourse if they do not pay enough attention to contextual variations in metaphor use.

3. Fragmentation of the discourse community

A question can be raised how to reconstruct the polyphony (Bakhtin, 1981) of the metaphor discourse or diverse voices of metaphors' users and recipients. A simplified model of discourse could be represented through the display of verdicts or assertive statements issued by a prudent authority, otherwise known as a power group, together with the reproduction of conformist voices of discourse community members. Such a model was used in the construction of totalitarian discourse (Inkeles, 1950). If I followed this sample for recreating voices participating in the metaphor discourse, I could have limited the study by the analysis represented in Sections 4.1 and 4.4. Unfortunately, dissenting voices, altogether with variations in the interpretation of events and statements among the supporters of the power group, could be located even in totalitarian discourse.

Furthermore, in contemporary mediated society many recipients of messages from the government also participate in the co-construction of political arguments (Didriksen & Gjesdal, 2013; Kjeldsen, 2013; Noren, 2013). Ordinary representatives of the discourse community negotiate values in statements made by the power group as these discourse participants need to defend or criticise the big players whose views are interpreted and mediated by the discourse community members in their own virtual communication with other discourse participants. The boundaries of modern public discourse become fuzzy since it accommodates a wide range of political, national and personal voices participating in negotiation of issues of public importance (Fløttum, 2013, pp. 8–9).

The complexity of contemporary public discourse, as discussed by Fløttum (2013), Didriksen and Gjesdal (2013), Kjeldsen (2013), Noren (2013), and Porto and Romano (2013) has several consequences for metaphor researchers. For instance, several linguists point out that in the process of negotiating claims, discourse participants often adopt and adapt the verbal repertoire of their opponents as much as that of their own in-groupers (Musolff, 2013, pp. 140–141; Porto & Romano, 2013, p. 71). Similarly, Didriksen and Gjesdal (2013, p. 88) argue that utterances of discourse community members contain traces of several different 'voices' or points of view, not only the ones associated with a given fraction but also those of the opposite one(s). In a similar vein, Kjeldsen (2013, p. 22) observes: "When the words have been disseminated, new players throw themselves into debates, and the use of decontextualized utterances set their agendas".

Metaphor researchers point out that in these instances metaphor vehicles are 'appropriated' (Cameron, 2010, p. 19) by different parties in discourse, but at the same time do not represent the matching ideological positions. The change of a viewpoint does not require total replacement of the repertoire of metaphors.

A popular concept can be further elaborated or recontextualized to alter its initial cognitive import. In a face-to-face conversation, the appropriation of another person's metaphor can be taken as a sign of acknowledging the other's perspective through language (Cameron, 2010, p. 20).

Yet some studies on the functions of metaphors in public discourse, i.e. in the virtual communication between and within communities (Musollf, 2004, p. 5), suggest that 'appropriation' happens when the opponents attempt to trump the claims of their adversaries (Musolff, 2013, pp. 138–142; see also A'Beckett, 2012, pp. 186–188). In such instances, an opponent can truncate, elaborate or twist the original analogy to provide an alternative cognitive underpinning of the discussed issue (e.g. the metaphoric exemplary 'family' invoked by a power group can be presented as a 'dysfunctional' one by an oppositionist). The opponent undermines the validity of the assertion not by rejecting the metaphoric proposition of the speaker, but through shifting the ground for analogy in this proposition.

Since discourse participants can adopt and adapt metaphor vehicles of other parties, the ubiquitous use of the same concept in discussions cannot be taken as a testimony of homogeneous beliefs in the discourse. The metaphoric proposition stimulates a play of voices among different interest groups in the community and becomes the focal point of public debates (Musolff, 2013, pp. 140–141). The range of attitudes and evaluative stances evoked by the metaphor can vary. Conflicting viewpoints, such as the government's and oppositionists' reading of the situation, may rely on the same cognitive foundation (Chiang & Duann, 2007).

It is still possible to hypothesize that among the supporters of the same position we can find similar attitudes toward a metaphoric analogy (e.g. acceptance, countering, questioning or rejection). Nevertheless, the cognitive input and the frame of reference of a ubiquitous metaphor are subject to continuous alteration and negotiation in context. Consequently, the metaphor on its own cannot be permanently associated with a particular viewpoint.

As previously stated, in the case study on the functioning of the metaphor UKRAINIANS AND RUSSIANS ARE BROTHERS in the Russophone public discourse, some dialogic positions toward the metaphor (i.e. acceptance, negation, questioning and elaboration, and extension of the metaphoric analogy) will be taken as a broad indicator of differences among interest groups in the discourse community. Such patterns of argumentation or play of voices around a statement were discussed by Martin and White (2005, Chapter 3) under the term 'dialogic engagement'. I will show in this paper that communicative operations of speakers on the metaphoric proposition NATIONS ARE BROTHERS (such as acceptance or rejection) cannot always serve as indices of specific ideologies.

4. NATIONS ARE BROTHERS in Russo-Ukrainian debates

The conceptualization of friendly nations in terms of a 'brotherhood' has a long history in Russian discourse (A'Beckett, 2012, pp. 188–189). The metaphor has been entrenched in public memory as it features in the new Russian anthem. Sergei Mikhalkov's lyrics represent Russia as "the eternal union of fraternal people" (*братских народов союз вековой).* In such a representation, the relations between Russia and "fraternal nations/peoples" have become the epitome of shared values, mutual understanding, trust, reciprocity, solidarity and equality (A'Beckett, 2012, pp. 177–178).

Nevertheless, the reality of living together with, or next to, Russia is different from the glamorized version. Recent events in the neighboring state of Ukraine have generated prolific public discussions on Russia's role in the military conflict in the south-east of this state. Russophone social media are full of claims concerning the 'fraternal and family relations' between the two countries. Ukrainians are also active participants of these public debates since Russian is still the mother tongue or a second language of many of them (Pavlenko, 2008).

The position of the Russian government, which frequently uses the metaphor BROTHERS when commenting on the situation, has been actively discussed. The discussants include Russian oppositionists, prominent public figures and unknown opinion holders. At the same time, Russian government loyalists have voiced positions which are hard to reconcile with the stance presented by top-ranking officials.

For the purpose of this research, 300 statements containing instantiations of the NATIONS ARE BROTHERS metaphor, such as the words 'fraternal', 'brothers' or 'brotherhood', were collected from Russophone social media (Facebook, Lifejournal and Odnoklassniki).[1] The investigation focused on the patterns of usage of this metaphor. In my analysis of the data I attempt to reconstruct the attitudes of the discussants towards the proposition UKRAINIANS AND RUSSIANS ARE BROTHERS, as well as to identify the argumentative strategies adopted by the participants. The time frame covers the period between the beginning of the Euromaidan in Ukraine in November 2013 (which resulted in ousting President Yanukovych) and the beginning of 2015. This period was marked by the annexation of Crimea by Russia and by the growth of a separatist military standoff in the Ukrainian regions of Donetsk and Luhansk.

---

1 Facebook, Odnoklassniki and LifeJournal are social networks which provide services for communication in forms of blogs and comments. Both types of texts provided via these social media can incorporate references to mainstream media publications as well as images and short films.

4.1. The use of BROTHERS metaphors by Russian officials

A consistent pattern of the use of the metaphor by Russian top-ranking officials can be observed. For instance, Sergei Lavrov, the Russian Foreign Minister, commented on the country's attitude toward Ukrainians as follows:

(1)

Украина *для нас — самый близкий,* ***братский народ****, имеющий общие с нами исторические, культурные, мировоззренческие и цивилизационные корни, не говоря уже о языке и литературе.*

[**Ukraine** for us is the next of kin, **fraternal nation** which shares with us common historical, cultural, ideological and civilizational roots. Let alone language and literature.]

(Lavrov, 2014)[2]

Lavrov's statement follows the tradition of addressing former Soviet Republics and allies of the Soviet Union as 'brothers', in particular at the time of conflict. The metaphor BROTHERS embodies the idea of a perpetual political and cultural partnership. A similar strategy was used by Dmitry Medvedev, former Russian President, in his addressing Georgians at the time of the Ossetian war (A'Beckett, 2012, p. 170). He was keen to reiterate that the Georgian people are 'brothers for Russians'. According to Medvedev, the only problem was the 'demoniac' Georgian leadership – the party to blame for the conflict among the 'brothers'. Another case in point is President Putin's talk about fraternal love for Ukrainians at the time of talking Yanukovych out of the treaty with the European Union and encouraging Ukraine to join the Russia-led Customs Union (see example 2).

(2)

Владимир Путин объяснил, что ***братскому*** *государству выгоднее объединяться с бывшими* ***сестрами*** *по СССР. По подсчетам экспертов, от вступления в Таможенный союз выигрыш* ***Украины*** *составит $9 млрд. в год.*

[Vladimir Putin explained that the **fraternal** state will be better off if it is united with former **sisters** from the USSR. The calculations of experts show that **Ukraine's** benefit will be equal to 9 billion dollars per year.]

(Beroeva, 2011)[3]

---

2 Lavrov, S. (2014). Для России Украина - это братский народ, а не марширующие в Киеве нацисты [For Russia Ukraine is a brotherly people, but not the Nazi who are marching in Kiev]. *Novaya gazeta*, 19 October 2014. Retrieved from http://www.novayagazeta.ru/news/1688414.html; DOA: 07.11.2016.

3 Beroeva, N. (2011). Владимир Путин предложил Украине открыть карты. [Vladimir Putin suggested to Ukraine to lay the cards on the table]. *Komsomol'skaia pravda*, 12.04.2011. Retrieved from http://www.kp.ru/daily/25667/829109/; DOA: 07.11.2016.

Similarly, Putin's 2014 address to brothers-Ukrainians, as shown in example (3), is no different in this respect:

(3)
несмотря на всю трагедию, которую мы сейчас наблюдаем, особенно на юго-востоке, украинский народ всегда был и остается самым близким для нас, ***братским*** *народом. Нас связывает общность этническая, духовная, религиозная, историческая.*

[notwithstanding the tragedy that we are witnessing, especially in the southeast, the Ukrainian people has always been closest to us, the **brotherly** people. We are tied by ethnic, spiritual, religious, historical unity.]

(Putin, 2014)[4]

As shown in examples (2) and (3), the conceptualization of the relations between Russians and Ukrainians in terms of 'brothers' performs several pragmatic functions. The metaphor entails the belief that the political union with Russia is perpetual since the 'family', or ethnic, bond is of a nearly sacred nature. If this is the case, then it is hard to refute something that allegedly manifests the will of the ancestors and involves practical aspects in sharing culture, economy and history.

The Russian users of the metaphor often accuse the 'Ukrainian brothers' of 'extremism' and 'fascism' (Pushnova, 2014), causing the confrontation between the two nations. At the same time, they shy away from a critical assessment of the role the Russian government played in the conflict. 'Fraternal feelings' expressed in such statements are hard to question or dismiss as they epitomize a long historical tradition. The cognitive base of the analogy carries an evaluative and attitudinal bias: family ties and obligations are binding for civilized or moral people; breaking the former implies that the agents responsible are anything but moral and civilized. Also, the assumption about family-like relations between the nations leads to other political implications, e.g. the right to interfere with the affairs of a 'brother' with 'good intentions'.

4.2. Attitudes of nationally conscious Ukrainians towards the 'fraternal bond'

Ukrainian responses to the 'brotherhood' imposed by Russians have been fairly consistent. Assiduous efforts have been made by Ukrainian discourse participants to dissociate themselves from the undesirable union and to reject the 'fraternal care'. The dissociation took the form of overt negation, questioning the grounds

4 Putin, V. (2014). Украинцы являются ближайшим братским народом для России. [Ukrainians are a brotherly next of kin nation to Russians]. *Pressa Ukrainy*. 02.10.2014. Retrieved from http://uapress.info/ru/news/show/41454; DOA: 07.11.2016.

for assuming such a state of affairs, as well as irony and tacit dismissals with the use of such terms as '**former** brothers' (***бывшие** братья*) and '**so-called** brothers' (***так называемые** братья*).

Both overt and forceful refutation of the 'fraternal bond' can be found in the lyrics of a young Ukrainian poet Anastasia Dmitruk (see example 4). Her poetic lines have become a subject of many discussions in Russophone social media (Strannik, 2014). Her message provoked a wave of responses from several Post-Soviet countries.

(4)
Никогда мы не будем братьями
Ни по родине, ни по матери.
Духа нет у вас быть свободными
Нам не стать с вами даже сводными.

[**We will never be brothers** (to Russians – L.A.)
Neither by (common – L.A.) Motherland, nor by maternity.
You don't have the spirit to be free
You can't be even our step-brothers.]

(Dmitruk, 2014, see also Strannik, 2014)[5]

Dmitruk claims that the 'fraternal union' between Russians and Ukrainians cannot be accepted even if their relations have been enforced by some circumstances, cf. *Нам не стать с вами даже сводными* [You can't be even our step-brothers]. Dmitruk raises objections as to the belief that there are similarities between Russians and Ukrainians or historical ties between the nations. According to Dmitruk, the spirits of the two nations, their tastes and likes are dramatically different. Russians and Ukrainians are not the same even if they are born of interethnic marriages (e.g. by maternity). Thus, in example (4), no possibility of reconciliation between the nations is envisaged.

Another Ukrainian author, in this case a blogger, expresses similar sentiments, but by means of a more tacit dismissal.

(5)
Но вот незадача: среди украинцев, которые посещают Евросоюз, неизменно прибавляется желание там жить, а вот у тех, кто ездит в Россию, дополнительного

5 Dmitruk, A. (2014). Никогда мы не будем бртьями. [We will never be brothers]. 19.03.2014. Retrieved from https://www.youtube.com/watch?v=Qv97YeC563Y; DOA: 07.11.2016. See also Strannik, I. (2014). Все ответы Анастасии Дмитрук. [All responses to Anastasiya Dmitruk]. 10.04.2014. Retrieved from http://agv.mirtesen.ru/blog/43607718234/Vse-otvetyi--na-stih-Anastasii-Dmitruk; DOA: 07.11.2016.

настроя быть с ней или туда переезжать не наблюдается. Вот на чем надо работать, ***братья вы наши бывшие.***

[But here's the thing: Ukrainians who visit the EU always bolster their desire to live there, but those who travel to Russia do not acquire any passion to stay there or to move there. This is the line of work for you, **our former brothers**]

(Hetmanchuk, 2014)[6]

Examples (4) and (5) illustrate a coherent pattern in the use of the metaphor BROTHERS by Ukrainian participants in public discourse. Nationally-conscious Ukrainians refute the similarities between themselves and Russians as much as the 'fraternal' obligations to live in a perpetual unity under the constant threat of 'fraternal assistance', otherwise understood as an 'intervention'. Also, many examples of irony have been found (see example 6) that can be defined as negation without a negation marker (Giora, 2003, pp. 15–17).

(6)

Антон Геращенко. ***"Русские братья"*** *пришли в Украину по указке Путина убивать наших людей. И мы будем защищать нашу независимость.*

[Anton Gerashchenko (an MP and spokesman for the Interior Ministry of Ukraine – L.A): **'Russian brothers'** came to Ukraine on Putin's orders to kill our people. So we will be defending our independence.]

(Fanailova, 2014)[7]

On the other hand, among Ukrainians there are also participants in public discourse who do not repudiate the fact of there being a 'fraternity' relation, but question the role of Russian 'brothers' in it (see example 7).

(7)

Братская *страна, говорящая о нашем общем прошлом, отказывается покупать нашу продукцию - и это, по словам ее же лидеров, может привести к значительному ухудшению уровня жизни у нас. Ничего себе* ***братья!***

---

6 Hetmanchuk, A. (2014). Почему нам не по пути? (предназначено для русских). [Why don't we go along one way? (Intended for Russians.)] 13.04.2014. Retrieved from http://blogs.pravda.com.ua/authors/hetmanchuk/534a9868b726d/; DOA: 07.03.2017. 19.03.2014. Retrieved from https://www.youtube.com/watch?v=Qv97YeC563Y; DOA: 07.11.2016. See also Strannik, I. (2014). Все ответы Анастасии Дмитрук. [All responses to Anastasiya Dmitruk]. 10.04.2014. Retrieved from http://agv.mirtesen.ru/blog/43607718234/Vse-otvetyi--na-stih-Anastasii-Dmitruk; DOA: 07.11.2016.

7 Fanailova, E. (2014). Лицом к событиюю. [Facing the event]. The script of the program *Украина: Патриоты и предатели.* [Ukraine: Patriots and traitors]. 18.07.2014. Retrieved from http://www.svoboda.org/a/25461853.html; DOA: 07.11.2016.

> [The **brotherly** country, which is talking about our common past, refuses to buy our products – and this, according to her own leaders, may lead to a significant deterioration in living standards in our country. Wow **brothers**!]
>
> (Portnikov, 2013)[8]

Examples (4–7) show that Ukrainians are not homogeneous in their perception of the country's past. Some Ukrainians deny the existence of the 'brotherhood' and appropriateness of this term (example 4). Some admit that there were ties between Russia and Ukraine but these 'fraternal' relations are meaningless at present (examples 5 and 6). Finally, example (7) demonstrates that there are Ukrainians who do not denounce the foundation of the 'fraternal' relations with Russia but accuse Russia of behaving in an 'unbrotherly' manner.

4.3. Russian oppositionists' attitudes toward Ukrainian 'brothers'

If we analyze the statements made by Russian oppositionists, i.e. those people who express strong disagreement with the policy of President Putin, it can be easily noticed that they differ significantly in terms of usage of the metaphor 'brothers' compared with 'Russian officials', as discussed in section 4.1. More specifically, the former represent three modes of metaphor application. The first category of speakers follow the Ukrainian denunciation exemplified in the poetry by Anastasiya Dmitruk: they deny cultural similarities and the perceived political and historical bonds between Russians and Ukrainians. The second category of speakers, similarly to Portnikov in example (7), acknowledge commonalities in mindset but blame the Russian government for turning 'brothers' into 'enemies'. The third category of speakers uses the term 'brothers' as sign of endearment and admiration. The first pattern can be illustrated by the statement of Alexandr Sokurov, a renowned film director.

> (8)
> *В наших отношениях с Украиной кроется очень старая проблема. Мы глубоко заблуждаемся, считая друг друга* ***братскими*** *народами, это не так. Мы два больших народа, которые являются соседями, но мы* ***не братья и сестры****. Русские никак не могут этого понять. У нас есть сосед, в жизни которого нам многое напоминает нас самих. Например, в культуре, но, тем не менее, мы не являемся ее частью, так же как и украинцы не являются частью русской культуры. Это иллюзия…*

8 Portnikov, V. (2013). Привет Путину. Украинцы меняют отношение к России. [Regards to Putin. The Ukrainians are changing their attitudes toward the Russians]. *Liga. net*. 05.09.2013. Retrieved from http://www.liga.net/opinion/142460_privet-putinu-ukraintsy-menyayut-otnoshenie-k-rossii.htm; DOA: 07.11.2016.

[In our relations with Ukraine there is a very old problem. We are deeply mistaken, considering each other as **fraternal** peoples, since it is not true. We have two great nations who are neighbors, but we are **not brothers and sisters**. Russians cannot possibly understand. We have a neighbor whose life reminds us a lot of our own. For example, in culture, but nevertheless we are not part of it, also – Ukrainians are not part of Russian culture. It is an illusion….]

(Sokurov, 2014)[9]

As can be seen, Sokurov invalidates the cognitive ground for the analogy between closely related or neighboring ethnic groups and the ideal family as exemplified in the Russian anthem by Sergei Mikhalkov. The analogy between neighboring nations or ethnicities and an idealized family could lead to the inferences that 'interdependent brothers' are destined to stay in one family/under the same roof and share their routine practices.

At the same time, Alexei Navalny, a Russian politician, does not deny the cultural proximity between Russians and Ukrainians and refers to his personal experience in communication to validate this point. According to Navalny, the rift between the 'brothers' was caused by the Russian intentional policy of confrontation and enforcement of political decisions (see also examples 6 and 7). Furthermore, Navalny uses the clichéd analogy 'Ukrainians and Russians are brothers' to blame the Russian leadership for ruining relations between the friendly nations. Navalny starts with the assertion of the 'fraternal bond' between the Eastern Slavs and proclaims it a valuable asset for Russians. Then he continues:

(9)

*…но всё-таки с Украиной и Белорусией мы как **братья** в разных квартирах, а не просто соседи. Понятно, что есть ньюансы, разные территории и тд. **Но творимый сейчас Путиным союз** с условным названием «Россия и Средняя Азия против Украины» для меня абсурден. Это извращение какое-то.*

[…nevertheless, Ukraine and Belarus for us are like our **brothers** residing in different apartments rather than simply neighbors. It is understandable that there are nuances, different territories etc. but the so-called **Union**, 'Russia and Middle Asia against Ukraine' **which is created by Putin**, is absurd, in my view. It is some sort of perversion.]

(Navalny, 2014)[10]

---

9 Sokurov, A. (2014). Мы, русские, украинцам не братья, мы им – просто соседи. [We, Russians, are not brothers to Ukrainians, we are just their neighbours]. *Argumenty nedeli* [Arguments of the week], 10.05.2014. Retrieved from http://argumenti.ru/society/2014/05/337375; DOA: 07.11.2016.

10 Navalny, A. (2014). Оппозиционер Навальный высказался по Украине. [Navalny, the oppositionist, has given his opinion regarding Ukraine]. *Belomorkanal*, TV

The assertion 'fraternal relations' does not carry the same intention as the statements of the government officials discussed in section 4.1 (see examples 2 and 3). It does not lead to the necessity of a political union. The intention of Navalny's argument is to blame the Russian Government for creating a gap in communication between the two Slavic nations and promoting artificial political alliances.

By contrast, example (10) demonstrates that the term 'brother' has been used as a sign of honoring the struggle of Ukrainian people with the corrupt President and government and does not derive from the assumption of sharing a long history of relations and reciprocal obligations in the perceived partnership.

(10)

Братья-украинцы*, простите нас!*

[Ukrainian **brothers**, forgive us!]

(A statement pronounced at an anti-government protest in Moscow)[11]

The statement in example (10) was made by a protester detained by the Russian police at an anti-government meeting. The claim was likely meant to show respect for participants of Euromaidan in Ukraine and to acknowledge the unfairness of the Russian policy on the matter. Here, the term 'brother' entails the solidarity and fondness for someone who is similar in spirit, which correlates with the metaphorical 'blood'.

To summarize this section, examples (8–10) show that there are different pragmatic functions attached to the assertion of 'brotherhood' between Russians and Ukrainians in the discourse of Russian oppositionists. In some instances, the term conveys respect and solidarity (e.g. in example 10), while in other contexts (see example 9) it is an excuse for expressing regrets about lost opportunities. Examples (8) and (9) illustrate that the perception of closeness and similarities between Russians and Ukrainians can vary among different speakers (i.e. Navalny and Sokurov; see also Dmitruk's statement in example 4). For instance, Navalny argues that Russians and Ukrainians are similar while Dmitruk and Sokurov deny similarities between the nations. We can conclude that metaphor users express different judgements as to whether cultural similarities allow for calling Russians and Ukrainians 'brothers'.

29.ru. 12.03.2014. Retrieved from http://tv29.ru/index.php?point=politic&bl62number=18106; DOA: 07.11.2016.

11 "No to the war!" protest, 11.03.2014. Retrieved from https://www.youtube.com/watch?v=ZP2Tb_GeQZ0; DOA: 07.11.2016.

4.4. Patterns of 'brotherhood' in the statements of Russian government supporters

The use of the metaphor by Russian government supporters reveals another cline of variations. Certainly, among these discourse participants there can be found examples which echo the statements of Putin and Lavrov. However, there is also a stream of comments which undermine the belief, expressed by the power group, in the perpetual bond between the two nations. These discourse participants have been engaged in expressing persistent denial of fraternal relations. If nationally conscious Ukrainians and some Russian oppositionists blame Russia for ruining the friendly relations, in pro-Russian statements it is Ukrainians who are usually presented as having uncivilized manners which are incompatible with partnership or 'brotherhood'.

Example (11) is testimony to the persuasive impact of government officials' discourse. The line of argument and the foundation of the analogy mirror examples (1–3).

(11)
*В любом случае мы **братские народы**. Наши корни, семьи, экономика прочно переплетены. Мы должны видеть разницу между политиками и их народом.*

[In any case, we are **fraternal nations** indeed. Our roots, families, and economies are strongly intertwined. We must see the difference between politicians and their nations.]
(Vatsenko, 2014)[12]

The blogger in example (11) dwells on the discursive frame of shared history which can secure perpetual connections on all levels of nationhood. It is argued that the deterioration in the special, 'brother-like' relations between the nations has been caused by a minority group, also known as 'fascists' or 'Nazis' (Lavrov, 2014). Moreover, any independent cause of actions such as a desire to join the EU has been perceived as an attempt to abandon the 'family'.

In short, the picture promoted by the Russian government, and then adopted by its supporters, can be verbalized in the following way: Russians and Ukrainians are members of an ever-lasting family/political union. Mad anti-Russian politicians and extremists endanger this friendly partnership of nations with common interests and an interconnected style of living. Other people among the 'brothers' have been either duped or left to suffer. Hence, all efforts should be made to

12 Vatsenko, A. (2014). Русские и украинцы объединяйтесь! [Russians and Ukrainians unite!]. 13.03.2014. Retrieved from http://rossiyanavsegda.ru/read/1815; DOA: 01.03.2016.

undermine the power of the 'mad people' and restore the normal functioning of the 'family'.

Nonetheless, not all anti-Ukrainian discourse participants adhere to this view. Example (12) features a post by a Russian blogger who claims that Ukrainians are the ones who imposed fake 'brotherhood' upon Russia. Ukrainians usurped the 'title' of 'brothers' when they needed business concessions. Otherwise, neither Russians nor Ukrainians could hold each other to be dear and beloved:

(12)

Украинцы же свято верили и верят только в то, что русские (москали) – это люди второго сорта, угнетатели, сволочи и гады, а ***сказку*** *про то, что мы* ***"братские народы"*** *– предъявляют нам тогда, когда хотят у нас что-то попросить или нагло потребовать.*

[Ukrainians also firmly believed and continue to believe exclusively that Russians (Muscovites) are a second-class people, the oppressors, swine and reptiles. They only tell us the **fairy tale** about the '**fraternal nations'** either when they need to ask us for something or to make some insolent demand.]

(SNTDPNI, 20th June 2014)[13]

In example (12) the portrayal of Ukrainian efforts to become 'brothers' at times when it suits them activates perspectives different from the government vision. If Russian high-ranking officials try to send a message that Ukrainians, as real 'brothers', are dear for Russians and that their interests, different from the interests of their politicians and extremist forces, should be attended to and protected, the blogger in example (12) implies that Russians should dissociate themselves from these imposters or punish them for their ignoble conduct. Many Russian discourse participants do accept the view that Ukrainians are their 'brothers', but at the same time cast them as treacherous ones. For this purpose, several subversive scenarios and metaphor stories have been deployed, including 'Cain and Abel', 'a black sheep in the family', 'Judas', or 'a prodigal brother' (A'Beckett, 2016, pp. 299–303). Thus, admitting 'ignoble brotherhood' between Russians and Ukrainians does not correlate with the government picture of caring [about] and respecting the interests of Ukrainians.

13 SNTDPNI. (2014). Наши украинские братья. [Our Ukrainian brothers]. A Russian blog, 26.07.2016. Retrieved from http://ru-polit.livejournal.com/1539770.html?utm_campaign=transit&utm_source=mirtesen&utm_medium=news&from=mirtesen; DOA: 07.11.2016.

5. Conclusions

This case study has demonstrated that the research model promoting the uniformity of beliefs and judgements among the users of the same metaphor needs to be considered with caution when metaphor discourse is analyzed. As has been shown in more recent studies (e.g. Musolff, 2013), the cognitive base of a ubiquitous metaphor is subject to contextual variations. For instance, as I have shown in my paper, the assertion about 'fraternal' relations does not necessarily lead to the objectification of trust, equality, common interests and solidarity attributed to the ideal of a 'brother'. If the speaker applies the metaphor 'brothers' but then specifies that they are the Cain and Abel type of 'brothers' (A'Beckett, 2016, p. 303), then the idealized prototype loses its relevance. Such occurrences in metaphor discourse undermine the assumption that it is important to change the set of metaphors in order to drive social changes. This point has been illustrated with example (9) and also in A'Beckett (2012, p. 187), which demonstrate that while Russian oppositionists, such as Navalny and Novodvorskaia, actually adapted the hegemonic metaphors of the Russian power group, they nevertheless used them to send a subversive message.

Does the circulation of a dominant metaphor warrant coherence of the expressed beliefs in discourse? The answer is both 'yes' and 'no'. If the coherence of discourse is viewed as a tradition of aligning certain issues with a distinct metaphoric frame then the answer is 'yes'. Yet, if we consider the variation of judgements and implications which come out of the application of this frame, then the answer is 'no'.

Discourse participants often use the same metaphor vehicle and put it in the same argumentative position (i.e. negation, assertion or question), but communicate dissimilar opinions. The detection of attitudinal biases requires a more fine-grained analysis which includes a juxtaposition of different frames of reference (i.e. attribution of roles of "bad brothers" and "good brothers"), as well as a comparison of pragmatic functions (i.e. expression of reproach, advise, blame or fondness and solidarity) and of the experiential ground for analogy.

It could be argued that Russian government officials adopted the metaphor to reinforce the idea of commonalities between nations and purport to please their neighbors by communicating fondness and a desire to care about their loved ones. The conceptualization 'brothers' in the speeches of Russian officials aims at evoking the perception of mutual trust, common values and reciprocity in dealings among nations. Regrettably, the metaphor has been consistently deployed to put a ruthless political agenda into effect since it reifies idealization rather than observations about real families. For instance, the use of the metaphor BROTHERS by Russian public officials sustains the perception that 'brotherly' nations should live in a friendly union and help each other. The extent of this help can be subject to speculation and distortion: as we could observe, it is often transformed into invasion and the practice of dictating the terms to a brotherly nation. The idealistic vision of NATIONS ARE BROTHERS who help each other has not found unanimous support in the addressed communities. Some opponents accept the idea of commonalities, but stress the ruinous state of the 'family'. Russian oppositionists blame officials for interference, while government supporters demand more action to protect the alleged 'family'. Other opponents and members of the Ukrainian discourse community reject the idea of commonalities between the two nations and the entailed partnership. The grounds for rejection vary, however, and the experiential ground of the metaphor undergoes constant alterations.

Ukrainians sometimes accept the idea of shared values and close relations, but put the blame for the destructive intrusions into their own matters on Russians. They recall trade wars, tall orders and meddling habits. Alternatively, Russians blame either the whole Ukrainian nation or a minority of 'fascists and extremists' for the dismal state of affairs within the 'family'.

Finally, some opponents of the Russian government have adopted the assertive term 'brother' as a means of expressing respect, solidarity, admiration and compassion. As was argued before, the official use of the metaphor alluded to the long family history which forged eternal relations between nations. However, in the statements of some government opponents the alleged 'brotherhood' was coined just recently upon the realization of exceptional bravery and achievements of 'Ukrainian brothers'. Thus, the patterns of BROTHERS metaphor use are not fixed and are subject to negotiation in discourse.

References

A'Beckett, L. (2012). The Play of Voices in Metaphor Discourse: A Case Study of 'NATIONS ARE BROTHERS'. *Metaphor and Symbol*, 27(2), 171–194.

A'Beckett, L. (2016). Interpretation of metaphoric evaluation: Contextual shifts in the semantic organizations of prototypes. In O. Laguta & A. Savchenko (Eds.), *Slavica Formosana 1. Humanitarian Values in Slavic Languages and Cultures*. Taipei: National Chenghi University, 283–309.

Bagshave, T. (2010). *Scandalous*. London: Harper Collins.

Bakhtin, M. M. (1981). *The dialogic imagination*. Translated by C. Emerson & M. Holquist. Austin: University of Texas Press.

Cameron, L. (2010). What is Metaphor and Why Does It Matter? In L. Cameron & R. Maslen (Eds.), *Metaphor Analysis*. London: Equinox, 3–26.

Chiang, W.-Y., & Duann, R.-F. (2007). Conceptual Metaphors for SARS: "War" between Whom? *Discourse and Society*, 18(5), 509–602.

Cisneros, J. D. (2008). Contaminated Communities: The Metaphor of 'Immigrant as Pollutant' in Media Representations of Immigration. *Rhetoric and Public Affairs*, 11(4), 569–601.

Deignan, A. (2010). The cognitive view of metaphor: Conceptual metaphor theory. In L. Cameron & R. Maslen (Eds.), *Metaphor Analysis*. London: Equinox, 44–57.

Didriksen, A. A., & Gjesdal, A. M. (2013). On what is not said and who said it: Argumentative connectives in Nicolas Sarkozy's speeches to the European Parliament. In K. Flottum (Ed.), *Speaking of Europe*. Amsterdam: John Benjamins, 85–111.

Fløttum, K. (2013). Speaking of and within the EU- Introduction. In K. Flottum (Ed.), *Speaking of Europe*. Amsterdam: John Benjamins, 1–19.

Giora, R. (2003). *On our mind: Salience, context and figurative language*. Oxford, UK: Oxford University Press.

Howe, N. (1988). Metaphor in Contemporary American Political Discourse. *Metaphor and Symbolic Activity*, 3(2), 87–104.

Inkeles, A. (1950). *Public opinion in Soviet Russia. A study in mass persuasion*. Cambridge (USA): Harvard University Press.

Kjeldsen, J. E. (2013). Speaking to Europe: A Rhetorical approach to Prime Minister Tony Blair's speech to the EU Parliament. In K. Flottum (Ed.), *Speaking of Europe*. Amsterdam: John Benjamins, 19–43.

Koller, V. (2004). *Metaphor and Gender in Business Media Discourse: A Critical Cognitive Studies*. New York, NY: Palgrave Macmillan.

Koller, V. (2005). Critical discourse analysis and social cognition: Evidence from business media discourse. *Discourse and Society*, 16(2), 199–224.

Lakoff, G., & Johnson, M. (1980). *Metaphor we live by*. Chicago: Chicago University Press.

Lakoff, G. (1996). *Moral Politics: What Conservatives Know that Liberals Don't*. Chicago, Il: University of Chicago Press.

Lakoff, G. (2013). Metaphor and war: The metaphor system used to justify war in the gulf. *Cognitive Semiotics*, 4(2), 5–19.

Lavrov, S. (2014). *Для России Украина - это братский народ, а не марширующие в Киеве нацисты*. [For Russia Ukraine is a brotherly people, but not the Nazi who are marching in Kiev.] *Novaya gazeta*, 19.10.2014. Retrieved from http://www.novayagazeta.ru/news/1688414. html; DOA: 07.11.2016.

Ly, A. (2013). Images and roles of the European Union in the climate change debate: A cognitive approach to metaphors in the European Parliament. In K. Flottum (Ed.), *Speaking of Europe*. Amsterdam: John Benjamins, 151–169.

Martin, J. R., & White, P. R. R. (2005). *The language of evaluation: Appraisal in English*. New York, NY: Palgrave.

Musolff, A. (2004). *Metaphor and political discourse*. Basingstoke, UK: Palgrave.

Musolff, A. (2006). Metaphor scenarios in public discourse. *Metaphor and Symbol*, 21(1), 23–38.

Musolff, A. (2013). The *heart of Europe*: Synchronic variations and historical trajectories of a political metaphor. In K. Flottum (Ed.), *Speaking of Europe*. Amsterdam: John Benjamins, 135–151.

Nerlich, B., & Jaspal, R. (2012). Metaphors we die by? Geoengineering, metaphors and the argument from catastrophe. *Metaphor and Symbol*, 27(2), 131–148.

Noren, C. (2013). Doing politics or doing media? A linguistic approach to European parliamentary debate. In K. Flottum (Ed.), *Speaking of Europe*. Amsterdam: John Benjamins, 43–65.

Pavlenko, A. (2008). Russian in post-Soviet countries. *Russian linguistics*, 32(1), 59–80.

Porto, M. D., & Romano, M. (2013). Newspaper Metaphors: Reusing Metaphors across Media Genres. *Metaphor and Symbol*, 28(1), 60–73.

Pushnova, T. (2014). Toppling Lenin and His Legacy. *New Eastern Europe*, 5, 25–28.

Ritchie L. D., & Cameron, L. (2014). Open hearts or smoke and mirrors: Metaphorical framing and frame conflicts in a public meeting. *Metaphor and Symbol*, 29(3), 204–223.

Santa Anna, O. (1999). 'Like an animal I was treated'; Anti-immigrant metaphor in US public Discourse. *Discourse and Society*, 10(2), 191–224.

Schȍn, D. (1993). Generative metaphor: A perspective on problem-setting in social policy. In A. Ortony (Ed.), *Metaphor and thought* (2nd ed.). Cambridge, UK: Cambridge University Press, 137–163.

Semino, E., & Masci, M. (1996). Politics is Football: Metaphor in the discourse of Silvio Berlusconi in Italy. *Discourse and Society*, 7(2), 243–269.

Strannik, I. (2014). Все ответы Анастасии Дмитрук. [All responses to Anastasiya Dmitruk]. 10.04.2014. Retrieved from http://agv.mirtesen.ru/blog/43607718234/Vse-otvetyi--na-stih-Anastasii-Dmitruk; DOA: 07.11.2016.

Sahadete Limani-Beqa

University of Prishtina, Kosovo

Approaches to Critical Discourse Analysis in interaction: Analyzing the political transformation in Kosovo with CDA methods and tools

Abstract: This article presents a research design developed for analyzing political transformation in Kosovo with the methods and tools of Critical Discourse Analysis (CDA). The model that I developed for the purpose of the research is a combination of different complementary approaches of Critical Discourse Analysis. It aims to provide a sample that is representative enough to generalize the results of the study, and, based on the existing research designs of different CDA approaches, to develop a hierarchy of categories, primarily of linguistic nature, needed to describe political discourse in the said context.

1. Introduction

This paper describes the methodology used in the research project entitled *The process of political transformation and language use in Kosovo during the period 1999–2005. A Critical Discourse Analysis*. The research was carried out by the author of this paper during the years 2008–2009 in Kosovo.[1]

The research was conducted by combining different approaches complementary to Critical Discourse Analysis (CDA), such as the dialectical-relational approach, (e.g. Fairclough, 1992, 1995, 2005; Mautner, 2000, 2009); the discourse-historical approach (e.g. Wodak, de Cillia, Reisigl & Liebhart, 1999; Jäger, 2001, 2012) and the socio-cognitive approach (e.g. van Dijk, 2001, 2009; Chilton, 2004), which share theoretical foundations (in particular the focus on the relations between language, power, ideology and domination), yet have no unique methodology. In consequence, to ensure that the basic criteria for quality assessment are fulfilled by the findings of my research, it was necessary to develop a methodology built on a number of existing methods and tools within different CDA paradigms.

The aim of this article is therefore not so much to provide a detailed account of the research findings on the political transformation in Kosovo and its discourse

1 For more about this research, see Limani-Beqa (2011).

as to show how a combination of different CDA approaches, methods and tools makes such research feasible.

2. Background information

The research for which the model was designed deals with the discursive dimension of Kosovo's post-war political transformation during the period from 1999 to 2005. From the end of the war in 1999, until the declaration of independence on 17 February 2008, Kosovo was under the administration of the international community[2], represented by the United Nations Mission in Kosovo (UNMIK).

Political transformation was supposed to change Kosovo's society from a conflict-driven to a democratic one. This meant building governmental institutions of a democratic and multi-ethnic society, which would later solve the issue of the region's political status.[3] Kosovo's post-war society was deeply divided ethnically and had to implement the principles, norms, and rules of Western liberal democracies.

In order to implement this scenario, the international community chose a top-down approach, which meant cooperating closely with Kosovo's political elites, mainly with the leaders of political parties, who in turn were to persuade their voters to accept the model proposed by the international community. These political elites had to be legitimized by both local voters and the international community, which proved hard to achieve as there were disagreements between local voters and the international community over the political rule in Kosovo. Specifically, Albanians opted for an independent Kosovo ruled by Albanians and respecting minority rights, while Serbs insisted that Kosovo remain under Serbian governance.

The process of political transformation in Kosovo is reflected in discourse. Apparently, the international community had started the country's political transformation in discourse: its main objective of establishing democratic structures of a multiethnic society meant, among others, rejecting old discourses and enacting a

---

2 The term *international community* is as such very vague, but for the purpose of this research, this term includes international organizations which were responsible for the administration of Kosovo in the Period 1999–2008, i.e. the United Nations Interim Mission in Kosovo, OSCE, KFOR, and the Representatives of the Countries of the G8 Group: the US, Germany, Italy, Russia, UK, France, Canada and Japan.

3 According to Resolution 1244 of the Security Council, Kosovo, under the protectorate of the United Nations, was to be democratized up to the point where political tensions between the two ethnic communities of Serbs and Albanians would be firmly relaxed, after which both communities would negotiate to settle the political status of the country.

new one. The old discourses were characterized by the binary opposite 'us' versus 'them' and a hatred language used by two ethnic groups: Serbs and Albanians against each other. The majority of the Kosovo population, the Albanians, considered Kosovo as an Albanian land, whereas the Serbs, who were ruling for many decades, wanted Kosovo to be theirs as the Serbian holy land.

Following the war, ended by NATO intervention in 1999, until the declaration of its independence in 2008 the land was governed by the international community under the umbrella of the United Nations. The international community was trying to enact a new discourse that featured human rights and liberal discourses and was part of a strategy to impose new identity on both ethnic groups, Serbs and Albanians, who were to identify themselves as 'us' – Kosovars. Whether the international community has succeeded to inculcate the new discourse is questionable. In one of its reports, the International Crisis Group (ICG), which looked at the political situation in Kosovo and the impact of the international community on shaping it, suggests that: "Kosovo Albanians have become so used to wearing the masks that the international community requires of them, that is probably not even clear to themselves if the masks have now become a true face." (International Crisis Group, 2006)[4]

The objective of this research is therefore to explore whether such masks – as constructed in discourse – have become the real, discursively created faces of Kosovars. The study covers the period in which Kosovo was under direct protectorate of the international community represented by UNMIK. Due to the limits of this paper I have narrowed my focus to the following research questions and hypotheses:

Research Question 1: Has the discourse of the international community colonized the local political discourse in Kosovo?

Hypothesis 1: Political elites in Kosovo have not implemented the discourse of the international community.

Research Question 2: How have discourse and power relations conditioned one another?

2.1 How does the political discourse in Kosovo change under the pressure of various political situations?

2.2. Do politicians in Kosovo use a dual discourse in order to gain and keep power, depending on the audience, i.e. one for the local voter and one for the international community?

---

4 International Crisis Group (ICG) is an international think tank, which has dealt with the developments in Kosovo since 1998. Many findings of ICG's research have served the international community in Kosovo in its political decisions.

Hypothesis 2: As a consequence of considerable differences between foreign and home players on the political scene of Kosovo, political leaders, in order to gain and keep power, used two types of discourses, one for local voters and one for the international community.

3. Theoretical Framework

This research is not a purely linguistic study; it focuses on the phenomena linking linguistic and non-linguistic issues – in this case, the political reality of Kosovo in the process of transformation and its discursive representation. The most prominent scholars of Critical Discourse Analysis (CDA) such as Ruth Wodak, Teun van Dijk, Norman Fairclough, Sigfried Jäger or Paul Chilton offer a suitable theoretical framework. The following paragraphs present the key aspects of the CDA approach, which should also justify its use in the present study.

By definition, CDA is basically interested in analyzing both opaque and transparent structural relationships of dominance, discrimination, power, and control as manifested in language (Wodak, 2009, p. 10). CDA explains, on the one hand, the relationship between linguistic means and concrete discursive actions that enhance certain discourse practices[5], and, on the other hand, the inter-dependence between discourse practices and political, social, and institutional reality.

For scholars in this field[6], discourse (understood as the use of language in written, spoken and visual media) is seen as an element of not only social practices, but also of material actions, institutional rituals, social relations, norms and values. As a result, discourse has a productive force, being capable of shaping the social reality. What is more, discourse practices can have major ideological effects – that is, they can help produce and reproduce unequal power relations between (for instance) social classes, women and men, and/or ethnic/cultural majorities and minorities, through the ways in which these groups represent things and position themselves and others (Wodak & Fairclough, 1997, p. 258). This productive force of discourse as a political practice is explained by Norman Fairclough in the following terms: "Discourse as political practice establishes, sustains, and changes

---

5 The term *discursive action* is used to describe each communication act, be it a single conversation, a single text or a single visual in which language means are used for a strategic purpose. When this single act becomes a practice, it is described under the term *discourse practice*.

6 See e.g. Fairclough (1992, 1995, 2001, 2005), Jäger (2001, 2012), van Dijk (1993a, b, c, 1998, 2005, 2007), Wodak & Fairclough (1997), Wodak (et al., 1999; Wodak, 1999, 2009), Chilton (2004).

power relations and the collective entities (classes, blocks, communities, groups), between which power relations obtain" (Fairclough, 1992, p. 68).

According to Fairclough (2005, p. 3), discourses not only have an impact on the ongoing processes of social change and other elements which inspired them, but also some changes actually begin with and in discourse. In situations of social crisis and instability, of which Kosovo under transformation is an example, different social agents develop strategies for change, including discourses representing the visions of new forms of social life and narrations which build a more or less coherent relationship between what happened in the past and what could happen in the future. In order to make this type of discourse a social reality, such visions are operationalized and become effective once they have been officially ratified (enacted) and become part of socially shared memory (inculcated).

Despite many theoretical approaches in discourse studies and their diverse methodologies, the 'core' of the new discipline remains the systematic and explicit analysis of various structures and strategies at different levels of text and talk (van Dijk, 2007, p. 5). Based on these components, analyzing discourse can provide findings about different social phenomena, including socio-political transformation. In this case the social meaning of transformation can be elicited by analyzing the related discourses.

As for defining the concept of discourse, for present purposes I use two definitions of the term. First, discourse can refer to the "flow of knowledge through time" (Jäger, 1999, p. 255). This definition was used when addressing the first research question (see above): *Has the international community discourse colonized local public discourses?* In order to answer this question, I used a sub-question: *Does the knowledge that the international community is trying to transmit about the kind of political system to be built in Kosovo circulate in the Kosovar society?* Second, discourse can refer to language use in text and speech (e.g. Wodak & Fairclough, 1997), which approach was used to address the following questions (Research question 2.2; see above): *How does the political discourse in Kosovo change under the pressure of various political situations?* And, more specifically: *Do politicians in Kosovo use a dual discourse? What kind of discursive strategies do Kosovar politicians use to legitimate their power? What kind of argumentation and language means do they use to realize these strategies?*[7]

7 A reviewer asked about an attempt at defining 'political discourse' which I made in this brief introduction via the definition of *discourse* by Jäger (1999, 2001, 2012) and Fair-clough and Wodak (1997), and which could be cosnidered a simplification or generali-zation. It must be taken into account, however, that my analysis is a critical-political analysis rather than an analysis of political discourse *per se*. The discourse of

4. CDA methodology: problems and challenges

To obtain valid and representative findings regarding the research questions, a research design compatible with the CDA theoretical framework was needed. As stated above, while diverse CDA approaches may have certain theoretical common points, in working to create an empirical research design I have encountered the following problems:

4.1. Lack of a unified methodology for data gathering

For my research to obtain findings that fulfill the criteria of rigorous research, a diachronic and synchronic analysis is required. The former results from the fact that the process of political transformation can be traced only by taking into consideration a long time span; the transformation of societies does not happen in a day or a month. Whichever definition of *discourse* is applied – the use of language in text and speech (e.g. Wodak & Fairclough, 1997; see also section 3) or the flow of knowledge during a period of time (e.g. Jäger, 1999, p. 255; see also section 3) – a study of discourse as presented in this paper requires an analysis of a large quantity of texts. Nevertheless, few CDA scholars, with a prominent exception of corpus-based CDA researchers such as Mautner (2000, 2005, 2009), offer a research design applicable to analyzing large quantities of texts, or to selecting a sample that is representative enough of such a large corpus. As Wodak and Reisigl (2009, p. 28) stated, "there is no CDA way of gathering data." As a result, CDA researchers often analyze a number of texts taken to be typical of the whole discourse in a given context, sometimes even without justifying why these texts can be treated as typical.

Also, research designs differ from one author to another. Some of them (e.g. Jäger, 2001, 2005, 2012) choose a two-phase approach: firstly, they make a more general analysis of the whole corpus; secondly, they conduct a micro-linguistic

main political actors is a sample of the public discourse, and the object of the study is the political transformation in Kosovo. In this context, the concept of discourse presented by Jäger was more useful to answer the main research question, which deals with the colonization of the local public discourse by the international community. Second, this definition was more useful to narrow the corpus (macro-analysis). Fairclough's definition, in turn, was used for capturing the discourse structures (micro-analysis). The political discourse as defined by e.g. van Dijk (1997) seems too narrow to define the research object in the present study. In terms of the context (namely of institutional settings, actors, events, time) and the discourse structures (text properties), my object of research is broader than van Dijk defines it, hence a different set of definitions was used as a theoretical point of departure here.

analysis of some texts chosen from it. Among different approaches applying this two-level model of analysis, one can indicate Jäger's (2001) model, differentiating between *structural discourse analysis* and *fine analysis*, or Fairclough (1992, 1995, 2005, 2009), who proposes to start analyzing the *socio-cultural practice* and the *discourse practice* (both related to the context at the general level), and only after that to analyze the text itself. These two-level analyses have their advantages since they help to structure the material; nonetheless, using such models does not solve the problem of gathering representative and unbiased data. Another methodological challenge lies with the definition of context: CDA underlines its importance in research in order to demystify the meaning of the discourses analyzed. Yet scholars applying CDA methods (e.g. Fairclough, 1992, 1995, 2005; van Dijk, 1993a, b, c, 1997, 2004, 2005; Wodak et al., 1999; Wodak, 1999, 2001, 2009; Jäger, 2001, 2005; 2012; Panagl & Wodak, 2004) often do not propose a unified definition of context, nor suggest the ways of defining it (e.g. how broad it should be).

4.2. Differently labeled and/or unstructured analytical categories

Scholars in CDA[8] have developed a wide range of analytical categories to describe text corpora systematically, at textual, semantic, syntactic and/or lexical levels. In some cases the authors of such categorizations draw on sociological theories (e.g. Fairclough, 1995, 2005; Chilton, 1998; Mautner, 2000; Jäger, 2001), but in general they rely on different linguistic theories for this purpose. However, regarding these analytical categories in general, two main problems arise: (1) different labeling of the same conceptualized categories by different scholars, and (2) lack of a structured hierarchy of categories.

Ad. (1) *Different labeling*: In some cases there is a risk of getting confused when referring to different categorization models if their authors have labeled differently the same categories. This may happen when the models are oriented towards different theoretical fields: functional linguistics, theory of social cognition, rhetoric, etc. For example, in many models argumentation is used as an analytical category meant to capture the formal structure of a text. Yet while some authors label argumentation in terms of *argumentative scheme, text schema,* or *argumentative structure* (e.g. van Dijk, 1991, p. 125), others call it an *argumentative process* (e.g. Fairclough, 1992; Mautner, 2000), and still some other authors label it *argumentation strategies* (e.g. Jäger, 2001) or *topoi* (e.g. Wodak et al., 1998, 1999, 2009). Another example

---

8 E.g. van Dijk (1985, 1991, 1993a, b, c, 1997, 2002, 2007), Fairclough (1992, 1995, 2000, 2003, 2005, 2009), Chilton (1998, 2004), Wodak et al. (1999), Wodak (1999, 2001, 2004, 2009), Girnth (2002), Geissner (2004), Spieß (2006), or Mills (2007).

are categories that are developed for analyzing the structures of the text content at the text's surface or underlying level. The content, which is very vaguely defined, includes meaning structures and is captured under such categories as *topics* (e.g. van Dijk, 1991, 1997, 2002, 2009; Wodak, 1999), *macropropositions* (van Dijk, 1980, 1997, 2002), and *themes* (Fairclough, 1992; Jäger, 2001; Jung, 2001).[9]

Ad. (2) *Lack of a structured hierarchy of categories*: Regarding the relations between language and society, CDA does not take this relationship to be simply deterministic, but rather invokes an idea of *mediation* (Wodak, 2009). In other words, as van Dijk (2009) argues, there does not exist any direct influence of social context on the variation of discourse. And because social structures and discourse structures do not interact directly, they need the mediation of some interface. In order to identify the categories that mediate between social structures and discourse, different CDA approaches use different theories originating from different disciplines. For instance, the dialectical-relational approach (e.g. Fairclough, 1992, 1995, 2005; Mautner, 2000) draws on Halliday's (1985) systemic-functional linguistic theory on the one hand, and Foucault's (1981) concept of *orders of discourse,* on the other. By contrast, the discourse-historical approach (e.g. Wodak et al., 1998, 1999, 2009) and the socio-cognitive approach (e.g. van Dijk, 2001, 2009; Chilton, 2004) make use of theories of social cognition (e.g. Moscovici, 2000), and critical theory and symbolic interactionism (e.g. Wodak, 1999, 2009), respectively. Jäger (2001, 2005) relies on critical theory and on the concept of discourse as defined by Foucault (1981).

When it comes to the operationalization of the theoretical concepts, researchers use linguistic categories analysis. The corpus is analyzed at the macro-structural level and at the micro-linguistic level. Yet the analytical categories at each level are not always clearly structured. For instance, van Dijk (1995) differentiates between the *underlying structures* and the *surface structures* of discourse. Surface structures refer to the forms of language use as classified within linguistic or semiotic models, while underlying structures refer to the meaning or interaction deriving from

---

9 All these labels are used to refer to the content or the subject, which is called *Inhalt* in German. In one of his works van Dijk (1997) stresses the difficultness to identify the possible topics as structures of political discourse. As he says:

> This seems to open up a Pandora-box of possible topics and to suggest that formulating topical constraints in political discourse seems pointless. However, even with this broad scope of topics, there are such constraints. (Incidentally, one of the major fields lacking in discourse analysis is a sub-discipline of 'Topics' (Topica) or 'topology' which studies, among other things, what various types of discourses in what situations may be 'about'.)
> (van Dijk, 1997, p. 26)

these surface structures. Underlying structures are expressed through surface structures, while surface structures are crucial to the comprehension of discourse. Nonetheless, in terms of empirical analysis van Dijk does not always make such a clear cut. Other scholars as well (e.g. Wodak, Jäger or Chilton) use categories that can be classified into two groups: the form and the meaning. Such a classification of categories, however, is not made transparent – it can only be implied from the studies of these scholars. Categories of meaning imply argumentation strategies, *topoi* or topics, while categories of form imply lexis, syntax or grammar.

In order to overcome the two major problems, a separate study design was developed that combines different CDA approaches and Corpus Linguistics.

5. A research model combining different CDA approaches and Corpus Linguistics

As argued above, within current CDA approaches it is hard to identify one holistic research design which can serve as a methodological framework that meets the criteria of rigorous research. Nevertheless, since the existing approaches focus on one or more dimensions, but in separation, to solve CDA's methodological problems, combining different existing models and developing a new model can make the findings more representative and the research more in line with the standards of validity.

With regard to data collection and corpus sampling, the model of Siegfried Jäger (2012) seemed to be the most suitable since it offers ways of accessing data that would be representative of the whole discourse under investigation. Thus I borrow the concepts of *discourse strand*[10], *discourse fragments*[11], and *discursive events*[12] from Jäger (2001, 2012). According to him, since it is impossible to analyze the discourse of a given social context as a whole, the analysis must be based on a selected strand of discourse and on one level of discourse – for example, media discourse, newspaper discourse, political discourse, parliamentary discourse, discourse of political speeches, discourse of political campaigns, etc. To limit the corpus even further within one strand or level, Jäger (2001) suggests that a researcher should concentrate

10 A *discursive strand*, according to Jäger (2012, p. 80), consists of flows of discourse that center on a common topic. Each discourse strand comprises several discourse topics.

11 A *discourse fragment*, according to Jäger (2012, p. 81), refers to a text or part of a text that deals with a particular topic.

12 *Discursive events* are those events that appear in discourse planes of politics and the mass-media intensively, extensively and for a prolonged period of time. See Jäger (2012, p. 81).

on discursive events, that is important events discussed intensively in public and, as such, in the media as well. Discursive events affect the orientation and quality of the discourse strand. Such a selection of empirical material is significant and representative of the whole discourse (see Jäger, 2001).

Based on Jäger's (2001) approach, I selected the discourse of the political leaders of the largest political parties in Kosovo, as delivered during certain discursive events that were reported by the local media and discussed extensively and intensively for a prolonged period of time as public discourse topics. The discursive events included in the corpus were national election campaigns, memorial days and events regarding the dialog between Serbia and Kosovo in the period 1999–2005. These events where selected based on the criterion of being largely discussed in the media and affecting the direction and the quality of the discursive strand[13], in our case public discourse at large. Another main criterion for this selection was the targeted public and the subject under discussion. For an event to be included in the corpus it had to have the power relationship between UNMIK, Serbs and Albanians as its subject and/or have local Albanian politicians and local Albanian voters as main communication actors. Although the borderline is very fluid, it is still possible to differentiate between discursive events with the local voter being the main addressee and discursive events in which international actors appear as the targeted audience. Based on the primary audience I divided these discursive events into two groups. In the first group (Sub-corpus 1), I included discursive events in which international actors appear as the targeted audience, and in the other group (Sub-corpus 2), I included discursive events which had local voters in Kosovo as the primary audience.

In order to establish connections between the text and the context, I used the model of Norman Fairclough (1995), according to which every communicative event must be seen as a text, as a discursive practice (which is equivalent to the production and reception of a text), and as a socio-cultural practice. These three levels interact: the socio-cultural practice, through the discursive practice, leaves its traces in the text, and vice-versa, through the discursive practice the text affects social practice. For this reason, every discursive event must be examined in terms of these three dimensions. Specifically, in the textual dimension, we must examine the text's linguistic traits; at the level of discursive practice we must examine different aspects of production and reception; and at the level of socio-cultural

13 According to Jäger (2001, 2012), this is a criterion that defines certain events as discursive events.

practice we must examine the underlying social and cultural contexts and their effect on the discourse.

Finally, for the systematization of analytical categories, I used the categorization model of Gerlinde Mautner (2000) since it uses a more structured system of categories. Mautner's categories are not equal but hierarchical. The superordinate analytical category is the *strategy*, which Mautner (2009, p. 83) defines as "the specific selection, structuring and placing of contents in order to achieve a higher persuasive aim". Next on the scale are such categories as *motives* and *argumentation schemes*, the former being semantic categories, and the latter – formal structures. These, in turn, consist of linguistic means, which are the smallest units in this model and the building blocks of their superordinate categories. What is more, Mautner's approach is useful in one other respect. The use of corpus linguistics as a methodological tool provides additional linguistic devices for a thorough analysis of the data (Wodak & Reisigl, 2009).

To summarize, a model combining the three different approaches described above offers a clearer and more logical scheme of analysis; with its help we can connect qualitative and quantitative methods in CDA because it broadens the traditional tools of analysis by corpus linguistics methods. This is necessary to conduct an analysis of micro-linguistic categories and at the same time include statistics in the conducted research and thus ensure representative findings.

Regarding the conceptualization of analytical linguistic categories and their classifications with respect to the level of the text's surface I have used the terminology used by three authors: Ruth Wodak (1999, 2008, 2009), Norman Fairclough (1992, 1995, 2005, 2009), and Teun van Dijk (1991, 1993a, b, c, 1995, 1997).

In my research model the process of analysis operates in two phases:

Phase I: Data collection and preparation

First step: Selection of the corpus. The utterances of the leaders of three biggest political parties, expressed during the selected discursive events and reported in the three biggest daily newspapers serve as a representative sample of public discourse. The selection was restricted at three levels. First level: selection of the public speeches by three main political leaders: (1) *Ibrahim Rugova*, President of the party *Lidhja Demokratike e Kosoves* (LDK) and President of Kosova in the period from 2001 to 2006; (2) *Hashim Thaqi*, President of the political party *Partia Demokratike e Kosoves* (PDK); (3) *Ramush Haradinaj*, President of the party *Aleanca per Ardhmerine e Kosoves* (AAK) and prime Minister of Kosovo in the period 2004–2005. Second level: selection of discursive events during which the speeches were given: (1) *national election campaigns of 2001 and 2004*; (2) *national memorial days* (The Albanian Flag day, 26–29 November during the period 1999–2005); (3) *the memorial days of the last war in Kosova called "Epopeja e UCK" during the period 1999–2005*; (4) *discursive events regarding the dialog between Serbia and Kosovo in the period 1999–2005*. Third level: selection of newspapers that quoted the speeches: three main daily newspapers (*Koha Ditore, Bota Sot,* and *Epoka e Re*).

There are two reasons why the speeches of political leaders were selected as representative samples of political discourse. The first is based on the thesis of CDA theory, according to which political elites have power over discourse, and gain and hold that power through discourse. Secondly, the international community, in order to realize its political strategy in Kosovo, as defined in the UN resolution 1244, chose political leaders as the main partners, through whose speech the international community discourse was to be dispersed in Kosovar society at large. In the absence of original speeches, their mediated records and/or quotations appearing in newspapers were used.[14] The total number of words in the corpus is 41 058.

Second step: preparation of the corpus for analysis. Articles coming from newspapers which were originally available only in hard copies were prepared electronically. All citations of the selected politicians were digitalized; this is how the corpus was created.

Third step: classification of the data based on the primary target audience. At this step, the corpus was divided in to two sub-corpora. Sub-corpus 1 contained texts from discursive events that had the international public as their primary target audience and Sub-corpus 2 contained all the texts that had the local people in Kosovo as their primary target audience. The primary target audience was identified on the basis of the situational context.

Phase II: Data analysis

First step: Analysis of the social context of discourse. According to the Text Oriented Discourse Analysis (TODA) model of Norman Fairclough (1995), discursive practice and social practice are mutually related, which is why in the first step of analyzing the corpus I reflected on the broad social context in which the analyzed discursive events took place. Specifically, I identified three levels of the

---

14 The United Nations Mission in Kosovo (UNMIK) did not allow me to access its archive of relevant political speeches and the political parties concerned did not have their leaders' speeches archived. That is why speeches quoted in the main daily newspapers were chosen. The selection of newspapers was based on the criterion of high circulation and on the editorial policy. E.g. *Bota Sot* supported LDK and President Rugova, PDK and AAK were supported by the daily *Epoka e re*, and the newspaper *Koha Ditore* is more balanced regarding editorial policies and does not support any particular political party.

context in question. At the first level I made a summary of the historical dimension of the conflict in Kosovo and of the socio-political situation during UNMIK administration. At the second level I described the institutional context in which particular politicians delivered their speeches. In this aspect I summarized the qualities and outlooks of the political parties in Kosovo, and of the newspapers in which the speeches of the political leaders analyzed were quoted. At the third level I presented the narrow situational context in which the discursive events occurred, including their institutional framework, cause, location, participants, and recipients. Information regarding the context was drawn from diverse sources of knowledge including history books, think tank organization reports, monographs from the field of political sciences, press reports etc. The incorporation of context into the analysis was done with the aim of further expanding the analytical approach as well as justifying and interpreting the findings obtained in linguistic analysis. Moreover, understanding the context helped explain the social preconditions of linguistic expressions and their political functions. It served as a tool to ensure intersubjective data interpretation.

Second step: *Quantitative content analysis*. This was undertaken to answer the question of whether the topics of the discourse of the international community were also part of the agenda of the discourse of the local political leaders in Kosovo. For this purpose I used the research model design of Gerlinde Mautner (2000), which uses the tools of corpus linguistics to obtain the statistics on the most frequently used lexemes, and, based on these data, to identify the topics most frequently discussed in the discourse. Using the *Mini Longmann Concordance* software I compiled a relevant list of lexemes with the highest frequency in the corpus. Afterwards I ranked them according to broader semantic fields (macro topics): for example, words such as *Kosovo, independence* or *state* were grouped under *Political status*, whereas words such as *war, hero, freedom, Adem Jashari* or *Kosovo Liberation Army* belonged to the topic *Political past*. Another topic was *Relation with international community in Kosovo*, which was also used for the legitimization of political leaders, and which included words such as *NATO, EU, USA* or *UNMIK*. Finally, words such as *Serbs, Serbia* or *minority* belonged to the *Interethnic relations* topic.

After the identification of the topics I made a comparison between the two sub-corpora to measure the frequency of the topics in Sub-corpus 1 and Sub-corpus 2. The statistics obtained show that the *Political status of Kosovo*, especially the independence of Kosovo, was the main topic in both sub-corpora. This result indicates that the discourse of the international community did not have much influence on the agenda of Kosovar political leaders. While the international community was neutral regarding the political status of Kosovo, as set forth in United

Nations Resolution 1244, the topic of the political status was the main topic in the discourse of local political leaders. However, regarding other macro-topics, there was a difference between the two sub-corpora. In the texts targeted at local voters the most discussed topic was the *Political past*, especially the war for independence, whereas in communication with the international community the agenda of Kosovar political leaders was dominated by such topics as *interethnic relations* and *democratic development of Kosovar society*.

Third step: *Qualitative analysis*. The two general questions which I attempted to answer in this phase were: (1) What did Kosovar politicians say about the topics identified, and how did they say it? What discursive strategies did their speeches serve?; (2) Did Kosovar politicians use a dual discourse, one for local voters and one for the international public?

In order to address these questions, I analyzed the semantic environment in which the identified key words[15] of each topic appeared. The semantic environment involved collocations of the key words in a concordance row of 15 words to the left and 15 words to the right of the key word. For example, in order to analyze the status of Kosovo (the macro-topic *Political Status*) as represented in the discourse of political leaders I investigated the semantic aura of the word *Kosovo* in the two sub-corpora so that I could see if there is any difference in the semantic quality of this lexeme between them. The corpus analysis showed that in Sub-corpus 1 this word was accompanied most often by such words as *independence, state, democracy, freedom, liberation, heroic, fatherland, sublime sacrifice, war, altar of freedom, century dream, bloodshed*, and *experience*. This lexicon can be analyzed, in turn, in the wider semantic category of *nationalism*. The collocations build an emotional semantic aura[16] around the word *Kosovo*. This can be taken as a sign that the Kosovar political leaders ascribe an affective meaning to the status of Kosovo when they have the local Kosovar voter as the primary target audience. Kosovo means more than simply a land.

In Sub-corpus 2, the word *Kosovo* was mainly used with the words *institutions, citizens, progress, state, independence, peace, consolidation, preparation*,

---

15 For the purposes of this study, *keyness* is defined as particular words or clusters that have statistically significantly higher frequency in compare to other words or clusters in the corpus under analysis in comparison with another corpus. Their purpose is to point the 'aboutness' of the text (Scott, 1999), namely the topic and other central elements of the content. For more about keyness, see Baker, Gabrielatos, Khosravinik, Krzyzanowski, McEnery & Wodak (2008, p. 278).

16 *Semantic aura* is defined as a "consistent aura of meaning with which a form is imbued by its collocates" (Louw, 1993, p. 157).

construction, final status, constitution, international standard, inseparable territory, human rights, democracy, security, representation, advance, respect, aspire, etc. Here the lexicon of collocations with the word *Kosovo* can be presented in the broader semantic aura of democracy, with a more neutral vocabulary than in the case of the above-presented nationalism-related collocations of Kosovo in speeches targeted at the local audience.

After the semantic field identification, the description and analysis were extended to the level of sentences and text. For the textual analysis, I selected linguistic categories prominent in those parts of speeches which concerned language and power, legitimacy, and politics. For example, the category of *perspective* (Fairclough, 1992, 1995, 2005; Mautner, 2000) was researched on with the categories of *time, modality* or *transitivity*; the category of *referent* (van Dijk, 1989, 2001; Wodak, 1997, 1999, 2001) was analyzed against such categories as *pronouns, allusions, metonymies,* and *metaphors* (Wodak, 1999; Jäger, 2001, 2005; Chilton, 2004).

For example, when analyzing the collocations of the word *Kosovo*, a syntactic regularity was noticed, namely that *Kosovo* was not presented as a part of an adverb group, which would otherwise determine its geographical location, but more often it was found in the position of a process participant. According to Halliday's (1994) system of semantic roles, Kosovo was represented as an *AGENS* or *PATIENS*, sometimes as *GOAL*; in general then, Kosovo was presented as the subject or object of a sentence. Also, the findings indicate that Kosovo was personified in political leaders' speeches. In order to analyze the personification of Kosovo and its role in political discourse, I focused on the figures of metaphor and metonymy as used in the sub-corpora. According to Wodak et al. (1999, p. 18), these tropes are important components of the discursive construction of national sameness and uniqueness.

The analysis of tropes such as metaphors and metonymy led to the conclusion that in Sub-corpus 1 independent Kosovo was conceptualized as a HOUSE that is being built, where the traditional Albanian family lives; as a HOUSE that needs a head of the household to lead it. Moreover, Kosovo's political independence from Serbia was glorified as the realization of a century-long Albanian dream. In Sub-corpus 2 Kosovo was again presented with the HOUSE metaphor, but as a house where all residents live, with no exception regarding ethnicity or religion. Meanwhile, an independent Kosovo was represented as being supportive of peace and stability in both the region and the world.

The analysis of other linguistic categories such as tense, verbs, modal verbs, and verb forms, shows the double perspective regarding Kosovo's independence. In Sub-corpus 1 independence was presented as a fact rather than an event that might happen. In Sub-corpus 2 an independent Kosovo was presented more as a desire or a request than a real event, expected to happen very nearly.

Based on the results from the analysis of these categories, I wanted to see which general structures, e.g. *motives and argumentation* (Mautner, 2000), were most often used in the discourse of political leaders, as well as which *persuasive strategies* (Wodak, 2001) were realized through the use of these linguistic categories. The results of the analysis are presented in Table 1.

Table 1. List of categories identified in the discourse of political leaders in the two Sub-corpora

Topic	Strategies	Argumentation[17]	Language means
Political Status	**Sub-corpus 1:** Glorification of an independent Kosovo in the past and the future. Glorification of the political leader as a hero who fights for the nation. **Sub-corpus 2:** Glorification of an independent Kosovo as the key to the peace in the world. Glorification of political leaders as heroes who fight for peace and prosperity in the world.	**Sub-corpus 1:** An independent Kosovo, belonging to Albanians is the salvation of all Albanians from all evils. I have to fight during the war and I will fight also in the peace for the independence of Kosovo. **Sub-corpus 2:** An independent Kosovo, a country where all ethnic groups will live in freedom and peace together will contribute to peace in the world. I am working to convince my electorate to accept a Kosovo where Albanians and Serbs will rule together.	Collocations, semantic aura, tropes, allusions, modality, transitivity, pronouns, implicatures. Collocations of words *Kosovo / Kosovo's*: **Sub-corpus 1:** *independence, state, democracy, freedom, liberation, heroic, fatherland, sublime sacrifice, war, altar of freedom, century dream, bloodshed, experience.* **Sub-corpus 2:** *institutions, citizens, progress, state, independence, peace, consolidation, construction, final status, constitution, international standard, inseparable territory, human rights, democracy, security, advance, respect, aspire*

17 In this column are presented the summaries of the most common argumentation strategies derived from the analyses of the micro linguistic features.

Topic	Strategies	Argumentation	Language means
Interethnic relations	**Sub-corpus 1:** 1. Distancing oneself from the Serbs. 2. Representing Serbs as the most horrible enemy ever. 3. Valuing the members of one's own group, who fight against Serbs and Serbian dominance. **Sub-corpus 2:.** Distancing the self through hidden devaluation of Serbs.	**Sub-corpus 1:** Serbs where dominating us in the most brutal way. The Serbian regime was the most brutal, violent regime. We have fought the Serbian enemy for centuries. We have beaten them and we have liberated the people from violent Serbian dominance. Serbs are still the enemy that we have against the independence of our country. **Sub-corpus 2:** **Yes,** the Serbs are citizens of Kosovo, **but** they are the minority, we should rule. **We** do offer the Serbs to enjoy their minority rights, we are doing the best we can, **but they** are not willing to cooperate. The scapegoat argumentation form. Serbs do not want to integrate themselves in Kosovo.	Collocations, semantic aura, allusions, tropes, modality, pronouns, perspectivation. Collocations of words *Serbs, Serbia, Serbian* **Sub-corpus 1:** War lexis: *barbarity of Serbs, boots of the Serbian army and police, paramilitary forces and Serbian gangs, dictatorial Serbian regime. Liberation from Serbs, victory against Serbs, KLA, Adem Jashari.* **Sub-Corpus 2:** lexis related to Human Rights, International norms: *minority, community, Serbian representatives, Serbian party.* Allusions: *war, the past. The referendum of Albanians for independence from Serbia in 1992.*

Topic	Strategies	Argumentation	Language means
Democracy	**Sub-corpus 1:** Emphasize the semantic features of the word *democracy*: 1. Collective self-determination; 2. Rule of representation; 3. Rule of the majority; 4. Accepting the rules of the game. Promoting "ethnic democracy". **Sub-corpus 2:** Emphasize the semantic features of the word *democracy*: 1. The right of individuals to self-determine. 2. Recognition of the plurality of ethnic groups. Promoting civic democracy.	**Sub-corpus 1:** Democracy is the will of Albanians for self-determination. **Sub-corpus 2:** Kosovo will be a democratic system where the citizen's rights will prevail.	Collocations, polysemy, semantic features, allusions, implicatures. Collocations of the words *democracy, democratic* **Sub-corpus 1:** *Kosovo, state, institutions, parliament, will of people, power of people, self-determination, rule, elections, Adem Jashari, values.* Semantic features: representatives, will of people, collective self-determination. **Sub-corpus 2**: *parliamentary democracy, civic democracy, civic identity, citizens, process, Kosovo, elections, society, power, institutions, system, developments.*
Relations with international community	**Sub-corpus 1 & 2:** Representation of NATO, USA and the EU as saviors and friends. Representation of UNMIK as partner vs. Distancing oneself from UNMIK.	**Sub-corpus 1 & 2:** Thanks to USA and NATO we enjoy our freedom. We will build a permanent friendship with the USA. The integration in NATO and the EU will bring us prosperity and wellbeing **Sub-corpus 1:** UNMIK is the partner with whom we are building the state. **Sub-corpus 2:** UNMIK is hampering our way to independence.	Collocations, modality, speech acts, tropes. Collocations with words *war, future, integration, values, freedom, partner, friends.* Speech acts: *praising, acknowledging, thanking, pledging.*

6. Conclusion

This article aimed to present a new research design to study the discourses of political transformation by methods and tools offered by Critical Discourse Analysis. At the beginning *discourse* was defined as language used as a form of social practice in order to achieve aims that are of a nonlinguistic nature. Political transformation was understood here as dissemination of Western values of democracy, subject to study with the research techniques of discourse analysis; however, the existing methods and tools of CDA have been shown to have some shortcomings. On the one hand, they offer findings which are not based on a sufficient amount of quantitative data; on the other hand, the analytical categories are not distinctive enough and/or hierarchized; in consequence, validity and representativeness of the research findings thus obtained can often be put into question.

The model I have developed aims to overcome these shortcomings; it is based on a combination of different models that exist within the current CDA approaches. This model links qualitative and quantitative research techniques, which is unavoidable if one wants to analyze the transformation process through textual data. The corpus (in this case study: a corpus of 41 058 words) is composed of texts representing a given genre (in this case study: political speeches as quoted in newspapers) and sharing certain specific discursive strands and discursive events. In order to link linguistic with non-linguistic phenomena – in this case, with the political transformation in Kosovo – a multi-dimensional model of context was necessary, combining the historical, institutional and situational levels. In order to ensure methodological purity, it was helpful to build a hierarchical model of analytical categories, including categories at the micro-, meso-, and macro-linguistic levels. The application of corpus-analysis software made it possible to systematically identify, highlight and describe analytical categories in the whole corpus.

The model applied ensures that the condition of the data being representative enough is fulfilled. In order to further develop this model, it would be necessary to also deal with issues related to the definition and different labeling of the same analytical categories at the macro- and micro-linguistic levels. Since this problem cannot be handled exhaustively within the scope of this publication, it remains to be dealt with in another research paper.

References

Baker, P., Gabrielatos, C., Khosravinik, M., Krzyzanowski, M., McEnery, T., & Wodak, R. (2008). A useful methodological synergy? Combining critical discourse analysis and corpus linguistics to examine discourse of refugees and asylum seekers in the UK press. *Discourse and Society*, 19(3), 273–306.

Chilton, P. (1998). Making sense of cold war's collapse. In P. Chilton, (Eds.), *Political discourse in transition in Europe 1989–1991*. Amsterdam: John Benjamins, 15–25.

Chilton, P. (2004). *Analysing political discourse. Theory and praxis*. London: Routledge.

van Dijk, T. A. (1980). *Macrostructures. An Interdisciplinary Study of global structures in discourse, interaction and cognition*. New Jersey: Lawrence Erlbaum.

van Dijk, T. A. (1985). Semantic discourse analysis. In T. A. van Dijk (Ed.) *Handbook of Discourse Analysis. Vol. 4. Discourse Analysis in society*. London: Academic Press, 103–136.

van Dijk, T. A. (1989). Mediating racism. The role of the media in the reproduction of racism. In R. Wodak (Ed.), *Language, Power and Ideology*. Amsterdam: John Benjamins, 199–226.

van Dijk, T. A. (1991). *Racism and the Press*. London: Routledge.

van Dijk, T. A. (1993a). Principles of critical discourse analysis. *Discourse & Society*, 4(2), 249–283.

van Dijk, T. A. (1993b). Analysing racism through discourse analysis. Some methodological reflections. In J. Stanfield (Ed.), *Race and ethnicity in research methods*. Newbury Park, CA: Sage, 92–134.

van Dijk, T. A. (1993c). Denying racism. Elite discourse and racism. In J. Solomos & J. Wrench (Eds.). *Racism and migration in Western Europe*. Oxford: Berg, 179–193.

van Dijk, T. A. (1995). Discourse analysis as ideology analysis. In C. Schäffner & A. Wenden (Eds.), *Language and peace*. Adlershot: Dartmouth Publishing, 17–33.

van Dijk, T. A. (1997). *What is political discourse analysis?* Keynote address at the Congress of Political Linguistics. Antwerp, 7–9 December 1995. Published in J. Blommaert & C. Bulcaen (Eds.), *Political linguistics*. Amsterdam: Benjamins, 11–52.

van Dijk, T. A. (2001). Discourse, ideology and context. *Folia Linguistica*, XXX(1–2), 11–40.

van Dijk, T. A. (2002). Political discourse and political cognition. In P. Chilton & C. Schäffner (Eds.), *Politics as Text and Talk. Analytical approaches to political discourse*. Amsterdam: Benjamins, 204–236.

van Dijk, T. A. (2004). Text and context of parliamentary debates. In P. Bayley (Eds.), *Cross-cultural Perspective on Parliamentary Discourse*. Amsterdam: Benjamins, 339–372.

van Dijk, T. A. (2005). Contextual knowledge management in discourse production. A CDA perspective. In R. Wodak & P. Chilton (Eds.), *A New Agenda in (Critical) Discourse Analysis*. Amsterdam: Benjamins, 71–100.

van Dijk, T. A. (2007). The study of discourse: an introduction. In T. A. van Dijk (Ed.), *Discourse Studies. 5 vols. Sage Benchmarks in Discourse Studies*. London: Sage, xix-xlii.

van Dijk, T. A. (2009). Critical Discourse Studies: a socio cognitive approach. In R. Wodak & M. Meyer (Eds.), *Methods of Critical Discourse Analysis*. London: SAGE, 62–86.

Fairclough, N. (1992). *Discourse and social Change*. Cambridge: Polity Press.

Fairclough, N. (1995). *Critical discourse analyses: the critical study of language*. London: Longman.

Fairclough, N. (2001). *Globaler Kapitalismus und kritisches Diskursbewusstsein*. In R. Keller (Ed.), *Handbuch Sozialwissenschaftliche Diskursanalyse. Band 1: Theorien und Methoden*. Opladen: Leske, 335–352.

Fairclough, N. (2003). *Analysing Discourse. Textual Analysis for Social Research*. London: Routledge.

Fairclough, N. (2005). Critical Discourse Analysis. *Marges linguistiques. M.L.M.S. Numéro 9, Saint Chamas*, 76–94.

Fairclough, N. (2009). A dialectical-relational approach to critical discourse analysis in social research. In R. Wodak & M. Meyer (Eds.), *Methods of Critical Discourse Analysis*. London: SAGE, 162–201.

Foucault, M. (1981). Orders of discourse. Untying the text. In R. Young (Ed.), *A poststructuralist reader*. London: Rootledge & Kegan Paul, 28–48.

Geissner, K. H. (2004). Political change without rhetorical change. In H. Barthel & K. M. Carragee (Eds.), *Communication and political change*. Band 20. St Ingbert: Röhrig Universitätsverlag.

Girnth, H. (2002). Sprache und Sprachverwendung in der Politik. Eine Einführung in die linguistische Analyse öffentlich politischer Kommunikation. *Germanistische Arbeitshefte*. 39.

Halliday, M. A. K. (1985). *Introduction to functional grammar.* London: Edward Arnold.

Halliday, M. A. K. (1994). *An Introduction to functional grammar*. 2nd edition. London: Edward Arnold.

International Crisis Group. (2006). *The Challenge of Transition*, Crisis Group Report No. 170.

Jäger, S. (1999). Zwischen den Kulturen; Diskursanalytische Grenzgänge. In A. Hepp & R. Winter (Eds.), *Kultur-Medien-Macht. Cultural Studies und Medienanalyse*. Opladen: Westdeutscher Verlag, 327–351.

Jäger, S. (2001). *Kritische Diskursanalyse. Eine Einführung*. Duisburg: DISS.

Jäger, S. (2012). *Kritische Diskursanalyse. Eine Einführung*. 6. Vollst. Überarbeitet Auflage. Duisburg: DISS.

Jung, M. (2001). Diskurshistorische Analyse – eine linguistische Perspektive. In R. Keller, A. Hirseland, W. Schneider & W. Viehöfer (Eds.), *Handbuch Sozialwissenschaftliche Diskursanalyse. Bd. 1. Theorien und Methoden*. Opladen: Leske+Budrich, 29–53.

Limani-Beqa, S. (2011). *Transformationsprozesse von Politik und Sprache in Kosova in der Zeit von 1999 bis 2005. Eine kritische Diskursanalyse*. Frankfurt: Peter Lang Verlag.

Louw, B. (1993). Irony in the text or the insincerity in the writer? The diagnostic potential of semantic prosodies. In M. Baker (Ed.), *Text and technology. In honor of John Sinclair*. Philadelphia & Amsterdam: John Benjamins, 157–176.

Mautner, G. (2000). *Der britische Europa-Diskurs. Methodenreflexion und Fallstudien zur Berichterstattung in der Tagespresse*. Wien: Passagen Verlag.

Mautner, G. (2005). Time to get wired. Using web-based corpora in Critical Discourse Analysis. *Discourse & Society*, 16(6), 809–828.

Mautner, G. (2009). Checks and balances: How corpus linguistics can contribute to CDA. In R. Wodak & M. Meyer (Eds.), *Methods of Critical Discourse Analysis*. London: Sage, 122–143.

Mills, S. (2007). *Der Diskurs. Begriff, Theorie, Praxis*. Tübingen & Basel: A. Francke.

Moscovici, S. (2000). *Social Representations. Explorations in Social Psychology*. Cambridge, UK: Polity Press.

Panagl, O., & Wodak, R. (2004). *Text und Kontext. Theoriemodelle und methodische Verfahren im transdisziplinären Vergleich*. Würzburg: Königshausen und Neumann.

Scott, M. (1999). *WordSmith Tools Help Manual, Version 3.0*. Oxford: Mike Scott & Oxford University Press.

Spieß, C. (2006). *Zwischen Hochwert und Stigma- zum strategischen Potenzial lexikalischer Mittel im Bioethikdiskurs*. In H. Girnth & C. Spieß (Eds.), *Strategien politischer Kommunikation. Pragmatische Analysen*. Berlin: Schmidt, 27–45.

Wodak, R. (Ed.) (1997). *Gender and discourse*. London: Sage.

Wodak, R. (2001). The discourse-historical approach. In R. Wodak & M. Meyer (Eds.), *Methods of Critical Discourse Analysis*. London: Sage, 63–95.

Wodak, R. (2004). Sprache und Politik. Einige Grenzen diskursanalytischer Vorgangsweisen. In T. Krisch, T. Lindner & U. Müller (Eds.), *Analecta homini universali dicata. Festschrift für Oswald Panagl zum 65. Geburtstag*. vol. II. Stuttgart: Hans-Dieter Heinz, 648–661.

Wodak, R. (2008). 'Us' and 'them': inclusion/exclusion – discrimination via discourse. In *Migration, Identity, and Belonging*. Liverpool: University of Liverpool Press, 54–78.

Wodak, R. (2009). *The discourse of politics in action: politics as usual*. Basingstoke: Palgrave Macmillan.

Wodak, R., & Fairclough, N. (1997). Critical discourse analysis. In T. van Dijk (Ed.), *Discourse. Studies: A Multidisciplinary Introduction*. Vol. 2. London: Sage, 258–284.

Wodak, R., de Cillia, R., Liebhart, K., Reisigl, M., Hofstätter, K., & Kargl, M. (1998). *Zur diskursiven Konstruktion nationaler Identität*. Frankfurt: Suhrkamp.

Wodak, R., de Cillia, R., Reisigl, M., & Liebhart, K. (1999). *The discursive construction of national identity*. Translated by A. Hirsch & R. Mitten. Edinburgh: Edinburgh University Press.

Wodak, R., & Meyer, M. (2009). Critical discourse analysis, history, agenda, theory and methodology. In R. Wodak & M. Meyer (Eds.), *Methods of Critical Discourse Analysis*. London: Sage, 1–34.

Wodak, R., & Reisigl, M. (2009). The discourse-historical approach (DHA). In R. Wodak & M. Meyer (Eds.), *Methods of Critical Discourse Analysis*. London: Sage, 87–121.

Studies in Language, Culture and Society

Edited by Łucja Biel, Andrzej Kątny and Piotr Ruszkiewicz

The editors of this series invite books addressing the nexus between language, culture and society. Contrastive studies are welcome in particular, whether of a synchronic or diachronic orientation. Various perspectives on language / communication are of interest: grammatical, pragmatic, sociolinguistic, discursive and semiotic. A wide range of theoretical and methodological positions is accepted: cognitive / anthropological / corpus linguistics, as well as pragmatics, interactional sociolinguistics, (specialized) genre analysis, and critical discourse studies.

The cutting edge of the series is to publish innovative research elucidating the processes of *inter-* and *intra-*language variation and change, and – at the same time – relating them to flows *in* and *across* cognate categories of culture, community and society.

The series publishes monographs and edited volumes reporting on data-driven research that carries a potential for application in translation studies, language teaching, multilingual (multicultural) education, and interdisciplinary critical discourse studies.

The languages of publication are English and German, yet book proposals in other major languages will also be considered, if centrally contributive to the main aim of the series.

Vol. 1 Ewa Kucelman: Self-based Anaphora in Early Modern English. 2013.

Vol. 2 Łucja Biel: Lost in the Eurofog: The Textual Fit of Translated Law. 2014.

Vol. 3 Marek Kuźniak / Agnieszka Libura / Michał Szawerna (eds.): From Conceptual Metaphor Theory to Cognitive Ethnolinguistics. Patterns of Imagery in Language. 2014.

Vol. 4 Grzegorz Kowalski: Claim-making and Claim-challenging in English and Polish Linguistic Discourses. 2015.

Vol. 5 Małgorzata Tryuk: On Ethics and Interpreters. 2015.

Vol. 6 Anna Duszak / Grzegorz Kowalski (eds.): Academic (Inter)genres: between Texts, Contexts and Identities. 2015.

Vol. 7 Alicja Witalisz: English Loan Translations in Polish. Word-formation Patterns, Lexicalization, Idiomaticity and Institutionalization. 2015.

Vol. 8 Agnieszka Kampka / Katarzyna Molek-Kozakowska (eds.): Rhetoric, Knowledge and the Public Sphere. 2016.

Vol. 9 Maria Załęska / Urszula Okulska (eds.): Rhetoric, Discourse and Knowledge. 2016.

Vol. 10 Łucja Biel: Lost in the Eurofog: The Textual Fit of Translated Law. Second Revised Edition. 2017.

Vol. 11 Karolina Broś / Grzegorz Kowalski (eds.): Discourse Studies – Ways and Crossroads. Insights into Cultural, Diachronic and Genre Issues in the Discipline. 2017.

www.peterlang.com

www.ingramcontent.com/pod-product-compliance
Ingram Content Group UK Ltd.
Pitfield, Milton Keynes, MK11 3LW, UK
UKHW041824100926
8556IPUK00002B/16

9 783631 739488